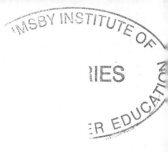

CRITICAL PRACTICE IN SOCIAL WORK

ADAMS, ROBERT

Critical Practice In Social Work

<u>1st</u>

Basingstoke: Palgrave, 2002   033392553X

Also edited by Robert Adams, Lena Dominelli and Malcolm Payne:

Social Work: Themes, Issues and Critical Debates *

Other titles by Robert Adams:

A Measure of Diversion? Case Studies in IT (co-author)
Prison Riots in Britain and the USA
Problem-solving with Self-help Groups (co-author)
Protests by Pupils: Empowerment, Schooling and the State
Quality Social Work *
Self-help, Social Work and Empowerment
Skilled Work with People
Social Work and Empowerment *
The Abuses of Punishment
The Personal Social Services: Clients, Consumers or Citizens?
Social Policy for Social Work *

Other titles by Lena Dominelli:

Community Action and Organising Marginalised Groups
Women in Focus, Community Service Orders and Female Offenders
*Love and Wages: The Impact of Imperialism, State Intervention and Women's
    Domestic Labour on Workers' Control in Algeria*
Anti-racist Social Work, 2nd edn *
Feminist Social Work (co-author)
Women and Community Action
Women Across Continents: Feminist Comparative Social Policy
Gender, Sex Offenders and Probation Practice
Getting Advice in Urdu
International Directory of Social Work
Anti-racist Perspectives in Social Work (co-author)
Anti-racist Probation Practice (co-author)
Sociology for Social Work *
Community Approaches to Child Welfare
International Perspectives Beyond Racial Divides
Ethnicities in Social Work (co-authors)

Other titles by Malcolm Payne:

What is Professional Social Work?
Social Work and Community Care *
Linkages: Effective Networking in Social Care
Modern Social Work Theory, 2nd edn *
Writing for Publication in Social Services Journals
Social Care in the Community
Teamwork in Multiprofessional Care *
Power, Authority and Responsibility in Social Services: Social Work in Area Teams
Anti-bureaucratic Social Work

*Published by Palgrave – now Palgrave Macmillan

Critical Practice in Social Work

Edited by

Robert Adams, Lena Dominelli and Malcolm Payne

Consultant editor: Jo Campling

First published 2002 by
PALGRAVE MACMILLAN
Houndmills, Basingstoke, Hampshire RG21 6XS and
175 Fifth Avenue, New York, N.Y. 10010
Companies and representatives throughout the world

PALGRAVE MACMILLAN is the new global academic imprint of
St. Martin's Press LLC Scholarly and Reference Division and
Palgrave Publishers Ltd (formerly Macmillan Press Ltd).

ISBN-13: 978-0-333-92553-9
ISBN-10: 0-333-92553-X paperback

This book is printed on paper suitable for recycling and
made from fully managed and sustained forest sources.

A catalogue record for this book is available
from the British Library.

Editing and origination by
Aardvark Editorial, Mendham, Suffolk

10 9 8 7 6
11 10 09 08 07

Printed in China

Contents

Notes on the Contributors

Robert Adams is a qualified social worker who worked in the penal system for seven years, before running a community-based social work project for Barnardo's. He has written extensively about youth and criminal justice, social work, social policy, protest and empowerment. He is Professor of Human Services Development attached to the Social Policy Research Centre at the University of Lincolnshire and Humberside and Visiting Professor in the School of Health at the University of Teesside.

Di Bailey is the Co-director for the Interdisciplinary Centre for Mental Health and Director of the postgraduate MA in Community Mental Health at the University of Birmingham. She has practised as an ASW in different settings, working for the past six years as an educator and trainer. Her particular interests are in the mental health social work contribution to interdisciplinary working.

Sarah Banks is Senior Lecturer in Community and Youth Work in the Department of Sociology and Social Policy at the University of Durham. Her research interests centre around professional ethics and community development. She has just completed a second edition of her book, *Ethics and Values in Social Work* (Palgrave) and recently edited a collection on *Ethical Issues in Youth Work* (Routledge, 1999).

Greta Bradley is Senior Lecturer in Social Work at the University of Hull where she researches and teaches in community care for vulnerable adults. Her current work includes a follow-up study of care managers and translating findings from a multidisciplinary study on ethical dilemmas and administrative justice into practice guidance. She is joint editor of *Practice*.

Helen Cosis Brown is the Course Director for the MA in Social Work at South Bank University. She was a social worker and team leader for ten years in an inner London borough. She has continued to offer training in the field of fostering and adoption and has produced a number of publications relating to social work practice with lesbians and gay men.

Beverley Burke is a Senior Lecturer on the DipSW at Liverpool John Moores University. She trained as a generic social worker and her practice and current research interests are in the area of children and families.

Chris Clark is Senior Lecturer and Head of the Department of Social Work, University of Edinburgh. His research and teaching interests cover professional ethics, community care and voluntary action. Recent publications include *Social Work Ethics: Politics, Principles and Practice* (Palgrave, 2000) and (as editor) *Better Days: Adult Day Services and Social Inclusion* (Jessica Kingsley, 2001).

Caroline Currer is Field Leader for Social Work at Anglia Polytechnic University, where she teaches about loss and social work. She is a supervisor with a local branch of CRUSE Bereavement Care. Her PhD (1986) examined the mental health of a group of Pakistani women in Bradford, drawing on language and other skills from previous social work practice in Pakistan. She is author of *Responding to Grief: Dying, Bereavement and Social Care* (Palgrave – now Palgrave Macmillan, 2001).

Jane Dalrymple is a Senior Lecturer at the University of the West of England. She trained as a generic social worker and her practice and current research interests are focused on children's rights and advocacy.

Lena Dominelli is Professor of Social and Community Development in the Department of Social Work Studies at the University of Southampton where she is Director of the Centre for International Social and Community Development. She is also President of the International Association of Schools of Social Work. She has been a researcher and educator for more that twenty-five years and has published widely, her most recent books being *Feminist Social Work Theory and Practice* and *Anti-Oppressive Practice*, both with Palgrave – now Palgrave Macmillan. Lena has also worked as a community worker, social worker and probation officer.

Nick Frost is Senior Lecturer in the School of Continuing Education, University of Leeds. He was formerly a social worker and policy officer in the voluntary and statutory sector. His research interests include family support, evaluation and professional training. He has published widely, including *Family Support in Rural Communities* (Barnardo's, 2001).

Kevin Haines has a long-standing interest in youth justice. He has been a committee member of the National Association for Youth Justice for eight years and is a board member of the Reseau International de Criminologie Juvenile. His research interests are focused on young offenders and the youth justice system.

Previous publications include *Understanding Modern Juvenile Justice* (Avebury, 1996) and *Young People and Youth Justice* (Macmillan – now Palgrave Macmillan, 1998), with Mark Drakeford. He has also written critically about developments in restorative justice, see Goldson, B. (2000) *The New Youth Justice*, Russell House Publishing. Kevin Haines is currently working mainly in Romania on the establishment of community sentences for juvenile offenders.

Margaret Lloyd trained and worked as a social worker in Manchester before lecturing in social work and social policy at Manchester University and currently at Sheffield University. She researches community care with particular emphasis on the health and social care interface. She is Chair of the Welfare Research Committee of the Parkinson's Disease Society.

Jill Manthorpe is Reader in Community Care at the University of Hull where she teaches and researches in gerontology and services for vulnerable adults. She is Chair of the Hull and East Riding Adult Protection Committee and has a background in work within community development, the voluntary sector and the NHS. Recent research has been in the area of student mental health, local government reorganisation, and risk and care management. Currently she is working on a study on older nurses.

Judith Milner is a former Senior Lecturer in Social Work at the University of Huddersfield. She currently works as a counsellor and as a freelance trainer.

Kate Morris is a Senior Lecturer at the University of Birmingham where she has management responsibilities for qualifying and post-qualifying social work programmes. She is active in research relating to family involvement in childcare planning and family involvement in adoption planning. She is working currently on a publication *Bringing Together Family Involvement in Child Care Planning*.

Audrey Mullender is Professor in Social Work at the University of Warwick and an elected Academician of the Academy of Learned Societies for the Social Sciences. She was, for four years until the end of 1999, editor of the *British Journal of Social Work* and has herself produced well over a hundred publications in the social work field, including ten books. She has recently jointly authored studies of children's perspectives on living with domestic violence, women's voices in domestic violence services, groups for domestic violence perpetrators and mapping family support services in domestic violence across the UK.

Patrick O'Byrne is also a former Senior Lecturer in Social Work at the University of Huddersfield. He currently works as a family mediator.

Joan Orme is Professor of Social Work at the University of Glasgow. She has researched workload measurement from the perspective of both trade unions and management and is firmly committed to the need to ensure that workload issues are considered as part of effective practice for the protection of both service users and workers.

Terence O'Sullivan is a Senior Lecturer in Social Work at the University of Lincoln and author of *Decision Making in Social Work* (Macmillan – now Palgrave Macmillan, 1999).

Malcolm Payne is Professor and Head of Applied Community Studies at the Manchester Metropolitan University, having worked in probation, social services departments and the local and national voluntary sector. Among his many books are *Teamwork in Multiprofessional Care* (Macmillan – now Palgrave Macmillan, 2000), *Anti-bureaucratic Social Work* (Venture, 2000), *Modern Social Work Theory* (2nd edn, Macmillan – now Palgrave Macmillan, 1997), *What is Professional Social Work?* (Venture, 1996) and *Social Work and Community Care* (Macmillan – now Palgrave Macmillan, 1995).

David Peryer is a former Director of Social Services. He was social services adviser to the Association of District Councils at the time of local government reorganisation. He works in the public sector as a management consultant, and chairs two large national voluntary organisations.

Judith Phillips is Professor of Social Gerontology and Director of the MA/Diploma in Gerontology course at Keele University. She qualified and worked as a social worker before becoming a lecturer in social work at UEA, Norwich and Keele University. Recent publications include two co-edited books, *Women Ageing: Changing Identity: Challenging Myths* (Routledge, 2000) and *The Social Policy of Old Age – Moving into the 21st Century* (Routledge, 2000).

Julia Phillipson has worked as an independent consultant and trainer since leaving the National Institute for Social Work and moving to west Wales in 1990. Her varied work includes practice teaching, service user involvement, inspection and writing training materials. Through all of these she tries to weave her abiding concerns of tussling with inequalities, sustaining creativity and ensuring social work makes a positive difference.

John Pinkerton is Senior Lecturer and Head of the School of Social Work at the Queen's University of Belfast, Northern Ireland, where he is involved with post-professional qualification training. His publications include *At Home in Care – Parenting, the State and Civil Society* (Avebury, 1994), *Embracing Change as Opportunity: Reflections on Social Work from A Northern Ireland Perspective* (Arena, 1997) *Making Research Work: Research, Policy and Practice in Child Care* (Wiley, 1998) and *Family Support – Direction from Diversity* (Jessica Kingsley, 2000).

Keith Popple is Professor of Social Work and Community Development at Southampton Institute. Previously a practitioner in the statutory social work and youth work services, he has considerable experience teaching on social work and community development courses. He has directed a number of research projects and is author of *Analysing Community Work: Its Theory and Practice* (Open University Press, 1995) and joint editor with Sidney Jacobs of *Community Work* *in the 1990s* (Spokesman Press, 1994). He is editor of the international quarterly *Community Development Journal*, published by Oxford University Press.

Mo Ray has worked as a qualified social worker in a variety of community settings, specialising in working with older people and developing a special interest in working with people with dementia. At present, she works half-time at Keele University on a European research project examining intergenerational relationships. She spends the rest of her time teaching at the Open University, practice teaching and training.

Alastair Roy is a Senior Lecturer in the Department of Social Work at the University of Central Lancashire. His teaching and research interests are in the field of substance misuse and criminal justice. He is a qualified youth and community worker, whose professional experience has focused on vulnerable young people. Prior to taking up an academic appointment, Alastair was manager of a therapeutic residential home for children. He still works as an independent visitor.

Bob Sapey is a Lecturer in Applied Social Science at Lancaster University. His publications include the second edition of *Social Work with Disabled People* (Macmillan – now Palgrave Macmillan, 1999) with Michael Oliver. Prior to his academic career, Bob was a social worker and training officer, specialising in work with disabled and older people.

Tim Stainton is a Senior Lecturer and DipSW Programme Director at the Centre for Applied Social Studies, University of Wales, Swansea. He spent ten years as a social worker in Canada, working mainly on resettlement of people with a learning disability. He is an active lobbyist and consultant and has written widely on issues related to learning disability and social work. He is currently completing a book on the social construction of learning disability from antiquity to the present.

Corinne Wattam is Professor leading the Child Care Research Group at the Unversity of Central Lancashire. She has developed, coordinated and been involved in a number of childcare research projects both in the UK and in Europe, including the Concerted Action on the Prevention of Child Abuse in Europe (CAPCAE). Recent publications, *Child Sexual Abuse: Learning from the Experiences of Children* (Wiley, 1999, with Nigel Parton) and 'The Prevention of Child Abuse' (*Children and Society*, **13**), confirm her commitment to the development of services informed by and with children and young people.

Frances Young is a Senior Lecturer in the Department of Social Work at the University of Central Lancashire. Her practice experience was in local authority childcare, specialising in adoption and fostering. Frances currently lectures on the DipSW, BA and MA programmes in the area of childcare and is a tutor to DipSW students. She has recently completed research on managing the external childcare placement market with the North West ADSS and NCH Action for Children.

Introduction

Robert Adams, Lena Dominelli and Malcolm Payne

In this book, we provide an essential grounding in social work practice for all students and practitioners. We place critical practice at the centre of all social work practice. The book offers the opportunity to explore the variety of critical practice and understand the principles and processes involved in all its aspects.

Critical practice is an essential part of being an effective social worker. We introduce here the multifaceted nature of social work practice. We show that just as criticality is more than just being critical of things, critical practice is more than doing. It requires reflectiveness, reflexivity and expertise in putting matters of practical concern into their wider context. The three parts of this book bring out the different components of practice, values, knowledge and skills, and those aspects of management that are central to good practice. This book complements our companion volume, *Social Work: Themes, Issues and Critical Debates*, (Adams et al., 1998) on different debates that arise over values, theories and approaches in the different areas of social work.

Many of the major points in the chapters that follow arise from discussion of examples of situations and cases. There is detailed analysis of the principal areas where the practitioner is likely to encounter particular issues, problems, tensions and dilemmas and may be working with complex situations, in changing conditions with widespread uncertainties.

In covering the major aspects of social work practice, this book highlights the positive opportunities for critical practice not to become stuck with the problems with which practitioners struggle, but to remain optimistic and become genuinely transformational.

We hope that our straightforward style and use of many examples from practice will make the book more accessible to you, the reader.

What critical practice is and why it is important

Critical practice is not social work per se but is integral to social work that makes use of criticality as the route to excellence in performance and advancing expertise. The 'being critical' is integral to the social work and not tacked on, marginal, a mere technical task or just a stage to be gone through. Criticality enables us to question the knowledge we have and our own involvement with clients – including our taken-for-granted understandings. It enables us to assess situations so as to make structural connections that penetrate the surface of what we encounter and locate what is apparent within wider contexts. It is unlikely that critical practice will resolve the contradictions and dilemmas we encounter in practice but it will enable us to retain an understanding of them while we act. This questioning approach is transforming. It transforms our own understanding and sometimes it can enable us and the client to change an aspect of the situation. We cannot claim that it will change the world, but the constant interplay between our actions and the deconstruction and reconstruction that comprise our critical reflection gives us access to advancing our practice.

Thus, the critical component of our expertise is crucial to good practice and practice development, a continuous and never-ending process.

What you can gain from this book

In this book we aim to make it easier for you to put criticality onto every agenda in your social work. This means developing a confident approach to questioning everything. Asking questions about what we are doing in practice often slows the action down, or halts it for a while, but that does not mean the practitioner should feel paralysed. In many of the chapters, critical reflection and practice proceed together. This is a deliberate method we have used to illustrate what we mean by criticality.

We do not separate theory from practice. This book is rooted in theories about social work, but its main purpose is not to interrogate those theories, but to examine the practice in which they are embedded. If you want to go further into the theoretical debates, we suggest that you use this book in combination with our companion volume *Social Work: Themes, Issues and Critical Debates* (Adams et al., 1998), which introduces the main currents and controversies in social work theory, research and approaches to practice.

The discussion of the major topics relies on practice illustrations rather than taking place at one remove from practice.

The authors and editors of this book are not exempt from the process of being critical. We have tried to include critical reflection on our own ideas in places, to indicate how criticality extends to every aspect of social work, including commentary on it.

How the book is structured

Introductory chapter We introduce the book with Chapter 1 on what critical practice entails. Each of us leads into each of the three major parts of the book with a chapter setting the scene for that aspect of critical practice.

Part I starts with the broader value-based questions that permeate every aspect of critical practice and in its later chapters focuses in more detail on some illustrative aspects that highlight the contradictions and dilemmas for the practitioner.

Part II takes many of the commonest areas of practice and uses examples from practice as the pegs on which to hang discussion of many issues arising for the practitioner.

Part III explores how management in its various forms is embedded in good practice.

Further reading At the end of every chapter, the author offers a short, annotated guide to further reading for those who want to take that topic further.

How you may use this book

We suggest you might turn first to the introductory Chapter 1, which discusses what critical practice is. Thereafter, the layout of the book enables you to dip in and out of whichever aspects are of most immediate concern.

If you are a student or beginning social worker, this book offers an introduction to critical practice.

If you are a practitioner, at whatever level of experience, this book will enable you to develop your social work practice.

On Being Critical in Social Work

Malcolm Payne, Robert Adams and Lena Dominelli

Critical practice is *still* relevant in social work

Increasingly, social workers and other professionals are asked to follow guidelines and meet national standards. Their agencies are organised to 'deliver' through 'joined-up government'. Of course, every user of social care services wants to be dealt with consistently and gain the benefits from policy and service objectives. If they are being supervised or checked up on through social work's social policing role, they want to be dealt with in justice and compassion. However, meeting guidelines, standards and objectives is not simple, because nearly all of them refer to *how* we should meet the aims. Usually, we have to use our judgement to decide the best way of doing our job.

Furthermore, social work has greater ambitions, because it seeks growth and empowerment as human beings for the people we serve, development and social progress for the communities we work in and greater justice and equality in the societies to which we contribute. It is not that every act of social work will achieve such large goals, but these values help to guide us in using our judgement about what is best. Critical thinking helps to implement these values by testing our practice against them. Making social work values practical is so important that the first part of this book focuses on making value objectives central to practice.

The needs and wishes of users and carers for the best social services is, however, a crucial element in all practice, and the second part of the book demonstrates how moving from critical thinking towards critical action creates a practice that can help us to develop the best social work. The specialist authors examine a wide range of situations in which people call on social work. Each chapter outlines a critical approach to the situation and ways of becoming involved, understanding and acting within it. The people, families and communities that social workers serve do not fall into easy categories, and so all of these chapters overlap. Working with an elderly person (Chapter 20), for example, may well involve dealing with preparing for their death and the bereavement of family members (Chapter 21), and subsequently childcare and family issues may emerge (Chapters 11–14), since grandparents are often important carers for children. It is never possible to separate out different aspects of human lives into social work specialisms, and one of the advantages of developing critical practice is that it helps us to identify the mutual impact of shared life events.

Management is also part of critical practice and forms the focus of the third part of the book. This is for three reasons. First, policy and organisational aims form legal and structural contexts, which enable us to practise, and condition and direct our practice. We do not practise in isolation from society, and it is through the management of agencies that society exerts some of its influences: hence the guidelines and standards. Second, the people we serve and the people who pay for us expect good value from our work, so managing our work well responds to their expectations and needs. Third, our practice interacts with the people we serve and with others who work alongside us, so that the structures within which we work and the ways in which we practise need to respect the boundaries and enhance the links between all we do. Since managers do things, management is itself a practice and, for just the same reasons as social work, it involves being critical. However, because managing is an essential part of social work, critical thinking about how we manage is central to social work practice.

Critical practice in social perspective

How can we 'be critical'? And how do we do that 'in practice'? Brechin's (2000: 26) account of critical practice in health and social care defines critical practice as: 'open-minded, reflective appraisal that takes account of different perspectives, experiences and assumptions'. She sees it as a way of managing uncertainty. Thus, critical practice speaks to a contemporary anxiety, because, as Beck (1992) argues, recent globalisation of economic systems brings previously separated views of the world into contact and potential conflict, raising ambiguity and controversy about what once seemed rational and ordered. Our world seems more unsafe and uncertain than it once did, and we seek mechanisms to help us to control potential risks to our equilibrium. Critical practice gives us a way of organising our thinking and action to respond to uncertainty and risk.

Brechin (2000: 31–3) identifies two guiding principles within critical practice. The first is 'respecting others as equals', placing a crucial interpersonal value as the starting point. While we share this emphasis on values, this book develops a stronger focus on including wider social values within critical practice. Brechin's second principle is 'an open and "not-knowing" approach'. Here, she focuses on accepting uncertainty and finding ways of dealing with it, rather than relying on old or inadequate certainties that do not reflect the world as people experience it. While we share this emphasis on openness, this book develops openness and uncertainty as an opportunity for creative practice. Brechin's (2000: 35–44) pillars of critical practice are based on forging effective relationships, so that practitioners may respond to and incorporate multiple perspectives on the situations that they deal with. Critical practice, to her, must also empower others, rather than restricting their opportunities and advancing our own power and it must seek to make a difference to the lives of the people we serve. While we share these elements of practice, this book develops interpersonal practice towards enhancing collective relationships, empowerment and change. Making a difference involves not only personal changes and gains for the better, but also seeing these as part of a movement towards empowering oppressed and disadvantaged groups in society. This should enhance their relationships in interaction with wider social progress, rather than their being excluded from participation in it.

Critical thinking leads to critical action, forming critical practice. Inevitably, because critical thinking will use the experience of action and its outcomes to inform further thinking, critical practice is a cycle in which thinking is bound up with action. We see this as part of a reflexive cycle. *Reflexivity* means being in a circular process in which social workers 'put themselves in the picture' by thinking and acting with the people they are serving, so that their understandings and actions inevitably are changed by their experiences with others. As part of the same process, they influence and change others and their social worlds.

Thinking critically: working with families

To make a start on how we might think critically in a practice setting, we consider here some ideas about working with families. So many people think that living in families is good that it is a conventional assumption in many societies. Arguments are brought up that it provides for mutual support between a couple, and allows for bringing up children while they are dependent on others. Our approach to critical thinking looks first at the *language* used, because this helps to test our undisclosed assumptions. The word 'good', above, immediately alerts us to the fact that this sentence makes an evaluation. It considers the value that might be attributed to families. Less obvious value-words, such as 'interesting' or 'worthwhile', have a practical feel to them, causing us to miss their value-laden content. Alternatively, the tone may be positive or negative, without any specific value-words being present at all. Critical practitioners remain alert to the use of language. This extends beyond values. For example, 'couple' and 'children' reveal hidden assumptions about families, potentially excluding single-parent and childless families. In the next paragraph, we indicate in square brackets some, but only some, of the language issues that you might consider critically, to remind you that this is a constant issue.

The next stage [one thing after another, rather than all entwined] of critical thinking is to explore [rather than, say, analyse] *agenda-setting*. In a book, the process of agenda-setting is not interactive, but in the control of one party. In this case, the people in control are us, the authors, but in social work, it is often the agency and its managers or workers themselves who are in control of agendas, rather than clients [tone shift from referring to 'users']. You might surmise, here, that we picked 'families' from a number of possibilities because it will allow us to make our points easily, in a topic that is universal to most human audiences. The critical reader will be thinking: 'Are there topics where it is not so easy? Do the authors' arguments work then?' In social work, you can imagine clients thinking similar things about why your agency is interested in them and what your aims are. Clients may accept or resist [term with historical, intellectual connections to psychoanalysis] the agendas that officials or professionals impose upon them. Whichever it is, the critical social worker will be alert to who is setting the agenda. Mostly, it is more effective [hidden value-word] to make agenda-setting interactive and include [hidden value-words] clients in the process [tone-setting word implying continuing participation].

Critical practice also includes considering the *content of judgements* that we make. Here, the content of the judgement is that living in families is good. Obviously, critical points are possible. Thinking reflexively here, we can put ourselves in notional families to interact with the idea. This allows us to see that there are families, and many of them, where there are poor relationships, leading to divorce, for example. Most murders and much violence also take place within family relationships (Chapter 7). So, in social work dealing with families, the critical social worker would want to be careful about making the assumption that the client's family is of a particular kind, which is more or less acceptable. Clients' experiences of their families may be anything but 'good'. Thinking reflexively could also mean that, rather than notional families, we put ourselves in this particular family and imagine what it might feel like to them. Social work often involves using reflexive thinking to generate empathy with the client's experience in this way. As we work critically, we often find that our professional discourse questions the assumption behind family legislation that maintaining families is a positive policy objective. We may need to question politicians' or managers' assumptions about restoring or maintaining family relationships, in general, or in a particular case. Our own experience of good or bad family life may condition how we respond to what our agency or our clients ask of us. If we are not aware of this, thinking it through and thinking reflexively how our reaction will affect the family we are working with, we are not giving clients the opportunity to participate on equal terms with us.

Critical practice also involves questioning *ideology*. Thinking does not emerge anew every time we come across a situation. An ideology is a system of thought, often derived from political or moral theories or principles. Ideologies are extensive or even comprehensive in the areas of personal or social action that they cover, so they offer guidance in a wide range of situations. They are logical constructions, built on evidence about the world, but they usually contain an element of belief or faith. Examples of ideologies are Marxism or feminism; religions are also ideologies. The advantage of using ideologies is that their extensive coverage means that we can take a consistent approach to a number of situations. The disadvantage is that, used everyday, an ideology seems so systematic that we forget the elements of belief and value that are integral to its system.

Oversimplifying, we could say that Marxists would see families as being constituted as they are to meet the needs of the economic system; to reproduce conveniently a compliant workforce. The personal needs of the individuals involved are subordinated to these covert objectives built into society, and that is why there are conflicts and violence in families. Feminists might say that social responses to gender differences are more important, and that society assumes patriarchy, control by men, citing the fact that most violence in families is by men against women to lend support to this view. Looking critically at another assumption underlying Marxism, it takes a 'conflict' view of society, seeing different groups in society as having opposed interests. Marxism is also 'materialist', because it proposes that economic interests, that is, material conditions, have an important impact on people's lives. An alternative 'spiritual' ideology, common in religions, emphasises shared humanity. Picking up these assumptions discloses that our original statement about families represents another contradictory ideology, a 'functionalist' view of society. Oversimplifying again, functionalists say that social institutions such as families perform a function in human relationships. The function knits societies together in a social 'order' or structure. Our arguments for saying that living in families is good reveal hidden functionalist assumptions. We are assuming that an ordered society is valuable, rather than, say, creative chaos, and that family life contributes to that order, rather than, say, making society inflexible and hidebound.

Although we have simplified and selected from these ideologies, trying to unpick all their implications seems very complicated. Therefore, we want to re-emphasise the point that everything we act on includes assumptions that come from these complex ideological systems of thought. This is a helpful way of coping with complexity but, because many of the assumptions that underlie ideologies are taken for granted, we may not be open enough to rethinking them. Working with a client, the critical social worker would put themselves reflexively in the client's family, asking what views of the value of family life exist in this particular family, and how these views conflict or connect with wider conceptions of family life.

All this seems complicated, so we must justify working in this way. So far, we have emphasised the value of openness and how this contributes to maintaining equality, inclusion and participation between workers and clients.

We value the views of the drama or music critic for their careful and detailed analysis of the work that they have experienced, based on the broad knowledge and understanding that they have of the field. Their work helps us to understand and appreciate a play or piece of music that we experience. In exactly the same way, social workers help others by being alive to and meticulous about possibilities or implications in their work. The practitioner needs to watch for possibilities and implications that might spell risks. We do not want to miss the risk for a child who might be abused, for the wife whose violent husband has not been painstakingly assessed, or the isolated elderly woman whose risk of falling has not been properly evaluated against the environment in which she lives. Also, as with the value that we gain from the theatre and music critic, being critical in social work means being thorough in building up our understanding of the world we are dealing with. Otherwise, we might not have built up the knowledge and understanding of social, psychological and interpersonal processes that will protect, help and offer opportunities to our clients. Finally, reviews entertain us. We are enthused to go to a performance or warned about it by the communicative skill of the critic. It is no use thinking critically if we cannot communicate it to the people who can make a difference to our clients.

Practising critically

Social work is about action, so critical thinking must lead to critical action. Practising within social work requires three aspects: thinking to inform the practice; actions that we take; and actions and their consequences which inform continuing critical thinking. The analogy with music or drama criticism in the previous section draws attention to four aspects of critical practice which take us beyond merely thinking critically:

- Examining the evidence in detail, from different perspectives through reflexive involvement, so that we avoid risk and open up opportunities.

- Contextualising the examination of evidence by placing it explicitly within the context of theoretical and value positions and within the range of other phenomena that might have an impact on the judgements being made. Contextualising is a twin process with reflexiveness: both are about allowing ideas and actions to interact together.

- Developing an overview, so that we and others involved see the full implications of the situation.

- Presenting our judgements to an audience, such as a case conference, clients or their families, or people in the community in ways that may assist, guide or influence their own understanding and evaluation.

The idea of practice contains two partly hidden assumptions:

- The idea of 'a' practice implies that in some way what we are doing is an accepted, acknowledged method of doing something, with the authority of convention or evidence of appropriateness or the likelihood of a successful outcome to support it. We says things such as: 'It is our practice to do it this way'.

- The idea of 'practice' conveys that what we do is not, and never will be, final. We are trying it out, on the basis of its authority as an acknowledged form of action, but it is provisional. If we compare it with the musician practising, or the actor rehearsing, we are practising our activity in a way that we *intend*, not hope, which does not carry the implication of a planned effort to achieve the outcome we want, but *intend* that it will improve the situation and improve our ways of acting in such situations.

For an actor or musical performer, practice has two elements: it intends to act on the present, but also it intends to improve similar actions for the future. Every time performers practise or rehearse, they intend to get better for the next time they practise. Eventually, performing in public, they build on the practice to present the best performance possible for them. No final complete achievement of results, therefore, exists. We sometimes sit through a wonderful performance of a piece of music or we are inspired by a striking production of a play. It may seem that nothing could be more perfect. Yet, another recording, another production next year, next century will be a further revelation of what the work contains. This will be the result of practising in two ways. First, more people trying to make things better again and again will produce improvements in technique. Second, that practice will build upon past practice but will present it in a new context.

Social work is like that. Workers have general knowledge and skill that they can apply to particular situations. That is why social work theories and training are generic. We can learn what to do in general, and adapt the ideas and practices to dealing with, say, children's special needs or practising in groups rather than with individuals.

We do this by being reflexive. For example, when we start working with a looked-after child (Chapter 12), we apply theory about anti-oppressive practice and realise that children will often have experience of being oppressed by adults, who may forget to allow children to think things out for themselves and express their own wishes and feelings. The phrase 'wishes and feelings' is drawn from the Children Act 1989, which requires us to take young people's views into account when making decisions. In this way, we take our professional theory and legal knowledge, reflexively, into the situation with the child and use it to help us to put ourselves in the child's place, rather than being like a 'typical adult'. We are thinking critically about that way of being. By doing this, we hope that the child will react positively to our approach, and we will be able to gain a better understanding of what they are thinking and planning. This can then influence how we are going to act as a social worker and make what we do more effective, or at least more responsive to the child's wishes. These perceptions build up, so that after a while, this child comes to see us not as a 'typical adult' but a more helpful and responsive person than the general run of adults. We gain experience of how this works for us in our 'practice', which is a good basis for more 'practice' with other children in the future.

Social work is an improvisation, like jazz, built up during the moments of performance, in the style of the performer, around a theme. Jazz musicians rely on experience and develop a style of responding to the stimulus of a musical theme. They also train their skills, so that they can play in many different ways and respond to many different kinds of themes and varying contexts. All this is exactly what social workers do. One of the frightening things about being a social worker is that we cannot know what situation we will face when we knock on a client's front door or invite them into the interview room. However, social workers have developed their knowledge and skills to that they can respond in the best possible way. If they are going to do social work of the best quality, they, like musicians, will take every opportunity to practise. It is not hard to find opportunities, they come with the job. Each time we do something, we have the opportunity to learn from it. Most people are accustomed to keeping information about people to contact, or about services to call on, and many teams carry out projects to build up and share information.

It is possible to do the same with skills. A skill is a capacity that has been developed and trained so that it is more clearly defined, can be used more flexibly and, in social work, can be applied to influence social situations. More widely, skills are practical, they are about how to do things in the best way. Hidden in that sentence, though, is a value-statement: an assumption that we know what is best. Also hidden there is the point that using skills implies using knowledge because knowing how to do something does not tell us what to do. These points lead us to the next section, in which we discuss using theory in being critical.

Using theories in being critical

In this chapter, we have emphasised the importance of action. We said that social work is always 'action' and that being critical both is and contributes to action. Recognising this emphasis is important, because conventionally people distinguish thinking and acting, in sayings like 'look before you leap' or 'engage your brain before setting off'. Thinking and acting are bound together in social work, through the reflexive cycle. Being critical in social work means being aware of this cycle and alert to how our thinking and others' ideas affect it.

However, this approach to being critical places great emphasis on reason. That is, we are assuming that the world is an organised or ordered place. If this is so, reasoning skills allow us to think out how to act and have an impact on the world, alongside other human beings such as our clients and colleagues in our team, in the reflexive process of being critical that we have been discussing and modelling. The problem is that, as we noticed when discussing the example of views about families, this is an assumption. It is a commonplace assumption, by which we organise our lives, but an assumption nevertheless.

Some social theories set out to challenge this assumption of reason and the ordered nature of the world in various ways. Because of this, they are often referred to as critical theories. There are three groups commonly referred to: Marxism deriving the work of Marx in the mid-nineteenth century; the Frankfurt School of sociologists, such as Horkheimer (1978), Adorno (Adorno and Horkheimer, 1979) and Marcuse (1964), who were working from the 1920s and 30s; and, finally, their modern successor, Habermas (1984, 1987), writing in the late twentieth century. When many writers discuss being critical, they mean using these theories.

Historically, much social thought depends on the assumption of a fixed social order, often based on important social beliefs, such as religion, and the authority of national leaders, such as the government. When this began to be rejected, rational thinking using the scientific method became important. This emphasises that understanding through gaining evidence about the world can make us more effective in dealing with the outside world. Through using such methods in physical science, human beings have achieved considerable control of natural forces. Some sociologists, such as Durkheim (1972) and Weber (Gerth and Mills, 1948), emphasise how understanding the social world enables us to operate more effectively in relation to one another. So, if we understand how social relationships work, we will be able to achieve our objectives in society. In this statement, however, there is an assumption that social relationships exist and can be clarified and understood so that we then can act upon them.

Much social work thinking is like this. It assumes that we may understand what is going on in social relationships through practices such as 'assessment'. Having assessed a social situation, we can plan to do something about it through activities such as 'care management' and thus we may be able to change social relationships for the better (having made a value judgement about what is better), using interpersonal relationships between the social worker and the client.

Critical theories challenge this assumption of the existence of a social order that we may understand, and consequently they lead us to question practices that seem natural parts of it. Marx (1972) argues, for example, that we treat the current, capitalist system of economic theory as natural and given, whereas he sees capitalist societies as using a particular mode of economic organisation that has particular, and in many respects unfortunate, social consequences. Marxists would say that conventional social work practices support and extend the oppressive power of social institutions in capitalist states. For example, people with disabilities often argue that social workers' assessments of them assume a society in which they are impaired and less than human, rather than acknowledging that much of their disability stems from the way that society is organised for the able-bodied (see Chapter 19 for more discussion of this). The Frankfurt theorists argue that we treat our cultural and ideological heritage as given, whereas these elements of society are crucial elements in how we may be dominated by a capitalist, authoritarian state (for example Horkheimer, 1978). Thus, in social work, we sometimes assume, as we did earlier in this chapter, that cultural ideas such as family or community are fairly universal, whereas there are many different interpretations and uncertainties in them. Habermas (1984, 1987) distinguishes between the 'system' and the 'lifeworld', which interact and to some extent conflict with each other. By the system, he means the current mode of capitalist economic organisation, operating through such social structures as government, together with the rational mode of developing knowledge, which has had such benefits for technological and scientific progress. The lifeworld comprises such aspects of the world as education, family life and the media, which operate by a process called 'communicative reason', in which moral and social ideas are worked out in a widely shared social debate. The system and the lifeworld develop different ways of viewing and acting on the world through their different forms of reason. We might see social work as part of the 'lifeworld', interacting uneasily with the 'system' of managerialism in agencies; this is among the themes of the third part of this book.

To use these theories for critical purposes in social work is beyond the scope of this book, and would require extensive study of these writers and their modern interpreters and successors. However, we take three points from their ideas.

First, they emphasise social change and the importance of developing collective action to achieve it. Much social thought assumes that there is an identifiable social structure, which we can analyse and describe. What these theories all emphasise is that society does not exist in an unchanging or slowly changing social order, but that it evolves, or may be subject to revolutions. Therefore, we should be concerned with social change and what factors bring it about or act to slow it down. It is a short step from this to being concerned with how human actions can alter social structures. These theories, therefore, place importance on human agency, that is, how human beings may have an impact on the social world in which they live. Much conventional social thought assumes that general social forms have a significant impact on individuals; critical theories emphasise how human beings may act to change general social forms. This produces a very different sort of 'acting on' social relationships from the actions of assessment, care management and interpersonal change: it is a form of political agency (Batsleer and Humphries, 2000). That is, critical theory proposes that when we say social work is concerned with action, acting within the interpersonal situations is always part of a wider action concerned with broader social forms.

Such action is always political in the sense that interpersonal action always has an impact on the interaction of wider groups in society.

Second, critical theory focuses on intentionality. Earlier in this chapter, we stressed that thinking critically in social work leads us to act, not in a haphazard way, but with the intention of creating a planned change. Critical theories suggest that we need to scan the origins of our intent warily for exactly the same hidden value assumptions about how society is or ought to be organised. However, agency implies more than simply movement, but impulsion, towards some intention based on our values and ideologies. So, critical theories are concerned with how our everyday actions are part of continuing streams of either social change or stability. We are part of social movements that form around important ideas, such as environmentalism, feminism and social development. Some critical theorists regard it as crucial that action, intention and social movements are transformational and emancipatory in the way they work. The argument is that social movements transform the way people experience society and emancipate us from the limitations of present economic, cultural and ideological heritage.

Third, the implication for social work, and other intentional actions, of these theoretical ideas is that being critical does not only involve the use of reasoning or thinking in the technical way we have been discussing in the early part of this chapter. Being critical in practical thinking and practice takes place within social movements that are directed towards transforming societies and our intentions therefore need to be formed by our analysis of how societies are changing and might be changed towards greater freedoms for people. Thinking and acting critically therefore needs to be placed within analyses of how the limitations of social divisions such as class, gender and social assumptions about disability, sexuality and ethnic origin are created within social ideas that appear rational and that we take for granted, but are also changeable and changing. Some critical theorists argue that thinking critically in this way reveals important social movements and enables us to participate in them, pressing them forward.

The importance of language and understandings

Ideas and how they are represented in societies are, therefore, part of the process that creates our intentions. If we want to have an impact on individuals and societies, we must also be aware of ideas and their representation and how they affect the situation within which we are working. This element of critical theories reminds us of the importance of language and how we use it in expressing our understandings about the world. These came out in a pragmatic way as we were looking at thinking critically earlier. They relate to a range of ideas that are particularly in debate at the present time, arising from the work of social constructionist writers such as Shotter (1996) and Gergen (1999). What these writers propose is that our understanding of how societies, and relationships within them, operate is constructed and represented by the language that we use. We saw in the example of thinking about families that the words used revealed assumptions and ideas that we held about families. As with the critical theorists, the argument is that we express social relationships in how we behave and speak about the world. Because we come to share these social relationships through interacting with one another, we take part in a set of conventions about how the world is. Our participation means that we both mould and control and also are moulded and controlled by these ideas.

The implication of these writers for social work is that we can only become free of this control by taking apart these ideas through exploring rigorously the language and the social ideas it represents. By operating reflexively in social work processes, we can understand and construct or reconstruct the aspects of life that are causing people problems through developing shared social understandings and structures for action. In our professional role, by becoming reflexively part of a family with debt problems, we can see how destructive the fear of debt may be to relationships. In this way, our understanding and thinking becomes more empathic, reconstructed from a bureaucratic concern with the loss of the house. We can then help the family to explore the consequences of various possible actions. Should they run away? Should they reconstruct all their debts? Social work participation identifies options and priorities and in doing so identifies who might do what. Do we understand with the family that the credit company is oppressive in its policies? Do we confront the family with the perception that they have been unrealistic? Operating reflexively means that we have a better appreciation of what different responses may mean for the family, and what their meanings may imply for practical actions.

Thinking critically in the way discussed in this chapter, therefore, moves towards greater freedom by making apparent our assumptions and representations about the world. A crucial element in this is how social work, its organisation, its language and the practices that it pursues are ideas that mould and control us and our clients as part of ideas that mould and control the social worlds in which we all move. We should not see this as a conspiracy of those in power or as an evil; this is how social worlds operate. Worlds in which people live collectively rather than as individuals inevitably generate collective understandings. It is a characteristic of social interaction that it creates these oppressions and limitations in our interactions with each other.

CONCLUSION

This chapter has explored some important general features of two important constituents of critical practice: critical thinking and critical action. The first part of the book on values identifies an extension of critical practice beyond interpersonal interaction between social workers and clients. Equality treats people equally, and also seeks greater social equality. Openness offers a critical dialogue between people, both clients and colleagues, and offers opportunities for creativity. Making a difference means not only pursuing betterment for services users in their world, but in the wider social worlds that we live in.

Understanding and exploring language, how it is used in interactions and how it forms our views of the world, is an essential element in critical practice. Through a process of critical thinking, by interacting reflexively in relationships with others, we can examine agenda-setting, the content of judgements that we make and the ideologies that underlie them. Using these understandings, we can build a critical practice of examining evidence and perspectives in detail, contextualising information, developing an overview and then presenting our thinking effectively to our audiences. As we practise, we develop and refine skills. The second part of the book builds on the value base of critical practice to identify how these processes may be applied in a multitude of practice situations. The third part extends this to critical management practice and the management contexts of practice.

The theoretical ideas of critical sociology emphasise that social work must go beyond a technical form of thinking and practice, following guidelines and standard practices to empower people, both colleagues and clients, with political agency to achieve collective and social objectives as well as personal growth. A reflexive focus on language and understanding incorporates within daily practice our wider social objectives, but grounds them in the lived experience of the people that we work with. Critical theory and critical action thus become participation with intentionality in a critical practice within social work, extending the interpersonal towards the social. It is the value base, practice and management of these processes that the following chapters seek to capture, explore and extend.

FURTHER READING

Arato, A. and Gebhardt, E. (eds) (1978) *The Essential Frankfurt School Reader*, Oxford: Blackwell. This reader provides access to the main writers in the tradition of critical sociological theory.

Taylor, C. and White, S. (2000) *Practising Reflexivity in Health and Welfare: Making Knowledge*, Buckingham: Open University Press. A good practical account of how practice may be reflexive in its thinking and response to language and social construction.

Waters, M. (1994) *Modern Sociological Theory*, London: Sage. This book offers a good introductory discussion to a range of sociological theories, including those discussed briefly in this chapter.

Values Into Critical Practice

Values in Social Work: Contested Entities with Enduring Qualities

Lena Dominelli

Values are concepts that provide a philosophical basis to social work practice (Compton and Galaway, 1975). They furnish the foundation for ethics as a set of principles that guide practice and are an important part of any profession. Values underpin the norms that ensure ethical behaviour on the part of practitioners and elaborate a basis for holding them accountable for their actions (Hugman, 1991). Values justify particular types of behaviour, giving those that conform validity and legitimacy. They are used in setting parameters around what can be considered defensible behaviour in professional practice and outlining the responsibilities of different participants in a particular intervention. These functions lead social workers to expect values to ensure continuity or have enduring qualities through which practice can be judged or evaluated across different settings and at distinct points in time.

Values have an aura of stability about them that enables practitioners to talk to other colleagues about their work and traverse various divides, giving the impression that they are talking about similar entities, even when they hail from different countries and cultures. However, when discourses about values and their application in practice are explored more carefully, several problems emerge. One is that to focus on values as concepts or consider their similarities, values have to be defined at high levels of abstraction, which denude them of their context. Another difficulty is that once values are contextualised to locate their specificity, significant differences in interpretation become more visible. Finally, different stakeholders in the social work enterprise contest values as they argue over their symbolic signification. This can produce conflict, but it also allows growth and change to take place. The fluid movement of values through complex interactions in helping relationships suggests that the certainty and stability that surround values are illusory. Indeed, some theorists argue that social work is an exercise in ambiguity and uncertainty (Parton, 1998).

In this chapter, I explore values in social work – their meaning and relevance for practice, their shifting nature and their implications for critical practice. I conclude that values are contested entities and that, as practised, they express both continuities and discontinuities between the past, present and future of the profession. As guides to ethical behaviour, values seldom provide the clear-cut principles demanded by those at the receiving end of social workers' ministrations or their employers. And, in trying to resolve moral and ethical dilemmas, social work values may simply produce new ones.

Defining values

How do social workers define values and are these defining values? The task of defining values can be an elusive one (Shardlow, 1998). There are a number of different kinds of values: personal, professional, institutional, organisational or agency, political, religious and cultural. The list might easily be extended, but a common feature of each is that they are socially constructed and historically specific. They are usually derived from values that permeate a given society at a particular historical conjuncture. Personal values are those that an individual holds and uses in guiding his or her individual behaviour and actions. They are important in constituting the person as a moral agent and support continuity between and across generations. Professional values are those that practitioners define as being specific to their particular profession. Their formulation is usually the explicit product of discussions and agreed among professional colleagues who advise upon them and, acting as a peer group, monitor each other's activities with relation to their stipulated code. In older professions such as medicine, professional values are backed by a code of ethics that is enforced by professional peers.

In social work, professional values are usually promulgated through professional associations, but their enforcement is more problematic. This is particularly the case in countries where social work does not have a protected title and the professional association has no legal powers of enforcement. In Britain, social workers have a code of ethics that draws on generally held professional values. Developed by the British Association of Social Workers (BASW), it is currently not legally enforceable, although this situation may alter when the General Council for Social Care (GCSC) is set up and running. On the international front, the International Federation of Social Workers (IFSW) has attempted to devise an international code of ethics. However, this is voluntary and acts more as a guide in the formulation of local, usually national codes that are devised by the relevant associations on the spot. There is considerable variability in these codes, although the dominance of Anglo-American paradigms is also evident. Some practitioners have countered Western hegemony by developing locally specific or indigenous codes, for example, First Nations[1] practitioners in Canada and Maori ones in New Zealand. These have sought to incorporate collectivist or community considerations and responsibilities missing in Western models.

Alongside Afrocentric models, these also focus on continuities in values and cultural traditions that ensure the survival of ethnic groups experiencing oppression over centuries (John Baptiste, 2001).

Organisational values can distort professional values by narrowing down options when practitioners seek to broaden them out. This occurs when social workers wish to increase the options available to 'clients'[2] but existing organisational resources reduce them. Budgetary limitations on community care assessments exemplify this practitioner dilemma. The fanfare of client empowerment surrounding community care raises the question of whether organisations can be ethical if they raise false expectations about the range of choices accessible by them. Research into this issue by Khan and Dominelli (2000) demonstrates how marketisation and globalisation have skewed professional priorities and contributed to practitioner disillusionment in their ability to deliver the best quality services in their organisations.

Values seem contradictory and difficult to define. Yet most social workers claim to adhere to a discrete set of values that represent their commitment to certain principles that both guide their behaviour and can be used to evaluate their performance. The most commonly recognised values in social work emanate from Biestek (1961) and consist of the following:

- individualisation

- purposeful expression of feelings

- controlled emotional involvement

- non-judgemental attitude

- self-determination

- confidentiality.

Respect for others and the dignity of the person underpin these and are fundamental to black perspectives (Ahmad, 1990), anti-racist approaches (Dominelli, 1988) and other anti-oppressive positions. Banks (2001: 27) argues that the underlying theme in Biestek's values is the Kantian one of 'respect for the individual person'. While this formulation of values has been criticised for its modernist bias and overreliance on scientific rationality (see Chapter 1) to back its claim to 'truth', it has been recognised by practitioners worldwide and can claim universal applicability. Indeed, Healy (2001) proposes respect and dignity as essential values in international social work.

Putting to one side the question of interpretation, reducing a set of values to one statement highlights the abstract nature of these values. When boiled down to one, it reaches levels of agreement and universality, which in practice become difficult to sustain in certain circumstances. If we are asked whether respecting the person is a key social work value, the question is cast in a decontextualised form and it is hard to imagine a social worker who would not overtly endorse it. However, posing the question in terms of practising values in context, the answers would be more nuanced and complex. For example, in working with a sex offender, social workers draw a distinction between the person whom they claim to respect and his (most sex offenders are men) behaviour which they cannot condone. Although a myth, acting as if these are two entirely separate entities allows social workers to address the difficulty of not endorsing unacceptable behaviour while maintaining the validity of the principle of respect. Similar dilemmas occur with counselling people on death row to become reconciled with their demise. While their professional ethics demand respect for the person and the sanctity of life at the same time, the practitioners involved are colluding with the elimination of that person through state-sanctioned violence, the validity of which is contested. Unequal power relations cut across the emancipatory dimensions of social work values and create oppression through practice, as literature challenging racism (Ahmad, 1990; Dominelli, 1988), sexism (Dominelli and McLeod, 1989; Hanmer and Statham, 1988) and disablism (Oliver, 1990; Morris, 1991) indicates.

Social workers have to become skilful mental acrobats who can juggle contradictory positions with ease when it comes to putting their values into practice. A further value or principle that practitioners use to deal with dilemmas they face is that of not treating people as means to other ends. However, as demonstrated above, it is not always possible to maintain this concern. Nonetheless, it has helped social workers to maintain their commitment to social justice, where they have argued that the means used to achieve a particular end must reflect the end that is being sought (Dominelli, 1996).

Biestek's (1961) principles have also been criticised for being highly individualistic and culturally specific, that is, tied to Western culture. Yet they are often used in ways that claim universal validity and applicability. This means that other cultural traditions, especially those Eastern ones which emphasise collective rather than individualistic bases to their societies, are excluded from these or are seen as totally irrelevant to their way of working. The issue of confidentiality is a particularly relevant one in this critique. For example, in a project that I was involved in some while ago, white community workers in a British Muslim Gujerati community in northern England expressed unease when interested members of this community accompanied a person who had a problem into the office and insisted on participating in the ensuing discussions. Several of the white practitioners found this behaviour incomprehensible because they defined it as one that violated their expectations about confidentiality. Their discomfort abated when it was explained to them that confidentiality was seen differently by this group of clients and that they welcomed the presence of kin and friends. At the same time, these clients were not willing to have their business discussed outside this group. Thus, they had criteria that stipulated boundaries or points at which their interpretation of confidentiality took substance, and they expected the white practitioners to honour these.

Whether Biestek's (1961) values are defining values, in the sense of being crucial to the profession or setting its parameters, is another question. Reference to them can be found in most social work texts on values. Their continued presence over the past four decades suggest that they have been influential, albeit they have been modified to more closely reflect contemporary linguistic usage. The process of reformulation and development is indicated by empowerment, which extends self-determination in new directions. Their adaptation has also furnished them with slightly different meanings. For example, in becoming empowerment, self-determination has acquired a more active sense even though the clients' rights to make decisions about their lives remain germane to both. And, as Jane Dalrymple and Beverley Burke remind us in Chapter 6, 'empowerment is overlain by contrasting and conflicting aims and expectations'.

Empowerment goes beyond the value of self-determination in that it makes power relations an explicit part of its analytical and practice repertoire, thereby making it a more contextualised concept than self-determination as defined by Biestek (1961). Moreover, the term has been developed conceptually in a number of different directions (Humphries, 1996; Dominelli, 2000). Are the terms synonymous, as some texts suggest, or are attempts to find similarities between them exercises in futility?

Some of the changes leading to innovation in social work's value system have been driven by a desire to identify values that are relevant to critical practice. Within this framework, respecting the person would remain a central one, but it would not simply focus on the individual as a decontextualsed person. Instead, it would see him or her as a social being operating within a social context which would include social institutions and a host of external factors that would have to be taken into account in translating this value into practice. Respecting the person would also be linked to dignity and the recognition that a person has socially sanctioned rights, although rights present another conceptual minefield.

In examining the relevant context, practitioners also need to look underneath the presenting problem, an important part of the holistic practice to which critical practitioners aspire (Ife, 1997). Asking probing questions to delve deeper into issues has also been part of traditional training (Compton and Galaway, 1975). So, there has been less innovation in this arena than appears at first glance.

Controlled emotional engagement is more likely to permit becoming non-judgemental. But even this value would be contextualised in today's critical practice. For, without contextualisation, it could be interpreted as meaning the acceptance of behaviour that harms others, whether this ranges from minor lying to theft or violence against the person or a cold detachment that precludes the formation of a professional helping relationship. Critical social workers would acknowledge that they are in the business of making judgements and that these are often finely balanced ones. For example, making decisions about whether a particular sex offender poses a potential risk to a given child requires practitioners to make judgements. However, as *professional* judgements, these are based on assessments of risk rather than arbitrary personal prejudices. Although risk assessments are not straightforward calculations and their use also needs to be critiqued, the basis for their judgements can be articulated and social workers held accountable for the decisions they make.

What counts as acceptable or plausible remains problematic. Do these terms mean the same thing? These questions cannot be answered except in a specific context, and maybe not even then. The complexity of implementing any set of values in practice is illustrated in Sarah Banks' example of the social worker's failure to disclose knowledge about a client with the potential to sexually abuse others (Chapter 3).

Individualisation would now be expressed more in terms of validating the uniqueness of each individual. But, in critical practice, particularly as advocated by feminists and black people, the individual would at the same time be seen as part of a wider group. In this, identity issues would be treated as more self-determining while a greater awareness of their diversity would be evident to simultaneously ensure that the space for the individual is safeguarded from bureaucratic encroachment.

Purposeful expression of feeling is the most awkward of Biestek's (1961) terminology for use in the present day. Most contemporary social workers would subscribe to the view that professionals should not allow their personal views to impact upon their work, and would only share their feelings or experiences with clients under very limited circumstances. Despite their caution in this regard, they would insist on being aware of what their personal views were to ensure that they are kept in check.

Critical practitioners would add that, in understanding themselves, practitioners would be able to handle the boundaries between the public and private domains more effectively. To some extent, their capacity to maintain the public–private divide would confirm their ability to be 'neutral' in relation to the client, in the sense of keeping a respectful objectivity or distance from him/her rather than being neutral, in the sense of having no views on the subject. On the other side of this boundary is the requirement that practitioners express empathy with their clients, an injunction that is at odds with the previous one.

Empathy requires the social worker to be in the clients' shoes (Egan, 1998; Chapter 1) or enter their epistemological and ontological worlds. This value is aimed at enabling practitioners to cross social divides and be with the client in a supportive way. Demonstrating empathy can be extremely difficult to achieve, as white workers tackling racist practices have found (Dominelli, 1988). Conflict between the practitioners' personal and professional values can also block the realisation of empathy, especially if the former prevents them from complying with statutory duties. They may be unable to express empathy in certain cases and find that curbing their private views becomes a source of considerable personal stress. This is an issue that can easily crop up in work involving child molesters or murderers, where a practitioner may have difficulty in being empathetic. Such situations also reveal that values are experienced emotionally as well as being thought about and implemented in practice.

On the practical level, it is crucial to ask how the values of a profession can be enforced so that ethical practice occurs as a matter of course. What are the roles of the individual practitioner, their employers and professional associations in ensuring that accepted values, standards and norms are adhered to by each of them? Who will monitor compliance? What happens when they are violated? Who will enforce them and how? None of these questions have easy, let alone automatic, answers. They constantly have to be posed and responded to in specific contexts. So, a practitioner's peers may more readily overlook a colleague's reluctance to empathise with a child molester or murderer, but they would not be so forgiving of a failure to prevent harm being inflicted upon a child in their care.

The descriptions of values-in-action provided above evidence a crucial point: values are not neutral, particularly when applied in practice. Conflicts of interest between the different participants – clients, victims, practitioners, policy-makers, service providers, and others, abound. Mediating conflicting interests draws on another principle – protection from harm. But in resolving conflicts, protection issues involving the self, others, workers and society can remain problematic. On what basis, that is, values, does a practitioner say that a child's right to safety overrides an adult's right to privacy and protection from the stigma caused by an investigation into an alleged abuse, especially when the case becomes 'not proven'? This scenario forms the most likely outcome in child protection investigations as most of these do not substantiate the allegations (Department of Health, 1995a).

Social workers constantly prioritise one set of principles over another. In taking action, social workers weigh different priorities. Establishing priorities to facilitate action in particular situations is one way of creating certainty in an ambiguous and contradictory world. Without some way of finding at least a temporary or transient certainty in difficult moral and ethical terrain, social workers would be unable to act.

To make matters even more complicated, the entire basis on which professional values rest is also subject to questioning. That is, the alleged superiority of professional or expert knowledge is today challenged by clients who reject the exclusion of their voices (Wendell, 1996) and postmodern theorists. Their demands can involve practitioners in conflict with traditional professional values that prioritise professional knowledge over client knowledge. But clients have led the way in emancipatory practice and given enormous impetus to the idea that practitioners should support their strivings for social justice. In this, clients have introduced the idea of citizenship as the basis of their relationships with caring professionals. However, citizenship in the welfare market is a limited or qualified one (Banks, 2001). The reduction of clients to users who follow an exit strategy when they cannot exercise a meaningful choice in the marketplace introduces commodity relations to a non-commercial sphere (Dominelli, 2000).

Practising values

The word 'values' is grammatically a noun, but it is derived from a verb, to value or hold in esteem. While easy to talk about applying values or values in practice, the phrase 'practising values' sounds odd. But it portrays a dynamism that is essential in (re)conceptualising values as values-in-action and in addressing the complexities and dilemmas that realising them entails. The difficulties in defining values are replicated in their application in practice. The problems encountered are not only about differences in interpretation and meaning, but also of values in conflict or contradiction with one another. This situation is further complicated by issues of accountability.

Social workers are accountable to a range of stakeholders – service users, other practitioners, employers, policy-makers, government and the general public. To begin with, these groups may or may not share the same values. So conflict can arise from these sources. But even if they do hold similar values, each has different imperatives that contextualise these. Contextual exigencies emanating from organisational priorities also have an impact on how values can be applied in practice. Practising values is not a straightforward matter. Social workers become embroiled as co-accused as a result of holding a case in situations where their clients have been adversely treated and their vulnerability increased, as in the case of the death of a child on an 'at risk' register. Whether or not the practitioner was directly responsible for this outcome, the social worker's practice will be subjected to intense scrutiny. The inquiry into their practice may be conducted in a manner that does not reflect the values of the profession in terms of showing respect for the person. The social worker may be scapegoated for a number of structural inadequacies, as Sarah Banks indicates in Chapter 3 when recounting the experience of an overworked, distraught social worker who is treated in a manner that ignores her own personal state. A crucial issue here is that social work practice is distinctive in that no matter what the psychological or emotional state of the social worker is, she or he must not endanger the life of a client through her/his actions.

In this case, the abuse of one child in a home by another might have been prevented had the social worker passed on crucial information to the home manager. Banks' example also raises a number of other value-laden questions: How do social workers value or weigh the information they receive? Does knowledge that the boy had previously perpetrated sexual abuse become valued in hindsight because it is now possible to see a causal connection between knowledge and action? Would conducting a more thorough risk assessment upon the young man's admission to the home have highlighted the weightiness of this piece of information beforehand so that preventive action could have been taken? But evaluation, as Nick Frost shows in Chapter 5, is not a one-way street. The social worker needs managerial support if evaluation is to become part of an ongoing process of intervention. Yet this ingredient is in remarkably short supply in the case cited. In addition to this, the evaluative tools at the practitioners' disposal do not always measure up to the task. For example, Quinsey's (1995) research has found wanting the capacity of risk assessment to effectively predict dangerousness in particular offenders.

Practice at this level is currently hampered by our inadequate knowledge about risk. The possibility that an event may occur is not the same as its actual occurrence. We cannot readily distinguish between the two before the event. And, in playing safe by assuming that it will occur, individuals suspected of being potential sex offenders may find a utilitarian approach to their rights. This is likely to mean that the presumption of innocence until proven guilty will be put aside in favour of ensuring the safety of those who might become their victims.

Other concerns to be addressed include issues of social justice, rights and fair play. As Chris Clark indicates in Chapter 4, these are contentious and at times in conflict with each other. Clearly, the children in the home have the right to live in an environment free of sexual abuse, and all those running the home and working within it are responsible for ensuring that it is such a place. Research (Kelly et al., 1991) reveals a high incidence of sexual abuse in society. Thus, it is possible to conclude that children who have been abused and those who are abusers are likely to be found in any general sample of the child population. Campbell's (1995) research indicates that the majority of sex offenders have been neither identified as such nor convicted. In this context, it would be reasonable to assume that every home would have systems in place to take account of the possibility that they might have sexually abused children and sex offenders in their midst and ensure that its duty to protect children is effectively discharged. This should be an institutional responsibility that those working within the home discharge collectively. Thus, practice has to be conceptualised as more than the sum of its constituent parts. This view of it has implications for the institutions responsible for caring for a particular child.

Formal inquiries seldom comment on institutional responsibilities except at the level of refining existing or introducing new bureaucratic procedures to hold individual practitioners more accountable in future. The issue of institutional responsibility for ensuring that employees have appropriate working conditions, including adequate support and supervision, is rarely detailed in the ensuing reports (Blom-Cooper, 1986; Butler-Sloss, 1988). Having fragmented services reliant on individual, atomised practitioners each responsible for covering an entire spectrum of provisions sets dangerous precedents for achieving maximum effectiveness in difficult and sensitive areas. The exclusion of practitioners from positions where decisions about policy and procedures are made exacerbates the problem of lack of fit between formal policies and the realities of practice. Consequently, the politics of practice become skewed by bureaucratic exigencies at the expense of practice ones.

Besides institutional responsibility, there is personal responsibility. If prevention of future abuse and the rehabilitation of the offender are to be valued, individual case notes should at least contain information that identifies a particular individual who may have experienced sexual abuse and/or perpetrated it. Providing information conflicts with not labelling people or placing them into a strait-jacket from which they cannot escape, even though it may be shared only among the few who need to know so as not to label a child unnecessarily in further stigmatising ways or hinder future work aimed at promoting their capacity to relate to others in non-exploitative ways. Such situations are potentially difficult to manage and become sources of considerable pressure for individuals to resolve. Nonetheless, personal responsibility enables a practitioner to play specific roles in interventions with a given individual and to take additional measures/precautions alongside the general ones instituted by the institution.

Issues of confidentiality are also complicated in such scenarios. A social worker's commitment is to change individual behaviour so that it becomes more socially acceptable. In pursuing this course of action, the right of the offender not to have his past held against him in the interests of rehabilitation and change, or when serving his time if he has been punished, is no longer automatically assured. In the case of a sex offender, one set of values – that of protecting others from harm – supersedes his rights to privacy, and the Sex Offenders Act 1997 has enshrined this contradiction in law. This demonstrates anew that values can never be practised in the abstract, but only in specific circumstances. Here, social workers have to make decisions which prioritise one value over another in particular ways. In such circumstances, most social workers will give priority to the rights of the most vulnerable person(s).

Fine balances in judgement often have to be made and, sometimes, the weighting that a specific practitioner gives to a particular situation or factor turns out to be wrong, as in the illustration provided by Sarah Banks. Yet, the crucial question remains: How can social workers minimise the number of inadequate decisions made in such circumstances? Responding to this question requires discussion among employers, policy-makers, trainers and the general public as well as the specific people involved in the case. However, contemporary discourses on the subject seldom focus on holistic responses to the problem. As countless inquiries into the death of looked-after children or their continued sexual abuse indicate, it is usually the practice of an individual practitioner that is scrutinised and held responsible when things go wrong.

Trust is an important element in practising values that promote ethical behaviour among professionals. Although not often considered, trust is itself a value that underpins other values and must be evident throughout an entire operation if it is to permeate all social interactions within a given case. At the same time, trust is created (or not) in and through the interactions of the individuals concerned, although they may draw on an institutional context that may (or may not) support it. Hence, trust is created through negotiations between people as well as being taken as given in a supportive workplace. A social worker has to 'trust' that the organisation will facilitate his/her work and back it in particular ways. Similarly, clients 'trust' practitioners to do their job effectively and in a manner that safeguards their interests and vulnerability. Trust is needed at many levels, none of which can be presumed in practice. But trust should be there as part of the taken-for-granted context in which helping relationships occur. As I show in Chapter 8, the climate in which reproductive rights are being simultaneously extended and curtailed both betrays and draws upon trust.

Understanding power relations and the roles these play in the various levels of people involved in client–worker relationships is essential in a framework that appreciates the political and contested nature of values. Power relations can be practised as a zero-sum game that divides people into those who have power and those who do not. However, I would argue for a more refined consideration of these. Following Giddens (1987), power can be conceptualised as a negotiated reality in which neither party is either completely powerful or powerless. In other words, the interaction between them is one that can either reproduce or challenge existing power relations (Dominelli, 1986; Dominelli and Gollins, 1997). Practitioners can respond to clients as agents who can take responsibility for their behaviour rather than being treated as passive victims who have everything done for them by experts. Thinking about power as multifaceted allows for more empowering forms of practice that enable clients to voice their own opinions and views, and participate in shaping the outcomes of intervention. Reinforcing client agency ties in more closely with putting substance behind the value of self-determination, even when practitioners have an eye on clients' potential to engage in further abuse of others as in the case of sex offenders.

Each situation is affected by a number of different and sometimes competing values. Audrey Mullender's Chapter 7 demonstrates how what is valued or prioritised can change over time. For example, feminist actions aimed at safeguarding the interests of women and children who have been at the receiving end of domestic violence have ensured that this particular form of cruel and degrading treatment is addressed and taken seriously in and through practice as it rises up the social work agenda. This issue also reveals how different client groups are valued and treated differently. Being treated differently does not always result in better or more appropriate responses, as the experiences of abused black women (Mama, 1999; Wilson, 1993) and lesbian women (Arnup, 1997) have shown. For this to occur, being treated differently has to be accompanied by a valuing or seeing the worth of a person undergoing that experience. It means being treated with dignity as human beings whatever the circumstances and is where humanism as a value comes through.

Values and critical practice

Critical practitioners have an important question to answer. In doing critical practice, are they practising different values? In other words, do professional values for critical practice differ from professional values for other paradigms of practice? In my view, there are overlaps between the two. In critical practice, professionals are considered as moral agents engaging in a moral activity. That is why the value of social justice is so important to practice. Promoting this value may constitute the key difference between traditional practitioners and critical ones.

Critical practice can be about a variety of different positions, and, as this book demonstrates, its definition is a matter of continuous dialogue and examination of different points of view. There appears to be some agreement about the importance of reflexivity in the processes of critical practice, and in defining social work as both a moral and technical activity. However, even this delineation of what counts in social work does not deal with difficult situations such as those where social workers or carers abuse those they care for. Caring for someone does not necessarily mean caring about them. The latter implies a different sort of relationship. It conveys the idea that a non-exploitative arrangement can be expected. What happens when these associations go wrong and the opposite is delivered? Do we say that a person was not a carer, only an abuser? Or has the person been both? The depiction of each of these values as discrete and separate entities does not help in clarifying this situation. This is because it covers both life-affirming and life-destroying values. An individual or organisation can espouse both simultaneously. It is only in their behaviour and its outcome that a firm judgement can be made about what values the person has prioritised (a decision about which value was more important to them personally).

The dichotomous thinking that divides behaviour into either one or the other may help us to establish the harm that has been done to the victim-survivor of the abuse. It does not help us to understand the position of abusers who claim to endorse life-affirming principles through their behaviour, as sex offenders often do when they claim they were demonstrating 'love' for their victims and not abusing them (Snowdon, 1980). Although practitioners tend to dismiss their comments as cognitive distortions if not outright lies, the sex offender may genuinely believe his statements. The challenge for practitioners is to get these men to revise their views. Practitioners can only do so if they believe in some absolute value that supersedes that of starting where the client is at, have knowledge that enables them to discount the offender's story, or use powers that entitle them to define what is acceptable behaviour and what is not, such as those vested in them through legislation, social approbation or professional codes. This may mean that social workers have to hold uncertainty and ambiguity as defining characteristics of their work, even when called upon to act with certainty in difficult situations.

Critical practitioners would engage in these situations by trying to find ways of assisting both the carer and the cared-for, but in different ways, and may insist that different practitioners undertake each particular piece of work. A traditional practitioner would struggle with similar issues and thus might find at the end of the day that they have more in common than they expect, except for the critical practitioner's overt commitment to social justice. Their practice with individual people may be remarkably similar. This possibility guides claims that, at the end of the day, all practitioners are about good practice and why CCETSW, when it lost the battle over anti-oppressive practice in the mid-1990s, asserted victory on the grounds that the value base had been retained intact.

CONCLUSION

Values provide tools for determining merit or worth. An important contribution of postmodernism to debates about values is its capacity to make explicit what has been implicit in much of the 'practice wisdoms' that practitioners draw upon in their practice. Although important, this contribution has been less about innovative insights into values than about presenting previously known ones in new ways. This has articulated the contingent and contextualised nature of values and highlighted the difficulties encountered in putting them into practice.

Critical practitioners need to start where clients are at. But this, like other values, is a contingent, not an absolute, value. Its conditionality still leaves much of the power in the helping relationship in the hands of the professional. This is not in itself an undesirable feature. It depends on how this power is used by the professional and for what purpose. And it is at this point that reflexivity in process and a commitment to social justice and client agency differentiate a critical practitioner from a more traditional one. Thus, critical practitioners can expect their practice to be constantly evolving. Their practice development is always unfinished. A social worker is always in the process of becoming a critical practitioner even when acting as if she or he were one already.

Notes

1. 'First Nations' is the term used by Canadians of indigenous descent to describe themselves in preference to either native Canadians or Indians, identifiers to which they object.
2. The term client is a contested one, but I prefer it to user or consumer. Similarly, the terms black and white when used to refer to people should not be taken to mean homogeneity in their physical, social and cultural attributes.

FURTHER READING

Banks, S. (2001) *Ethics and Values in Social Work*, 2nd edn, Basingstoke: Palgrave – now Palgrave Macmillan. A comprehensive consideration of the issues and dilemmas that practitioners encounter in implementing their values in practice. This second edition makes some international comparisons.

Dominelli, L. (2002) *Feminist Social Work Theory and Practice*, Basingstoke: Palgrave – now Palgrave Macmillan. Examines the differences that feminist values make to work that is undertaken with clients at the centre of the helping relationship. Arguing for a reconceptualisation of power relations between service users and practitioners, it considers how social workers can work in empowering ways.

Wilmot, S. (1997) *The Ethics of Community Care*, London: Cassell. Considers the complexities of practice and ethical dilemmas that need to be addressed when delivering community care.

Professional Values and Accountabilities

Sarah Banks

This chapter explores the concept of accountability and its implementation in social work practice. Although accountability is not a new concept, concern with accountability is currently a high priority. This chapter considers the implications for critical practice in social work, drawing on interviews with local authority social work managers and practitioners.

The importance of accountability

A social work team manager, being interviewed about ethical issues in her work, made the following statement:

> More than ever before, because I've been in social work for a long time, it seems like accountability is very hot on the agenda – demonstrating outcomes and having to have almost number crunching type pieces of information that you can give.

This interviewee made two important points. First, concern with accountability seems greater than previously. Second, she referred to a particular type of accountability, which she later described as especially onerous – the production of quantifiable outputs and outcomes in response to demands by employers and central government.

Accountability has always been important for professionals. According to Tadd (1994: 88), it is 'the sine qua non of any professional group'. But the kind of accountability stressed by professional bodies is that owed to clients or service users. Service to clients is the essence of professional practice; and any professional, whether a doctor, lawyer, or social worker, must be prepared to account for their actions to people using their services. Although we may dispute how well professionals have implemented it, accountability to service users is integral to the core values of social work of respecting service users' freedom of choice, promoting their welfare and challenging discrimination and oppression. Indeed, professional codes of ethics stress that the social worker's primary responsibility, and hence accountability, is to the service user and community (BASW, 1996: para. 9).

In addition to professional accountability to service users, social workers have always had a duty of public accountability to the wider political community (Clark, 2000: 78–9; Pratchett and Wingfield, 1994: 9). They often work directly or indirectly for public bodies, with a role to promote the public good by, for example, protecting the vulnerable and treating or controlling dangerous people. Social workers and their employers are therefore accountable to the public for the effectiveness of the services they deliver. So, notions of professional and public accountability are at the heart of social work, and in both areas demands are increasing. The two are interconnected, as employers are introducing quality standards, standardised assessment forms, contracts and complaints procedures, partly in response to demands from service users for their rights to more effective services, to participate in decision-making and to complain. But the accountability demands of different parties may also conflict, and one of the themes of my interviews with social workers is that, in striving for organisational and public accountability, the voices, needs and rights of individual service users and their communities may get lost.

The nature of accountability

Accountability is an integral feature of everyday as well as professional life. The eighteenth-century philosopher Reid suggests it is a distinguishing feature of humans: 'that which makes them moral agents, accountable for their conduct, and objects of moral approbation and blame' (Reid, 1977 [1788]: 69). It is not just that we must be prepared to describe, explain or justify what we have done in order to be apportioned moral praise or blame, but 'giving an account' is an essential feature of our means of communicating with others, being understood and establishing our identities (Buttny, 1993; Heritage, 1983). What I have called professional and public accountability are part of this wider system of moral and social accountability.

To be accountable is literally to be liable to be called upon to give an account of what one has or has not done. The account may include all or some of descriptions, explanations, excuses or justifications. Frequently, giving an account is associated with the occurrence of a problematic situation and the apportioning of blame. Indeed, Holdsworth (1994: 42) defines accountability as 'the obligation to lay oneself open to criticism'. Buttny's concern in his sociological study of accountability is with 'talk used to transform pejorative ascriptions and resolve problematic events' (1993: 16). Hence, the main types of accounts tend to be excuses and justifications. Buttny acknowledges that accounts can be 'descriptions', 'ordinary explanations' or 'self reports' which would also include unproblematic situations (p. 15) but, his main concern, along with other sociologists, is with accounts as attempts to mend a social breach resulting from a problematic situation. Accountability is linked with laying oneself open to blame and criticism, and trying to counter any negative evaluations that might be placed on one's action. As Buttny (1993: 2) comments:

> This distinctively human capacity to be blamed and to be held responsible for actions creates the practical necessity for the communication of accounts.

This suggests an important relationship between accountability and responsibility. Being held responsible for my actions means that I am able to make rational choices and decisions and therefore should 'own' my actions. If something goes wrong, if I am accused of making a bad decision or causing a bad outcome, then I may be asked, or I may wish, to give an account of what happened, my reasons for acting as I did, perhaps pointing to circumstances of which others may be unaware.

Although some commentators treat accountability and responsibility as synonymous (Clark with Asquith, 1985: 40), and others just use the terms interchangeably (Clark, 2000; Tadd, 1994), this is unhelpful. Fairbairn (1985) lists four senses of responsibility, only one of which means the same as 'accountability'. The first relates to causing a state of affairs. For example, when we talk of someone having 'responsibility for an accident', we may mean that they caused the accident. Another sense of responsibility is that of having a duty to someone or to do something. For example, we might say: 'you have a responsibility to look after your daughter'. We may also use 'responsibility' to describe a person's character or behaviour, for example, 'she acted with responsibility' in the sense that she was trustworthy and reliable. In none of these three usages of 'responsibility' could 'accountability' be substituted without changing the meaning. The final sense of responsibility is being liable to explain or justify action, that is, accountability. Accountability, therefore, is just one sense of 'responsibility', and is not always synonymous with it.

Accountability and blame

A senior social worker being interviewed on ethical issues in practice described a situation for which the worker had been 'called to account', held responsible and blameworthy:

> One of the really bad experiences that I did have last summer, and it was because I was working – I had too much work to do. I said I had too much work to do, and it was perceived as a kind of weakness on my part, you know, it wasn't responded to positively at first. And also I had various personal problems. My son was ill at the time and one thing and another. I placed a 15-year-old young man with learning disabilities in a group care home. I was told to do so by my team manager. I'd written a very comprehensive case conference report, in which I had alluded to various sexualised behaviour that this young man had exhibited in the past. I was pressurised by the people who were currently looking after the young man to move him within a very short space of time, took the young man to the care home, did an introductory visit. I completed the essential information pack that we have from the Department of Health – the essential information. There is no question in that pack: 'Has this child exhibited sexualised behaviour?' So the

information, the documentation that you fill out is flawed anyway, because it doesn't contain the essential information. The young man then went on to sexually abuse one of the young women living in the home. And then there's a big enquiry about it and I'm to blame.

We will now analyse this account, also bringing in information given later in the interview, to elucidate what is involved in giving an account in the context of a problematic situation in social work.

1. Contextualising the worker

First the worker situates herself. Not only is she a social worker with the standard skills and responsibilities expected of all social workers (her professional identity), but she is also a person with events happening in her personal life that affect how she feels and performs. Later she also locates herself as 'part of a system' – particularly the decision-making system that includes a team manager, care home manager, and members of the case conference. The worker feels it is important to contextualise herself partly because she felt exposed:

> You feel a bit like Lee Harvey Oswald, you know, on the top of the Book Depository Building with a smoking gun ... where's everybody gone? Where have all the case conference members gone who actually knew about it? ... Where is the team manager who told me to place? Where is the supervision?

2. Descriptive narrative

The worker tells the story of what happened: she placed the young man in a care home; she completed the forms correctly and handed them over; the young man then abused another resident. Obviously this is not 'pure description', but a selection of what she thinks is the most relevant information to construct the case.

3. Explanations, justifications, excuses

Some of the descriptions may be serving as explanations, justifications or excuses – it is not always clear which until later in the interview. Explanations are about giving reasons for action. Justifications involve accepting responsibility for an action, but denying it was wrong. Excuses deny full responsibility for action, but admit that it was wrong or inappropriate (Scott and Lyman, 1970: 114). The fact that the worker was suffering from stress and that she followed the procedures and completed all the required documentation may serve as excuses for not informing the care home manager about the young man's sexualised behaviour. The fact that she was responding to orders from her manager and family pressure explain the rapidity of the placement. There are no obvious justifications in this extract, although later in the interview the worker considers whether she could reasonably have been expected to regard the boy's previous behaviour as a danger signal, important enough to have communicated it to the care home manager. If she could not, then although she might accept responsibility for not passing on the information, and accept that the outcome in this case (abuse of a young woman) was bad, it could be argued that her action (not passing on the information) was not wrong.

4. Ascriptions of moral responsibility

The worker says 'I am to blame'. At this point in the interview it is unclear whether she accepts blame, or is merely reporting that others are blaming her. Later, when referring to the care home manager's comment that had she known about the sexualised behaviour then she would have taken protective measures, the worker adds 'quite rightly'. This implies that the worker agrees that the care home manager had a right to this information. Although clearly taking some of the blame for not informing the care home manager, the worker later suggested in the following statement that she was not sure that workers can always be expected to spot a danger signal:

> My mind would have had to be more like a computer than something created by God, you know, to draw in all that information and see it. You can see it instantly now that an abuse has happened.

This case illustrates the kind of account this worker chose to give in a research interview. It will not be the same as she gave to the others who requested accounts from her, but it is likely to be informed by the kinds of question she had already been asked, and her view of what counts as a plausible or acceptable account in this context. I would suggest that the kinds of account expected and given in social work tend to be in terms of:

- *Technical accountability:* With reference to commonly accepted knowledge and skills about what works (evidence-based practice) and how to do things (such as a risk assessment). One of the questions at issue here was whether the type of behaviour exhibited by the young man previously was a likely predictor of his potential to commit sexual abuse. In this case, the social worker suggests that, although a computer might predict this risk, the technical competences of the human mind are limited.

- *Procedural accountability:* With reference to a set of rules or protocols about how to do things. In this case, the worker had completed the relevant 'Looking After Children' documentation (see Chapter 12) and passed it to the care home manager, so she could justify her actions in terms of following the required procedures for cases like this.

- *Managerial accountability:* With reference to orders or requests from a senior manager. In this case, the team manager had sanctioned the rapid placement in the care home.

- *Ethical accountability:* With reference to commonly accepted values about what is right and wrong. These may be personally held values, the stated values of the profession or prevailing societal values. The extract given above does not contain any justifications or excuses for actions in explicitly ethical terms. Later in the interview, the worker affirms the care home manager's right to have had the information about the young man in order to protect other residents. This implies that the worker thinks that the rights of service users to protection are important and are a material ethical consideration in this case. The social worker later reports being questioned about exactly what she knew about the boy's sexualised behaviour. The implication is that if she had had this information then she should have passed it on to the care home manager. Had the information not been in the worker's possession, then the outcome might be regarded as regrettable, but the worker might not have been held blameworthy (see Banks, 2001: 17–21 for a discussion of the distinction between blameworthy and regrettable outcomes).

Multiple accountabilities

This case illustrates the many different people and organisations to whom social workers are liable to give accounts of their actions. She first learnt of the incident of abuse from a colleague. As she put it in retrospect: 'the residential care manager came running down the corridor saying "I'm so annoyed with you. You should have realised..."' An internal investigation followed, also drawing in people from outside agencies. Senior managers were calling the worker to account to them and to 'impartial' outside experts representing the 'profession'. The care home manager was also asking for explanations, as was the father of the young woman who had been abused. Finally, after the father persisted with a complaint, the ombudsman was called in. The local authority complaints officer sought explanations in order to respond to the ombudsman.

Clark (2000: 83) claims that 'complex accountability' is an important feature of social work, with workers having accountabilities to many different parties for a range of different and often conflicting responsibilities (in the sense of duties). Social workers are constantly faced with conflicting duties, for example to respect parents' rights as well as to protect children, to promote the well-being of service users and to distribute resources in accordance with the rules and regulations of the employing agency. The kinds of account expected by the different parties may often be in terms of these different duties. Often a decision is made to give one duty priority over another, for example protection of children over parents' rights to care for their children. In such a situation, parents might seek an account in terms of their rights and competences (a focus on ethical accountability). The employing agency will expect technical and procedural accountability. If the social worker gives an account of her action to the parents with reference to procedures and rules, it is quite likely that the parents will remain dissatisfied, not just with the unwelcome decision, but the explanation or justification given.

Buttny (1993: 127–41) discusses a transcript of a 'welfare interview' featuring a white American caseworker and a mother and daughter of African-American origin seeking financial assistance. The caseworker justifies her decision to refuse assistance with reference to institutional procedures (an application to court must take precedence). The mother and daughter put their case in terms of obvious needs and the fact that all other channels have failed. Buttny comments on the asymmetry in this interview and the impossibility of the applicants successfully challenging the caseworker's decision without a specialised bureaucratic knowledge:

Decision-making involves not only explicit institutional rules and procedures, but also tacit conventions and criteria based on cultural assumptions of the situation, appropriate ways of structuring information, and preferred ways of speaking. Those ignorant of such conventions and criteria are put at a disadvantage in attempting to attain their goals. (Buttny, 1993: 128)

Accountability, transparency and critical reflection

So far we have stressed the importance of accountability in the context of problematic situations; its role in apportioning blame; and accountability to the employing organisation in terms of procedures. If we consider accountability from a critical practice perspective, then we might pay more attention to routine accountability in everyday situations; collective responsibility for untoward events; and transparency of communication with service users.

In social work, routine accounting is very important – making recordings of everyday unproblematic encounters with service users. Of course, social workers always have an eye to the case going wrong, having to answer a complaint, to appear in court, to justify a decision to a team manager or a case conference. As one of the social workers interviewed by the author put it:

> One of my clients hung himself in the garage, yesterday afternoon. The first thing I was asked was: 'Is the file up to date?' Because it's so important that the file is up to date and that nobody can be held to be responsible.

Nevertheless, at the time they are made, these routine recordings are primarily descriptions and opinions rather than excuses or justifications. They may enable the social worker to engage in 'reflective practice', to clarify the nature of the situation and her role within it and to reflect on possible courses of action. She may also go beyond this to 'critical reflection', which involves developing awareness of the political context of social work and the potential for change (Fook, 1999).

Supervision in social work (see Chapter 24) is also a routine way in which social workers give accounts of practice. Certainly, these accounts can be framed in such a way that workers present their practice in a good light and demonstrate that they did the right thing so they cannot be blamed if things go wrong. But accounts in supervision can also be about sharing mistakes and uncertainties. Supervision should be a process that allows workers to reflect on and learn from their mistakes. The worker in the abuse case described earlier felt her supervision was inadequate and commented that a new policy was now being established requiring supervision to occur free from interruptions and to involve 'thinking things carefully right through'. In relation to the abuse case she commented:

> I think that if I had thought carefully about ... [the sexualised behaviour], I might have remembered, as it were. I hadn't even forgotten. It just hadn't been in my mind.

Unless workers trust their supervisors and are clear about what information is confidential between the two of them, and what is on record for the organisation, then the potential for reflective learning and hence the value of supervision is considerably diminished. In a climate of blame and defensiveness this can be difficult to achieve, as can any 'safe space' within a team or agency where open dialogue can happen. Rossiter et al. (2000) note the importance of 'ethical deliberation' as a vital part of developing a critical awareness of the political and ethical context of social work. It is also an important step in moving beyond the individual worker as the locus of responsibility and blame. As McNamee and Gergen (1999: xi) point out in their exposition of relational responsibility: 'the tradition of individual responsibility – in which single individuals are held blameworthy for untoward events – has a chilling effect on relationships'. The abuse case is an example of this, where, during the course of the investigation, the worker reported feeling as if she was 'some kind of pariah, a child abuser by proxy'.

The importance of honest and open dialogue and sharing responsibility both among social workers and between workers and service users is one of the key features of critical social work. In the relationship with the service user, the emphasis is on transparency, which means acknowledging the power of the worker and sharing that power when possible (Healy, 2000: 30). It requires giving clear accounts to service users of why a social worker is involved, what her powers are and what might happen. It involves listening to service users' own views, hearing the stories of their lives, cultures and identities, recognising their experiences of racism or homophobia, responding in language that is comprehensible and with a commitment to challenge the structures in society that perpetuate their negative experiences. As was stated earlier, such an approach to relationships with service users reflects the commonly accepted values of social work (see Chapter 2), which are about respecting and promoting the self-determination of service users, promoting their welfare and working for social justice.

So why do we need to restate these values? Surely all social workers believe in them and act on them? They may certainly believe in them, as most of the social workers I interviewed evidenced, but the difficulty is in interpreting and implementing them. To do this, debate, dialogue and discussion is needed (Banks, 1998). In the past, the stumbling block may have been 'paternalism' or parentalism – the belief that social workers know best and should be trusted by service users without question to work in their best interests, or the best interests of society, whichever was the most important. Trust in the professional meant there was little need for detailed and 'user-friendly' accountability. Today, according to many social workers, one of the main threats to user-friendly accountability comes from a certain type of overzealous accountability demanded by employers and central government. Although aspects of this accountability may be about improving the standard of services and giving users the right to complain, its development is often largely in terms of organisational language and needs.

The team manager quoted at the beginning of this chapter referred to the ongoing accountability required of individual social workers to their organisations and of social service agencies to central government. This is creating demands for massive documentation to demonstrate that the work is being done to prescribed standards. This requires not just the collection of statistics, the inspection of practice, but changing the way the work is done in order to facilitate the accountability process. Many of the procedures and protocols that have been developed to aid social workers in conducting a fair and comprehensive assessment, reviewing and monitoring needs and outcomes for service users, are designed both to improve practice and demonstrate that good practice has occurred. The extensive 'Looking After Children' documentation (Department of Health, 1995d; see Chapter 12) referred to in the abuse case is a good example. The documentation was devised to standardise practice, improve the outcomes for young people and give more information to all the parties involved (Jackson, 1998). Since the forms are prescribed, they also facilitate social workers being able to demonstrate, when asked, what they have done. But social workers report spending so much time filling in the forms that they neglect to develop a relationship with the people they are working with. As one social worker commented: 'You can spend so much time ticking boxes that you can actually forget that there's people that need to be helped.'

Although the forms may ask questions about ethnic identity, use of language, health needs and preferences, this does not guarantee that the social worker will behave in an ethnically sensitive way, will spend time communicating and getting to know the person, and helping them to express the hopes, fears and desires that cannot be accounted for on the form. Reliance on the forms can also cause workers to neglect to reflect more broadly on factors that are not covered on the very comprehensive forms, as the abuse case detailed above demonstrates. The social worker may be lulled into a false sense of security once having completed them in full. Many of the practitioners interviewed were cautious about over-reliance on set procedures. One group leader in adult care summed this up:

> Procedures are guidelines, and not tablets of stone. You've got to use your intelligence, you've got to kind of look at them in the context of people, and in the context of situations, and procedures can't cover every eventuality. There are times when you just have to use your brain and judgement, and people say: 'Well, what if I get it wrong?' and I say: 'Well, you know, you get it wrong then'. If we're not paid for our judgement, then what are we paid for?'

CONCLUSION

Much of the literature on accountability focuses on problematic situations, where something has gone wrong and there is a desire to allocate blame. In social work, routine accountability in the form of recordings has always been important, as has supervision as a learning process. It is important not to lose sight of the potential for reflective learning and the development of critical practice through these traditional means, rather than focusing excessively on ever-more bureaucratic and detailed procedures and forms. The association of accountability with problematic situations and with criticism and blame can lead to defensive practice and a reluctance to take risks; to a focus on public accountability (to the employer, the public at large) at the cost of professional accountability (to the service user). Critical practice involves a refocusing of attention on the importance of the communication with the service user, recognition of and honesty about potential conflicts and powers and a striving to change the organisational culture of social work agencies through shifting the focus from individual to collective responsibility.

Acknowledgements

I am grateful to the practitioners who gave interviews, to Robin Williams for references to sociological studies of accountability and to the Leverhulme Trust for a research fellowship during which this chapter was written. Some of the identifying details of cases have been changed to preserve anonymity.

FURTHER READING

Banks, S. (2001) *Ethics and Values in Social Work*, 2nd edn, Basingstoke: Palgrave – now Palgrave Macmillan. An overview of social work ethics, including discussion of blame and responsibility, the role of codes of ethics and analysis of practice dilemmas.

Buttny, R. (1993) *Social Accountability in Communication*, London: Sage. An exploration of the use of accounts in everyday and professional talk, with analyses of a variety of examples of conversation, including a 'welfare interview'.

Chadwick, R. (ed.) (1994) *Ethics and the Professions*, Aldershot, Avebury. Includes useful contributions by Holdsworth and Tadd on accountability.

Fook, J. (1999) 'Critical Reflectivity in Education and Practice', in Pease, B. and Fook, J. (eds) *Transforming Social Work Practice: Postmodern Critical Perspectives*, London: Routledge. A useful chapter covering the importance of critical reflection.

Identity, Individual Rights and Social Justice

Chris Clark

Rights and justice in social work

Social work is committed to individual rights. Every prescription for good practice holds that the client has the right to respect, autonomy, proper consideration of their interests and so on. Bad practice is often described as a failure to satisfy the relevant rights. We say, for example, that a young person who was abused in residential care was denied their legitimate right to a safe and wholesome upbringing conducive to proper growth and development.

Social work is equally committed to justice. Every plausible conception of social work builds in some ideal of social justice, such as the belief that individuals experiencing the effects of structural inequalities in society are entitled to fairer treatment because a morally wrong state of affairs needs to be corrected. Justice is a large and complex aim and, like rights, can seldom be perfectly achieved; but like the denial of rights, manifest injustice in service practice is always a priority concern. Nowadays it is widely felt, for example, that requiring older people to sell their assets in order to pay for care is unjust.

The different faces of rights and justice can be illustrated by thinking about policies for the welfare of children. In Western countries, nothing attracts more popular outrage than the violation of children's rights in publicised but isolated cases of gross abuse and murder – especially when the social services are seen to have failed in their job of protection. In other places, social leaders may be more concerned about the systematic injustices and wholesale damage to human rights perpetrated on entire populations of children who do not have access to clean water and adequate food.

Rights and justice are not necessarily opposed in principle. Justice can be defined precisely as the satisfaction of rights, and the satisfaction of rights as the necessary outcome of truly just social arrangements. However, in the situated reality of service practice there is a tension between the pursuit of *social* justice – with the emphasis on collectivity – and the fulfilling of *individual* rights – with the emphasis on individuality. The tension can be illustrated between two contrasting fields of practice: community development (see Chapter 15), and community care assessment under the NHS and Community Care Act 1990 (see Chapter 16).

Community development workers in social work, adult and community education and other related fields work in an enabling capacity with members of local communities to address issues of local concern. Community development differs from the mainstream of social work (with which it has had a lifelong ambiguous relationship) in that the primary focus is on the needs and aspirations of communities as a whole, rather than on the individuals who comprise them. Thus, it comes naturally in community work to cast its objectives as the pursuit of social justice. For example, a community may argue that the lack of effective and accessible public transport constitutes for its members a systematic injustice in comparison with the privileged position of car owners – who benefit from hidden subsidies denied to public transport users. Community workers tend to judge their efforts in terms of improvements in social justice brought about by global changes in that community; their concern for justice in the lives of particular individuals is secondary to their concern for systemic improvements in social justice. As a rule, community workers give priority to working with groups on local public issues over working with individuals and their private troubles, although in practice the distinction is often difficult to see and harder still to adhere to.

Community care assessment is the cornerstone of social work responsibilities for adults with disabilities since the 1990 Act. On behalf of the local authorities, social workers carry out assessments of adults who may have difficulty in managing the ordinary demands of everyday life. Social workers, and their clients, may well see this process as aiming to satisfy individual rights: for example, someone's right to choose to continue living in their own home despite disabilities, and entitlement to receive the publicly funded services that would make it possible. For social workers in community care, the individual user's rights are at the top of the agenda. While it might be expected they should be concerned for social justice in the wider arena of publicly sponsored social care, that concern is secondary to securing improvements in the rights of the individuals with whom they are actually working. They will advocate for their client, whose interests in a world of scarce resources may be in competition with others. The possibility that successful advocacy in a particular case may actually decrease the justice of the system as a whole is not an issue that the case manager can afford to consider.

Practising rights and justice: five models

Rights and justice are both indispensable in social work (Clark, 2000), but seem to be in tension and perhaps even contradiction. Critical practice demands, at the very least, a provisional answer to this tension. This section discusses several different models of the identity of the client or service user (to borrow two of the common terms). From these follow a number of ways of understanding rights and justice in social work practice. It will be seen that the appropriate term for 'client' itself depends on the understanding of the client's identity. I shall argue that it is by seeing the *participant* (as I prefer to say) as citizen that the tension between rights and justice is best addressed.

In a recent text on the 'imaginary relations' between the public and the state in the sphere of welfare, Hughes and his co-authors (Hughes, 1998) argue that the post-war, social-democratic idea of the welfare state has disintegrated under attacks from both the political left and right. They propose three models that might replace it: 'consumerism', 'community' and 'citizenship'. This typology will be adapted here and expanded by adding a further model based on feminist ethics of care. We begin with the social-democratic model that some presume is obsolete.

The social-democratic welfare state: clients

The social-democratic welfare state assumes that it is the responsibility of the state to guarantee certain standards of conventionally defined welfare, especially in the traditionally recognised areas of income protection, health, education, housing and – to a much more limited extent – social care. The public as *clients* are treated as largely passive recipients of services devised by an expert elite of policy-makers and delivered by professionals or lower grade staff working under professional supervision. Rights are fulfilled and social justice is served by ensuring that the public actually receive what policy is supposed to provide; the public are deemed not sophisticated or knowledgeable enough to need any substantial influence over the content of services or policy aimed at them.

While nostalgia for the old social-democratic dream of comprehensive, socially provided, expertly administered welfare services is by no means extinct, it entails a model of professional authority that is no longer tenable. The public have lost faith in the promises and purported expertise of professionals – perhaps more in social work than in some other areas of welfare. In the public mind, rights to welfare can no longer be restricted to what experts decide is good for us. Moreover, the social-democratic notion of justice is biased by the working assumption that all members of society who share a particular condition of need – say, for example, help with childcare – should be satisfied with a similar choice and level of services – say, institutional daycare from a certain age. However, this is insensitive to differences arising from personal and cultural background or different social values.

Critical practice must therefore be dissatisfied with the old social-democratic ideal of welfare. Its concept of rights is too limited, since the selection of rights identified by experts as the proper targets of welfare policy nowadays seems essentially arbitrary. Its notion of justice is biased towards a universalism that misfits the pluralism of postmodernity. The social consensus essential to the social-democratic model of welfare has disappeared; or perhaps it would be more accurate to say that the voices that were suppressed during the dominance of social-democratic welfare are now being heard, and they reject it.

The consumerist welfare state: consumers

The consumerist welfare state supposes that welfare needs are no different in principle from the other needs that individuals look to satisfy in the market. The essentials for welfare have always been partly supplied by the market even when, as for example in health, it was the aim of policy to insulate recipients and beneficiaries from the fortunes of markets. Marketisation of what were previously areas for direct public provision was crucial to the policies of the (now not so) New Right in the 1970s and 80s. For libertarians, it is a prime right of citizens to participate freely in markets. The effects of markets are in themselves neither just nor unjust, but interfering with markets is an infringement of liberty and therefore a source of injustice.

While there is now little support for distribution based on pure libertarian market principles, there is a much more pervasive general reliance on contrived and regulated, rather than free, market mechanisms. Thus, for example, transport, communications and public utilities are regulated markets in which private and public organisations compete on terms controlled by state agencies. In social work, these principles apply in community care and are increasingly being adopted in other areas of service provision.

In the consumerist welfare state the client is, precisely, a consumer and professionals become primarily oriented to customer relations. For at least some user groups, this new consumerism may bring what they have long sought: for example, in the case of service users with disabilities, the possibility of becoming their own care managers, or their relatives undertaking the care management, instead of being forced to depend on the discretion of service professionals.

The consumerist welfare state promises some improvement in rights. On the other hand, it is founded on a meagre and unsatisfactory concept of justice. To regard citizens as no more than consumers ignores the wider contexts of social living and public responsibility. It is widely argued that the consumption of community care can never be equivalent to the consumption of groceries. This is partly because market mechanisms do not, in reality, function adequately to deliver social care. The consumers of publicly supported social care are in an inherently weak position and their power as consumers is highly circumscribed. But further, giving and receiving social care is a qualitatively different activity from buying groceries; the complex issues of social relationships and social value are not comprehended within the functional commodity transactions of the market.

The communitarian welfare state: community members

The social-democratic and consumerist welfare states are familiar from recent history and current experience. The remaining models are much more tentative and exploratory. The communitarian welfare state is represented in the protests and proposals of a number of minority interests who have not so far greatly influenced the mainstream of welfare policy and practice.

For communitarians, it is fundamental that people's very identity is created in the statuses and relationships established and continually renewed in the communities to which they belong. Communitarianism rejects the abstract autonomous individual of liberalism, who – once basic human needs are satisfied – is considered to have no values and no projects beyond those he freely chooses for himself. For communitarians, the point is that no meaningful identity and no life worth living are conceivable apart from the concrete obligations and benefits entailed by one's own particular tradition, culture and enmeshment in a particular set of relationships. Communitarians stress the mutual responsibilities of community members, and their shared duty and right to participate in the daily political processes (Tam, 1998).

There is no single or leading project for a communitarian welfare state. Indeed, that would be fundamentally incompatible with the community focus and pluralist principles of communitarianism, which expects and entitles communities to develop their own particular versions of welfare. Reflections of communitarianism are found in several versions of community social work. The locally based and personally committed approach to working with individuals and groups in areas of high social deprivation long advocated by Bob Holman (Holman, 1993) bears many of the characteristics of communitarianism. The Barclay Committee (Barclay, 1982) proposed a reformation – or reaffirmation – of social work that would widen its focus to address the social functioning of communities; and its first minority report (Brown et al., 1982) argued that the way forward was patch working. Similar approaches continue to be advocated (Smale et al., 2000).

In the communitarian welfare state it hardly makes sense to speak of the 'client' at all. Instead we should think of *community members* who from time to time may need particular support, which should primarily be provided by other members of the community on a basis of reciprocity and in a spirit of common membership or fellowship. This does not preclude the employment of professionals, but where they are employed they should be subject to the active governance of involved community members. Of course this is a far cry from the bureaucratic state services that currently dominate welfare provision.

Despite some affinities between communitarianism and the elusive Third Way, there is apparently little prospect of communitarian models being adopted as the favoured template for social work services in the UK. To do so would involve a renunciation of power and financial control from central government to local communities that runs altogether contrary to the centralist tradition and practice of British politics. Nevertheless, there are elements in communitarianism that merit a place in the wider debate about reforming welfare.

Feminism and the welfare state: partners in relationships

The feminist critique of welfare is many-sided and far-reaching (see for example, George and Wilding, 1994, Ch. 6). Everyone knows that feminists have demolished the presumption that caring ought to be primarily a female activity, provided by mothers, wives, daughters and low-paid female servants. Many feminists have argued that it is the state, not female family members, that we should look to when care is needed for children and dependent adults. In some ways, the argument has been won, in theory if not yet in practice. It is no longer tenable that women should be systematically disadvantaged in the many areas of social life where men's interests have traditionally been dominant; and the public roles and private behaviour of men and women have begun to shift as a result.

There is another aspect of the feminist critique that is perhaps less widely appreciated. In the liberal tradition, persons are seen in the abstract as moral agents and bearers of universal rights. In this view, rights are not affected by one's specific obligations to the particular, real individuals with whom one happens to have actual, ongoing relationships. Some feminists argue that women think differently, choosing instead to give priority to their real primary relationships over abstract theoretical obligations. They hold that our understanding of moral responsibility has been unbalanced by universalist models of human relationships that are excessively abstract, impersonal and decontextualised – products of essentially masculine thought. Other feminists have wanted to celebrate the virtues of subjectivity without abandoning the rights that feminism has hard won out of liberalism, such as a woman's right to control her fertility. They resist giving way to any new essentialism about gender as false as the ones that feminism has spent so much energy in repudiating (Sevenhuijsen, 1998).

Feminism provides no single, coherent answer to the question of how best to understand the identities of the givers and recipients of care, whether in the private sphere of personal relationships or in the public domain of welfare services. What feminism does put irrevocably on the welfare agenda is that users of formal services are, among other things, individually known persons to whom professionals as well as their own kin are bound by partly subjective ties of *partnership* in actual *human relationships*. The relations of welfare, therefore, are not accurately described or properly prescribed by the abstract role obligations favoured in the traditional discourse of the human service professions.

Citizenship

The identity of the participant in welfare services is most fruitfully addressed through the idea of citizenship (Clark, 2000; Coote, 1992; see also Chapter 22). Citizenship invites us to think of the rights and duties of the individual as supported, enmeshed and realised in society. Civil and political rights are promised under law and the constitution. Formal social, or welfare, rights reflect the rising expectations of human living that follow upon prosperity. However, citizenship does not end with formal legal provisions and duties: it acknowledges that the individual's identity is realised in relation to innumerable informal filaments of social obligation and trust; it requires citizens to recognise each other as mutually obligated and equally responsible. Citizenship thus incorporates the valuable attributes of the four preceding models, while offering checks on their less desirable features.

Social rights rest as much on the informal expectations and commitments that members of the community have in relation to each other as on the agencies and professions that constitute the formal services. In social services, it is convenient to speak of service *participants* (a term that deliberately dims the traditional distinctions between professionals, clients and the wider community). We should think, first, of professionals, participant-recipients, their carers and dependants, and the wider community as fellow citizens; as commonly protected and obligated by the shared rights and duties of citizenship. The policy papers of the 'modernising' New Labour government and the writings of its intellectual mentors (Commission on Social Justice, 1994; Giddens, 1998b) suggest one interpretation of citizenship rights. Critics of social services who advocate greater user involvement and participation in the provision and evaluation of social care have a different and more radical emphasis. But it is the discourse of citizenship that best contains the debate over rights and justice.

Critical practice and citizenship

The pursuit of individual rights may lead to the neglect, if not the contradiction, of social justice. How should critical practice address this tension?

A *critical* approach combines reflective and sceptical observation with positive and committed activism. Critical practice is alert to flaws in the veracity of observation, to defects in the basis of alleged evidence, to faulty inference and deduction and other common types of empirical and logical error. The critical observer accepts the reports, explanations or teachings of others only after attempting to subject them to some degree of independent scrutiny and evaluation. Moreover, the critical observer treats received knowledge and doctrine as matters to be questioned, as embedded in ideology whereby the content of knowledge is necessarily formed by its conduit.

The critical activist or practitioner, however, knows that the scope for mere scepticism is infinite, and that no practical progress is possible without accepting the risks of committed action under conditions of inescapable empirical uncertainty and moral doubt. Critical practice is thus engaged in the world as well as contemplative of it. Critical practice embodies a theoretically informed vision: 'Theory ... helps practical actors deal with social change by helping them see beyond the immediacy of what is at any particular moment to conceptualise something of what could be' (Calhoun, 1996: 436). A mentality of critical practice accepts the tension of the perpetually irreconcilable demands of reflection and action.

The five conceptions of the identity of service recipients or participants – as clients, consumers, community members, partners in relationships or citizens – are all powerfully (but unequally) influential in the contemporary world of welfare. Critical practice teaches that each perspective has its value as a particular interpretation of rights and justice. But critical practice is sustained by having a common language within which conflicts of value can be articulated. Indeed, it is arguable that without such a common language the attempt to improve rights and justice will necessarily fail – since we should have, in the end, no mutually intelligible way of judging progress. The dialogue on citizenship provides the best route to a resolution. In the pursuit of rights and justice, critical practice must embrace the concept of citizenship; yet remain somewhat dissatisfied with every reading of it.

================ **FURTHER READING** ================

Brechin, A., Brown, H. and Eby, M.A. (eds) (2000) *Critical Practice in Health and Social Care*, London: Sage. A useful collection of essays on problems of contemporary welfare practice.

Campbell, T. (1988) *Justice*, Basingstoke: Macmillan – now Palgrave Macmillan. A clear textbook on theories of justice.

Clark, C.L. (2000) *Social Work Ethics: Politics, Principles and Practice*, Basingstoke: Macmillan – now Palgrave Macmillan. Provides a general ethical and political theory for social work, and develops the idea of social work as welfare citizenship.

Hughes, G. (ed.) (1998) *Imagining Welfare Futures*, London: Routledge. Focuses on changing ideas of the place of welfare in contemporary societies.

Sevenhuijsen, S. (1998) *Citizenship and the Ethics of Care: Feminist Considerations on Justice, Morality and Politics*, London: Routledge. A particularly reflective application of feminist insights to the provision of care under official auspices.

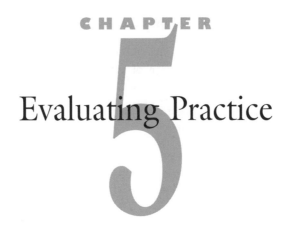

CHAPTER

Evaluating Practice

Nick Frost

This chapter examines the problematic relationship between two forms of practice – social work practice and the practice of evaluation. The aim of the chapter is to examine the nature of this relationship and to suggest approaches to evaluation that maximise the relevance of evaluation as a practice for social work. The focus of the chapter is on evaluation, as opposed to research. By evaluation, we are referring to formal evaluation which aims to assess the effectiveness of interventions in terms of their aims and objectives – such evaluation can be undertaken by project workers, or by external evaluators. Illustrations of the main arguments will be provided from a project evaluation recently co-written by the author (Frost and Ryden, 2001). Drawing on the author's practice, as a fieldworker, policy-maker and evaluator, this chapter begins by confirming that evaluation is a form of practice, examines some issues, tensions and controversies involved in the evaluation process and tentatively suggests a form of evaluative practice which addresses some of these difficulties.

Evaluation as a form of practice

A commitment to evaluation as a form of practice is central to the development of a critical perspective on social welfare initiatives. There is often a danger that evaluation can be seen as a purely technical enterprise – the application of value-free 'instruments' that in some straightforward manner measures 'outcomes'. However, it is argued here that the evaluator necessarily has a value commitment to change within the project or topic they are working with. Evaluators, be they internal or external, will bring with them values about, for example, listening to people and utilising findings as part of the change process. Evaluation is therefore at heart an ethical and value-driven process. It will challenge the practitioner who wishes to engage critically with their own practice.

The practice of evaluation 'has grown massively in recent years' (Pawson and Tilley, 1997: 1). Funders have become more demanding in requiring independent evidence of the outcomes of projects they fund: 'the demand for social workers and their managers to identify the effectiveness of their work is now very great' (Cheetham et al., 1992: 3). Extensive evaluation programmes have been put in place in relation to a number of the New Labour policy strategies, including, for example, Sure Start and the various Youth Justice Board initiatives. These policy initiatives involve both specific individual project evaluations and overall national evaluations.

Additionally there has been a new emphasis on dissemination of findings. This sometimes takes an institutional form involving the establishment of organisations such as Research into Practice. A related development has been the growth of publications promoting evaluative evidence as central to practice and professional development. A successful and extensive example of this is the Barnardo's 'What Works' series, which now consists of almost 20 publications (see Stein, 1997, for example). The Department of Health has adopted a strategy of producing readable summaries of its funded research projects, which have been accompanied by sophisticated publicity and dissemination processes (see Weyts et al., 2000, for an evaluation of Department of Health strategy).

There can be little doubt that evaluation as a practice has grown and developed in recent years. Social workers and related practitioners are likely to have their practice evaluated at some time during their career; academics are likely to be approached about undertaking evaluations and practitioners will be expected to evaluate their own practice as a continuing process.

Issues, tensions and controversies

In 1975, Stan Cohen wrote a chapter entitled 'It's all right for you to talk', in which he analysed some of the tensions between social work practice and practices whose primary aim is the production and dissemination of knowledge (Bailey and Brake, 1975). In his title, Cohen neatly summarises the reservations that social workers may have about the research and evaluation community. Frontline practitioners and policy-makers may question whether evaluators can grasp the complexity and shifting nature of the real world. More concretely, in the contemporary environment of a culture of targets and contracts, social workers may be concerned about the outcomes of an evaluation. Could it lead to closure of a project, changes to existing practice, or criticism from management?

External evaluators will share some of these concerns and have some of their own. Will they be allowed unfettered access to the data? Is the evaluation budget sufficient for the task that needs to be undertaken? Are the methods robust enough for the task? Will the report gather dust once produced, rather than being a real contribution to the development of the project?

Before I can move on to examine creative approaches to evaluation, I have to unpick the underlying causes of some of the tensions and problems involved in evaluation. We need to be aware of the complex and inherently problematic relationship between practice and evidence. Three specific underlying issues will be addressed:

- the question of methods
- the application of evidence to practice
- the relationship between evidence and service users.

The question of methods

It is important to recognise that, as Trinder (1996: 233) suggests, 'the future direction of social work research is contested'. There is a great diversity of possible evaluative methods available and, within the research community, there are differences and controversies, sometimes referred to as the 'paradigm wars'. Some would argue that the randomised controlled trial (RCT) should set the 'gold standard' (Macdonald, 1996), while others would argue that the theoretical basis of RCTs is flawed (Pawson and Tilley, 1997: 30–54). Some would advocate 'action research', or quantitative methods, or single case methods, or ethnographic methods, for example. Others would propose solving these dilemmas by suggesting that an eclectic approach to methodology has much to recommend it (see Fuller, 1996).

The question of methods, then, is a controversial one: different methods will uncover different forms of evidence and analysis will interpret them differently. It is argued here that this debate should be exactly that – an open debate. It is not helpful to exercise some form of closure – to propose in an unproblematic way that some method should be privileged over another. Knowledge is not static and is enhanced through debate and critique. Later in the chapter, I will argue that methods have to address issues of relevance and 'fit' with the project that is being evaluated. This can be managed through the formation of advisory groups that include a range of stakeholders (see Frost and Ryden, 2001). Issues around methods then should not be taken for granted.

The application of evidence to practice

Let us, for the sake of argument, accept that evaluators are able to gather robust and reliable evidence. Even if this were possible, there remains a problematic relationship between evidence gathered and social work practice. Pawson and Tilley (1997) argue convincingly that evidence tends to be situational and we should be wary of transferability. For example, much has been made of the Head Start projects in the US. While the evidence can be seen as 'rigorous', the transfer to a different context such as the UK or to a different time is problematic. One might be able to produce rigorous evidence on a given topic in year x but inevitably, given the pace of legislative, policy and social change, the context for this work will change, quickly and sometimes fundamentally, year by year.

Thus, even if we could agree the basis for collecting evidence, we need to examine its application to practice in detail without assuming that evidence can be transferred to instructing social work practice in some unproblematic way. To give a concrete example, generally, children looked after by relatives do better than children looked after by foster carers they have never met before (Wheal, 1999). This seems to be a perfectly acceptable and unproblematic finding. However, how can we translate this into practice? All we can say is that in general a child is likely to do better if placed with a relative than another foster carer. It does not mean that placement of a *particular* child with their grandmother will necessarily be successful, or even generally better than placement with another foster carer. Thus, while the evaluative knowledge is contextual and informative for policy, it cannot be determinative of practice in given concrete situations.

A second problem in the application of evidence to practice is presented by the considerable volume of evaluation and research findings in circulation. Writing personally, as an academic specialising in child welfare, I know there are always journals, books and research reports in my area that I have not read. While academics and the Department of Health have recently made serious efforts to disseminate research evidence in summary and 'popular' form, the scale of the task of keeping up to date for busy practitioners and managers should not be underestimated.

A third area for concern is that the pleas for practitioners to apply research and evaluation findings in practice should not undermine the role of 'tacit' knowledge. Educational theorists have identified knowledge as 'codified' (explicit) and 'tacit' (implicit) (see Polanyi, 1983). Codified knowledge is that which is written down, can be taught and assessed. In contrast, tacit knowledge is that which we pick up from doing the job, and is more difficult to communicate.

Let us take an example of a social work team leader who chaired the team meeting last week. She has 'tacitly' picked up that the team seem to be unmotivated and generally uninterested by the meeting. She makes a mental note to be more upbeat next week – perhaps to start and end the meeting a positive note. While there may be some professional guidance on chairing meetings and some limited research, this is an example that relies on 'tacit' knowledge, which is crucial to professional competence. Even if the topic has been extensively researched, the knowledge is clearly situational and specific. There remains a crucial role for 'tacit' knowledge.

The relationship between evidence and users of services

Adherents of evidence-led practice argue that social work practice should be led by rigorous evidence. For example, Newman et al. (1996) argue that:

> Practitioners who adopt a particular approach must be able to describe what evidence has led them to do so, what the intended outcomes will be and what the probability is of such outcomes occurring.

While it might be that evidence-based practice is applicable in technical areas such as engineering and medicine, the dimension that makes it difficult in social work is its human and relational nature. Social work is fundamentally about recognising human subjectivity and responding with some form of partnership and cooperation with the service user. Thus, most forms of practice need to be actually negotiated and agreed. Relationships are the key to social work practice – relationships that cannot be reduced a formulaic 'evidence-based approach'. Even if in theory the evaluator and the practitioner 'know' that approach x is 'what works', the service user may not wish to cooperate and might indeed prefer y as a form of intervention. This is the very complexity of social work – negotiation, conflict and compromise. It the human and relational nature of social work that makes the relationship between practice and evidence a complex and problematic one.

I would argue that a dogmatic adherence to evidence-based practice immediately dismantles the possibility of any partnership approach to working with service users. For indeed if I, as a professional, possess the evidence, then I have no choice but to implement it, even if you, as a service user, disagree. Thus the claim made by Newman et al. (1996) is spurious, when they argue that professionals have a duty to base their work with 'the poor' on evidence and that a failure to do this is a breach of trust. If we do indeed base all our practice on 'evidence', then by default any room for negotiation, partnership and compromise with the service user is lost.

Indeed the proponents of evidence-led practice tend to privilege RCTs (Macdonald, 1996), which by definition tends to exclude any user involvement in the research and evaluation process. In RCTs the research subjects are allocated as recipients or non-recipients of the service to be evaluated and therefore excluded from full knowledge of and participation in the evaluative process. This can be contrasted to more inclusive forms of research and evaluation, which tend to be more qualitative in nature (see, for example, Priestley, 1999). In such research, the views and perspectives of the user are privileged over researcher imposed 'outcomes'.

Thus far we have identified three main problems in the relationship between evidence and social work practice. In summary these are that:

■ there is no universally agreed evaluative methodology

■ there is no straightforward manner of applying evidence to practice

■ there is an uneasy relationship between the application of evidence and working in partnership with service users.

Having recognised these problems, and having distanced myself from those who would see the evidence and practice relationship as more one dimensional, I now go on to examine a basis for establishing a positive, but critical, relationship between evaluation practice and social work practice.

A creative evaluation practice?

What might a creative approach to evaluation practice look like? This section goes on to examine some of the 'micro'-aspects of evaluation practice, before concluding with a proposed model for the use of evaluation in social work and social care. The connecting thread is that power and knowledge should be shared between evaluators, managers, practitioners and service users, with the aim that evaluation becomes an empowering tool for change.

Establishing the task

Evaluation practice can only be as good as the task that has been agreed and established, thus agreeing exactly what the task is forms an important stage of the evaluation process. What is the context of the evaluation? How is it funded? Whose idea was it? What methods will be needed? Who will be involved in any steering group? And so on. Some of these are detailed and even mundane questions but they are crucial to the success of an evaluation.

It is possible for an entire evaluation to founder following a failure to address a question of detail. Take, for example, the issue of confidentiality. Let us say that the evaluators wish to undertake a postal survey of service users. Should service users' addresses be given to the evaluators? Should service users' permission be gained in advance? These are small but fundamental points – one mistake here and the credibility of the entire evaluation project could be undermined. Successful evaluation involves the detailed negotiation of ways of working, drawing on the expertise of the evaluator, the practitioners and, wherever possible, the service users (see Frost and Ryden, 2001).

Clear and regular liaison

As part of the process of clearly establishing the task, it is necessary to set up clear and regular points of liaison for the evaluation process. If power is to be shared, then this involves sharing information and decision-making on a regular basis. There are a number of reasons for ensuring effective liaison:

- to help in the commitment of the organisation, its practitioners and service users to the evaluative process

- to enable discussion of any changes to the evaluation methods or within the organisation. Inevitably the detail of the evaluation process will change over time. Rarely is an evaluation plan delivered as initially envisaged

- to allow the evaluator to check the micro-aspects of the evaluation process with the various stakeholders. As we have argued above, in evaluation practice seemingly technical questions – such as when a set of interviews should take place – involve a series of complex issues in relation to timing, place, confidentiality and so on.

Effective liaison is central to sharing power in the evaluation process. Evaluation should not be seen simply as an 'expert-led' process. Indeed evaluation can be undertaken by users, staff or service users; all will require support and training. Evaluation issues can be discussed in advisory groups, which are one form of empowering users and other stakeholders.

Adopting methods appropriate to the organisation

As I have already attempted to establish, there is a range of evaluative methods that may be adopted. It is important in any empowering approach to evaluation that the methods utilised are appropriate to the organisation. This issue has two specific dimensions:

■ Methods adopted in any study must be consistent with the value base of the organisation. For example, where an organisation holds partnership with service users as a central value, it would be inconsistent, to say the least, if the evaluation methods did not fully involve service users in the design, execution, writing up and dissemination of the evaluation.

■ Methods need to be appropriate to the organisation in the technical, methodological sense. To take an obvious example, adopting largely quantitative methods in a small-scale organisation, with an emphasis, say, on counselling would clearly be inappropriate.

Implicitly, I am taking an unapologetically eclectic stance here. Methods should be suitable to the nature of the organisation and the specific expectations of the evaluation. The methodological debate should be open and not closed, dynamic and not fixed. Indeed many of the best evaluative studies will involve a variety of methods; for example, surveys and questionnaires, face-to-face interviews, observation of practice, documentary study and so on. Qualitative data, such as users' perspectives on the service, can often be supplemented by quantitative data such as statistics outlining the frequency a service is used.

Involving stakeholders

A creative approach to evaluation has to avoid assuming that the evaluator is the holder of some magical key which will unlock the 'truth'. The traditional 'expert' model would hold, probably in an implicit rather than explicit way, that the evaluator has a privileged position in relation to 'knowledge' and has some form of privileged access to this. An alternative model would rather emphasise a process of evaluation which is empowering – which shares knowledge and expertise, and which mobilises, for example, practitioners' and service users' perspectives on how the project works. Pawson and Tilley (1997) identify distinctive roles in evaluation for the different participants:

■ Subjects, or service users, 'are likely to be far more sensitized to the mechanisms in operation within a program' (p. 160). These can be uncovered using in-depth face-to-face interviews or through focus groups.

■ Practitioners, 'translate program theories into practice and so are to be considered the great "utility players" in the information game' (p. 161). They can act as partners in the process or as self-evaluators.

■ Evaluators, according to Pawson and Tilley (p. 161), 'carry theories into the encounter with the program'.

Each party to an evaluation then has a valuable and clear role. Indeed effective evaluation can be carried out as part of an ongoing quality enhancement mechanism by staff, which is part of developing a continuous critical reflection on practice. Evaluation then becomes an element of practice in the same way that counselling or campaigning is seen as a form of practice.

Dissemination

Of course, the evaluation process does not finish with the production of a 'report'. The dissemination process is essential and needs to build on the model we have outlined above with all parties being involved. As Trinder (1996: 238) argues, dissemination is itself 'a political process'. Dissemination is about sharing knowledge and using information as part of a change process. Effective evaluation findings should be fed into a process by which current policy and practice are critically reflected upon. This is a cyclical process of 'critical reflection', and is an important aspect of being a 'reflective practitioner' (see Payne, 1998: 119–37). Imaginative methods of feedback need to be adopted. A recent evaluation in which the author was involved was disseminated as part of a 'fun day' involving jugglers and other entertainment (Frost and Ryden, 2001).

Utilising and integrating evaluative evidence – a model

Thus far, I have established that the practice of evaluation has increased significantly in recent years. I have argued that the relationship between evaluative evidence and social work practice is complex and problematic. Having recognised these issues, I have discussed some of the detailed practice issues arising from evaluation. I conclude by proposing a model that places evidence generated by evaluation within a wider context.

This model can be given the acronym 'RIPE'. It demonstrates that policy, practice and professional development are determined by the combined influences of research and evaluation findings (R), ideological positions (I), politics (P) and economics (E) – which I shall now briefly examine in turn.

We have explored the generation of evaluation and research-based evidence. In the real world, direct links between evidence and practice are far from straightforward. In reality, evidence enters a melting pot with other influential factors such as ideologies, politics and economics.

By ideology, I mean the values and perspectives that social work practitioners use to guide and steer their practice.

By politics, I mean disputes over the distribution of power and decision-making. Politics, organisational, local and national, is evidently central to the policy-making process. But again, the relationship between evidence and politics is contested. Sometimes politicians will ignore even the most robust of evidence for political reasons, an often quoted example being former Home Secretary Michael Howard's view that 'prison works', despite evidence to the contrary (Pawson and Tilley, 1997: 3). In other cases there may be political reasons for publicising and emphasising a particular element of evidence.

Economics is also crucial to this debate. For example, robust evidence may suggest a particular policy direction, for which resources are not made available. Equally, there may be economic reasons for hanging on to a practice which evidence has questioned.

The RIPE model proposed here is an attempt to recognise the complex interaction of factors that influence social work practice. The reality of social work practice is that there is a role for clear and well-disseminated research and evaluation findings, but that they have to exist in a world of competing ideologies, political conflict and economic possibility and restraints. This complex mix forms the context in which reflective social work practitioners and managers practice. The evaluator then becomes part of the change process, contributing from a committed perspective to the process of change.

CONCLUSION

This chapter has examined the role of evaluation and its complex link with social work practice. Having examined a number of problems, we have explored the elements of evaluation practice that enjoy a creative partnership with social work practice. We have concluded by proposing a model of policy and practice formation which takes the role of evaluation seriously, but which recognises that, in the real world of policy and practice formation, evaluation has to take its place alongside ideology, politics and economics.

FURTHER READING

Department of Health (1995) *Child Protection: Messages From Research*, London: HMSO. Probably the most influential of the series of Department of Health texts aimed at disseminating research findings to practitioners.

Pawson, R. and Tilley, N. (1997) *Realistic Evaluation*, London: Sage. A sophisticated guide to the theory and practice of evaluation.

Robson, C. (1993) *Real World Research: A Resource for Social Scientists and Practitioner-Researchers*, Oxford: Blackwell. Probably now the standard text for practitioner research – practical guidance on issues such as designing surveys, analysing data and so on.

Stein, M. (1997) *What Works in Leaving Care*, Barkingside: Barnardo's. A good example of the 'What Works' series – it includes some interesting reflections on the relationship between social work practice and research evidence.

Trinder, L. (1996) 'Social Work Research: The State of the Art (or Science)', *Child and Family Social Work* 1(4): 233–42. An excellent discussion of what the author argues are the three main tenets of social work research – empirical, pragmatic and participatory/critical.

Intervention and Empowerment

6

Beverley Burke and Jane Dalrymple

To assist us in writing this chapter we asked Dawn, a mother with learning difficulties, to share her story and allow us to use her narrative. In telling her story, she gives voice to the experiences of parents with learning difficulties. Their voices can often be lost, particularly those unable to read and write (Atkinson and Walmsley, 1999), raising the complex question of whose voice is finally reflected in the text (Clifford, 1998). The challenges are to ensure that Dawn's narrative is true to her account and is heard and respected, while acknowledging that she is not an equal party in any ongoing dialogue concerning intervention and empowerment strategies (Cedersund, 1999).

We have interspersed the text with excerpts from Dawn's story as told to us through her advocate. She relates her experiences with various professionals: Anna the social worker, who is based in a children and families team, Clover, a community nurse specialising in working with parents who have learning disabilities, and Bernie from a family centre. While placing Dawn's story in the foreground, we are aware that her children also have their own stories to tell. Finally, to protect confidentiality the names and situations are disguised.

Intervention and empowerment in critical practice

I know that I did everything I could to get my kids back, you must fight back. It's still not any easier living without my children and I still want them back. It's so painful and I still feel really angry that I've been let down by not having more support.

(Dawn)

It could be said that the term 'intervention' is oppressive. It indicates the moral and political authority of the social worker to invade 'the social territories' (Payne, 1996: 43) of service users. Many of us find it difficult to reconcile the invasiveness of our professional role with the concepts of critical and empowering practice and have developed terminology such as 'working together', 'partnership', 'participation' or 'user involvement' in our attempt to portray a more equal and cooperative relationship between ourselves and service users.

Examination of the term 'empowerment' indicates conceptual disagreements, rooted in how power is conceived. Given its hybrid political ancestry, the notion of empowerment practice in contemporary social work creates ethical, moral and practical dilemmas for practitioners (Lupton and Nixon, 1999). However, we argue that the radical potential of empowerment practice cannot be realised if professionally driven intervention strategies are seen as key to the promotion of empowerment (Croft and Beresford, 2000). We concur with Simon (1990) that service users 'who are empowered by their social workers have, de facto, lost ground ... in their battle for autonomy and control over their own environment and existence' (Simon, 1990: 37 cited in Mullaly, 1997).

Critical practice is based on an understanding of how the concepts of power, oppression and inequality determine personal and structural relations. Practitioners are required to analyse how the socially constructed divisions of 'race', gender, class, sexuality, age and disability, and the impact of differential access to resources, interact to define the life experiences of individuals and communities. Critical practice is informed by a political perspective which takes account of diverse experiences of oppression, is critical of existing social and political institutions and is 'emancipatory in intent' (Mullaly, 1997: 109). The critical practitioner engages in meaningful dialogue with service users to facilitate the telling of their stories so that, in the process, their situations can be better understood and more creative intervention strategies can be developed. Fundamental to these strategies is the idea of promoting radical change. To achieve this aim the critical practitioner needs to be political, reflexive and reflective (see Chapter 1).

As writers, our theorising regarding critical practice is rooted in an understanding of how users experience social work intervention (Healy, 2000; Mullaly, 1997; Parton, 1999). The testimony of Dawn in this chapter illustrates how professional intervention can be experienced as disempowering and oppressive. This highlights the challenges of defining empowering practice when intervening in people's lives, particularly within a practice context that is characterised by bureaucratisation, resource constraints, concerned with managing risk (Parton, 1999) and places limitations and restrictions on social workers (Fook, 2000). Competing discourses around concepts such as risk and need, parenting, rights of parents with learning difficulties and children's rights (see Chapters 10–13) add to the complexity of practice. The practitioner therefore has to be aware of the organisational context, deal with a range of situations involving many players with competing and conflicting interests and be cognisant of how the competing discourses shape the practice context in relation to defining priorities and intervention strategies.

> My partner would hit me in front of the children and I'd try to move out of the way when it happened. It was terrible for the children to see. I was too scared to tell anyone at first as he said he would knife me. The children were getting naughtier and they would sometimes copy him. They would hit, kick and bite me and each other.

Actively involving Dawn in decision-making will be difficult as this has not been part of her experience. Dawn has not only been silenced by the violent environment in which she lived, but also her status as a young, white, heterosexual, working-class mother from the north of England who has learning difficulties contributes to her marginalised position and experience of oppression. Self-location is an essential element of empowerment practice (Dalrymple and Burke, 1995). Therefore the social worker Anna actively needs to consider how her social class, personal experiences, training and practice experience with adults who have learning difficulties will affect her relationship with Dawn.

Children and family work in statutory agencies is dominated by legislation and policy mandates built on welfare principles with the notion of partnership as a central tenet. The dilemma for Anna in developing partnership practice is that she is working within systems and procedures that create tensions between herself, Dawn and the children through coercive and legalistic approaches. As a case manager, this forces her to assess risk and monitor and evaluate progress. Anna may find herself driven towards defensive and reactive forms of practice (Parton, 1999; Lupton and Nixon, 1999) where intervention becomes focused on collecting information or evidence, rather than working with Dawn and trying to understand the situation of her children (Cooper and Hetherington, 1999).

Constructing critical practice with Dawn and her children

Countering bureaucratic mechanistic ways of working, Parton and O'Byrne (2000) posit a constructive social work approach which focuses on dialogue, listening to and talking with the service user. It is concerned with narratives of solutions to problems which are necessary for change to occur. Instead of focusing on gathering information about the causes of Dawn's problems in order to make an expert assessment, Anna should help Dawn in the difficult process of telling her story so that she can gain control and meaning. It will only be an empowering process, however, if Anna is aware of the potential for language to reflect power differentials; it is important to use words that Dawn understands and are meaningful to her and can use to define herself and her situation. So, for example, if Anna described the behaviour of the boys as 'disturbed', this would indicate her theoretical and value perspective and impact on her ability to understand Dawn's narrative.

> The children had a social worker, Anna, and me and the children went to the family centre twice a week. I had a keyworker there called Bernie. Eventually, I told Anna and Bernie what was going on and they were concerned about the boys' behaviour. At this time, I got a community nurse, Clover, and a social worker of my own.

Numerous professionals with different personal and professional values, membership of diverse social classes and varying levels of experience and training are now involved in Dawn's life. It could be argued that Dawn is actively contributing to the assessment process by attending the family centre and talking openly about the difficulties she is experiencing. Dawn believes that by complying with the social worker's plan she is getting help to be a 'good parent'. *Eventually*, as she says, when she feels able to trust them she talks to Anna and Bernie about her concerns. But her insight and the act of her telling also provide the evidence for possible care proceedings. The various players are gathering information in relation to their roles and responsibilities. As the keyworker managing the complexity of the situation, Anna needs to take into account how far her own assessment of the welfare needs of the children and Dawn's parenting capacity is confirmed or disconfirmed by other specialist assessments. How does Anna evaluate information provided by workers promoting the rights of Dawn as a parent as compared with those holding a more protectionist perspective regarding the children's right to welfare? Whatever decision is eventually made, Dawn needs to be constantly involved in the planning and decision-making process. This requires Anna to have an ongoing honest dialogue with Dawn.

Interagency sharing of information in child protection focuses on the welfare of the children, which marginalises and excludes Dawn. The dilemma for Anna is that she cannot directly empower Dawn. Anna's advocacy role is compromised by her location within the agency and her legal mandate regarding the welfare of the children. However, by linking Dawn with Clover and ensuring that she has her own social worker, Anna is recognising the need for Dawn's voice and agency. The engagement of an independent advocate drawn from a local group with expertise and experience of working with people with learning difficulties would contribute to Dawn's power resources (Mullaly, 1997).

> Anna said I should leave my partner, either make myself homeless or go to a refuge. But I was too scared that my partner would find me and hurt me if I did this. I was also scared to go to a place where I didn't know anyone. I felt Anna wasn't helping me because I wanted me and the boys to be protected but she was only interested in the boys. I wanted to stay with my children; no-one else had ever looked after them and I thought they would be scared.

Oppressed groups 'experience obstacles to develop their capacities and participate fully in society' (Mullaly, 1997). Domestic violence reduces the ability of women to make life-changing decisions. Dawn's experience is that no choices have been offered because she does not understand the notion of a refuge or making herself technically homeless. Anna's use of language here is disempowering, indicating an assumption that Dawn has a particular level of understanding and ability to seek ways out of domestic violence. Therefore Dawn has been denied the opportunity to consider all the information presented to her, which in turn has implications for any decision she might make. Dawn's decision-making capacity is compounded by her learning difficulty. Therefore, Anna needs to consider different forms of communication. The narrative approach discussed above would provide Anna with the opportunity to examine with Dawn her previous decision-making experiences and identify and develop her skills in this area.

I think I need help with parenting, there are some things I can't do very well and I needed advice. I didn't get this from Anna. I also can't read or write, so when Anna wrote to me or sent me anything, my partner always had to tell me what to do. I don't think that Anna really thought about the help I needed, and sometimes I find it hard to explain myself properly to other people. I did all that Anna had asked me to do.

Evidence from international research on parenting by people with learning difficulties shows that they receive a service that is characterised by an 'over zealous' approach to the assessment of risks (Social Services Inspectorate, 1999). Booth (2000) suggests that professional practice serves to undermine rather than support parents with learning difficulties wanting to care for their children. They are scrutinised and policed, their vulnerabilities exposed rather than their abilities worked with. This is Dawn's experience. Anna's focus on the children should not be at the expense of Dawn's needs. Dawn's wishes and feelings appear to be overlooked, her right to parent denied. Dawn asks for help with her parenting, but this support is not initially provided, and the children's right to experience improved parenting by their mother is therefore also denied.

The problem for a practitioner attempting to work from a child-centred perspective is balancing the range of needs identified within the family. The interconnectedness of these needs should be explored and should inform the assessment and intervention strategy. The question to be considered is the precise nature of Dawn's parenting and the justifiability of judging it adequate or inadequate. Is Dawn providing minimum standards of care for her children to thrive, and is her parenting comparable to other women in similar social circumstances? Dawn has to be respected as a person and her human right as a woman to be a mother to her children also has to be respected. But this has to be balanced against her ability to 'parent'. If Dawn is doing *all that is asked of her*, then it could be said that she is doing all that she can to be a good parent. Ultimately she will never be able to fulfil all the 'Dimensions of Parenting Capacity' (Department of Health/Department for Education and Employment/Home Office, 2000: 21) identified in guidance for social workers. However Anna, in partnership with the family centre, could work with Dawn to identify the positive aspects of Dawn's relationship with her children. For example, Dawn can provide basic care and secure attachments but due to her own cognitive ability finds it more difficult to facilitate the children's intellectual development. By undertaking a comprehensive assessment of her strengths, an empowering strategy for 'working with' Dawn could then be identified.

Eventually Clover contacted my sister who my partner had not allowed me to see for quite a few years. She helped me leave with the children. I was really scared during this time, but I knew I had to do it. Anna then said that the children had to go and stay with foster carers. I was upset about this and so were the boys. I visited the boys several times a week, and we all got really upset; it was very sad. I felt angry towards Anna and Bernie because I felt they should have helped me with the boys sooner.

At this stage, Clover, in her specialist role, has used a different approach to help Dawn leave the violent situation. The language used by Anna in suggesting options to Dawn earlier was not helpful. By listening to Dawn's narrative, Clover has established not only that a sister exists but that there is therefore somewhere for Dawn to go. The act of leaving is a first empowering step for Dawn. Dawn's networks are now developing and her social situation changing, which will have an impact on her life experiences. These changes are an indication that Dawn is attempting to take control of her life and resolve her own relationship problems. Booth (2000) reminds us that in focusing on the needs of the children, practitioners often overlook the needs of the parents who may be unable to do their best by their children until their own problems are resolved. At this point, intervention could be refocused to recognise Dawn's resilience, moving practice away from a problem-solving approach towards a strengths perspective (Jessup and Rogerson, 1999).

A family group conference (FGC – see Chapter 13) could be an alternative decision-making process. The FGC approach emphasises collective family decision-making and, through the use of an independent coordinator, tries to manage the tension between compulsory intervention and family choice (Lupton and Nixon, 1999). While there is limited research about the outcomes of FGCs, Lupton and Nixon (1999) suggest that messages about the empowering potential of FGCs consistently indicate that professionals and family members find it a more enabling process. Using such an approach with Dawn could be problematic by replicating her feelings of powerlessness if her learning difficulty is not taken into account. However, it could also provide the opportunity for the telling of her story and modelling a more constructive and democratic way of working with professionals as well as developing supportive familial networks.

A supported parenting model also offers an empowering perspective on working with families headed by parents with learning difficulties (Booth and Booth, 1998). This requires moving from a punitive to a positive approach and rejecting traditional deficit models of service delivery. For Dawn, it would mean focusing on her strengths and resilience (already demonstrated by her) rather than on risk. Anna would need to move from a concern about promoting dependence to the goal of building Dawn's competence, and work in partnership with her rather than maintain the role of 'expert'.

> I then found out that Anna wanted my children to be adopted and this made me feel even more upset and angry. I felt I was losing control but wanted to fight to keep them even though this was hard and I was scared. There were lots of meetings and trips to court and I didn't always understand what was going on. Clover and my solicitor spent a lot of time trying to explain. I had to make decisions about what to do – I wanted to fight. There was a lot of arguing in court and my solicitor fought hard for me but it wasn't enough.

It could be argued that although the children are the most vulnerable in the scenario, once the child protection system becomes activated they are subject to the protective gaze of professionals charged with the responsibility of ensuring that they are adequately cared for. Their vulnerable position is now transformed, because their welfare is supported and maintained by a powerful legal system and professional surveillance. Dawn does not have the benefit of such support, instead she is subject to a system that appears to be intent on destroying her family.

Too often empowerment means reconciling people to being powerless (Langan, 1998). If this is to be avoided, Dawn needs to be made aware of the realities of practice in order to avoid unrealistically raising her expectations. Dawn was invited to attend 'lots of meetings and trips to court'. This professional-led attempt at empowerment actually meant that she was complicit in the state intervention into her life and that of her children. Professionals wanted to be supportive and Dawn acknowledges this. However, Dawn still felt she was not given a chance. Any attempts at empowerment were negated by the system and Dawn eventually felt that she was losing control despite wanting to fight.

In terms of assessing Dawn's parenting ability, it is likely there would be sufficient evidence to indicate that the children's welfare would be better served by their removal. However, this decision has to be balanced against research evidence which shows that corporate parenting fails to provide stable consistent care once children are removed from their family of origin (Jackson et al., 2000). Having left a dangerous relationship, Dawn has demonstrated her commitment to being a 'good' mother and making life changes to enhance the welfare of her children. With a supported parenting package, Dawn could therefore continue to be a mother to the best of her ability and share the parenting tasks with others.

The welfare of the children and that of Dawn are not entirely separable and the future placement of the children has to be considered in the light of the existing bonds and the culture and ethnicity of the children. Therefore management of the process to ensure Dawn's involvement is essential from both her own and the children's perspective, in order to maximise the potential for continuing constructive involvement of the one parent who is able to maintain links with their past.

> They are now looking for parents to adopt my boys, I don't think I'll ever get over it (crying). I feel like I wasn't given a chance. I was with my partner all the time the children's behaviour was bad and I wanted a home of my own with the kids. I needed some help with parenting on my own, but if I had got this help I would have managed.

Dawn does not accept the decision to remove her children and the ideological, professional and structural power, which Anna and Bernie use to achieve their desired result, served only to crush Dawn. She feels the full power of the invasiveness of professional intervention.

Continuing reflections

Anna had to assess and balance the risk to the children and the needs of a mother with learning difficulties who clearly wished to care for her children. As a critical practitioner, Anna will now need space in supervision to deal with feelings generated by the situation and support to reflect on and evaluate her experiences, and further develop her practice. This should be the start of a dialogue, which could contribute in the future to the development of policy and practice. Clover used the energy generated by her anger and frustration immediately after the court case to write a discussion paper for the community learning disability team concerning practice with parents with learning difficulties. Through this, she aims to bridge the organisational gap between child protection teams and adult services for people with learning difficulties.

How far we have facilitated Dawn telling her story can only be confirmed by her. Our personal histories, ethnicities and experiences of being social workers and users have had an impact on our deliberations. The writing of this chapter presented us with the opportunity to consider the contradictions of empowerment practice that is provoked by the intrusiveness of intervention. Dawn's experiences provide the impetus for us all to engage in practice informed by a politics of challenge and resistance.

FURTHER READING

Booth, T. and Booth, W. (1998) *Growing Up with Parents who have Learning Difficulties*, London: Routledge. Challenges taken-for-granted ideas about the process of parenting, the roles of parents, especially disabled parents, and the needs of children.

Brechin, A., Brown, H. and Eby, M. (eds) (2000) *Critical Practice in Health and Social Care*, London: Sage. Argues that professionals should be strategic as well as reflexive thinkers and understand and work with conflicts and changing structures.

Healy, K. (2000) *Social Work Practices: Contemporary Perspectives on Change*, London: Sage. Outlines critical theoretical perspectives and indicates their implications for social work practice. The book considers potential ways of working which are informed by postmodern theory.

Lupton, C. and Nixon, P. (1999) *Empowering Practice? A Critical Appraisal of the Family Group Conference Approach*, Bristol: Policy Press. Examines the nature and meaning of empowerment, which is evaluated and operationalised using the family group conference approach as an example.

Parton, N. (1999) 'Reconfiguring Child Welfare Practices: Risk, Advanced Liberalism and the Government of Freedom', in Chambon, A.S., Irving, A. and Epstein, L. (eds) *Reading Foucault for Social Work*, Chichester: Colombia University Press. Analyses the changing discourses of social work, focusing on the discourse of risk and risk management.

Persistent Oppressions: The Example of Domestic Violence

Audrey Mullender

Since the early 1990s, social work has belatedly begun to accept domestic violence as within its legitimate sphere of interest. Prior to that, the typical response was to reject domestic violence as 'not a statutory responsibility'. The shift in attitude came when a link was established between the abuse of women and the safety and well-being of children. This made the issue 'core business' for social services departments, but has tended to result in a narrow focus on domestic violence as a child protection concern, rather than a recognition that social work skills have a great deal to offer to all the parties involved. These encompass emotional support and practical assistance for abused women, direct work with children who are recovering from living with domestic violence and tackling violent men's behaviour.

This chapter will explore these domains of practice from a critical perspective, raising issues such as the following:

Regarding women:

■ Why do women feel unable to tell their stories to social workers?

■ What could social work offer women that would actually help them to be safe and improve their quality of life?

Regarding children:

■ Why is practice not child-centred?

■ Could models of direct work with children be more widely adopted that focus on safety planning and recovery from distress and upheaval?

Regarding men:

■ 'What works' with men?
■ Is there room for social work skills in preprogrammed cognitive behavioural intervention?

This chapter will conclude by highlighting how the skills of social groupwork could be particularly helpful in challenging the behaviour of violent men and helping women and children to move forward with their lives. In respect of all three areas of intervention – with women, children and men – what will be revealed is that social work holds many of the answers to domestic violence, particularly through the use of groupwork. First, however, to explain the title of the chapter, we will turn to a brief consideration of the persistence of domestic violence over time and across cultural and socioeconomic groupings.

The persistence of domestic violence

Domestic violence will be understood here as typically combining physical, sexual and emotional abuse and intimidation and, characteristically, as the misuse of power and the exercise of control (Pence and Paymar, 1990) by one partner over the other in an intimate relationship. It is predominantly perpetrated by men against women (across all ethnic and socioeconomic groupings), sometimes the other way round, and also occurs in same-sex couples who may find it even more difficult to obtain help owing to homophobic attitudes and heterosexist assumptions. Disabled women may be particulatly vulnerable to abuse, for example when their abuser is also their carer. Domestic violence also forms one aspect of elder abuse.

Although there has never been a national prevalence study of domestic violence in the UK, the figures from well-designed, generalisable local surveys are remarkably consistent. Mooney (1994) found 1 in 3 women in a random household survey in north London admitting to having experienced, at some point in their lives, violence in an intimate relationship worse than being grabbed, pushed or shaken, with similar rates across all social and ethnic groupings. Earlier, McGibbon et al. (1989) had had a similar result in a GP surgery survey in west London, while a later shopping centre survey in Surrey came up with 1 in 4 (Dominy and Radford, 1996). These figures indicate that domestic violence is endemic right across society. Further confirmation comes from the Violence Against Women Survey of 12,000 women in Canada (Johnson, 1998) which once more reported just under 1 in 3. At the fatal end of the spectrum, approaching two women a week are killed by male partners and ex-partners (Home Office, *Criminal Statistics for England and Wales*, year on year).

Turning to incidence, when women are asked about events in the 12-month period prior to interview, figures are again consistent, with 12 per cent in the Mooney study having been victims during that period and very slightly fewer (11 per cent) telling Stanko et al. (1998) in a GP surgery survey that they had required medical attention following violence in the past year.

Proportions of disabled women who have experienced abuse may be higher still (see Nosek and Howland, 1998, for a summary of North American research). In the home, if her partner is also a carer, the woman's dependency may trap her in the abuse, as may the daunting prospect of reconstructing a complex care package elsewhere. Her disability may also be used against her if her abuser restricts her mobility, her outings or her access to medication (London Borough of Hounslow, 1994).

The predominant pattern across society is one of men's violence towards women (see summaries in Dobash and Dobash, 1992; Mullender, 1996), although women may also be violent to men, and there is certainly abuse in some same-sex relationships (Renzetti, 1992; Island and Letellier, 1991).

Recent Home Office statistics (Mirrlees-Black, 1999) show roughly equal levels of minor violence by men and women, but the more persistent patterns chiefly involving men's violence, with women more likely to be injured and to feel very frightened. Choking incidents and forced sex are shown to be virtually entirely male-on-female phenomena.

Abusers trade on the fact that men were traditionally not only expected but required to keep women in order in the household (see Freeman, 1979). Also, the issue is still emerging from being a butt of humour into construction as a potentially resolvable social problem. The turning point in the UK came when police policy shifted to regarding a domestic assault as a crime like any other crime and men as responsible for their own abusive behaviour (see Morley and Mullender, 1994). More recently, the Protection from Harassment Act 1997 has also allowed intervention in situations where more subtle methods are used to sustain intimidation.

The failure to offer women effective help

Although domestic violence is now on the sociopolitical agenda as never before, women still report that assistance is patchy, and often accompanied by judgemental and woman-blaming attitudes (Mullender and Hague, 2000). Too little has changed since women in the classic studies (for example, Binney et al., 1981; Dobash et al., 1985) spoke of trying one agency after another and encountering constant obstacles and delays. Homophobia (Violence Against Lesbians in the Home, 1998) and inaccessible services (London Borough of Hounslow, 1994; Nosek and Howland, 1998) make the situation worse for lesbian and disabled women.

Institutional racism has also been identified in domestic violence responses from statutory agencies (Mama, 1996; Rai and Thiara, 1997). Women who do not have British nationality may have been lied to by their abuser about their citizenship and residence rights. Officials dealing with immigration, asylum and refugee status do have an element of discretion, which they can operate in cases of real danger, but may tend to demand proof that abused women are not always in a position to provide.

Yet women turn to professionals only when the violence has become frequent and severe and they have exhausted all the resources of self, family and friends (Dobash et al., 1985). Encountering a lack of effective help may then escalate the danger (Hanmer, 1996), especially as many professionals continue to believe that, if the woman leaves, she will be safe, ignoring the dangers of post-separation violence for women and children (Hester and Radford, 1996). Some statutory agencies fail even to convey information about local women's organisations, and neglect language and cultural needs (James-Hanman, 1995).

Overall, mainstream agencies pay too little attention to safety (London Borough of Lewisham's Community Safety Team, 1998). Refuges are the only agencies that women consistently believe can offer them safety and which they entrust with the full details of their experiences (Hague et al., 2001). Women's organisations specialise in offering survivors of violence respect (Sissons, 1999), with emergency, outreach and advocacy projects all playing a key role. Consequently, women evaluate such services positively (Mullender and Hague, 2000). In all other contexts, they fear disbelief, revulsion, blame and possible consequences in terms of child protection intervention.

Rediscovering social work skills – a way forward?

Because the problem of domestic violence thrives in isolation and intimidation, behind closed doors, groups are one of the most powerful ways of challenging its impact. They help women to see that 'if you, you and you are battered, it can't be your faults' (Mullender and Ward, 1991: 94), 'break the secret' for children who have lived in violent homes (Peled and Edleson, 1995) and create a context in which workers and other group members can challenge perpetrators to confront their own behaviour and its impact. These dynamics for change cannot be recreated through individual work. While recognising that feminist counselling and other interventions can also be helpful, groupwork is considered here as a particularly useful approach.

The remainder of this chapter will explore what groups can achieve with women, children and men in relation to domestic violence and will argue for a reclaiming of groupwork skills as a key element in the struggle to combat men's abuse of women as a persistent oppression.

Groups for abused women

Groupwork offered by women to women has always been the foundation of a feminist approach to domestic violence services. Such groups aim at a process of healing and growth. They focus on helping women to understand that the abuse is not their fault and that the abuser must take responsibility for his own behaviour. They support women in naming the abuse and in rebuilding self-esteem and an independent life. Groups may use participative exercises, discussion topics, role-playing and women's own stories and poems to highlight not only the causes and effects of men's controlling tactics and women's enforced submission, but also women's survival strategies and energy for change. The women's group manual from the world-famous Duluth programme in the USA (Pence, 1997) emphasises internalised oppression and cultural expectations in relation to class, age and ethnicity, as reasons for staying in a bad relationship. It combines individual valida-tion ('I am a lovable person, I deserve to be treated well'), with the need for social change ('What can we do that will make a difference?'). There are numerous British publications (for example, *Breaking Through*, 1989) which offer personal accounts of living with abuse and leaving it, including the use of art and poetry. Many of these could be adapted for use in groups to explode the myths about why women stay with abusive men (see also Mullender, 1996) or return to violent relationships, and how they survive, in most cases eventually separating.

Although groupwork with women would be hard to find in most statutory social work and probation settings, social workers do have the necessary tradition (Donnelly, 1986; Dominelli, 1990; Butler and Wintram, 1991) and could rapidly revive the skills. In recognition of this, the London Borough of Hackney's *Good Practice Guidelines* (1994: 46) state: 'Social workers who wish to run groups for women who are or who have experienced domestic violence will be encouraged to do so by the Department'. There would, in fact, be opportunities all over local authority settings for social services staff to facilitate supportive discussion wherever women gather together. Groups for women whose children have been identified as having childcare needs, for example (Butler, 1994), will always include women who are being or have been abused, and could be an ideal context for meeting women's as well as children's needs. In the community, too, any mother and toddler drop-in session, women and health course, or women's class in a minority ethnic community centre could be used to offer support and advice on living with or leaving abusive relationships and affirm women's experiences and plans.

An independent evaluation of support groups for women survivors of domestic violence in the USA found that group members experienced substantial improvements in social and emotional functioning and also a reduction in violence (Tutty et al., 1993). Although some caution must be exercised as to the generalisability of these findings (Abel, 2000), they nevertheless support the wisdom of rediscovering traditional social work skills in groupwork where domestic violence is concerned.

The failure to help children – and a way forward

A recognition that living with domestic violence often has an adverse impact on children's behavioural and emotional adjustment (see Mullender and Humphreys, 2000 for a summary) has frequently led to a narrow child protection response. Practice examples of this approach at its worst have included blanket registration on the grounds of emotional abuse (guaranteed to prevent women from mentioning their own abuse to social services), the sending of a routine letter warning of the impact domestic violence could be having on the children (taking no precautions to prevent the arrival of the letter from further exacerbating the man's violence) and numerous individual instances of statutory intervention used to protect children while taking no action to help the woman (Humphreys, 2000).

Although these interventions are intended to be child-centred, they do not meet children's needs, either to feel safe or to recover from their experiences. A patchier (Humphreys et al., 2000) but far more positive development, drawing on work in Canada and the USA, is that of offering groups for children who have lived with domestic violence.

Children's groups

Groups are an ideal way of bringing children together so that they know they are not alone in what they have experienced, as the atmosphere of secrecy at home has previously led them to believe (Peled and Edleson, 1995). Coming together helps children to talk more freely about feelings they have been keeping bottled up inside, to understand that the violence is not their fault and to learn new ways of keeping safe.

The Community Group Treatment Program for Child Witnesses of Woman Abuse (Mullender, 1994; Loosley et al., 1997) in London, Ontario, offers groups for 4–16-year-olds, divided into age bands of two to three years in each group and available to all agencies in the city to make referrals. A rolling programme of groups, drawing together workers from a range of agencies, operates to a set of core principles:

1. Is the group providing ample opportunities for children to tell their stories and be heard, believed and validated?

2. Does the group ensure that the children know how to protect themselves emotionally and physically by developing and practicing safety plans?

3. Does the group convey the message that all types of violence and abuse are unacceptable?

4. Does the group convey that abusive behavior is a choice and that responsibility lies with the person perpetrating the violence and abuse?

5. Does the group explore the expression of anger and other emotions and provide nonabusive alternatives?

6. Does this group explore alternative means of conflict resolution?

7. Does the group provide a positive environment where all the activities are learner centered and esteem building?

(Loosley et al., 1997: 6)

Groups are closed (that is, the same children attend throughout) and set their own ground rules, with 'confidentiality' and 'no violence' to the fore. Most are mixed sex and they normally run weekly for ten weeks, following a programme of topics approached through a range of age-related activities. Facilitators can be one, two or three women (the youngest children need three workers), or a woman and a man.

Group sessions may be varied as needed. One group of 8–10-year-olds were mainly speaking about their experiences for the first time and required several sessions before they could move on (Loosley et al., 1997: 28). A teenage group focused on the subject of dating violence, dealing with personal safety and forms of help available. It is part of the groupworkers' skill to vary content and activities as the life of the group and the needs of members determine. Younger children tend to respond to more activity and less talking, with a faster pace. A topic can be introduced during a snack, for example, rather than expecting 5–6-year-olds to sit still and listen.

Most groups are for children only. One issue that remains to the fore is how best to involve mothers in the work. A few groups are for mothers and children together, where talking about former family secrets can be very helpful, although it also takes skill to prevent agendas from then becoming too adult-centred. Most recently, a model of parallel groups has been spreading, with joint sessions at the beginning and end.

Effective outcomes have been demonstrated from children's groups. They can challenge children's assumptions of responsibility for the violence and teach them to seek help safely (Marshall et al., 1995; Loosley et al., 1997) and about non-violent conflict resolution. Groups are fun and can help to rebuild self-esteem (Peled and Edleson, 1995, based on similar groups in the USA). Thus, once again, the evidence from research shows groupwork as having much to offer where there has been domestic violence.

Working with perpetrators

Groupwork with the perpetrators of domestic violence also remains in short supply in the UK, although it is spreading – undertaken most often by the probation service or in the voluntary sector and typically based on cognitive behavioural techniques. It can certainly form one part of an active response to domestic violence, requiring abusive men to take responsibility for their own behaviour and attitudes, although completion rates are low and evaluation to date equivocal (Mullender, 1996; Mullender and Burton, 2000). Men's programmes need long-term monitoring, with feedback from partners to ensure that men are not simply using more subtle abuse tactics or claiming to have changed in order to preserve their relationships. The Home Office is conducting a large-scale study of the crime reduction potential of such work (Blumson, 1999).

In order to be successful (Mullender and Burton, 2000), groups need to be based on a clear recognition of domestic violence as an endemic crime. Anger management, for example, is not an appropriate response because men who abuse women are not out of control – they choose the time, place and victim. Issues of women's safety need to be prioritised, with a direct channel for the groupworkers to hear instantly if the woman is revictimised. Accountability to women more generally is also an issue in men's work, including not competing for resources with services for women and children. There remains a debate as to whether some forms of men's groups (those which divert from sentencing, or which are not linked to the criminal justice system) may themselves minimise or decriminalise domestic violence in comparison with other violent crime and thus become 'a substitute for justice' (Burton et al., 1998: 41). RESPECT (2000) provides a set of good practice principles and minimum standards for men's programmes which avoid many of these dangers.

Groupwork process: the key to change

Recent research has suggested that it may well be groupwork process which obtains the best results and not a simple instructional format. The evidence comes from a four-site, longitudinal study comparing different groupwork models (Gondolf, 1998), which indicated that altering gender attitudes may be the crucial element. At the 15-month follow-up, men saying that they had learned to 'talk things through' was statistically linked with the third of women who reported 'a great extent' of change in their partners.

The men were more likely to show attitude change if they had learnt to avoid violence through discussion or respect for women and their point of view. This cannot be achieved in a group simply by practising behavioural techniques such as 'time out' when the man begins to feel angry.

These findings are supported by Dobash et al. (2000), in a study of two programmes in Scotland, where discussions in the group were also said by the men to have had most effect on them, along with specific aspects of the content. The researchers comment (p. ix):

> Group work it seems is very important in providing a context in which violence can be discussed with others who have had similar experiences and with group leaders who focus clearly on the offending behaviour and provide new ways of seeing and understanding violence.

The skill lies in challenging directly and facilitating meaningful discussion, so as to draw men into confronting one another's denial, minimisation and projection (blaming others). The ability to do this cannot be learned from a manual; it requires adequate training and professional experience both in the groupworker and in their supervisor or consultant, as well as adequate resourcing.

Social work traditionally possessed and nurtured immense skill in groupwork (Brown, 1992) as an intervention for change. Our work is about more than assessment; we can also help people to move on in their lives.

CONCLUSION

We arrive, then, at a series of paradoxes:

- Why, when domestic violence is so high up the agenda, do women continue to feel unsafe and unbelieved?

- Why, when social work is obsessed with child protection, does it give children so little effective help?

- Why, when research has shown that attitudinal change towards women makes perpetrators less dangerous, do a rather rigid, mechanistic, cognitive behaviouralism and talk of 'anger management' persist in practice?

The greatest paradox of all is why the UK is allowing a precious national resource, in the form of the traditional social work skills of 'people change', to wither away in deference to managerialism. In fact, as this chapter has demonstrated, skilled and carefully evaluated groups have a great deal to offer in helping survivors recover and in challenging perpetrators, yet they are little used nowadays. When the need is so pressing, as it clearly is in relation to domestic violence, this failure to harness the appropriate tools for evidence-based practice looks like wilful neglect.

FURTHER READING

Brown, A. (1992) *Groupwork*, 3rd edn, Aldershot: Ashgate. This is the best general introduction to social groupwork in the British context. The third edition includes content on anti-oppressive groupwork practice, particularly in relation to gender and ethnicity.

Mullender, A. (1996) *Rethinking Domestic Violence: The Social Work and Probation Response*, London: Routledge. This is a comprehensive overview of current research-based knowledge on domestic violence, covering best practice with women and children and also intervention with perpetrators.

Taylor-Browne, J. (ed.) (2001) *What Works in Reducing Domestic Violence? A Comprehensive Guide for Professionals*, London: Whiting & Birch. Written by experts in their respective fields, this edited collection provides the most up-to-date information on strategies for tackling domestic violence in a multiagency context.

'Glassed-in': Problematising Women's Reproductive Rights under the New Reproductive Technologies

Lena Dominelli

Women's reproductive rights are contested rights. So, it is not surprising that the advent of the new technologies in women's reproductive lives has created new sites of struggle and exacerbated old tensions in this arena. But what is interesting about recent developments is that this particular instance of the (re)gendering of social relations between men and women has not been acknowledged as a 'sex war'. Rather, it has been clothed in silence as technical and gender-neutral language is used to cover the gendered bodies that are at centre stage (Steinberg, 1997). Secrecy and silence have disempowered women as active participants in the life-giving process, a point poignantly expressed by a woman I interviewed for this article when describing how confined and confining her choices were. She said:

> I felt glassed-in. Just like my babies on those petrie dishes. For years, I came and went, came and went, with nothing to show for it. I got so I dreaded the next appointment. But I couldn't talk to anyone about it. And the doctors never asked.

The absence of discussion of the impact of the new reproductive technologies on women's (or even family) lives on social work courses and in statutory practice is equally marked. In this chapter, I consider the importance of the new reproductive technologies for social workers and argue that its potential to disrupt our thinking about work with women, children and families is enormous. Social work educators and practitioners need to engage in public discourses about its significance and meaning and take a more active role in rethinking the implications of the new reproductive technologies on social work theory and practice.

The new reproductive technologies: forces for changing thinking and behaviour

Secrecy was the key word that came to mind as I endeavoured to find out what social workers in Britain were doing with regard to the new reproductive technologies. It was also difficult to find anyone willing to talk about their experiences of either childlessness or attempts to overcome it. Social work practitioners in mainstream agencies, including hospital settings, claimed they seldom dealt with the issue and knew little that could help in my research. As far as they could tell, these services were being provided by voluntary agencies and health professionals. Even the counselling of distraught women, they felt, was better done by others who had the time to spend with them. This suggests that the changing nature of social work is having a profound impact on daily practice routines, including the 'takeover' of social work activities by health professionals and the blurring of the boundaries between health and social care. But it also indicates the appalling working conditions of many practitioners. They had more than enough work on their hands without adding yet another new area to it.

The term 'the new reproductive technologies' covers a lot of ground. It can mean hi-tech interventions such as *in vitro* fertilisation (IVF) and a range of other treatments used to address infertility and childlessness including artificial insemination by donor (AID), surrogate mothering and the human tissue transplant market in eggs and embryos. Inman (1998) claims there are 2,200 children born as a result of sperm or egg donation and 100 surrogate births. Often left out of the equation is the number of professional interventions and range of medicalised processes that women undergo in order to give birth. The exclusion of social work from this process symbolises, for me, the medicalisation of women's reproductive rights. This danger was identified by Stanworth (1987) when she first applied a feminist lens to these developments. Since then, the new reproductive technologies have advanced at such a pace that even lay discourses encompass the cloning of babies, the substitution of human body parts by those of animals, or even artificially created ones, and the 'purchase' of babies via the internet. Thus, the question 'Who am I?' no longer has a straightforward answer, if it ever did. And tracing one's genealogy becomes an identity puzzle that would exercise the mental agility of a Sherlock Holmes. Indeed, finding one's ancestors can become a traumatic quest that challenges existing legal and practice definitions of parenthood, whether motherhood or fatherhood, and what or who constitutes the family, extended or nuclear. One health practitioner I met claimed that a child could have as many as six parents. Moreover, it also raises enormous questions about the different, often competing and irreconcilable rights to information or anonymity of the different parties involved in the processes from conception to birth (Blyth, 1998). These are difficult questions that social workers have traditionally addressed in their practice.

Under the cloak of medical interventions, however, there has been both a serious erosion in the rights of women to become active participants (Klein, 1989b) in the process of giving birth, while at the same time producing increased possibilities for women to have children and reaffirm their mothering roles (Steinburg, 1997). The power of and roles played by doctors, particularly consultants with research interests, have been crucial in defining the terms under which discourses in this area occur and have privileged the voices of those professionals involved in multidisciplinary teams. They have promoted this as a highly scientific medical enterprise or capital intensive venture, whose espoused aim is to benefit childless women (see Winston, 1987). When services become commercial businesses controlled by hi-tech medical experts and pharmaceutical companies whose eye is on making profits for shareholders (Burfoot, 1990), they can lose their focus on women's experiences of these technologies and operate at the expense of women (Steinberg, 1997), often as an unintended consequence.

Britain has a pioneering place in the history of the new reproductive technologies. IVF was invented here. In 1978, Louise Brown was announced as the world's 'first test tube baby'. Also, the first clinical use of genetic screening of IVF embryos occurred in the UK, and the Warnock Report (1984) has been heralded as the first government document of significance on the subject. The Warnock Inquiry, which resulted in this Report, raised the moral and ethical dilemmas of the new technologies for human reproduction as a key concern. Another was not to undermine the ideology of conventional motherhood and the heterosexual nuclear family (Spallone, 1987). Scientific rationality dominated the discourses within the Warnock Committee and enabled the Report to both 'protect scientific progress' and respond to the embryo 'rights' lobby (Crow, 1990). Convergence between these two positions was reflected in the legislation that followed Warnock, particularly the Human Fertilisation and Embryology (HFE) Act 1990. This assumes that: IVF is a beneficial treatment; IVF is conducted not on or through women's bodies, but on gametes or other genetic material; and embryos acquire personhood at the moment of implantation. The implications of this for women are to deny women a say in what happens to their bodies. They become passive recipients of benign (in intention at least) medical interventions and have their rights and access to abortion eroded, including through the setting of new deadlines during which terminations can be carried out. Hence, section 37 of the HFE Act has reduced the time during which abortions can be sought from the 28 weeks stipulated by the Abortion Act 1967 to 24 weeks. These issues are germane to social work practice with women.

The HFE Act 1990 and the Human Fertilisation and Embryology Authority (HFEA) provide the basic framework within which both scientific research in this area and the treatment of women and their partners is conducted in Britain. They aim to tightly control the conditions and period under which medical research and interventions on women's bodies can be carried out. However, as Steinberg (1997) has pointed out, this framework has heightened medical control over women's bodies, virtually erasing them from the scientific discourses, which now dominate. Ironically, this means that the struggles that women have historically waged to wrest control of pregnancy and childbirth away from male medical professionals (Ehrenreich and English, 1979), symbolised by the resurgence in the use of midwives, have to be rewon on new terrain.

The Warnock Report and the HFE Act affirm a disablist approach to human reproduction by legitimating the production of perfect embryos. This validates the continued viewing of disability as a medical condition rather than a socially created one (see Oliver, 1990; also Chapter 18). Scientific research on human beings, particularly when it seeks to eradicate human deformities or disease, is defined as technically neutral and ethically unproblematic. Ultimately, this approach feeds into desires for 'designer babies', as the media labels them, that conform to racist, sexist and ablist stereotypes. This issue was aired to an extensive degree when Molly Nash's parents used genetic screening and IVF techniques to produce an embryo that was 'disease-free and a perfect match' in terms of providing her with blood cells from the forthcoming baby's umbilical cord to substantially increase her chances of surviving Fanconi's anaemia (Thompson, A., 2000). This procedure, lawful in the United States where it was performed, is illegal in Britain. Yet it led to further demands for assistance from worried parents, including a couple, Alan and Louise Masterton in Scotland, who, having lost their daughter in a tragic accident a year earlier, demanded this treatment to 'restore the "female dimension" of their family' (Thompson, A., 2000). Few people would argue against the technology's beneficial potential, although the eugenicist dimensions of these 'choices' are cause for concern. The examples above also demonstrate the ethical minefields that such technologies can produce. The possibilities of exploiting women for disreputable purposes, including racist, sexist and ablist, ones have to be consciously addressed. These techniques are not inherently abusive, but how they are used can be. For the question of who decides what is acceptable and what is not is an inherently political one that can exclude those that are normally marginalised in society. For example, non-hearing disabled parents might want to ensure that their children have normal hearing, but who are they to decide that disabled parents must also have 'perfect' children? We know that how society answers this question can have devastating consequences, as the Nazi determination to preserve the 'Aryan race' has demonstrated. RADAR and Mencap have also been vocal in raising these concerns (Fletcher, 1999).

Although apparently a spoof perpetrated by jokers at the end of the twentieth century, the 'designer baby' attitude is best typified by a group of attractive women models using the internet to sell their eggs to the highest bidder. This was followed later by a real life 'tug of love' as two childless couples, one British and the other American, both 'purchased' the same set of twins through the Web. The commodification of children thereby acquired new twists as national boundaries became blurred at the same time that problem-solving based on solutions rooted in national jurisdictions revealed their inadequacies. The racial and class dimensions of this saga are not commented upon, although obvious. The two sets of 'adoptive' parents are white; the twins and their biological parents are poor African-Americans.

The question of who is a fit parent is a major concern of social workers. And, in the case cited above, social workers were called upon to take the children into custody and find legal ways of solving the dispute. The 'best interests of the children' was advocated as the way forward. And, while important in its own right, an equally troubling set of questions, implied in the affair, received little considered attention. The needs that the two sets of parents were trying to fulfil, their motivations in choosing an unorthodox manner for becoming parents and their suitability for such a role were sidelined. The problem that the twins' biological mother was trying to resolve was also left as an unaccompanied apostrophe in the air. How important were poverty, racism, and sexism in her decision? Did the internet offer a vehicle for decision-making that she could control?

The concern about who is a 'fit' parent (although the focus is usually on the mother) was also addressed in the debates surrounding the creation of a regulatory framework to control both the clinicians and the putative parents. So, the issue of who could be a 'donor' and a 'recipient' received an airing in the media on other occasions where stereotypes of able-bodied heterosexual couples in their youth were endorsed. The outrage that erupted when the newspapers revealed that a 60-year-old woman in Italy had been assisted through the new reproductive technologies to give birth was a clear indication of the gendered and ageist character of the discourses. Little sympathy was given to the woman's right to choose (or not) motherhood. Yet, as was demonstrated by the lack of comment in the media shortly afterwards, it was permissible for men in their eighties to become fathers.

Issues for social worker involvement

Social workers have traditionally held key roles in working with children and families, where questions about fertility, pregnancy, childbirth, childlessness and family networks have been discussed in the context of the social problems that they seek to address. These practitioners' absence from the scene in the context of the new reproductive technologies is a cause for concern. One outcome resulting from this situation is that their expertise in handling complex moral and ethical dilemmas is being/will be lost. Certainly, it is not being made available to those in the voluntary sector who are replacing them. The other is that, according to research that has explored this area, the medical profession is not meeting women's needs as individuals who have their own specific interests that merit attention as well as those of the subsequent implanted embryo or child to whom she gives birth (Sewpaul, 1998). In my view, social workers should become an integral part of the multidisciplinary team that deals with women undergoing fertility treatment of whatever kind, and they should be involved in responding to women's needs at all points in the process. This includes helping a woman to examine the meaning of being childless for her, including acknowledging the acceptability of being childless. This is crucial given the low success rate of fertility treatments including IVF (Sewpaul, 1998). If she decides to go ahead with the treatment, its invasiveness should be considered carefully and the difficult moments that the woman might encounter have to be considered. Women have found medical practitioners too busy and lacking training for handling the complex emotions and dilemmas that they experience when the treatment does not work or when they feel demoralised after years and years of 'trying' and still finding that they are unable to have the child they want.

In Britain, surrogacy arrangements are shaped by the Surrogacy Arrangements Act 1985. This legislation prohibits the sale of babies. Surrogate mothers are only entitled to receive 'expenses' incurred in the course of their pregnancy, although what counts as expenses is open to debate. The government is considering tightening up the current rules (Inman, 1998). However, as Steinberg (1997) argues, this definition of the situation reaffirms sexist social relations because women are expected to provide free labour to the reproductive technology medico-commercial complex. Men who donate sperm have often been paid for their contributions to human reproduction, even though the risks associated with sperm donation are hardly comparable to those experienced by women during the invasive procedures they undergo in the process of egg extraction, being pregnant and/or giving birth.

The issues that women will confront depend on whether they are considering fertility treatment or surrogacy arrangements. Although women undertaking one or the other of these treatments will share some concerns, others will be different. Points of convergence include: worries that someone else's gametes may be involved; questions about whether the child is hers and her partner's; and concerns that the partner may or may not go on to become the ensuing child's father. Another revolves around how she will explain genetic differences to any resulting offspring. Although responding to these queries may be avoided for a while, or may be unproblematic if they arise while she is in a stable relationship, the situation can deteriorate rapidly and she may find that she is unsupported and isolated when she is most in need of help. Not having considered these matters during the good times can intensify her feelings of vulnerability. Appropriate and sensitive social work intervention before this dilemma arises and afterwards can ease the transitions between these different states.

Surrogacy arrangements also have the added complication of having to deal directly with other people, besides the surrogate mother, and this can exacerbate conflict, particularly if their motivations for engaging in surrogacy relationships differ. For example, this can occur if the surrogate mother wants to retain contact with the commissioning family while her partner does not. Alongside a conflictual relationship, the woman may be deprived of the support she urgently needs. On the other hand, the commissioning or social mother, having formed a relationship with the baby, might feel it is best to end contact with the surrogate mother. She may reach the same conclusion if she decides that she does not want her mothering capacities to be qualified, an issue she would constantly face if she saw the surrogate mother, for her mere presence would provide proof of her incapacity. Where the 'best interests of the child' lie in such situations and how this can be ascertained remain relevant and problematic, but are questions rarely asked. Another difficult one is whether these concerns can be left to one side until the child grows up and makes demands in his/her own right. These relationships raise moral and emotional dilemmas alongside contractual and legal ones for all parties in the transaction. Although a social worker is unlikely to have all the answers for these occasions, she/he would be able to provide practical and emotional support and/or refer them to other agencies or professionals for assistance.

A woman who acts as a surrogate mother also feels a range of, and at times conflicting, emotions. These include mood swings during pregnancy and uncertainty about whether or not she is doing the 'right thing'. Whatever the contract she has signed states, she may wish she had not agreed to part with 'her baby'. These feelings may be intensified after the birth and could lead to serious depression. Or, despite careful legal crafting of its content, she may refuse to comply with the contractual agreement, and have expensive legal proceedings initiated against her. Careful exploration of her motives and feelings before entering such agreements could be provided by a supportive social worker. Currently, this service, if available, is provided by voluntary or non-profit organisations, which operate networks that seek to put women who want to become mothers in touch with women willing to act as surrogates. Childlessness Overcome Through Surrogacy (COTS), an organisation started by Kim Cotton, a surrogate mother, has a nationwide network that includes counsellors as part of its services. Systematic research into who these counsellors are and their qualifications for practice is lacking, as is an analysis of which women seek and which act as surrogates. COTS claims to have arranged 200 surrogate births and has standards of openness that require prospective parents to tell their offspring about their origins. It carries out police and HIV checks on them and also provides counselling before matching the intending parents with a surrogate mother and afterwards (Inman, 1998). Thus, COTS tries to promote responsible surrogacy. Much of what COTS does is endorsed in the Code of Practice developed by the British government to set out minimum standards for surrogacy arrangements. This Code also declares that the interests of the children must guide the actions of the professionals involved in these situations.

Cotton has strongly defended women's rights to choose whether or not to become mothers or act as surrogates. Steinberg (1997) suggests that it is not enough to focus solely on choice issues because this ignores the context in which women make their choices. And, from their practice in other areas, social workers are aware that the context is often central in determining what women do. In this case, it would affect which women would go forward to use the new reproductive technologies and which would not. Questions about 'race', sexual orientation and age can intersect with views about fit persons for these treatments, and the availability (or not) of money can constrain women's decisions. Even for fertility treatments funded by the National Health Service (NHS), it can be a 'post-code lottery' where the chances of getting treatment or having it for a sufficient period to yield results can vary according to residential location and clinical discretion. Consequently, a worry expressed in the literature is that the donors and surrogates will be poor 'black' women in low income countries meeting the needs of wealthy 'white' women in the West, or poor 'white' working-class women doing the same for their wealthier sisters in high income countries (Steinberg, 1997).

Relationships between all those involved in these transactions can become complicated after the birth. The child may be disabled or less than perfect and, as the American experience demonstrates, the commissioning parents may refuse to accept delivery of their baby. This can set the scene for another expensive legal battle. Additionally, the arrangements for minimising or maintaining contact between the contractual parties may break down. Indeed, keeping the origins of their 'donors' a secret may prove to be extremely difficult, as adoptive parents in other contexts have discovered. In New Zealand, for example, sperm donors have found that their offspring can turn up on their doorstep, despite earlier assurances of anonymity. Indeed, legislation in New Zealand now permits children access to information about their genetic parent, however acquired (Blyth, 1998). One of the arguments in favour of a child's right to know has been tinged with eugenicist overtones. That is, there might be some rogue or disease-carrying gene that needs to be identified for medical purposes or by insurance companies for actuarial reasons. Such information can be devastating to the unprepared person who simply wanted to find out who their parent was. Again, social workers involved in assisting people in making difficult decisions that may profoundly alter their lives as they have previously understood them are in position to help to deal with such eventualities. Another strand of argument endorses the child's right to know by focusing on 'the best interests of the child'. In Britain, the Children's Society, COTS and Barnardo's, for example, support openness on these grounds. Although the HFEA collects this information, offspring are currently unable to have access to it. However, some non-identifiable information such as height and medical details and whether or not an applicant is related to their intended partner can be provided. But this data can remain beyond reach if 'parents' do not tell their 'children' that they are the product of donor gametes. Addressing identity issues, is therefore, a crucial area in which social work intervention could be helpful.

CONCLUSION

The new reproductive technologies have opened doors for women wishing to become mothers as well as pulled others shut by reducing the scope of their decision-making when it comes to having or not having children. The increased scientific input into human reproductive processes has remedicalised a normal activity for women and reaffirmed the powers of male medical practitioners and researchers to make decisions affecting fundamental aspects of women's lives. The legal framing of these opportunities and the media's involvement in public discourses of the issues contained within them have further reinforced conventional ideologies and norms regarding motherhood and family life.

Social workers have been in the background in these debates, even though they cover ground that they are more than familiar with, and for which they have the skills and knowledge base for responding sensitively. As a result, much of their expertise in dealing with complex matters in the human condition has not been accessible to women undergoing fertility treatments or engaging in surrogacy arrangements. They have also had little to say about women's roles as either women or mothers in these discussions. It is time for social workers themselves to find their voice and begin to provide the critical reflexive practice for working in anti-oppressive ways with and for women in an area of crucial importance to them. It also requires social work educators to start including this subject on the academic and practice curricula.

FURTHER READING

Feinman, C. (ed.) (1992) *The Criminalization of a Woman's Body*, New York: Harrington Park Press. This edited book covers a range of topics embedded within the practices of professionals intent on controlling women's bodies.

Scutt, J. (ed.) (1990) *The Baby Machine: Reproductive Technologies and the Commerciali-sation of Motherhood*, London: Green Print. An edited collection, this book examines the impact of reproductive technologies, and the opening up of choices for women wishing to give birth through these, on motherhood.

Steinberg, D.L. (1997) *Bodies in Glass: Genetics, Eugenics, Embryo Ethics*, Manchester: Manchester University Press. Providing a comprehensive examination of the new reproductive technologies, this book explains what these technologies are and considers their contradictory potential to both expand and limit women's choices because the medical model prevails.

Developing Critical Practice

Developing Critical Practice in Social Work

Robert Adams

The question that practitioners reading this book face is how to use the ideas in it to develop their critical practice. Part II of this book is devoted to exploring critical practice in the main areas of social work. This introductory chapter examines what it means to develop our own critical practice. This is a journey towards achieving an authentic practice which expresses our values and understandings as empowered practitioners as well as empowering the client. We have to acknowledge that in the early stages this will tax our energy, commitment and assertiveness, because the various contexts in which we make this journey are stacked against developing our critical practice in this way.

What it means to practise critically

In Chapter 1, we argued that critical thinking leads to critical action, which forms critical practice, in a reflexive cycle which links thinking and action. There is overlap here with the three domains that Brechin identifies as essential for successful caring work: critical action, critical reflexivity and critical analysis (Brechin, 2000), referred to in some detail in Chapter 20. Although distinct, these are inseparable components of critical practice. Inevitably, because critical thinking will use the experience of action and its outcomes to inform further thinking, critical practice is a cycle in which thinking is bound up with action. This is part of a reflexive cycle, as critical practitioners are engaged in and committed to the struggle to develop their practice through a questioning rather than a defensive approach.

Practising critically is an aspiration towards much more than technical, procedural or maintenance-based social work. In this chapter, we examine in more detail the demanding process of holistic engagement actually involved in practising critically: engaging with contexts, engaging with ourselves, engaging with knowledge, engaging with practice and engaging with paradoxes and dilemmas.

Engaging with contexts

Being critical requires that the practitioner acts like a critical researcher (Harvey, 1990: 11) and makes links between the particular situation and wider social structures and the way power operates, so as to get beneath the surface. This includes the way that ideology operates to cloak oppressive structural relationships, including class, gender, race, disability, age and other forms of oppression. To give an example that is reflected in social work education policy and practice, social work educators and students may be required to accept as natural certain factors which since the 1980s have threatened to undermine the critical component in social work and social care education and training courses. Three particular aspects of this can be identified:

■ Criticality has lost its prominence in many professional courses. There is a noticeable distinction between the primacy of criticality in the social sciences, for example, and its displacement by the emphasis on the demonstration of competence, based on functional analysis, which drives vocational and professional education and training. (Adams, 1998c: 257; Dominelli, 1996)

■ The notion of what is academic is often set against what is reckoned to be good in practice, rather than the meaning of academic extending to both. The consequence is an unhelpful dichotomy of ideas between what is academic and what is practice. The competence movement and pressure to establish NVQs at the heart of social care work have had an impact on closely neighbouring areas, especially in territory such as social work, where there is great complexity and uncertainty due to the intrinsically problematic nature of its subject matter. Instead of practice and academic wisdom working with each other in mutual clarification and reinforcement, they have been divided and set against each other. A struggle to shift the centre of gravity of practice development to the workplace, which in itself has benefits, has been perceived and represented as irrelevant academia being shed in favour of the work settings which have the answers on the 'true' nature of practice. Such stereotyping impoverishes the practice of theory and starves academia of opportunities to develop models of rooting concepts and critical reflection in practice.

■ The role of critic – whether as employee, social worker, other professional, academic, researcher, client, carer or member of the public – is precarious. This persists in spite of widespread rhetoric about supporting the outsider, promoting empowerment and espousing the positive features of whistle-blowing. Like attempts to protest about conditions in many services, whistle-blowing remains highly problematic for the client, service user, school pupil or patient, and a precarious activity for the professional in today's climate of contracts which try to reinforce obedience and conceal practice in confidentiality under the guise of 'commercial, in confidence'.

In health and social services agencies, criticality in practice has only been given formal recognition in agency procedures since the 1980s with the advent of quality assurance and inspection (Adams, 1998a: 50–62). Many professions working with people are noteworthy for their lack of positive mechanisms for dealing with criticism. There may be rhetoric about empowering clients, but in practice people are not consistently thanked for criticising and complaining about the professional services that they receive. Professional bodies may exist to protect professionals as much as to promote the rights of clients.

In contrast, for many decades disciplines such as literature have put the role of critic in the mainstream, rather than at the margins. Literature has a tradition of literary criticism, which may not be applauded by those criticised, but at least is institutionalised as part of the culture of cognate subjects. Critics are actually paid by newspapers and TV channels.

CASE EXAMPLE

The writer came across a case several years ago where a student in a college of higher education on an observation placement in a community home with education (CHE) responded to sexual harassment against her by a physical education teacher by writing up the incident in her placement report and complaining when she returned to college. Her tutor's response, before the writer and others intervened, was to fail her because by blowing the whistle she put at risk the relationship between the college and that establishment, thereby jeopardising other placements; she should have taken the incident in her stride. Viewed from a critical perspective, it was unacceptable for the student to have to accept abuse from a staff member, even though the tutor's response took the form of pressure to accept the situation. It was necessary to strip away the ideology that a certain level of harassment in that male-dominated CHE was 'natural' and that relations between the college and the CHE had traditionally been good and transparent, that is, collusive in maintaining the oppression.

Engaging with ourselves

Practice begins with us as practitioners. Before we act, we bring ourselves to a case, a situation, a problem. As part of this process, we engage with our own values, as discussed in Chapter 1. Robin Norwood, the therapist, argues that in order for an adult to develop a healthy relationship with another person, that adult must first develop a relationship with themselves (1986: 146). This, perhaps, is akin to not being alienated from ourselves and others. It is one expression of the wider reality that as practitioners we engage with other people as ourselves, experiencing certain emotions as we learn about the case, or the situation of another person. It is necessary to be in touch with our own feelings and understand our own emotional responses, in order to relate professionally to others. We have to grasp what our emotional responses signify, for our own continuing personal and professional development and for the person with whom we are working.

In Chapter 1, we described *reflexivity*. When Hall and Hall are discussing ethnography, in which the researcher seeks to capture and analyse the informants' experiences, they give useful insights into the nature of reflexivity. Reflexivity 'means the self-awareness researchers should have developed throughout the study about how they influenced the results' (Hall and Hall, 1996: 42). Hall and Hall make suggestions that may help critical practitioners to develop their awareness and self-awareness, powers of reflection and degree of engagement with people receiving services and others. Hall and Hall raise issues and questions that critical practitioners might ask themselves:

> How did they gain access to their informants and explain the research? How much did their gender, race or age affect the way they interacted with their informants? Data is seen not as something 'out there' to be collected or captured but as something created through a social process. Data is produced or generated through social interaction between the researcher and the informant, so that research itself is a creative process which you will be part of – as you design and negotiate your research, frame your research instruments and carry out your fieldwork.
>
> (Hall and Hall, 1996: 42–3)

Engaging with knowledge

As practitioners, we also engage with what we know. Knowledge about practice is difficult to grasp and apply critically (see also Chapter 5). This is partly because knowledge expands continually. The practitioner works in a rapidly expanding universe of research, reflection and critical commentary. We often encounter people complaining that there is too much to read in social work. Partly also, encountering new knowledge which conflicts with existing knowledge involves shaking up taken-for-granted aspects of what we know and re-evaluating them. This is a very demanding yet necessary process.

Other problems make it difficult to engage with knowledge about social work. Much of this knowledge relates to social science perspectives and theories. As Hugh England observes, such theories 'are rarely devised as prescriptions for practice ... they inform the worker's understanding and thus his action, but they do not const-itute that understanding' (England, 1986: 37). England explains that practitioners bring ideas and theories acquired by formal learning to bear on situations to give them meaning, but also understanding as part of intuitive consciousness.

> The theory cannot 'fit' because it is general; the worker's use is necessarily partial and selective; the situation changes with each moment and movement in the client's world. Thus the screening of available understandings is a constant process, fuelled by the worker's need to 'make sense', and revised and reasserted whenever sense is absent. It is an intuitive process. It is extended and articulated by the worker's familiarity with theory, but the appropriate use of theory and its integration into understanding and action is a matter of the accuracy of the worker's intuition.
>
> (England, 1986: 38)

But social science theories are themselves problematic and do not provide the direct rationale for social work activities.

John Pinkerton (Chapter 10) reminds us of the role of critical theory, from whatever perspective, in exposing what is hidden, and the role of academics in unmasking what we take for granted. It is important to appreciate also, as we see below, the value of critical practitioners assessing situations from different theoretical vantage points. David Howe shows that adopting a different theory can vary the observation and lead to a totally different explanation for the behaviour or the problem (Howe, 1996: 171). Language assigns meanings and so constructs social reality, as Milner and O'Byrne describe (Chapter 26). Tim Stainton (Chapter 19) provides a graphic illustration of two different constructions of a person with a learning disability, showing some of the consequences of this for practice. The meaningful dialogue that critical practitioners enter with people receiving services (Dalrymple and Burke, Chapter 6) enables them to recount their stories, improving assessment and the planning of more meaningful and relevant services.

Using reflection

Reflectiveness is a stage on the way to criticality. It is not sufficient to be reflective. We need to use the understanding that we gain from reflection to achieve change. Critical practice is not just reflective practice, because the critical practitioner does not take the world for granted and does not automatically accept the world as it is. Reflective practice contributes to critical, transforming practice. What is troubling, though, is the widespread and uncritical acceptance of the view of the reflective practitioner which often is read into Donald Schön's book (1991), as though this makes for 'good enough' social work; it does not. Perhaps this is because reflection could be regarded as a 'here and now' activity, which could be regarded as restricted to the status quo. Critical practice involves reflectiveness, but transcends it. One of the contributions of feminism has been to challenge the assumption that women should be content with achieving equal opportunities in a man's world, rather than changing this world. Reflection is apt to stop short of challenging in this way. Reflective practice contributes to critical practice but of itself is not sufficient. Reflection on its own views the situation unchanged, whereas critical practice is capable of change. Reflection on the situation *as it is* does not achieve transformation. Critical practice offers the prospect of transformation by not being bound by the status quo. The critical practitioner is capable both of being deeply involved in a situation and being detached from it and viewing it from an independent vantage point, bringing to bear on it contextual, theoretical and conceptual understandings. Thus, the critical practitioner can be both insider and outsider and can move between these positions.

Maintaining self-criticality

Critical practice is self-critical. Self-criticism is essential to good critical practice. The chapters in this book demonstrate in different ways how the writers turn their critical attention to their own writing. So, there is an element of modelling in each chapter. Critical practitioners can use self-criticism to highlight alternative contexts, perspectives, approaches and actions, as a means of critically appraising intended or past practice.

Critically analysing

Critical analysis, according to Brechin, involves 'the critical evaluation of knowledge, theories, policies and practice' (Brechin, 2000: 30). Joan Orme (Chapter 23) notes that if practitioners can analyse the systems introduced by managers at work, this will help practitioners to understand how different managerial discourses construct different personal, professional and organisational identities. It is important that such analysis is not regarded as the sole province of academics. Carter et al. comment on an edited collection of social workers' accounts of their practice that 'workers and students are just as much theory-makers as academics who write books' (Carter et al., 1995: 5). It is reasonable, as David Peryer implies (Chapter 30), for critical practitioners to expect transparency in the reorganisations of services, whatever the political imperatives giving impetus to the changes. After all, if the quality of services is to be maximised, the fullest possible participation by all stakeholders – from managers and professionals to people receiving services – is necessary (see also Chapter 29).

One way to focus on what is critical about critical practice is through the idea of networks. Malcolm Payne talks about social work forming part of a very complex network of services and agencies (Payne, 1996: 12). In different areas of work, the social worker is likely to draw on and develop different theories of practice in social work. Links can be made between different contexts. The more knowledgeable and experienced the social worker, and the more critically self-aware, the more readily these links can be made. However, greater self-awareness can generate a sense of being overwhelmed as the further possibilities and difficulties become evident.

Nick Frost (Chapter 5) illustrates the need for practitioners not to downgrade the importance of their own 'tacit' knowledge when they are faced with applying the 'codified' knowledge of research and evaluation findings in practice. The shift of the centre of gravity of critical reflection to the workplace has as part of its essential activities that of continual reference both to academic and practice traditions and wisdoms. The notion of what is academic practice needs to embody and bring together traditions of building on the best practice, bringing critical awareness of concepts and contexts to bear on the work done, as it is practised. In the process, traditions of 'academic' practice should be resited, so as to encompass both academic and practical, college and workplace. Julia Phillipson's (Chapter 24) notion of curiosity is relevant and can bridge the space between research and practice. It has resonance with research and also is firmly rooted in what critical practitioners do. Whitaker and Archer (1989) emphasise the need for the intending practitioner-researcher, before spelling out the purposes of the research, making the existing practice wisdom as explicit as possible, by writing down, completely spontaneously:

> brief accounts of four or five experiences or cases which sparked the interest in the issue or which intuitively struck the social worker as rich examples of it. Once down on paper, they can be examined with such questions in mind as 'What do these

accounts have in common?' 'How do they differ?' 'Are there identifiable turning points?' 'What do I think the client(s) thought about it?' 'At what point did I feel best about my involvement and why?' Thinking along such lines helps a social worker to see what he or she already knows or suspects about a practice interest. Almost always, a social worker knows more about an issue than he or she may have realised, because some of the knowledge and understanding has been held implicitly.

(Whitaker and Archer, 1989: 37)

Often, qualitative methodologies such as participant observation yield insights into the nature of people's experiences that are particularly relevant to social workers. However, the open style of participant observation, and the involvement of the researcher's own emotions and experience in the to-and-fro process of dipping in and out of data collection and analysis, exposes the researcher's own values, commitment and actions to critical scrutiny by others and self-scrutiny by the researcher. This can be far more rigorous than more traditional approaches to research, with the researcher's 'ethical dilemmas and the personal anguishes about them ... exposed not just in the collection of data but also in its publication' (Jupp, 1989: 61).

Adopting a critical approach to less inclusive, emancipatory methodologies

The workplace offers the unique and exciting possibility of developing emancipatory, new paradigm and collaborative research as the practice proceeds. Nick Frost (Chapter 5) argues that evidence-based practice, which tends to gives less weight to inclusive, often qualitative, research, should not be accepted dogmatically. Critical practitioners should adopt an open-minded approach and be prepared to take on board a range of insights from a variety of methodological perspectives.

If the research process is liable to be problematic, tortuous and precarious, the conventional assumption that the purpose of research is to translate the findings into improving the next wave of policy and practice is also questionable. The likelihood that this will happen is improved when the person evaluating practice exchanges the skills of critical scrutiny for those of active participation in the political process (Smith, 1995: 9).

Engaging with practice

It is easier to shy away here from the task of examining practice by keeping it at a distance, than it is to engage with it. We can endlessly discuss ideas about practice, rather than exploring and critically questioning the practice itself.

Payne describes how workers are constantly attempting to bring intuition and conscious thought to bear on evidence and the justification for their practice (Payne, 1996: 62).

This identifies the importance both of reason and of intuition in this process. The rational and intuitive traditions are deep rooted and often mutually antagonistic (Adams, 1985). It is difficult to capture briefly in words how these two components of the use of self contribute to critical practice. There are two main reasons: first, books about practice written by academics tend to emphasise the contribution of rational thought to this process, which inevitably marginalises emotions and intuitive awareness; second, the style of these books tends to highlight prose descriptions rather than poetic insights.

Using empathetic understanding of the client to inform practice

Reflectiveness depends on those capacities to feel as well as think which feed into empathy. Criticality depends on empathy in this complete sense. Empathy has long been regarded as a component of case-based social work. Empathy contributes to critical social work, although on its own its contribution is not sufficient to ensure criticality. Critical practitioners do more than empathise with people's circumstances. They engage with people's biographies when working with them. Their sense of assessment in the here and now is heightened by an awareness of context, which brings together the past and the present. They situate people's histories. Taking a history makes it possible to reflect on the whole life in its context. Biographical details are historical fragments that require contextualising. So, although assessment involves history taking, and history provides one kind of context with significant explanatory potential, the explanatory power of the historical account of a person's circumstances depends on how the critical practitioner relates it to other contexts.

Working purposefully

Practice could be any old work, but that would leave the benefit to clients as a matter of chance (see Chapter 1 on intentionality). We have to choose what to do in order to maximise the likelihood that it will benefit people receiving services. Our actions have to be purposeful.

Hugh England distinguishes social work from informal work with people by asserting that 'to do social work is to do purposefully and deliberately that which is primarily intuitive' (England, 1986: 39). In doing this, the worker's use of self

> extends far beyond the worker's emotional involvement and in fact determines the character of his professional knowledge and behaviour. Competence in social work therefore will be found not by seeking to avoid intuition, but by its recognition and development, by the creation of uncommon common sense. Social work is a matter of intuitive understanding, but it must be intuition which is unusually sound, unusually fluent and accessible, and subject to unusually careful evaluation.
>
> (England, 1986: 39)

Rojek et al. assert that social work needs to grapple with the dynamic and contradictory nature of social life and the often unforeseen and unplanned problems that arise. People's thoughts, feelings and actions are ever changing. So:

> the attitude which social workers adopt to established theoretical outlooks and methods of intervention must be not merely critical, but also self-critical. This is what dialectical thought means.
>
> (Rojek et al., 1988: 5)

Critical practice is not simply a collection of fragments of various radical and critical kinds, in a postmodern bricolage of flotsam and jetsam. Critical practice is not just an adjective bolted onto practice to give it the appearance of professionalism and respectability but purposeful, creative, assertive, committed to change, the promotion of people's rights and the elimination of injustice. The diversity of critical approaches has the potential to occupy the mainstream of practice, possessing conceptual robustness, theoretical cogency and practical coherence.

Promoting change

The notion of change is crucial to critical practice. It is vital that the critical practitioner seeks opportunities for change to occur. At the most basic level, people worked with are unlikely to experience benefit unless either the circumstances of a problem, or their responses to the problem change in some significant way. Of course, at its grandest, change may take place at the macro level. Kevin Haines (Chapter 14) uses international statements of principles of human rights as a lever to create pressure for change in policy and practice. Chris Clark (Chapter 4) argues that the critical practitioner must reject a social-democratic approach to welfare because it embodies a restricted notion of rights which underrepresents or excludes some people. He proposes the ideal of the communitarian welfare state, because it includes minority interests not previously empowered to influence policy and practice. Ideally, he suggests that the welfare state would be so inclusive as to make the word 'client' redundant since everybody would be a community member. The fact is, of course, that Chris Clark's solution does not have to be everybody's. We do not have to embrace the communitarian ideal to appreciate the value of celebrating diversity, which critical practice facilitates.

Engaging with paradoxes and dilemmas in developing our own critical practice

Critical practice is no exception to the rule that social work commentary may attempt to impose unifying perspectives and analyses on a diversity of activities that defy homogenisation. There can be no simple checklist of items that constitute critical practice. The diversity of chapters and approaches in this second part of the book shows how many different approaches can be taken to social work in different settings, justified under the banner of criticality. On the other hand, critical practice is more than diversity. It gains coherence and credibility through certain shared features of what is actually done. These can be grouped in different ways. The usefulness of these groupings is that they provide a starting point for reflection and debate. Ray and Phillips (Chapter 20) set out the main features of Brechin's view of critical action (Brechin, 2000), based on empowering and anti-oppressive principles. The development of critical practice makes it necessary to challenge certain aspects of current social and policy contexts. Dalrymple and Burke (Chapter 6) point out that critical practice is concerned with understanding the interaction between the concepts of power, oppression and inequality and personal and structural relations. Kevin Haines (Chapter 14) argues that the development of critical practice will be piecemeal and ad hoc unless at times it is located outside the current boundaries of government policy. Kate Morris (Chapter 13) argues that policies should be inclusive in order to combat the increasing fragmentation and specialisation of services which exclude many families from defining their needs and planning their services. Alastair Roy and colleagues (Chapter 12) suggest that critical practitioners need to go beyond promoting anti-discriminatory approaches, by valuing diversity as an alternative to monolithic conceptualisations of childhood.

Uncertainties and dilemmas: acknowledging or surmounting?

One of the salutary realities encountered by practitioners is that some situations are so complex and convoluted that simple solutions to people's problems are out of the question. Just as practitioners have to live with uncertainties, so dilemmas are often inescapable in practice. Critical practice is likely to involve the appreciation of dilemmas more often than being able to suggest ways of surmounting them. But because social workers often have to act, these have to be tackled. *Appreciation* is not enough. Critical practitioners have to develop strategies for *actually coping* with uncertainties and tensions.

Dalrymple and Burke (Chapter 6) point out that a child-centred practitioner working with the family faces dilemmas about whose identified needs to address. Roy et al. (Chapter 12) offer the dilemma posed by children's participation in decision-making where participants' current priorities may conflict with the longer term view. It may only be possible to work with the child in the context of a trusting relationship, where it is recognised that the child both needs protection and to be regarded as a thinking person with her own ideas. Bob Sapey (Chapter 18) shows the inadequacy of analysis which simply points to the dilemma that social work with disabled people is part of the problem by perpetuating their dependence. He shows that the practitioner needs to address the dilemma and may find it possible to approach problems from a different, more creative perspective. This echoes Sarah Banks' (1995) assertion, in her book on ethics and values in social work, that most of the time social workers have to resolve dilemmas, in that they have to take some action. A dilemma, by definition, involves a choice between two equally unfavourable options, but, whereas academics can comment from a distance, practitioners, by definition, are involved. Bob Sapey in this present book (Chapter 8) reminds us that critical reflection by the social work student working with Michael, a 19-year-old with spina bifida, leads to her not accepting Michael's mother's request that he be readmitted to the day centre he had been attending, because Michael did not want to do this. The dilemma for the student was whether to relieve the mother's concerns about how she would cope with Michael if he was left at home during the day, or to accept that Michael had the right to refuse to be sent to the day centre.

The student's decision to approach the dilemma from a different perspective, involved enabling Michael to meet a nearby coalition of disabled people. This, in effect, reframed the situation more critically, enabling Michael to develop his awareness of the political context and the potential for change beyond what a non-disabled social worker could offer. This shows how practitioners need to be able to distance themselves from the immediate situation and use techniques such as reframing to work out alternative actions.

Accepting there is no 'best' solution

The above example shows that the critical practitioner often works with the awareness that there is no single best answer to the situation, problem or case in question. Critical practice may not always be able to suggest a particular course of action, but may be strong on clarifying issues and – as in the situation of Michael – may be able to come up with a 'reframe' of the situation that empowers the client.

The decision about what to do is taken in the light of informed consideration of a range of possibilities. Critical practice in mental health practice, in Di Bailey's view (Chapter 17), should be located with practice rather than with received wisdom from the social sciences, focusing on 'working with' rather than 'doing to' people with mental health problems. O'Sullivan threads an example through Chapter 27 which offers a rational and purposeful agenda for decision-taking in practice settings often dominated by concerns such as risk management. In O'Sullivan's (1999: 16) book on decision-making, he distinguishes sound decision-making by the social worker, the preferred option in the light of available knowledge at the time, from effective decision-making, against which it may be unfair to judge social work, because of other factors operating which are beyond the limits of the practitioner's knowledge and powers. The task for the critical practitioner is to push the boundaries of sound practice as far towards effective practice as possible, thereby minimising this apparent gap, even when it is apparent that this or that piece of practice cannot be completed. Aspects of it will remain unfinished.

One way to deal with this is to consider how we face an apparently insoluble problem. Critical practice crosses and recrosses boundaries between what is public and private in people's lives and situations. We can try to move back and forth between outsider and insider positions, recognising, of course, the paradoxical reality that practitioners are inescapably insiders even when they try to reflect from outside. The relationship between insider and outsider positions is complex. Being an outsider may increase opportunities for independent appraisal and contextualising a situation. Being an insider may maximise the chance to empathise. Critical practitioners use empathy as a means of engaging their thoughts as well as their feelings. But knowledge of a person's circumstances is partial. The situation may be complex, different people's interests may conflict, uncertainties may beset the situation, not all the relevant facts and factors operating may be known, values and moral positions may be different and not all static. But at the very least, critical practice can help to clarify issues.

The critical practitioner acknowledges the inherently problematic situation and takes its essence into account rather than pretending that it can be simplified and the problem ignored. Thus, critical practice is likely to embody the conflict that the dilemma holds, rather than ducking it or working round it. This is extremely testing for the practitioner, who has to establish a direction for the practice, rather than yielding to the temptation to impose a simplistic, often inappropriate, 'solution'.

The connection between critical analysis and critical practice is intimate. The critical practitioner is committed to a transforming practice. There is no premature closure of issues, questions, debates, dilemmas and possibilities for action. Critical practice may not always be able to point to a single most desirable course of action. But it should enable us to move into new areas of analysis and practice as part of the dialectic between thought, reflection and action.

Engaging in lifelong critical practice development

Critical practice is not achieved overnight, or at the point that the student social worker qualifies. Critical practitioners engage in a lifelong process of becoming critical. Competence in particular areas of social work cannot be gained by producing evidence at a point in time of specific activities that are assessed as satisfactory. Social work, like other professions involving work with people, involves performance. Performances depend on professional expertise accumulated on an open-ended basis over a period of time, rather than vocational competence monitored as achieved in one set of specified circumstances. There should be no upper limit set on the level of expertise which it is possible to achieve. Expertise is linked with excellence, rather than with the pursuit of minimum standards of achievement (Adams, 1998a: 80).

Critical practitioners demonstrate expertise afresh every time they work in a new encounter with a new or existing client or situation. Critical practice is creative and part of that creativity involves the hope of achieving excellence and, realistically, the risk of disappointment or, in extreme circumstances, outright failure. Critical practice is optimistic and takes risks as part of a positive strategy of addressing issues and problems rather than avoiding them.

Developing creative approaches to uncertainties rather than simply following prescriptions

Rojek et al. (1988) observe that critical practitioners need to be able to deal creatively with uncertainty rather than simply following prescriptions. They comment that:

> so much exists in institutionalised social work to deter attitudes of thought which are consistently dialectical ... Before an individual can become a qualified and employable social worker it is necessary to pass through certain rules of accreditation. In order to 'belong' to the occupation, one must learn recognised occupational skills, knowledge, and the official language. The communication of authority and competence depends upon the efficient use of skills, knowledge, and language. However, the relationship between the social workers' perception of outward competence and their internal attitude towards it is very complex. Often, social workers may know what to do or say in order to give the external appearance of competence, but inwardly harbour feelings of self-doubt and confusion. Society requires social workers to do the right thing, even in circumstances where they do not know what the right thing is, and where several courses of action are seen as equally right. It follows that social workers labour under strong institutional pressures to camouflage and repress uncertainty and, instead, to appear decisive ... in these situations the normative framework produces rigid and inflexible actions and responses in the social worker which deny doubt and contradiction. In this way, social work can very easily fall from being an activity

which seeks to help clients and alleviate distress, into being an activity which responds to questions of client need, care and the nature of the social work task with mechanical stereotypes.

(Rojek et al. 1988: 5)

CONCLUSION

The ultimate paradox, of course, is that practice may reach a kind of conclusion, but more often than not this turns out not to be an ending so much as a transition to another situation. Critical social work does not follow a predicted course and sign off neatly, delivered at a price, and now a completed contract, on a particular date. Dalrymple and Burke (Chapter 6) end their chapter with a section under the title of 'Continuing reflections'. As Helen Cosis Brown (Chapter 11) acknowledges, critical social work does not occupy a predictable, stable world where resources are adequate. Critical social workers cannot anticipate with certainty. Much practice may be 'well-informed leaps in the dark'.

There may be pressure on social workers to deny problematic issues and artificially simplify the complexity of situations to make them manageable. In a fierce debate I witnessed about a practice study, the tutor wanted to fail the student for showing hesitance in specifying one social work approach. Eventually, I agreed with the practice teacher, who was able to demonstrate that the student's hesitance was soundly based in a critically reflective style, rather than a sign of incompetence.

The several tensions and dilemmas identified by Margaret Lloyd (Chapter 16), for the practitioner and care manager responding to the pressures created by a confusion of policy approaches, have to be addressed in the absence of one single, simple solution. However, there are ways forward. Alastair Roy et al. (Chapter 12) argue for the development of defensible rather than defensive practice, informed by, and progressing, research, theory and experience. As Caroline Currer (Chapter 21) states, the critical practitioner will need to tackle two tasks: first, to interpret general understandings and ideas and apply them in a particular setting; second, to challenge structures, policies and practices which may pose a threat or undermine the practice. This implies that the critical practitioner will be thoughtful, confident, assertive and resilient – a daunting but exciting prospect.

FURTHER READING

Brechin, A. (2000) 'Introducing Critical Practice', in Brechin, A., Brown, H. and Eby, M. (eds) *Critical Practice in Health and Social Care*, London: Open University/Sage. A clearly and concisely expressed view of the main features of critical practice, which can be used as the starting point for discussion and debate.

Child Protection

John Pinkerton

Introducing the practice

CASE EXAMPLE

We met quite by chance that day in the college car park. I was on the way to my office and Peter was arriving for the first day of a new post-qualifying childcare course. Ten years ago, we had spent a lot of time in each other's company. We were both active trade unionists, involved politically and intent on making a positive difference through social work. Changes in both our lives, domestic, work, political, had taken us in different directions. On the odd occasions that we now met, we just exchanged a few words, but, on this occasion, we agreed to meet later that day and 'catch up'. When we did, we talked about a lot of things including why Peter was doing the course. Unusually he had stayed in frontline practice. Not unusually, he often felt overwhelmed and dragged down as he struggled with the crises and chronic difficulties that beset the families he worked with, particularly where child protection was an issue. Over the years, he had used courses as a way of re-energising himself. He was on this one to see if there was new thinking around that could help him to develop the critical perspective he reckoned he needed to take the refocusing debate beyond the pages of policy documents and academic journals and into his practice.

I was not surprised to hear Peter's reason for coming on the course. He had always resented and resisted what he saw as the distortion of social work with families by procedural child protection. I was more surprised that he had also held on to what

---

had been our shared view that a searching, critical perspective was the best way to inform the understanding, decisions and actions of practitioners. For us, critical theory had never been 'a God too far' (Cohen, 1975) – a retort that in some form or other has greeted every attempt to kindle critical engagement within social work, whether from a Marxist, feminist, black or postmodernist perspective. Critical theory, to borrow a phrase from Day (1987) in his promotion of sociology for social work, is about 'making the implicit explicit'. For me that unmasking of the taken-for-granted is a core responsibility of a social work academic. For Peter it was a part of being able to cope better with the daily grind of practice.

Child protection practice based on a critical perspective demands constant questioning: not only of personal actions, both workers' own and those of their colleagues, but also of structural constraints and opportunities, both organisational and societal. Most important, it requires questioning of the relationship between personal action and structural opportunity and constraint. This is criticism not in the sense of blame but as informed judgement, providing the basis for more effective action. While time away from direct practice may be useful for reflection and preparation, critical questioning can only really be addressed in the context of the day-to-day delivery of services. This is not an easy task, especially in an area as fraught and demanding as child protection. This chapter argues that it is possible and that it can be supported by consistently coming back to three questions: how is practice measuring up to the worker's vision and values; what working hypotheses are being tested in practice; and how is the balance of power being negotiated.

Values: measuring up to a vision

In getting beneath the surface of child protection practice a critical perspective must make explicit the vision and values that constitute both the ideological context and the personal ideology of practitioners. The challenge is for practitioners 'to locate themselves, as fully conscious participants, within arenas where understanding and action will be contested' and that requires them 'to develop a conscious ideological position of their own' (Spratt and Houston, 1999: 315). Peter and I used to debate the difference between values and ideology and why the former got a good press while the latter was generally viewed with suspicion. In a dated but still useful discussion of ideology and power, Therborn (1983: 15), a Marxist sociologist, noted:

The operation of ideology in human life basically involves the constitution and patterning of how human beings live their lives as conscious, reflecting initiators of acts in a structured, meaningful world.

He makes it clear that ideology is neither a rigidly imposed world view nor 'false consciousness', meanings often associated with the term. Indeed, it is more than just sets of ideas.

Within social work, ideologies are expressed in the way in which a social worker dresses, the furnishing of an interviewing room, holding a case discussion in a family's home rather than a social services office, as much as in the ideas that hold sway at a case conference. The dominant ideologies within the societal context and the organisational structures in which social work practice takes place are neither intrinsically right nor wrong, accurate or inaccurate. The ideas and practices of existing ideologies, and how they are expressed, endorsed or challenged in the personal ideology of individual workers, provide the meanings required to live our lives as social actors. These meanings express contested views not only of how the world is, but also how it should be and how it could be.

Although no longer politically active, Peter still held to a socialist view of the world. Even in the way he dressed you could see he was holding out against 'the suits' of the new managerialism. He was angry about how the years of New Right conservatism had undermined confidence and pride in the welfare state and in particular what it had done for generations of children. But he was optimistic that this could be rebuilt and bettered. He was disappointed that New Labour seemed unprepared to use the state to intervene directly in the jungle economics of the free market but impressed by their ambitious plans for tackling social exclusion and child poverty. He also drew confidence from the way that the United Nations Convention on the Rights of the Child (UNCRC) (Hill and Tisdall, 1997) had established itself as the touchstone for policy and practice in all aspects of child welfare, including child protection.

For Peter the UNCRC provided a global vision for children that was immediately relevant for him in its bold assertion of the three key principles:

- children's rights to be available without discrimination of any type (article 2)

- children's best interests to be a primary consideration in all actions concerning them (article 3)

- children's views to be sought and taken into account in all matters affecting them (article 12).

In addition, article 19 of the Convention sets out in two paragraphs the obligation of states to protect children from all forms of maltreatment perpetrated by parents or others responsible for their care, and to undertake preventive and treatment programmes in this regard. Article 34 states in a single paragraph the child's right to protection from sexual exploitation and abuse, including prostitution and involvement in pornography. These were aims that Peter believed he was directly involved in pursuing through his child protection practice. The UNCRC gave expression and status to his beliefs and developed them further in relation to promoting children's active involvement in determining their own lives.

Article 5 of the Convention also sets out the duty of states to respect the rights and responsibilities of parents and the wider family to provide appropriate direction and guidance to children in the exercise of their rights. It asserts in a Preamble that:

> the family as the fundamental group of society and the natural environment for the growth and well-being of all its members, and particularly children, should be

afforded the necessary protection and assistance so that it can fully assume its responsibilities within the community.

(Hill and Tisdall, 1997)

For Peter this balancing within the UNCRC of authority, responsibility and rights between state, children and families, which can also be found in the Children Act 1989 for England and Wales (Ryan, 1994) and related legislation within Scotland and Northern Ireland (Tisdall et al., 1998), reinforced his view of the state's enabling and resourcing responsibilities. It also reinforced his personal values. A critical perspective requires self-criticism, including core values being held up to scrutiny. A simple way to identify these is for an individual, or group of social workers, to complete the sentence: 'Working in child protection expresses my/our belief that ...'. For Peter this would prompt statements such as:

- children have the right to a childhood free from all forms of abuse and exploitation
- the best interests of the child must always be the primary consideration of the adults on whom they depend
- every child is a unique human being and their individual wishes and feelings must be respected.

But it would also prompt other value statements attaching rights not only to children but also to parents, the state and child protection workers themselves:

- parents have rights through responsibilities in regard to their children
- children wherever possible should be brought up within their own families
- parents are individuals who deserve respect for their rights and the range of needs and strengths they have
- the state should be the ultimate guarantor of every child's right to safety and protection
- staff are individuals with needs and rights as well as being workers with authority and responsibilities.

Peter's experience had taught him that values are not neat, safe, feel-good phrases but challenging guides to action within particular circumstances. He had also found that values which may be regarded as of equal importance when considered in the abstract, compete against one another when applied in practice (Pinkerton and McLoughlin, 1996). Peter was constantly having to make judgements about the relevance and relative weighting to give to his different values according to the circumstances. This was not a weakness but one of 'the everyday creative accomplishments of professionals on the ground' (Spratt and Houston, 1999) as they engage in the social construction of the world.

Promoting the vision and holding to values consistent with the UNCRC are not just the responsibility of individuals like Peter. In signing the Convention, governments go beyond just declaring what 'should be' for children, they are also making a statement about what 'could be', and their regular reporting to the UN Committee on the Rights of the Child is the means to monitor their progress in making it so. Among the many ways that governments have to progress their commitment to the Convention is the work of child protection staff. Thus, enabling workers to engage with every case as an expression of the Convention's vision for children at risk is an obligation of government. This requires that agencies and staff, and families and neighbourhoods, are provided with the necessary resources to identify and assess children at risk and provide appropriate prevention and treatment programmes. Staff should not hold themselves responsible for failure to meet needs where resources are not made available by those with the power and authority to do so. In this way a critical perspective helps to draw attention to where power lies in order to effect change. This is not to say that resource allocation is not the business of practitioners but rather to clarify their responsibility within the limits of their power. They can only exert pressure through collective action in trade unions, pressure groups, professional organisations and political parties.

Knowledge: testing working hypotheses

Peter's dogged optimism was based on his calculations and hopes for change. In delving beneath the surface of phenomena, critical theory assumes nothing to be constant. For social workers within child protection, as in any other area of practice, change, and how it is managed through defining and redefining needs and services, dictates the circumstances in which they pursue their vision through practice. Change is absolutely central to any understanding of the present nature and future role of social work (Payne, 1997; Campbell and Pinkerton, 1997). It both structures the context and is the focus for social work in child protection as in any other area of practice. With change goes uncertainty. Corby (2000), in updating his comprehensive review of child protection, draws attention to a very different mood at the start of the twenty-first century from that prevailing in earlier decades:

> The certainty of purpose about the state's response to incidents of child abuse within the family which has previously informed many of the policy developments in this field (if not as obviously the practice of front line professionals) is beginning to evaporate.
>
> (Corby, 2000: 2)

The history of child protection shows a number of stages on the way to this loss of confidence (Corby, 2000; Parton, 1985, 1991). First, the recognition during the 1970s of child abuse as a major issue for social services, represented by the tragic milestone of the Maria Colwell inquiry report. During the 1980s came the promotion of assertive child protection as the dominant service response. This was first stoked by the findings of the various child death inquiries, such as Beckford, Henry and Carlisle, but then severely questioned by the reports into overintrusive intervention, such as Cleveland and Orkney. The general sense of growing concern about an overproceduralised child protection system was brought to a head with the publication of *Child Protection: Messages from*

Research (Department of Health, 1995a). From that review of the findings of 20 government-commissioned research projects, it was clear that however efficient the closed, professional child protection system might be, it was not effective. It was overidentifying child protection cases and failing to respond appropriately to the varying types of need identified. The system was failing even on its own terms. Workers, like Peter, who were uncomfortable with the dominance of a narrow child protectionism stand vindicated as child protection is refocused to align itself with the promotion of family support. They now find themselves better placed to retrieve something of their preferred style of practice as 'resourceful friends' (Holman, 1983). But this cannot mean a full return to the loose, enabling, problem-solving of the past. Change is not a circular movement.

Thanks to those years of preoccupation with child abuse and child protection, there is now a substantial and still growing literature which will block any return to the days before the 'discovery' of child abuse and the growth of the child protection industry. Professional practice and academic study within social work, medicine, history, sociology, philosophy, social policy and psychology have all contributed to a much fuller understanding of abused children and their families and how best to respond to them. Work carried out within the English-speaking world of North America, the UK, Ireland, Australia and New Zealand is increasingly informed by European and international material (Harder and Pringle, 1997). It becomes ever-more difficult for anyone, especially busy practitioners like Peter, to keep fully abreast of all this material. Developments in new technology can help and there is a growth in publications, particularly from government, which aim to draw together systematically practice experience and research findings. However, what is more important to recognise is that while Peter is keen to draw on this burgeoning knowledge base, he does not see this as ferreting out the one right answer for solving the problem of any one particular case he is involved with. Part of Peter's resistance to procedure-driven child protection was his conviction that people's lives are too complex to fit neat responses – especially in an area as socially and emotionally fraught as child protection. His practice is informed not by an illusory scientific certainty but by working hypotheses. These are based on knowledge that is only partly made up of the main messages on needs and services coming from the literature and research, and are at all times open to challenge and modification.

Certainly, the critical practitioner needs an understanding of how child abuse and child protection express the dynamic interactions within social systems and how these play out for individuals within the context of established patterns of human growth and development. To understand abuse, Corby has helpfully suggested:

> three main groups of perspective: psychological theories: those that focus on the instinctive and psychological qualities of individuals who abuse; social psychological theories: those that focus on the dynamics of the interaction between abuser, child and immediate environment; sociological perspectives: those that emphasise social and political conditions as the most important reason for the existence of child abuse.
>
> (Corby, 2000: 31)

Each of the three has its own strengths and weaknesses, as Corby usefully rehearses. The danger in all of them for the critical practitioner is that of reductionism. Sociobiologists' preoccupation with genes should no more be dismissed out of hand than feminist concerns with patriarchy, but neither should be seen as providing the total picture.

One thing made clear by the literature is the complexity of the dynamics of child abuse and the response to it. Attachment theory may provide a convincing and detailed explanation of the process whereby abuse and neglect can be derived from, and transmitted through, poor adult–child relationships. Both psychodynamic theories and behavioural approaches engage with and explain intra- and interpersonal dynamics and suggest intervention aims and strategies. Marxism, feminism and postmodernist explanations bring the structures and relations of power into clear view. But none of these theoretical perspectives is sufficient alone. Nor is it possible or even desirable to integrate them into a unified theory. They provide the basis for uneasy amalgams that usefully inform working hypotheses about what is at issue for the individuals caught up in child abuse.

Precisely because of the complexity and lack of a single, uncontested theoretical base, these hypotheses must be explored and open to challenge in order to be discounted or confirmed as useful in any particular situation. This requires another type of knowledge – knowledge of the particular history, characteristics and aspirations of the individuals involved. In order to gather that knowledge, it is important to avoid 'typification' (Marsh and Fisher, 1992: 38). This is where, often encouraged by agency procedures, the relationships between social workers and service users are defined by routine responses which place the users into preexisting, fixed, typical categories. Refusal to reduce people, workers and service users alike, in that way to either the victims or villains of child abuse or the heroes of child protection was always the hallmark of Peter's practice.

Skills: negotiating within a context of inequality

At the core of the skills of social work lies building, maintaining and realising the potential for change within relationships. The centrality of the relationship, 'that dreaded idol of traditional social work' (Leonard, 1975: 53), holds true for the critical practitioner. Power is what fuels relationships and what is distinctive about the practice of a worker like Peter is that the power differentials being expressed within relationships are openly acknowledged. Drawing as much on his political and trade union experience as on his casework, Peter always prided himself on being both aware and 'up front' about inequality in power. When he saw it, he acknowledged it and worked with it, whether it was adult to child, male to female, white to black, between worker and service user, among service users, or within and between social workers and their managers.

In child protection work, the relationship between worker, parent and child is generally tightly circumscribed by legal and procedural requirements. The power and status imbalance is firmly with the worker who is advantaged as a representative of the state. It is also likely to be reinforced by the parents being disadvantaged by factors such as class, gender, race and age, the issues raised in Part I. It is not surprising that such imbalance can prompt resistance through the extremes of either withdrawal or violence. At the same time, it needs to be recognised that social workers not only exercise power over service users, but are also subject to the very power they are exercising. Peter talked of being carried along by the logic of child protection procedures that he believed should never have been instigated; of supervising access visits in cases where he no more judged it to be appropriate than the parents did, but was bound by a management decision. Only when power was acknowledged could the imbalance be negotiated in a manner least likely to be oppressive. This Peter applied whether representing staff interests to management, ensuring that a parent was accompanied by an advocate at a case conference or seeking the exclusion of a violent partner.

Power is a complex and contested concept (Hugman, 1991). It is expressed within both process and structure: 'social workers' power is expressed not only in what they do but what they are' (Harris, 1997: 29). Power is interactional and ubiquitous. The various aspects of the imbalance of power within child protection are based on social inequalities of class, gender, age and race and the nature of state power. Social inequalities and oppressive state power are deep seated within the social and political structures of British society (Novak, 1997; Williams, 1991). The shifting configuration of state, civil society and ideology provides the structural supports and constraints of all social work intervention (Lorenz, 1994; Campbell and Pinkerton, 1997). Child protection is no exception. Structural contradictions find expression in the dilemmas of care and control that are found in all childcare, whether provided informally within the social institutions of civil society, such as family and neighborhood, or through the formal services provided by the state and the voluntary sector (Hill and Tisdall, 1997). These dilemmas are particularly sharply experienced in child protection work, where ensuring the safety of children can require the naked display of state power, but they are not peculiar to it.

The inequality of power relations within child protection has been explored through the considerable work done on partnership (Department of Health/Social Services Inspectorate, 1995; Thoburn et al., 1995). This work suggests that what is too often lacking is attention to the basic requirements for ensuring working relationships. Service users, like service providers, need written information, manageable practical arrangements, advice and emotional support. It is also the basic decencies of human relationships that have been stressed by service users. Advice from one group of parents with children deemed to be at risk included: use everyday language we can understand; be realistic about how well you really know us and only write reports on us when you do; don't put us 'under a microscope'; don't come across as threatening and sticking too rigidly to rules and regulations; deliver on what you say you'll do and don't expect of us more than you would of anyone else in our situation (Pinkerton et al., 1997). Children value social workers who listen, are available and accessible, non-judgemental and non-directive, have a sense of humour, are straight talking and can be trusted (Butler and Williamson, quoted in Bannister et al., 1997: 1).

Much of the problem of partnership working within child protection lies in the absence, confusion or difficulty in achieving agreement over what constitutes the shared goal of the worker and the family. It is crucial to be clear as to the mandate for working with families on particular goals:

These goals may be agreed with the user because they are what the user wishes to work on, or they may be agreed with the client as a result of some external authority placing them on the client's agenda via legal proceedings.

(Marsh and Fisher, 1992: 18)

That second mandate provides a difficult basis for partnership working but can be 'reframed' as part of a managed process of partnership (Tunnard, 1991; Pinkerton and Houston, 1996; Pinkerton, 2001).

Like many practitioners, Peter is sceptical about the term 'partnership', however reframed. Again, drawing as much on his political and trade union experience as on his casework, he prefers the term 'negotiated agreements'. Negotiation permits all those involved, whatever their status, to signal their needs and wishes so that there can be a search for a common goal, even if that is only an accommodation between differences. It provides the means to pool resources to work together in achieving the desired outcomes (Barber, 1991; Fletcher, 1998). Successful negotiation can require the professionals involved to relinquish power and status, something they can find difficult to do (Calder, 1995). This is not just out of a desire to be in control, the dominant reflex in any state functionary. It can also be hard for the professional to acknowledge that what they bring to any negotiation is only a contribution, and often a minor one, to the wider and deeper pool of resources that children in need and at risk require. As family group conferencing seems to be showing, many of these resources may be better accessed through informal networks (Marsh and Crow, 1998).

One other point stressed by Peter was that in negotiating and implementing agreements it is important to accept that the unexpected will occur – sometimes involving gains, sometimes losses. This can be anything from a sudden shift in the dynamics between a mother and her alcohol-abusing partner, to a child reconnecting with an important adult, to a job move by a key member of an interdisciplinary child protection team. Accepting the inevitability of unpredictability allows practitioners to respond earlier and more flexibly when the unexpected occurs, to take advantage of any gains and manage the impact of losses. Expecting the unexpected also reinforces the need to regard all outcomes as unfinished business – which is a way of saying that child protection is a creative process. The best-planned intervention will still need to be brought alive by the creative endeavours of individuals.

CONCLUSION

As Peter and I talked, I felt reassured that the critical perspective I had held on to over the years was not some throwback to the illusions of more optimistic times. Uncertainty and complexity may now be seen as the defining character of child protection, but that it was so was always the case put by critical theory, with its capacity to get beneath the surface of certainty. A critical perspective was never a means of tidying up reality, shoehorning it into a particular framework, but rather a way of opening it up to exploration, contest and change. Measuring up to vision and values, testing working hypotheses and negotiating the imbalances of power may not have the surface appeal of heroic child rescue or the cosy warmth of universal family support. But attending to those three imperatives of critical practice will support solid commitment to children for themselves, an informed sense of social and psychological perspective and attention to the fundamentals of human communication. Together it is those things that are most likely to nudge child protection to its rightful place as a crucial but minor aspect of the child welfare system. A critical perspective offers practitioners like Peter, and others like me who see it as our function to support them in their work, the means to dig down and dig in for the long haul.

FURTHER READING

Corby, B. (2000) *Child Abuse – Towards a Knowledge Base*, 2nd edn, London: Open University Press. A well-informed, clearly presented and thoughtfully considered review of the existing multidisciplinary knowledge base, covering the historical development, definition, extent, cause and consequences of child abuse.

Department of Health (1999) *Working Together to Safeguard Children: A Guide to Interagency Working*, London: HMSO. As the best way to get the most out of procedures and avoid being unnecessarily constrained by them is to be fully on top of them, this multidisciplinary and interagency guidance to policy, processes, structures and procedures is essential reading for anyone working in child protection.

Department of Health/Social Services Inspectorate (1995) *The Challenge of Partnership in Child Protection: Practice Guide,* London: HMSO. Through a clear statement of the principles of good practice in partnership, detailed discussion of how these can be applied at different stages in the child protection process and a useful set of team and individual exercises, this remains a very useful resource for skilling up for negotiating child protection.

Hill, M. and Tisdall, K. (1997) *Children and Society*, London: Longman. Child abuse and child protection, while given its own chapter, is convincingly presented as an integrated part of this book's ambitious but successful attempt at a holistic synthesis of empirical research, theory and policy relating to children in the UK, with particular attention to children's own perspectives (includes the text of the UNCRC as an appendix).

Hulme, K. (1985) *The Bone People*, London: Hodder & Stoughton. This Booker Prize-winning novel, which focuses on the strange and uneasy relationships linking a solitary artist, a lost boy she befriends and his abusive stepfather, is a powerful representation of the raw humanity, ambivalence and confusion of child abuse.

Parton, N. (1991) *Governing the Family: Child Care, Child Protection and the State*, London: Macmillan – now Palgrave Macmillan. Although this account of the historical development of child care is primarily about the 1980s and the introduction of the Children Act 1989, it remains the most coherent and instructive exposition of the political economy of child protection.

Fostering and Adoption

Helen Cosis Brown

This chapter aims to explore what critical practice in fostering and adoption involves, first by looking at fostering and adoption in their current context and second by considering the critical application of research to practice. Third, I explore the dilemmas and tensions in critical practice via a practice area pertinent to both fostering and adoption: 'safe care'. Social workers in the fields of fostering and adoption hold both children's and families' lives in the balance. Critical practice is essential to enable each family to facilitate the best possible start in life for an individual child.

Fostering and adoption practice in their current context

Fostering and adoption are two separate areas of practice governed by separate legislation and policy. However, they also have many similar features. They are both primarily concerned with enabling a child, in need of a family, to be placed in a new family, either temporarily or permanently. It is not within the remit of this chapter to outline the legislation and policy governing fostering and adoption but rather to concentrate on practice. That is not to suggest that knowledge of legislation and policy are not crucial for critical practice but rather that there is insufficient space within this chapter to cover these areas.

The placement of children with substitute families involves the recruitment of carers, assessment, matching children to carers and training and support of carers and children. There is a symbiotic relationship between fostering and adoption practice and social work practice with children and families, as fostering and adoption are dependent on the quality of work undertaken with birth families and networks as well as children. For a child to be adequately matched with a substitute family, there needs to have been a thorough and accurate assessment of the child's needs, personality, history, attachments, likes and dislikes and health and educational attainment. If the assessment was lacking, there is a much higher likelihood that the child will be misplaced and the placement likely to break down. The quality of the work done in trying to retain the child within their own family is also of great consequence to the fostering and adoption process, as well as to the child's future ability to make sense of the disruption to his or her life.

The processes of long-term fostering and adoption have become much closer as changes in adoption patterns have materialised. In England and Wales, the number of adoptions of infants under one-year-old has dropped dramatically from 1968, when 75 per cent of all adoptions were of infants, to 1991 when that percentage had dropped to 12 per cent (Triseliotis et al., 1997: 15). Currently, the majority of adoptions are in relation to children in public care, whereas in the past this was not the case. This has meant that social workers are having to make complex assessments as to whether or not the needs of a child in public care would be best met through being adopted or through long-term foster care. This assessment is not simple, involving the consideration of the prognosis of finding a suitable adoptive family who would be able to take on board contact arrangements for the child as well as his or her troubled and complex history. The critical practitioner would hold in mind that there are currently benefits and costs to both options. For example, adopted children and families often find that post-adoption resources and support are not always forthcoming, leading to serious difficulties for families caring for children with troubled pasts and multiple needs.

Recruitment

Adopters and foster carers are 'ordinary' members of the community. They come in all forms with different histories, cultures, strengths and weaknesses. Over the last 20 years, most fostering and adoption agencies, but not all, have become more inclusive in who they recruit. The stereotypical, white foster mother with husband out at work and birth children washed and scrubbed is still being recruited as an invaluable resource, but she has been joined by many other carers of different races and cultures as well as single carers, gay carers and some carers with disabilities. However, despite these changes, the traditional picture of the foster carer still prevails and they are numerically still the majority (Triseliotis et al., 2000). Given the changing nature of children placed either in foster placements or for adoption (they are older than they were and have more complex needs), there may be a tension between what the 'traditional' carer had to offer and what the current child needs. We need to revisit who we are recruiting as carers to make sure that they have a secure sense of self and are resilient, so that they can withstand the personal and public exposure of self that inevitably arises from caring for children.

Assessment of carers

Once recruited all carers have to be assessed. The National Foster Care Association UK Joint Working Party on Foster Care's National Standard (1999b) and Code of Practice (1999a) provide more clarity in respect of every aspect of fostering and specifically in relation to assessment. Prospective carers have to undergo a lengthy and rigorous assessment process and a number of checks to ascertain if they will have the potential to care for other people's children in their own homes.

The nature of adoption and fostering is now so diverse that it is often the case that the same carer may be suitable for one fostering project but not for another. For example, someone may be able to offer a considerable amount to a severely sexually abused seven-year-old child but not meet the criteria for a remand-fostering scheme. Some adoption applicants would make excellent parents for an infant but not for a troubled three-year-old child.

Practitioners have two current 'models' of assessment of carers to consider when undertaking assessments: the British Agencies for Adoption and Fostering's Form F (1991) and the National Foster Care Association's competence model (2000). We have yet to see whether the competence model will lead to a mechanistic approach to a highly individual and complex process or to a better critical and well-evidenced outcome.

Matching children and families

We have the benefit of the new *Framework for the Assessment of Children in Need and Their Families* (Department of Health/Department for Education and Employment/Home Office, 2000) as well as the *Looking After Children: Assessment and Action Schedules* (Department of Health, 1995c). This should mean that there is now a framework for assessing and recording children's needs, attainments, wishes, 'social presentation, family and social relationships, identity, emotional and behavioural development, education and health' (Department of Health/Department for Education and Employment/Home Office, 2000: 17). The *Looking After Children: Assessment and Action Schedules* for a child being placed from within public care should also record the child's 'care' history.

If the carer's assessment has also examined in detail what the family or individual has to offer as well as their limitations, then theoretically it should be possible to 'match' a child with a placement with the optimum chance of success. In a number of voluntary and independent projects, 'good enough' matching is possible, because the agency would have a number of carers ready to take children. Unfortunately, in many social services departments, it is recognised that there is a shortage of carers so that the sensitivity of matching is likely to be significantly blunted and reduced to 'who has space'.

Matching should involve consideration of the child's needs, wishes, abilities, age, race and ethnicity, care plan, and their need for contact with their own family. Thoburn notes the range of placement types, emphasising the enormous range of placements that are needed, from 'short-term "shared or relief" fostering right through a whole range to adoption' (Thoburn, 1994: 63), in order to satisfy the varieties of care plans. For critical practitioners to make good enough matching decisions and a placement for a child, there needs to be a range of carers available to meet the diverse needs of children needing placements.

Training and support of carers

Many agencies incorporate training into the assessment process. This gives the assessors the chance to see the applicants functioning in a group as well as seeing how they manage new information. Occasionally, through training, it becomes apparent that the applicants will not make appropriate carers or they decide themselves that they do not want to proceed. Training also is considered now by most agencies to be an essential aspect of support for carers. As new dilemmas arise, they can make sense of new information and try to apply it to their own circumstances. Training involves being in a group with other carers where similar and shared difficulties can be explored. Many agencies run carers' support groups. However, group support cannot be a substitute for individual support from a placement support social worker. Not all carers can take advantage of group settings and the confidential nature of much of what a carer may wish to discuss also means that group discussions sometimes have to be 'general'.

Most agencies now accept that training is their ongoing responsibility for carers who increasingly are caring for children with complex needs. This remains a tension between fostering and adoption, as the majority of adopters will not receive post-adoption training even though their needs may be as great as foster carers and the children they are caring for are often very similar to those in long-term foster care.

Support to carers is more than just training. Support is one of the laments of carers often feeling that they do not get enough. Fostering schemes and adoption agencies vary in what support they offer. One theme emerges; that actual or perceived lack of support or appropriate support is a major contributory factor to why carers cease to have children placed with them (Triseliotis et al., 2000). Sellick and Thoburn, discussing short-term placements, write: 'Firstly, supporting foster carers maximises their retention; second, it minimises agency costs; and thirdly, it prevents the breakdown of placements' (1996: 50). For the critical practitioner who is aware of this, there is a tension as a result of the current recruitment and retention crisis in social work. 'Support' is one of the first things to get less attention when an agency is under pressure, ultimately leading to disruption for some children's placements. Instability for children in public care is of national concern and the incorporation of a reduction in the number of moves for children has rightly been included in the Quality Protects agenda (Department of Health, 1998b). Given that children have entered the public care system because it was deemed to be in their interests, Jackson and Thomas's finding, that 'Research consistently points to a high level of instability and change for the majority of children in the care system when compared to children who remain with their own families' (1999: 41), has to be of grave concern.

Children also need to be supported in placement. They are often in need of ongoing effective social work to enable them to make use of the placement, to sustain meaningful relationships where appropriate, with their own families as well as, again where appropriate, form attachments to their new family. They may need many years of support to 'recover' from previous trauma. The children will need a consistent and effective social work input to make sure that their needs are being met and their voice heard. Support for a child and a carer is often delivered by separate social workers. Often they need to be liaising with education and health professionals in order to maximise the chances of the placement achieving stability and success. This means that both the child's and the carer's social workers need to be working interprofessionally.

The quality of the recruitment, assessment, matching, training and support contributes to the successful outcome of placements and bettering of outcomes for children in public care and those who need to be adopted. Critical practice is integral to bettering outcomes at each stage of the placement process but it is also reliant on sufficient resources.

Critical application of research to practice

Later than some professional groups, social work has entered the world of 'evidence-based' practice (see Chapter 5). This is an arena where critical practice has to be alert and vigilant. The mechanistic application of theory or research findings to an individual placement scenario could be as damaging as theoretical and research ignorance. As Jackson and Thomas write, 'the truth is that research is about generalisations but practice is about individuals' (Jackson and Thomas, 1999: 5). Practitioners need to be aware of theoretical perspectives and relevant research findings, hold these in mind and apply them thoughtfully to the individual circumstance and individuals with whom they are working. This necessitates the practitioner being research literate, able to form effective relationships to enable a full assessment to be made and then use his or her own critical thinking to assess whether or not some specific theory or research applies to a particular case. As Sellick and Thoburn write:

> When it comes to using research to throw light on specific decisions to be made about specific children, there is no alternative to a careful scrutiny of the studies which seem most relevant. An appraisal must then be made as to the validity of their conclusions in the context of the specific case.
>
> (Sellick and Thoburn, 1996: 26)

The practitioner needs sufficient confidence to remain flexible in relation to the application of 'evidence' to practice and focused on the individual child's interests.

Research literacy

Current practitioners are in the fortunate position of having a number of research reviews available to them that are accessible and user friendly (Berridge, 1997; Department of Health, 1991; Department of Health, 1999b; Jackson and Thomas, 1999; Sellick and Thoburn, 1996). There are also texts that incorporate research findings as an integral part, (Howe, 1998b) and relevant research reports (Quinton et al., 1998; Triseliotis et al., 2000). However, for the practitioner to make sense of this material they need to be research literate. By this, I mean they need to have the capacity to understand research findings as well as research outcomes, thus being able to make sense of the researcher's interpretation of the data. They need to understand a sufficient amount in relation to research methods to understand whether or not a specific research design was sufficiently rigorous to deliver findings that were valid.

CASE EXAMPLE

Tania had been a 'child in need' from age two when her maternal grandmother, with whom she and her mother lived, had died. Tania's mother, Jane, was a crack cocaine user and Tania's grandmother had undertaken the total care of her. Tania and Jane had then moved into Jane's boyfriend's flat, where she lived for five years. She had been cared for minimally by Jane but had received affection and intermittent physical care from the boyfriend's sister, Sarah, who was a neighbour. The family lived on income support and, by any criteria, Tania suffered from neglect. She attended her primary school intermittently and her health visitor had had to work hard for her first immunisations to happen.

The primary school head had referred Tania several times to social services but they had not visited, as concerns were vague and unsubstantiated. Jane's crack habit increased, as did Tania's neglect, neither receiving any help. Sarah visited on Tania's eighth birthday to find Jane unconscious and Tania sitting in a urine-soaked bed feeding herself baked beans out of a tin. Sarah managed to get Jane admitted to hospital and Tania was accommodated that evening and placed with 'short-term' foster parents.

After a month's assessment by social services, it became apparent that Jane vehemently did not want Tania to return home and Sarah, although wanting to remain involved, could not care for Tania. Neither Jane's boyfriend nor Tania's father could be traced.

The social worker for Tania, being mindful of the need to assess Tania's degree of attachment to significant people in her family of origin (Fahlberg, 1991) through a process of careful observation, noted that there was a significant attachment between Tania and Sarah. Sarah was involved in the care planning for Tania, but Jane was not, despite valiant attempts by Sarah and the social worker to involve her.

After three months (and a number of court hearings resulting in a care order) it was decided that a permanent substitute family should be found for Tania and that contact should be maintained with Sarah. The placement team only had three families available. The placement social worker needed to keep in mind the following research findings:

- The success of a placement lessens as the child's age increases at point of placement (Quinton et al., 1998)
- Outcomes for children are improved if contact is maintained for the child with significant people (Thoburn, 1994)

■ If the placement family has a child very near the age of the child to be placed, then the prognosis for success is poorer (Jackson and Thomas, 1999).

According to the above, Tania, now eight years old, was more likely to experience disruption than if she had been one year old. However, she may have had a number of 'protective factors' in her favour, for example she was attached to her grandmother and Sarah, which might mean there was a better prognosis for her attaching to a new family. It would be important to find a family that would encourage her contact with Sarah and help to maintain that attachment. It would also be better if she could be placed in a family with no children near her own age.

However, two of the families available to take children were reluctant to maintain regular contact permanently between Sarah and Tania and the other had a nine-year-old son. Tania urgently needed a family, as her short-term foster family were migrating to Australia and she would experience further disruption if she were offered another short-term placement.

Critical social work has never existed in a predictable, stable world of ideal resources. By the nature of practice situations, the practitioner is often choosing the least damaging option. This practitioner met the family with the nine-year-old son, as it was her belief that it was of paramount importance that Tania maintained the relationship with Sarah as her one remaining attachment. As a result of the thorough assessment and good observational skills of Tania's social worker, the importance of this relationship had been recognised. On visiting the family, the social worker was struck by the maturity and confidence of the nine-year-old son as well as the inclusive warmth of the family and its openness. When she returned to visit Tania, the frailty and lack of self-esteem of the child overwhelmed her in comparison to the foster family's son. She knew that either the foster son's confidence and maturity would give enough space to Tania for her needs to be met or that she would feel inadequate by comparison. However, she was also cognisant of the fact that outcomes in relation to human beings and their relationships with others are often unpredictable and unknowable. Even the best-informed critical and reflective social worker cannot predict the future. Much practice is about well-informed leaps in the dark.

Tania was placed with the foster family. Both children attended the same school in different years. Sarah visited weekly and Tania stayed with her for a weekend every month. Her new family formed a strong attachment to Tania as she did to them. As Tania became more settled and attached to the family, competition and conflict increased between the son and Tania. However, the practitioner worked with the family, including encouraging Tania to focus some of her increasing energy into judo, at which she excelled. After a year, the foster siblings were able to express feelings for each other and the competitive nature of their relationship decreased. Tania's social worker remained involved, helping Tania, Sarah and the family to secure the placement. After three years in placement, the family applied to adopt Tania, with the approval of Sarah and the consent of Tania's mother. Her father still could not be traced. Tania, post-adoption, continued to see Sarah every week and stay the monthly weekend. All parties had managed to be open enough to enable Tania to have a second start in life while maintaining what was important to her, her previous attachment to Sarah.

The social worker, through her awareness of the relevant research, as well as consideration of the unique and specific aspects of the case, had made a statistically risky placement, which she believed stood a good chance of permanence.

Dilemmas and tensions – 'safe caring'

When the National Foster Care Association published *Safe Caring* in 1994, it was much needed as a practice guide. The rate of allegations by children against carers had been increasing rapidly and some research showed that the majority were in relation to sexual abuse (National Foster Care Association, 1994). It was an area of uncertainty that provoked considerable anxiety. The extent of allegations against carers and actual cases of abuse have been difficult to measure accurately (Nixon, 2000). The rise in numbers was likely to be linked with adults being more ready to listen to children, resulting in them being more likely to divulge abuse, than was the case in the past.

As is sometimes the case with subjects that raise anxiety in social work, there was the occasional overzealous reaction to the increase in the number of allegations. For example, in the National Foster Care Association's very helpful guide, when advising carers to think carefully about their lifestyles in order to lessen the likelihood of allegations, they said; 'make sure that your family, and children joining your household, have a dressing gown and slippers as well as nightwear' (National Foster Care Association, 1994: 24). I, for one, have been left puzzled as to how 'slippers' were going to help.

When recruiting and assessing carers, the majority of agencies integrate assessment and preparation in relation to safe caring into the assessment and training processes. This involves helping families to reflect critically on their lifestyles in minute detail and think about how a child coming into a family might feel about, and interpret, that lifestyle. Inevitably, caring for a child, new to the family, requires practical as well as emotional adjustments to keep the family and the child safe. This does not involve simply helping carers to lessen the likelihood of allegations being made against them, but also involves practical matters, for example fire precautions and so on.

Why is this an area of dilemma and tension? Because, as in any area of practice that raises high levels of anxiety, social workers sometimes lose the capacity to think critically and can, as a result, fall back on mechanistic procedural processes or 'blame' one party, neither of which are in children's interests.

Drawing on training that I have run over six years with carers, work as a consultant in relation to complex cases involving allegations and as a foster panel chairperson, I have developed a simple model of categorising children's allegations. As with any model, it is only a guide and is in no way prescriptive or fixed. I have seen a pattern of allegations that fall into four groups as follows:

- *Actual:* the event described by the child happened

- *False:* the event described by the child did not happen

- *Perception of the child:* resulting from past experience and other factors, the child misinterprets the behaviour of the carer

- *Behaviour of the carer:* resulting from the impact of the child's behaviour and the dynamic between the carer (or the carer's household) and the child, the behaviour of the carer (or member of the household) is affected.

Many allegations fall into the last two categories and often overlap. Agencies regularly approach investigations of allegations through 'child protection procedures', throwing up the dilemma of, at the same time as investigating thoroughly, holding in mind that occasionally children make allegations about events that have not happened. The reaction to a 'false' allegation, which causes such agency and placement difficulty, can be to blame the child rather than consider the meaning of the allegation. Allegations are powerful tools for children who can feel as if they have, and often do have, little or no access to power or control over their own lives. They may want to move from a placement and know no constructive way to voice their wishes. The child's social worker has to contain the anxiety generated by an allegation. The practitioner, at the same time as offering appropriate support to the family or directing them to such support, needs to focus on the best interests of the child making the 'false' allegation. In one case, a young person made the same 'false' allegation against two carers before he was helped to disclose that the 'actual' incident had happened within his own family several years previously.

Placing children with troubled pasts in new families inevitably stirs up complex and difficult feelings for both the child and the family. The tension as well as the dilemma is making sure that carers are properly supported through the processes of investigation, while at the same time continuing to support and work with the child. To be a critical practitioner is to be able to 'hold in mind' a number of differing and often conflicting matters, feelings and dynamics at the same time; to retain the capacity to 'think' under pressure and to remain child focused. Once an allegation has been made, there is the potential for 'splitting' (one party becoming the 'goody' and the other the 'baddy') and the practitioner needs to hold on to complexity and the 'whole' in the child's interests.

CONCLUSION

Since the important work of Rowe and Lambert (1973), which identified the extent of drift and stagnation for children in public care, there has been a re-emphasis on trying either to return children as quickly as possible to their families of origin or to place them permanently in a substitute family either through adoption or fostering. However, we have made poor progress in creating stability for children in public care, many of whom have had unacceptable numbers of moves between foster families (Jackson and Thomas, 1999).

We currently have a shortage of carers to place children with and many troubled and upset children to place. The government has tried to tackle the situation partially via the Quality Protects initiative, which has released monies to tackle the problem. However, resources are not the only consideration. The quality of the social work being done, in assessing children's needs, in the recruitment and assessment of carers and the matching of a child with a family, is fundamentally important. These social work processes are dependent on the practitioner's capacity to think and practise in a critical fashion. This entails an awareness of self, theory, research, skills and values; to enable the analysis of dynamics, facts and processes in the interests of children. For a child to be separated from their birth family is a traumatic life-changing event. Those professionals responsible for children in public care and in need of adoption owe it to them to practise in a critical and reflective manner; to get it 'right enough' to enable them to have a stable remaining childhood within a family where they can develop their potential to the full.

FURTHER READING

Department of Health (1999) *Adoption Now: Messages from Research*, Chichester: Wiley. A useful outline of key research findings in relation to adoption.

Jackson, S. and Thomas, N. (1999) *On the Move Again? What Works in Creating Stability for Looked After Children*, Ilford: Barnardo's. A review of research looking at stability for looked-after children

Kelly, G. and Gilligan, R. (2000) *Issues in Foster Care: Policy, Practice and Research*, London: Jessica Kingsley. A collection of papers addressing current pertinent areas of foster care.

Triseliotis, J., Shireman, J. and Hundleby, M. (1997) *Adoption: Theory, Policy and Practice*, London: Cassell. A thorough overview of policy, theory and practice in adoption.

Looking After Children and Young People

Alastair Roy, Corinne Wattam and Frances Young

The best care involves the drinking of copious amounts of tea. For tea means talking face to face, talk means humans are interacting and interaction is appropriate to caring.

(Blaug, 1995: 433)

Introduction

The number of children and young people in the care population is falling but the levels and complexities of the needs of those within it continue to rise (Berridge and Brodie, 1998). Many practitioners argue that these needs can only be met through meaningful, consistent, positive relationships. At the same time as need is increasing, however, childcare policy and guidance appear preoccupied with the 'surface' managerial agenda of outcomes and accountability at the cost of the 'depth' of feeling, thinking and relationship (Howe, 1996). This brings an inherent conflict into practice, which must be dealt with in everyday relations between carers and children. One area in which the apparently competing agendas of policy and practice converge is that of the evidence base. It is from this base, that paradoxically underpins the outcome-led approach, that the importance of relationships and associated skills and environments can be defended. Despite current official and agency focus on outcomes, we argue that when working with children the process is equally important.

The following case example demonstrates some of the issues that childcare workers encounter when attempting to work effectively with a young person while fulfilling policy agendas.

CASE EXAMPLE

Kirstie is a 15-old girl of dual heritage who was accommodated at the request of her mother and herself when she was 14. Her mother said she was unable to cope with Kirstie and was concerned about self-harming behaviour that seemed to be getting worse. Since becoming looked after she has had three placements in residential units within eight months and consequent changes of school. Each placement has broken down in response to violence against other resident children. Kirstie has been pleased to move and easily makes new friends with peers. She relates well to adults, but as peers rather than adults. Each placement has resulted in an escalation in Kirstie's disruptive, violent and self-harming behaviour, culminating in a court appearance and two hospital admissions. In her current placement, Kirstie became involved in selling sex. A further placement is now being sought in the private sector at a cost of approximately £3000 per week.

Communication – relationship skills

Contemporary social work has neglected the development of skills involved in working directly with children. Winnicott (cited in Kanter, 1999) commented that children involved with social services tend to have been through painful experiences of one kind or another, which leads many of them to clamp down on feelings or to feel angry and hostile because this is more tolerable than feeling loss and isolation. Despite Kirstie's ease of communication with adults, it would appear to be only at a superficial level. Kirstie's behaviour spiralled further and further out of control with each move and her feelings were expressed by actions that did not include verbal communication with carers. Such behaviour may be confusing and traumatic for Kirstie and for those working with her. Trusting relationships are a prerequisite to the exploration of feelings and frequent moves inevitably inhibit the development of trust.

In order to achieve meaningful communication, the practitioner needs, first, to be able to build a relationship. Young people stress the importance of the relationship with their social worker and value professionals who find the time to build a relationship with them (Morris, 2000). Kirstie's relationship with her field social worker may prove to be critical owing to the large number of recent moves.

The process of developing relationships of trust becomes problematic in an atmosphere where practitioners have to obtain information to comply with instrumentalist and procedural agendas (see also Chapter 10). The bureaucratisation of the care system has created an environment in which relationships are pursued as a means to an end; an outcome-led agenda. Kirstie's current priorities may be significantly different to those of professionals and carers assigned to or involved with her case. A practice dilemma which has particular relevance to children's participation and attendance to their perspective, is that current priorities may not take account of a longer term view (see also Chapters 6 and 10). Eekelaar (1986) has argued this point in relation to children's rights, proposing that the duty of adults who care for children should be less about rights in the present and more about adult responsibility. Quite simply, would Kirstie thank her carers for promoting her right to freedom of association, for example, if this leads to sex work that as an adult she may claim she should have been protected from?

It is clear, however, that current outcome-led approaches deny children/ young people the opportunity to set their own agenda and spend time on issues that are of importance to them. The various *Looking After Children* (LAC) publications increasingly prescribe dialogue within their structured format. They were aimed at improving outcomes and have now been adopted by the majority of local authorities in addition to being used in a range of other countries (Department of Health, 1995f). While no one would argue against the need to improve the quality of care or general outcomes for looked-after children, there is less consensus between government, practitioners and children about what these outcomes should be and the methods for achieving this.

Within a critical practice framework, the needs of children are not viewed as fixed, but as socially constituted and open to change (James and Prout, 1997). There is not one childhood but many. The LAC publications (and all government guidance in relation to childcare) do not provide for the contested nature of childhood and children's needs. Instead, a developmental, ideal type (in a Weberian sense) childhood is unquestionably accepted as fixed, immutable, desirable and historically static. Children and childhood are viewed as one and the same. Thus, even practice directives to 'listen to children' and take account of their views and wishes (Children Act 1989) have little impact on the conflicts inherent in promoting one version of childhood. The way in which children are perceived and defined is largely through scientific and normative modes of understanding. Children are not authorised, in the same way as adults are, to speak within their own discourse. They are only 'heard' if adults sanction the sense of it; if adults decide that their feelings and wishes, statements and communications are first meaningful and second in their best interests. Kirstie may want to relate to her adult carers as peers but it will be difficult for them to reciprocate on an equivalent basis.

Power relationships between carers and children are inherently unequal. Most children are emotionally, physically and financially dependent on adults. The notion of child dependency has altered considerably over the last century, although this varies across cultures. In this context, there must be caution against child-centredness being a sanctioning of white, Western, middle-class notions of dependence (Boyden, 1997). Some argue that the circumstances of children and young people will not improve until they are waged. Kirstie may perceive accessing money as the only realistic way for her to achieve any level of independence and autonomy. The means available for young people generally to access money are distinctly restricted. This situation can be worse for looked-after children who are vulnerable to not fitting the mould of current policy constructions of childhood. Practitioners working with 'streetwise' children such as Kirstie are therefore left to bridge the gap between the outcomes directed by the state and lived experience which are often at odds.

The power of carers is both overt and covert. A sensitive study of 'hard times' for children (Chaput-Waksler, 1991) showed that 'hard times' were strongly related to adult control. She noted that all children are denied control of:

■ their bodies, such that others deal with their bodies against their will or without their permission. This is often legitimated through 'hygiene';

■ the activities in which they engage, ie, others determine where they go, how they conduct themselves, what they do, and what they cannot do;

■ appearance, and thus their presentation of self;

■ relations with others, including friends and enemies.

(Chaput-Waksler, 1991: 222)

Additionally, children may be frustrated by inabilities or inadequacies, much as adults may be, but may also lack control over resources to cope with, minimise or change their deficits (Chaput-Waksler, 1991: 222).

If we consider the above in relation to Kirstie, it is apparent that such issues may only be addressed within relationships of genuine concern and trust. While it may be deemed that Kirstie is in need of protection, she should also be engaged with as a thinking, autonomous individual with her own ideas. Such exchanges can be highly complex and the agendas are likely to be individual in nature and content. A successful intervention with Kirstie will require the dedication of a practitioner with a repertoire of interpersonal skills. If she experiences her ideas and thoughts as respected and important within the context of one relationship, a framework is developed from which further constructive involvement may be built. With reference to the self-harming behaviour, for example, decisions must be made as to whether Kirstie should be allowed to have access to sharp instruments and whether her wounds should be sympathetically tended to. Busy accident and emergency departments can make short shrift of teenage girls who present with these kinds of injuries, and preventive policies often involve ensuring no access to potentially damaging objects (Bracken and Thomas, 2000). An alternative practice approach is to respond in a non-judgemental but sensitive way that allows the young person to build up trust while retaining control over their own body to do what they want. This approach, carefully managed, has been demonstrated as effective (Spandler, 1996). Proceduralised responses may result in Kirstie feeling like an object to be processed rather than a subject to be engaged with. In addition, intervention that emphasises adult control can exacerbate feelings of disempowerment that can underpin self-harming behaviour.

Thus a further issue for the critical practitioner is the extent to which they can allow their power to be restricted and control by the child facilitated. This is relevant to issues such as 'passive' (on behalf of) or 'active' (by) advocacy with looked-after children (Boylen and Wyllie, 1999), confidentiality (on behalf of or with) (Wattam, 1999), involvement in decision-making/mediation (given information or participation) to name a few. From an adult's position, such as Eekelaar's (1986), giving children control could be viewed as damaging. The practice challenge is to take risks, to allow the child to retain control while encouraging less damaging behaviour, as in the self-harm example above. In doing so, practitioners need to empower themselves, have the confidence to take risks and know that they will be supported. Thus, critical and challenging practice requires a sympathetic organisational environment and cannot be practised in isolation. A requirement of this environment is that it accepts, makes explicit and works positively with uncertainty and ambiguity (Parton, 1998).

It may be thought that involving children/young people in decision-making processes is a further step towards enabling control to rest with them (see Chapter 6). Most local authorities have accepted the case for participation, although many remain at the early stages of this process. However, it is important to challenge tokenistic participation. Inviting children to adult-led meetings is problematic. Undoubtedly, Kirstie will have been invited to participate in a range of meetings but it is likely that the content will have been organised around adult-led agendas. Personal information about the child, their behaviour and relationships often forms the major agenda item. Far from experiencing such meetings as representing concerned planning and consultation, children such as Kirstie often report feeling humiliated. Hart (1992) has developed an eight-stage ladder to represent children's participation in decision-making. The various stages are not incremental or sequential and range from:

■ Manipulation (use of the child to get what the adult wants)

■ Decoration (meaningless use of the child for appearances only)

■ Tokenism (when children are apparently given a voice but have limited or no choice about the subject)

■ Assigned but informed (given roles which are symbolic and functional)

■ Consulted and informed (work as consultants for adults and are involved in all the stages)

■ Adult-initiated, shared decisions with children

■ Child-initiated and directed

■ Child-initiated, shared decisions with adults.

A critical practice framework would prioritise the last four stages.

Children, like adults, are not a homogeneous group and power relations between adults and children are mediated by other forms of difference such as gender, sexuality, ethnicity, class, ability, size and so on. All of these can provide a source of division and occasionally physical violence for children, as well as acting as positive foundations for identity formation and a sense of self. All practice must promote anti-discriminatory intervention (Thompson, 1993). However, critical practice would take this a stage further through valuing diversity as an alternative to monolithic childhoods.

The United Nations Convention on the Rights of the Child (UNCRC) (see Chapter 10) offers a baseline standard for all childcare systems: the UN is adamant that the Convention must be interpreted as a whole and not taken piecemeal. Some may take issue that the UNCRC does not go far enough, viewing it as an adult interpretation of childhood, along the 'best interests' theme. However, the following 'rights' can be helpful in practice as checks and balances, discussion points and underpinning principles (United Nations, 1989):

- All actions concerning the child should take full account of his/her best interests (there is an obvious issue here about who defines 'best interests')

- The rights and responsibilities of parents are respected (the issue here is about when these conflict with the child's)

- The child has a right to express an opinion and to have that opinion taken into account in any matter or procedure affecting him/her (the issue here is 'taken into account' – how far does that extend? This has recently been applied by pro-family lobbies in relation to divorce and separation, for example)

- The child has the right to obtain and make known information and express views unless they violate the rights of others (how much information and of what type? Kitzinger (1997) makes the point that sex education and safety messages steer clear of gender and power/empowerment issues, for example)

- The child has a right to protection from interference with respect to privacy, family, home and correspondence, and from libel/slander (the issue here is again the extent of application – how far is this a reality in most children's lives?)

- The state has an obligation to protect children from all forms of maltreatment perpetrated by parents or others responsible for their care (what about other forms of maltreatment; other children, acquaintances, strangers and so forth?)

- The right to freedom of thought, conscience and religion, subject to appropriate parental guidance and national law (that is, adult control).

Most of the UNCRC, ratified by government, is relevant to the Human Rights Act 1998. It therefore becomes a potential tool for leverage and improving conditions for children and young people. Where practitioners consider that a human right is violated, they are directed to seek legal advice (United Nations, 1989). The victim is the key complainant, but the practitioner must consider an advocacy role.

Access

Access to the 'looked-after' childcare system is an often neglected area when it comes to considering childcare practice. This is because the service is fragmented between community-based (field) social work and 'looked-after' (residential or foster) care. Kirstie is likely to be acutely aware of the differing roles and responsibilities undertaken by field social workers and residential childcare workers, and the potential for conflict. Critical practice can be a method that unites childcare professionals in reconstructing and finding new ways of organising and delivering services. For example, some local authorities have altered children's services to enable needs to be met across traditional boundaries, without recourse to multiple departments and the inherent bureaucracy that this entails. Others have built new approaches, on the basis of robust consultation strategies with a representative cross section of children, attending to a broad array of needs such as buildings, transport and community safety. The principle underpinning this approach is that whether children are in need, or looked after, their needs are often the same as all children.

A different organisational approach has been to reduce the numbers of children needing to be looked after. These are proactive attempts to identify the characteristics of the looked-after population and discern patterns behind their reasons for entry to care (Thorpe, 1994). Such analyses suggest services that can provide intensive home-based support can be effective in enabling children to remain in their own homes. These include interventions to address adolescent and parent conflict, the overrepresentation of unsupported single parents and comprehensive, accessible, community-based child and adolescent mental health services. If Kirstie and her mother had been offered a tailored, intensive, home-based support package, it is possible that the need to be looked after would not have arisen. Like many looked-after children, Kirstie's access to mental health services is likely to have been a lottery, influenced by geographical location and local authority resources (Department of Health, 1999d).

Once in the childcare system entrants have been distinguished as 'victims', 'volunteers' and 'villains' (Packman, 1986), all three of which arguably continue to be subject to the principles of deserving and undeserving candidates for care. Kirstie's request to be accommodated ensured that her care career began as volunteer, with her self-harming behaviour beginning to indicate a possible victim status. However, her sex work, violence and resulting court appearances could now see her categorised as 'villain'.

The treatment of young people who require looking after for reasons of criminality and challenging behaviour reflects their position as 'villains' and 'folk devils', masking their vulnerability. Incarceration involves the child's removal from the family and community, sometimes at great distances, where treatment regimes can involve being locked away for up to 22 hours each day. This exclusion is both physical and emotional, and also adds a powerful label, which has the potential to push individuals further in the direction of exclusionary lifestyles.

The overrepresentation of black young people in youth justice reflects that in the criminal justice system more generally. Awareness of the dynamics and effects of racism is therefore essential to childcare practice. In a 'post-Macpherson' climate racism must be addressed at a structural and organisational level, while supporting individuals in overcoming personal experiences of oppression (Dholakia, 1998). Gender differences in offending behaviour, both in terms of level and type of offence, are also acute. A high proportion of sexual and violent offences are committed by boys, however research on section 53 offenders highlights that high proportions (91 per cent in a study by Boswell, 1995) have suffered abuse and/or a significant loss. These statistics demonstrate the need for the critical practitioner to fulfil nurturing requirements in addition to addressing offending behaviour. Females who offend can be deemed to be doubly deviant, having transgressed laws and stereotypes of appropriate female behaviour. Thus, Kirstie's violent behaviour is more likely to be treated harshly within the criminal justice system by virtue of the fact that she is female.

Organisational context

There is a current preoccupation in childcare social work with the techno-rational managerial agenda of outcomes and accountability (see Chapters 4 and 22). Moves towards a consensus on standards, benchmarking and 'best value' have both positive and negative connotations for children. An improvement in service delivery and systems containing checks and balances represent progress. There is always a danger, however, that these markers for improvement become mechanistically applied and an end in themselves, losing sight of process and the 'best' way of getting to them.

Within a culture of criticism in social work, ambiguity and the unknown has become increasingly hard to live with (Parton, 1998). Practitioners are concerned that any intervention not officially sanctioned or approved may be open to misinterpretation and hence criticism. Such criticism could have serious professional implications for any individual social worker. Unambiguous directives have also become increasingly attractive to practitioners who can feel more confident with clearly defined objectives and targets. This leads to the development of defensive practice, which fails to address either the needs or the root cause of children's difficulties.

While few would argue against the need to improve the quality of care given to looked-after children/young people, the predominant focus on outcomes as a measure of success addresses one set of issues to the exclusion of other important areas. Garrett (1999) argues that the promotion and managerial enforcement of the 'outcomes' and measurement culture was closely bound up with the targeting of resources and using 'finite resources in the best possible way' (Garrett, 1999: 30). A continuation of the rational, outcome-led approach to resource management comes with the Quality Protects initiative. This three-year programme sets defined objectives for those providing children's services and allocates financial resources on the basis of targets. Thus, there is a need for practitioners to create flexible, responsive and meaningful indicators within the context of this agenda.

Evaluating the success or failure of childcare programme outcomes using measures such as GCSE results, movement and ethnicity can be inappropriate for some service users and too general to accommodate diversity. Attempts to develop methodologies of evaluation that are led by users and carers and adequately reflect the childcare relationship are still in their infancy (Everitt and Hardiker, 1996). Practitioners would do a great service if they could turn their attention on how best to reflect traditionally non-scientific concepts, such as meaning, trust, enjoyment, hope, nurturing, feelings, emotion and other features yet to be recognised, in ways that might be open to evaluation (that is, demonstrating their value).

In doing so, they must be supported by access to information (including research, current and relevant policy) along with regular and supportive supervision. It has been argued that supervision has increasingly been hijacked by an instrumental agenda, used to ensure that procedures have been followed rather than as a forum for workers to explore their practice.

> We are now just a short step from hiring managers for their (instrumental) administrative ability only, from discovering via an (instrumental) training survey that they require an instrumental workshop wherein they will be presented with a list of the twelve components of good (instrumental) supervision.
>
> (Blaug, 1995: 429)

Anxiety is an intrinsic part of the parenting task. Therefore, it is not possible to remove the anxieties that exist within childcare. They arise out of meaningful engagement with children. Developmental supervision is essential in providing the practitioner with the opportunity to manage anxiety in the context of creative solutions. It is probably the most effective antidote to negative risky thinking.

CONCLUSION

The critical practitioner needs to develop 'defensible' rather than defensive practice, adopting interventions that are informed by, and also progress, research, theory and experience. The current evidence base cannot be accepted uncritically if children and young people are genuinely engaged in a participatory practice. Thus, a foundational skill for critical practice is the ability to understand, scrutinise and appraise the knowledge base. So much of what has been taken for granted as 'best practice' is actually founded on little more than opinion and dominant ideologies of the time. Rigorous qualitative research can be liberating in the sense that it advances what cannot be known through quantitative positivist approaches. Calls for an evidence base to childcare work mean that research and its implementation must now be an intrinsic and constant feature of practice. This evidence must be able to reflect the uncertainty that is an inevitable part of human interaction and decision-making.

In this chapter, we have suggested that the location of critical practice is not necessarily with the individual practitioner or child; it also needs to be located in the structures and

Table 12.1 Conceptual framework for critical childcare practice

Context	Boundaries	Critical practice
Individual	Child's individual needs	Understanding, negotiating, meeting need, particularly for identity, safety, trust and health
Immediate	Extent of adult control	Negotiating inclusion (active/passive, partial/complete)
	Degree of participation	Critical evaluation
	Boundaries of imposed regulations and regulators	Prioritising relationship and process
Wider social	Ideologies of childhood (immaturity, incompetence, innocence, dependence)	Skill building for social inclusion
		Deconstructing childhood
	Sources of difference and diversity (ethnicity, gender, ability, size, sexuality, age, class)	Valuing diversity
		Promoting positive parenting
	Sources of regulation and control (risk society, mixed economy of welfare)	Critical qualitative evaluation

organisation of key agencies, supported by managers with confidence derived from a critical appraisal of the knowledge base. We consider that this can be approached through a conceptual framework that highlights the context and boundaries of childcare work (Table 12.1).

FURTHER READING

Blaug, R. (1995) 'Distortion of the Face to Face: Communicative Reason and Social Practice', *British Journal of Social Work*, **25**: 423–39. This article explores the changes in social work practice using Habermas's theory of communicative action. Offers some innovative ideas for social work which is practised in a bureaucratic and managerialist culture.

Brechin, A. (2000) 'Introducing Critical Practice', in Brechin, A., Brown, H. and Eby, M.A. (eds) *Critical Practice in Health and Social Care*, London: Sage. Explores the idea of critical practice and reflects the working challenges and dilemmas of practitioners to frame a three-way concept of critical practice. She suggests that critical practitioners are integrating analysis, reflexivity and action as they work and develop on a daily basis and are striving to establish and hold to principles of openness and equality.

Howe, D. (1998) 'Relationship-based Thinking and Practice in Social Work', *Journal of Social Work Practice*, **12**(1): 45–56. Examines the increasing bureaucratisation and proceduralisation in social work and promotes relationships as being of central importance in successful social work interventions.

Shaw, I. and Lishman, J. (eds) (1999) *Evaluation and Social Work Practice*, London: Sage. Provides a useful overview of the debates concerning what can constitute evidence for practice and helpful guidance on evaluation and empowerment, qualitative approaches to evaluation and different theoretical positions including feminist evaluation. Presents an informed and relevant challenge to performance culture.

Family-based Social Work

Kate Morris

Introduction

Traditionally, concepts of family-based social work have focused on professional intervention and achieving change in family dynamics that are perceived to be inadequate or appropriate, thereby enabling better care of children. Practitioner texts have argued the importance of professional intervention and the treatment of the family as a dysfunctional grouping. More recently, the emphasis has shifted to one of debates about family involvement and participation. Texts such as those produced by Thoburn (1992) and Marsh and Crow (1998) draw together the research and practice possibilities of partnership and participation. This latter theme informs the critical thinking for the framework for the following discussion. Family inclusion, and exclusion, will be critically explored in the development of child welfare services that aim to achieve better outcomes for children.

This interpretation of family-based social work means that the focus will not include a comparison of, or commentary on, effective models for professional intervention in family functioning. Instead, it builds on a framework that kinship networks are central to good outcomes for children, even when children are unable to live within these networks.

The diversity of family life and the range of 'family' models and types that child welfare professionals work with generate a particular demand for accessible and flexible approaches to practice. Structures and forms of family life have become increasingly complex; with this diversification have come various implications for childhood and childrearing (Hill and Tisdall, 1997). Child and family social workers face particular challenges given these demographic trends:

Yet while there are many commonalities about the ways in which people construct their family life, there is nothing set about the family as such ... There are many different families; many different family relationships; and consequently many different family forms.

(Allen and Crow, 2000: 21)

Hence the term 'family' is used broadly and refers to the child's extended network – not merely the primary carers – and does not propose a specific structure or form. Instead, concepts of 'family' are those defined and represented by those using the services and as such will vary enormously.

The framework explored in this discussion takes a critical stance in relation to methods of practice that perceive the family as a homogeneous grouping with common weaknesses shared by all. Instead of this essentially deficit model of practice, that is, the assumption that difficulties presented by one family member are shared by the entire network, a strength model is pursued. This framework for critical practice sees families as rich and varied mixes of resources, strengths and difficulties and aims to enable practice to develop accordingly.

The terms 'partnership' and 'participation' are used carefully and are not presented as interchangeable. Participation is seen as family member involvement in the professional processes affecting a child. The definition of partnership is drawn from Tunnard (1991: 1):

The essence of partnership is sharing. It is marked by respect for one another, role divisions, rights to information, accountability, competence and value accorded to individual input. In short each partner is seen as having something to contribute, power is shared, decisions are made jointly and roles are not only respected but are also backed by legal and moral rights.

A brief overview of some of the research that provides evidence for the importance of family connections in achieving good outcomes for children will be provided. The expectations of the Children Act 1989 and associated guidance and policy will be considered and their implementation reviewed. The model of family group conferences will then be used to illustrate emerging critical practice that challenges and addresses existing approaches to family involvement. The conclusion will argue for a significant shift in the value framework adopted by professional social work practice to enable inclusive child-centred practice to occur.

Legal and policy framework

In the decades leading up to the introduction of the Children Act 1989, family-based practice ranged across a continuum that stretched from perceptions of families as needy and inadequate to concepts of families as dangerously dysfunctional. At their extremes, both approaches were fundamentally incompatible with family partnership and participation. These frameworks for practice with children's families demanded the adoption by professionals of the role of primary 'expert' in relation to a child's needs and best interests. Such a position prevented the full exploration of the knowledge, skills and possibilities of the kinship network. The emergence of research during the 1980s began to question the usefulness of this approach. The evidence of increased use of formal powers in relation to children (Parton, 1991), coupled with the research that clearly indicated significant shortcomings in corporate parenting (Department of Health, 1991), helped to form the backdrop to the introduction of the Children Act 1989.

Embedded within this new legal framework were expectations about the principles underpinning child and family social work. Specifically the Children Act makes clear that:

- where possible children are best brought up within their families

- families should be supported in this task where difficulties emerge

- compulsory intervention must rest on evidence that such action is actively preferable to no formal court order being made.

To achieve the preferred outcome of children being brought up within their families, the Children Act implicitly and explicitly expects professionals to develop working partnerships with families. While the term 'partnership' is confined to the accompanying guidance and regulations, duties within the Children Act to consult, inform and support families form a framework for practice that renders some form of family involvement a legal requirement:

> The development of a working partnership with parents is usually the most effective route to providing supplementary or substitute care for children. Parents should be expected and enabled to retain their responsibilities and to remain as closely involved as is consistent with their child's welfare, even if that child cannot live at home either temporarily or permanently.
>
> (Department of Health, 1989c: 8, 9)

Part III of the Children Act lays out the framework for preventive and supportive services and in doing so introduced new thinking to underpin support services for children in need. The development of 'accommodation' (s.20) illustrates the intention that, even where substitute care of a child is needed, this should be achieved in a supportive, accessible framework:

> family support implies a potentially open ended approach, and one in which the views and preferences of service users are to be given greater weight.
>
> (Tunstill, 1997: 48)

Such thinking substantially challenged the basis on which some services had been, and indeed are, provided. The concept of informal, helpful, support services for a child and his/her family as needed created real tension with the demands of resource management. As research by Aldgate and Tunstill (1995) illustrated, many authorities managed this tension by defining children in need within very narrow, acute criteria. This research showed that, for the significant majority of local authorities, children in need were defined by criteria that focused on risk and harm. By working with these eligibility criteria, social work services continued to be based on crisis intervention. A consequence of this was the limitation of social work services only to those in extreme need and so enabled underlying professional concepts of 'inadequate families' to be maintained.

The most recent central analysis of the use of the legal framework for practice indicates the ongoing difficulties in implementing part III of the Children Act. (Department of Health, 1999a). Few authorities have established strategies for delivering family support services, echoing earlier findings that social work services are struggling to reflect the philosophy and principles of the Act and are locked into responding to acute need. Interestingly, running alongside this finding is evidence of an increasing use of formal intervention, specifically the use of care orders, with an accompanying reduction in the use of informal accommodation arrangements.

Central government guidance issued in relation to child protection and child assessment maintains the confusion and dilemmas of partnership practice. The new *Framework for the Assessment of Children in Need and Their Families* (Department of Health/DfEE/Home Office, 2000) outlines the core dimensions for effective assessment of children in need. These dimensions contain a range of references to the importance of families and family networks.

However, the document itself is targeted almost exclusively at a professional audience. Service users are not provided with guidance about best practice in assessment or what minimum standards might be expected. There is little that would enable a family member to be clear about their roles and responsibilities in the assessment process. While examples of information to share with families are offered, the central debate about the value or limitations of a purely professionally determined assessment process is not explored. The development of a working partnership, or effective participation, is limited when only one party has the necessary guidance and information about the service being delivered.

To summarise, the introduction of the Children Act 1989 presented important developments in the opportunities to incorporate research into practice and, as a result, achieve working partnerships with children and their families. The implementation of this legislation, and the more recent associated guidance and practice frameworks, has struggled to achieve these opportunities. The absence of service users in the development, design and piloting of practice-focused material has ensured that it remains a professionally dominated and determined framework for services.

Importance of family connections

There is now a substantial body of research that explores the role and value of kinship networks for children. Such research can be grouped around the themes of the emotional and psychological well-being of children, the impact on developing effective planning for children and the role in achieving good outcomes. Common to all this research and understanding is an acknowledgement that not all children can live within their families, nor can all families provide safe care. However, the value of maintaining kinship connections is apparent. Maintaining connections is not, as might be assumed, merely the promotion of contact. Maintaining connections can take a diverse range of forms, such as letters, oral histories, family meetings, but the critical issue for practitioners is the creative thinking necessary to enable connections to be respected.

The concept of 'clean breaks' for children that severed all links to their families has been recognised as flawed. Children perform better, emotionally, socially and educationally, where family connections are preserved. For children, their family can hold the means of understanding their identity and their heritage. While patterns developed within the family may not have been positive for the child, and indeed may even have been harmful, the family network still remains the key holder of the information about attachments, identity and heritage.

More positively, research shows that relatives remain the primary source of support for the majority of children. Research also indicates that, for many, times of particular need lead to increased contact with relatives and carers (McGlone et al., 1998). While the nature and pattern of this support varies according to need, economic circumstances, culture and ethnicity, the majority of children grow up within their kinship network. We have moved away from concepts of a 'standard' family life and, increasingly, the diversity of family composition, traditions and experiences is now acknowledged. Definitions of family as adopted by practitioners need to reflect and incorporate this broad interpretation. As established by Morrow (1998), children do not hold a rigid interpretation of family:

> Overall, children appeared to have an accepting inclusive view of what counts as family and their definitions did not centre on biological relatedness or the 'nuclear' norm.

Politically, notions of the 'family' remain potent. Recent policy and practice developments such as Sure Start, part of the raft of initiatives from the consultation document *Supporting Families* (Home Office, 1999) cite the strengthening of families as a desired outcome. Such political agendas are rooted in perspectives of family life not pertinent to this discussion, but evidence is clear that family networks remain a central source of support for child rearing and as such continue to provoke significant practice and policy debate.

As social work has shifted away from a primarily excluding, professional mode of decision-making, the role and value of families in planning for their children have been explored. Some aspects of practice have received considerable attention, such as child protection. Other areas such as family support have been less well researched. This may be a reflection of the professional anxieties involved in increased participation, areas of risk provoking more attention than areas of assumed cooperative practice.

Particular attention should be given to the experiences of children and families facing extensive barriers to participation and partnership. As research demonstrates (Bebbington and Miles, 1989), families in receipt of social work services are already facing economic and social disadvantage. The experiences of black and ethnic minority children living away from home highlight the extent to which professionally exclusive practices further exacerbate the oppression encountered. The take-up of family support services, such as family centres, demonstrates that for many black and ethnic minority families the services provided are not accessible or participative (Butt and Box, 1998).

However, the conclusions drawn from the research can be perceived as applicable to all areas of practice. Essentially, family participation is both possible and productive in the development of services to children. The more inclusive the approach to practice, the more likely that a child will either remain within their network, or will return to the network successfully. Such practice demands changes in professional approaches, and may require new and different skills. Where family and professional *partnerships* are explored, the findings become more complex. Actual, working professional/family partnerships form a minority of the material explored by research. As a result, messages about partnerships are less evident, and fewer conclusions can be drawn. The absence of substantial research can be seen to support the argument that professionals have struggled to find effective methods of practice that enable partnerships to develop. Professional and policy debate about the value of partnership practice continues to run alongside the struggle to develop methods and skills.

Family group conferences: an example of family involvement

Family group conferences (see also Chapter 6) offer a useful means of analysis of the critical issues emerging in the development of partnership and participatory practice in child and family social work. The family group conference model addresses the criticisms already outlined of existing childcare planning and allows innovative processes and plans to emerge.

Family group conferences are relatively new to the UK but form a central tool in primary childcare legislation in other countries (for example, the Children, Young Persons and their Families Act 1989 in New Zealand). The model originated in New Zealand, in an attempt to respond to highly critical commentary from the Maori communities about child welfare services. Specifically, Maori children were significantly overrepresented in the public care system and were predominantly placed with white carers (Wilcox et al., 1991) The model was introduced in England and Wales in the early 1990s (Morris and Tunnard, 1995) and has become increasingly recognised as an effective planning process. However, its introduction into childcare planning in England and Wales has generated some critical issues for practitioners and policy-makers and these will be explored in some depth.

Family group conferences are a kinship-led planning process. The term 'family' is widely defined and includes carers, relatives and others significant to the child. Where there is an established need for a plan to be developed to meet a child's needs, a family group conference is held. The child (or children) is assumed to be a full participant and arrangements are made to reflect this, for example the use of advocates, child-friendly facilities and the creative presentation of information. The meeting process is facilitated by an independent coordinator who should reflect the language and culture of the child's network. The role of the coordinator is crucial, and demands particular skills in mediation and negotiation. Those filling this role vary in their backgrounds, but include counsellors, guardians *ad litem*, foster carers, advice workers, social workers, teachers and lawyers. The process and meeting are held in the first language of the family and professionals must seek interpreters where needed. The coordinator holds the right to exclude members from attending, but should only do so in exceptional circumstances – such as a proven risk of violence. The family is brought together to hear from those professionals directly involved about their roles, concerns and resources. The family is also clearly informed about any professional responsibilities that they must accommodate in the plan and any powers that the professionals have to prevent particular courses of action. The family then meets in private to agree their plan, decide upon monitoring arrangements and specify contingency plans. Unless the plan places the child at risk of significant harm, the professionals should agree the principles of the plan and negotiate any resources.

A carefully linked research programme accompanied the introduction of the model in England and Wales. This has enabled clear evidence about the possibilities and limits of this approach (Marsh and Crow, 1998). In general, the model is perceived by service users to be highly participative and, although at times painful, the outcomes are preferred to those of professional planning processes (Lupton et al., 1995; Jackson and Morris, 1999). As a family member said:

> It's a reasonable method. At least you can air your views and make a contribution. In the past the professionals have made a decision and you don't feel it's the right one. The family can make a better decision because they have the larger picture. The social worker only has a small picture.
>
> (Lupton et al., 1995: 94)

Families identify the model as enabling them to have clarity about their roles and responsibilities and encouraging a wider harnessing of family involvement and support. However, this is not without some pain and stress, as another family member points out:

> In cases like this it would be useful for a counsellor or some one like the coordinator to talk to people after the meeting. It was quite traumatic. I haven't heard a word from social services or anyone and I've been getting quite a bit of abuse from [the mother] ... They have all kinds of expectations of her, and don't give any support.
>
> (Lupton and Stevens, 1997: 30)

The relatively recent introduction of the model has limited the longitudinal measures of outcomes but research begins to demonstrate that there is an increased use of family placements, that family plans are no more costly than professional plans, but are different in content. However, for families there is a key issue in professionals failing to maintain their initial undertakings or commitment to the plans (Jackson and Morris, 1999). Families recount their frustration and bitterness and a feeling that their plans were not given weight and credibility. The absence of professional accountability in the implementation of family plans can render the model a difficult process for families.

The development of the model has also enabled some exploration of the underpinning attitudes and values informing professional perspectives on family participation. Common to much work surrounding this model, and emerging from the research, are the difficulties in engaging professionals in the use of the model.

Research in one authority found that social workers were reluctant to refer to the family group conference project, despite clear criteria for doing so. Professionals also failed to predict with accuracy the potential of a network to create a working plan. Families seen by professionals as likely to be unable to reach an agreed effective plan often actually managed to do so, suggesting professional assessment of family potential to be limited (Shepherd, 1998; Morris and Shepherd, 2000).

More recent research, still being completed, has identified a pattern of referrals to the coordinator where families do not share the professional definitions of the problems and needs. While the family may perceive there to be difficulties, they may not agree with the professional description or assessment of these problems. Therefore professionals are seeking another mechanism from the model in order to gain family agreement to their agenda, rather than perceiving the model as a means of opening up creative planning opportunities.

The professional approach to this model can indicate how deep rooted are concepts of deficient families. Professionals are able to see a role for this model where families are perceived to be needy rather than failing or risky. The use of the model in situations where some family members have posed a risk to their children or have failed to meet their needs generates debate about the rights and abilities of such networks to plan for their children (Connolly and McKenzie, 1999). Informing this approach is the assumption that failure and/or harm by some family members means the entire network is unsafe. This is despite research such as that by Thoburn et al. (1995) that indicates how few of those adults known to social services intentionally harm their children.

The model is open to criticism, particularly when introduced without careful preparation and training. Not all families are able to come together and plan, and, in exceptional circumstances, to do so would be to place a child at further risk. Lupton and Stevens (1997: 65) note that:

> Important issues remain however about the way in which the FGC process engages with that of more traditional child protection procedures and about the extent to which the process would be appropriate for the full range of child protection cases.

Family group conferences cannot be the answer to all childcare planning needs; they are one way of exploring family involvement. Other methods need to be developed and evaluated, as to depend too heavily on this one model may institutionalise its use and remove its creative possibilities.

For those agencies wanting to develop the use of family group conferences, family support needs are perceived as the appropriate location for this model. Throughout the development of the model, attempts have been made repeatedly to locate it firmly within family support services. This belief is endorsed by central government guidance (Department of Health/Home Office/Department for Education and Employment/National Assembly of Wales, 1999b). However, there is no evidence to support this limit to the use of family group conferences. Research indicates that the model does not generate more or less successful outcomes dependent on the type of problem/need being addressed (Marsh and

Crow, 1998). The exception to this is the use of family group conferences in planning for adoption, where very limited piloting of the model means minimal research material is available. Assertions about the best practice use of this partnership-based model must therefore be based on particular values and attitudes about either the eligibility or ability of families to operate in partnership with professional agencies. Despite the extensive developmental material available (Morris et al., 1998) and the positive research outcomes, family group conferences remain relatively marginal to mainstream services.

CONCLUSION

The legal framework for social work practice with the kinship networks of children in need promotes and expects substantial inclusivity and participation:

> The Act rests on the belief that children are generally best looked after within the family with both parents playing a full part and without resort to legal proceedings.

> (Department of Health, 1989c)

As already discussed, professional practice guidance does not always reflect or take forward these expectations. The use of innovative family-based models of planning and decision-making, such as family group conferences, provides important opportunities for existing practice to be critically reviewed and developed. Research and practice experience indicate that such developmental opportunities have been limited in their impact on professional approaches to inclusive practice.

Critical commentary about the uses and abuses of partnership in childcare planning reflects the concern about inappropriate avoidance of intervention based on a collusive approach to practice. Family involvement can, if misunderstood, lead to children failing to gain better outcomes. Texts such as Stevenson's (1998) work on neglect indicate the dangers of partnership being defined in practice as being actions reflective of only adult family members' wishes. Such an interpretation is wrong: professional responsibilities are not removed or rendered irrelevant by a commitment to participative practice.

Underpinning examples of innovative practice developments are complex issues of professional attitudes and values. Central to the critical development of inclusive social work practice are core values about the worth and value of service user input (Morris and Shepherd, 2000). The continued adoption of a primarily deficit model of family analysis reduces the professional abilities to explore positively kinship knowledge and resources.

In child and family social work practice, extensive service user involvement in the design and delivery of services for children can be argued to be relatively limited:

> There were very few examples of users being involved at any level in the process of planning ... much less at all levels.

> (Social Services Inspectorate, 1998)

The repeated theme in research highlighting the particular exclusion experienced by families facing specific barriers, such as racism, means that for some communities and families the barriers to participation are extreme.

The evaluation of the consequences for children of exclusivity in practice must be linked to the substantial body of knowledge about their needs. Without inclusive practice, rich and indeed unique sources of knowledge, support and practical assistance can be lost. The history of corporate parenting is too problematic for the social work profession to continue to exclude the significant resource that families can represent. However, inclusion demands a respectful sharing of power, and a holistic approach to children that existing structures and professional cultures may inhibit. The growing fragmentation and special-isation of services prevent families from sharing in the process of defining need and the resultant planning of services. Recent professional debates in child welfare have focused on the structure of services (Parton, 1997) which may not usefully reflect actual need:

> I rang asking for help many, many times. On one occasion I was in tears on the phone, but nothing was done. Then things got really bad ... Suddenly social services were here next day.

> (Lindley, 1994: 8)

The commentary on the tensions between family support services and child protection services has, at times, failed to acknowledge the reality that for families there is a continuum of need that ebbs and flows.

The absence of service users in policy-making forums, and in central government representation, maintains the marginal state of families who experience difficulties in meeting the needs of their children:

> In a complex and potentially controversial area of service planning, the views of service users are not simply an extra burden which staff have to assume. They can, on the contrary, be of significant help in identifying new issues – and as a sounding board for new ideas.

> (Social Services Inspectorate, 1998)

The groups most likely to receive social work services for their children are the groups facing exclusion on a number of levels. Poverty, economic deprivation and social exclusion impact the skills and resources that families can develop to participate, with many families only able to gain help on an individualistic, crisis management basis. With professional input repeatedly confined to acute need, the possibility of empowering effective service user participation and partnership to achieve best outcomes for children remains the critical issue facing those developing best practice with children and families.

FURTHER READING

Bullock, R., Little, M. and Millham, S. (1993) *Going Home: The Return of Children Separated from their Families,* Aldershot: Dartmouth. A research-based text identi-fying good practice and key issues in work with children returning home, with messages that are transferable to other child welfare settings.

Marsh, P. and Crow, G. (1998) *Family Group Conferences in Child Welfare*, Oxford: Blackwell Science. This text offers both an overview of the development of FGCs in the UK and summarises the findings from the national research project.

Morris, K., Marsh, P. and Wiffen, J. (1998) *Family Group Conferences: A Training Pack*, London: Family Rights Group. A practical guide to implementing FGCs which also contains key information about the context for this partnership-based practice.

Parton, N. (1997) *Child Protection and Family Support: Tensions, Contradictions and Possibilities*, London: Routledge. An edited text that contains chapters exploring central contemporary issues in delivering and analysing child welfare services.

Thoburn, J., Lewis, A. and Shemmings, D. (1995) *Paternalism or Partnership? Family Involvement in the Child Protection Process*, London: HMSO. This text forms part of the Department of Health collection of child protection studies and specifically addresses issues of partnership and participation in protection.

Youth Justice and Young Offenders

14

Kevin Haines

CASE EXAMPLE

John is 15 years old. He is currently on remand and is being held in a private remand centre over 200 miles from his home. John has a short history of committing minor offences and has been made subject to a number of interventions.

Many of John's problems and his offences are linked to difficulties he has experienced with school. Since he started secondary school John has been the subject of bullying. A child of normal abilities and performance in primary school, John's school work has since deteriorated and he often plays truant. John's first offence, a minor act of criminal damage, was committed when he was 13, for which he received a reprimand from the police. Two months later, John was arrested again for an act of minor criminal damage, committed while he was truanting from school; this time the police gave him a final warning and referred him to the youth offending team (YOT). The YOT worker involved John in an offending behaviour programme designed to tackle his lack of respect for other people's property – John did not seem interested and he failed to complete the programme.

John did not reoffend until after the school holidays, when he again started truanting from school. This time he was arrested for shoplifting in a sports store. He had been under surveillance for some time and had been suspected by store detectives of theft on previous occasions. John was prosecuted and given a referral order by the youth court. The YOT, the police and the sports store were represented on the youth offender panel. Two magistrates participated as community representatives. John attended with his parents. During the panel John talked about his problems with school and bullying, he said he had taken the sports shoes (which were recovered) to try to 'fit in' with other kids.

The panel agreed a programme for John which included a letter of apology to the sports store manager, after-school-only visits to the shopping centre and then accompanied by his parents, 15 hours of community service and a requirement that he attend school. Monitoring quickly showed that John breached the requirements of his programme. His truanting continued but, more seriously, John reacted negatively to the punitive and restrictive elements of the programme.

Now 15, John's truanting and offending have escalated. On his 15th birthday John was arrested for theft (shoplifting) and bailed. One week later his school contacted the police, as he had been found in possession of a knife, and they suspended him. He was arrested for carrying an offensive weapon. John explained that he carried the knife because he had been threatened by other boys and was afraid. He was prosecuted and remanded in custody.

John is on remand in custody now. He was interviewed in custody by the YOT bail support staff who assessed him as unsuitable for the bail support programme due to his previous non-compliance. The YOT staff recorded, however, that John appeared isolated in custody, he had not received any visits from his parents and he reported being bullied and afraid. John was subject to special supervision by custodial staff.

Critical practice could have prevented John's situation. A critical practitioner would never have subjected John to an offending behaviour programme without evaluating John's behaviour in its full context. His school problems should have been dealt with more effectively by the youth offender panel. The YOT worker did raise the non-attendance of school at the panel, but expressed frustration at the way in which the YOT sought only to deal with offending behaviour and did not have working links with other agencies through which, for example, schools could be involved in problem-solving approaches. YOT staff know that bullying is prevalent in schools but schools try to hide this problem in the context of image management, and no anti-bullying programmes exist.

Throughout John's short teenage years, no-one has listened to his story and no-one has attempted to take his problems seriously or do anything constructive to improve John's situation. A lack of critical practice has failed John. Interventions have focused on John's offending and failed to respond to the causes of his behaviour. John has been perceived as a problem and an offender and the system has responded to him accordingly. As a result, John, an average 15-year-old child, sits alone and afraid in prison custody awaiting his fate.

The youth justice system in England and Wales has been completely overhauled by a raft of legislation that has left no area of the system untouched (see generally, Goldson, 2000; Pickford, 2000). The range and extent of these reforms make a detailed, point-by-point, critical analysis beyond the scope of one short chapter (but see, Goldson, 1999; Muncie, 1999a; National Association for Youth Justice, forthcoming). Indeed it would be a mistake to embark on a path of critical practice in a piecemeal and ad hoc manner, as this would subsume critical practice within the boundaries of the government's agenda and critical practice must, at times, step outside these boundaries. What is missing in the 'new youth justice', however, is a coherent and fundamental set of principles from which policy and practice can be both derived and measured. This chapter, therefore, will discuss reform of the youth justice system and develop an approach to critical practice that is grounded in a more coherent, concrete and robust set of principles.

The politics of juvenile crime

Throughout history, no area of public policy has attracted such sustained interest and controversy as crime, and none more so than juvenile crime. In recent times we have become accustomed to the politicisation of juvenile crime, and, all too often, particular juvenile offenders. The politics of juvenile crime, it seems, fuels the rhetoric of governments and political parties as they compete to capture the popular punitiveness of public opinion and electoral success (Pitts, 2000).

Doing something about juvenile crime is a constant feature of national politics. This 'doing something' inevitably leads to policies and calls from government to intervene more seriously and earlier into the lives of young people who have offended – the 'nipping offending in the bud' mantra. One of the most successful practices of recent times, however, has been the growth in diversion from prosecution. The development of the cautioning system and diversion from prosecution was an initiative led by juvenile justice practitioners and, although it was later adopted as Home Office policy in the mid-1980s, its origins and success are firmly located in local initiative and practices.

Critical practice, initiated, developed and extended through local networks of juvenile justice practitioners, has a long and important history. The need for critical practice is paramount. No matter how clever the government thinks it is, no matter how much it believes that it should steer and local agencies should row (Pitts, 2000), no matter how many tactics it seeks to employ to ensure local compliance with central policy, there is an enduring need and capacity for local agents to shape and mould national structures into local practices.

Intervention, intervention, intervention

Although a common-sense view might be that policies towards juveniles who have offended are generally tougher and more punitive under a Conservative than a Labour administration, this has not necessarily been the case in recent decades. It is true that the Conservative administration from 1979 to 1997 ushered in some overtly punitive measures, and it would be quite wrong to attribute the 'Thatcher years' as child friendly (Haines, 1997). In criminal justice terms, however, the Conservative administration quietly sanctioned and gradually adopted most of the practitioner-led developments which resulted, among other things, in a significant growth in diversion from prosecution and a reduction in custodial sentencing (Haines and Drakeford, 1998). These major trends overlaid some other notable practices. During the 1980s and early 1990s, there was no evidence that that system was net-widening (Bottoms et al., 1980) or up-tariffing – intensive community-based supervision was being effectively targeted at the so-called 'heavy-end' young people who would otherwise receive a custodial sentence (Bottoms, 1995). Thus, other lower tariff disposals remained important sentencing options. The conditional discharge, for example, remained a popular sentence of the court and an effective disposal in terms of low reconviction rates (Audit Commission, 1995).

High rates of diversion from prosecution, popular and effective low tariff sentences, properly targeted intensive supervision and low rates of custodial sentencing, plus no evidence of an increase in the amount or seriousness of juvenile crime were, therefore, the characteristics of the juvenile justice system as it operated under the Conservative government prior to the election of the Labour administration in 1997 (Haines and Drakeford, 1998). The type of work with young offenders promoted during this period (Haines, 1996; Haines and Drakeford, 1998) was based on professional knowledge about the effectiveness of different types of interventions, including the potential for inappropriate interventions to have negative short- and long-term consequences.

New Labour and youth justice

While one might expect to find a more interventionist core at the heart of Labour policy, one might also expect this interventionism to reflect a more child-oriented than offender-oriented character (Pitts, 2000). In just over a year after election, the Labour government enacted the Crime and Disorder Act 1998 (following the White Paper *No More Excuses;* Home Office, 1997), ushering in the major elements of its reforms of the juvenile justice system. The very title of the White Paper was to give an important indication of Labour thinking and policy. In his introduction to the White Paper, the Home Secretary said:

> An excuse culture has developed within the youth justice system. It excuses itself for its inefficiency, and too often excuses the young offenders before it, implying that they cannot help their behaviour because of their social circumstances.
>
> (Home Office, 1997: 2)

This statement is significant in a number of important ways. First, it demonstrates the policy of the Labour government to discredit the youth justice system and portray any claims for success in organisational, administrative or professional terms as obfuscations of the underlying realities. Second, this undermining of the 'old youth justice system' represents an attempt to establish a discontinuity with the past, thus creating the opportunity for the Labour Party to fashion the new youth justice in its own image. Thus, the heavy baggage of those who operated the 'old' system did not need to be unpacked and examined, it was simply to be left behind. Lastly, the home secretary's statement indicates that the government was not going to tolerate offending behaviour or those who 'made excuses' for it.

The strength of these anti-child (even if they are offenders) attitudes was both necessary and problematic for the Labour government. Necessary because of the Party's emerging interventionist philosophy and the need to manage the perceptions of the fear of crime, but problematic because of its anti-child sentiments and the contradictions with the broader social inclusion agenda. The contradictions and consequent bifurcation are clear:

> To put it more bluntly, current youth crime policy appears equally committed to preventing the social exclusion of children and young people at risk and increasing the exclusion of those who go on to offend.
>
> (Anderson, 1999: 83)

Such a strategy has precedents in the practices of previous decades (Thorpe et al., 1980). The resultant confusions, caused by competing political objectives, have led to a professional and morally undesirable outcome:

> By drawing the less problematic young people into an extended social control network at an earlier age, Labour has revealed how a logic of 'prevention' and 'risk management' is quite capable of being used to justify any number of repressive and retrograde means of dealing with young people in trouble.
>
> (Muncie, 1999a: 59)

Whatever the contradictions and conflicts, the moral or ethical vicissitudes of the Labour Party, its policy for youth justice is 'held together' by the official objective for the youth justice system of preventing offending by children and young people. While the previous Conservative administration tended to see criminal justice as an area for rhetorical rather than policy achievements, in contrast the Labour government has shown a determination to have its policies put into practice. To this end, it established the Youth Justice Board (YJB) for England and Wales (in September 1998), whose responsibility is to ensure that the policy, philosophy and practices of the new youth justice are implemented speedily and fully. Although, as a quango, the board has few formal powers, it has a considerable amount of money at its disposal to 'pay for' the development of 'desirable' practices in the new YOTs (see, for example, the board's corporate plan; Youth Justice Board, 1999). It also has control of a significant research budget to evaluate the introduction of new practices.

Since its creation in September 1998, the YJB has set about ensuring that the Labour government's policy for youth justice is implemented. Strenuous efforts went into ensuring that local areas established YOTs in the manner envisioned by the YJB. Fervent endeavours have been applied to the development and implementation of new practices in these YOTs. The YJB has made use of every opportunity and mechanism at its disposal to ensure that a new system is created in the image it intends. In short, from its inception to its implementation, the new youth justice is a top-down venture. It is thus important to unpick, a little, this broader context in which youth justice practice is now managed and conducted.

The managerialist approach

The postmodern approach to crime and offenders is centred on the management of insecurity in the present, not the guaranteeing of security or the promise of a better future (see Finer and Nellis, 1998). Are we just to accept this as the inevitability of our modern culture, or do we believe in the capacity of individuals to shape and reinterpret macro social structures in (sometimes different) micro or local practices? It is our capacity to give light to this latter possibility, that drives critical practice.

The framework in which we struggle to manage caseloads on a daily basis, or within which we try to create space for new or fresh thinking, is not normally one of our own making, but it is rather imposed from above. In the area of crime (and crime prevention in particular), Pitts and Hope (1998) have argued that a government policy has been superimposed on criminal justice agencies, which has been characterised by three distinctive concerns:

■ a focus on crime and solving the crime problem

■ a local lead in defining the specifics of the crime problem

■ the interagency approach.

Thus in Britain the aim has been to bring agencies together to focus on and take action against locally identified crime problems. Pitts and Hope (1998) contrast the British model with the distinctively different approach taken in France. In France, the approach was based on: the identification of local problems (that is, not assuming it to be crime per se and not ignoring underlying problems or causes); supporting the mobilisation of communities, including young people, to devise and implement local solutions; and integrating the work of local agencies to support these initiatives (Pitts and Hope, 1998; Bonnemaison, 1983). Following the introduction of these policies, recorded crime in the most deprived areas of Britain was increasing, while in France it declined (Pitts and Hope, 1998).

The French approach was distinctive from the British, therefore, to the extent that it focused on local social problems, broadly defined, as perceived by those living their lives in these localities, and it sought and supported organic responses to mitigate negative practices and promote positive responses. In Britain, however, despite a rhetoric of cooperation and coordination, local actors have found themselves operating within different agencies struggling to compete in an imposed interagency framework which did little to meet the daily work needs of staff and, more seriously, at best only tenuously made any positive impact on the lives of local people, whether they had committed offences or not (Haines, 1996). This brief discussion is important because it highlights the central characteristics of the British government's approach to policy development and implementation. Thus, the establishment of YOTs, the new framework of youth justice, the setting of objectives for the system, the development of administrative/professional tools, and the measurement of performance and so on have not been the product of local discussion, debate and action, but rather have been and continue to be imposed by the government and the YJB in an ongoing and ever-changing manner. The most significant problem that this approach gives rise to is the tendency of YOTs to take, as their primary reference point for the organisation and delivery of services, the national YJB and not those communities which the teams serve.

In practice, of course, there is a continuum between a YJB-focused approach and a community-focused approach, and the development of YOTs across England and Wales ranges across this continuum. While no YOT can operate to the exclusion of the YJB, we can nevertheless characterise two distinct approaches. YJB-focused teams have tended towards what may be termed the 'empire building' model in which the YOT has sought to draw in resources and carry out its work directly. More community-oriented teams, by contrast, have tended to seek partnerships and build relationships with other parts of the local authority and other agencies and community organisations and so on, and mobilise the resources and so on of these partners to deliver services.

Critical practice, therefore, begins from an understanding of the institutional context of youth justice and the implications of the choices that are made within this broader context. There are important connections between structural and organisational factors and the services that YOTs provide and, perhaps more importantly, the manner in which these services are provided. Processing a child through a final warning, recommending a referral order and running a youth offender panel, completing an ASSET assessment and supervising a child following a period in custody can be undertaken with different objectives. A team can pursue these activities because they comprise government policy, legislative requirements or because they are prescribed by national standards, or these activities can be conducted to promote the best interests of the child in a manner consistent with professional knowledge and objectives. These differing approaches are in tension and it is essential that practitioners understand these tensions and are clear about their objectives in planning and undertaking interventions.

The criminology literature is redolent with publications exploring and explaining the vicissitudes of managerialism (Brownlee, 1998; Feeley and Simon, 1992; Haines, 1996, 1997; McWilliams, 1992; Peters, 1986; Vanstone, 1995) and the pursuit of policy objectives through increasingly intrusive administrative control measures. Ranged against this is professional knowledge which often appears weaker or less certain, but in reality is simply more complex, as it deals with the real lives of real people and not simply organisational processes. In modern criminal justice systems, therefore, critical practice is rooted inevitably in professionalism.

Reconnecting with the past

Critical practice also begins with what we know. We have already noted how a central characteristic of the Labour government and YJB's strategy for implementing the new youth justice discredited previous practice and the professional knowledge that supported it, in order to disconnect the new (managerialist, administrative, policy-driven) future from the old (professionally based) past. Critical practice, therefore, must take as an important starting point an appreciation of what we do know about young people and the effectiveness of interventions and reconnect this knowledge with current practice.

The period from the early 1980s through to the late 1990s was, for youth justice in England and Wales, one of the most successful periods of criminal justice practice – in contrast to the pessimism of 'nothing works', repeated moral panics and a widespread culture of failure in criminal justice policy and practice. Cautioning was widely recognised as a success in both policy and practice terms, and it also worked for the approximately 80 per cent of young people who never came before the courts again. The conditional discharge was a successful and popular disposal (Audit Commission, 1996). Supervision packages enjoyed the confidence of the courts and were effectively targeted at those young people who would otherwise have ended up in custody. Nationally, diversion rates peaked at over 90 per cent for the youngest age group, and the proportionate use of custody declined dramatically. All of this took place during a period when there was no evidence of any increase in crimes committed by young people.

There were, of course, some problems which remained during this period. Bail support practices were significantly underdeveloped and the remand population of young people remained high. Similarly, information systems were not sufficiently well developed or widespread and consequently youth justice teams could not always fully demonstrate the effectiveness of their work. Perhaps paradoxically, the YJB has targeted these two deficiencies in particular for improvement, while simultaneously seeking to discredit and radically change practices in those areas where justifiable successes can be claimed. Lack of space precludes a full discussion of the achievements of youth justice teams and the professional knowledge that underpinned them (see, Haines and Drakeford, 1998; Muncie, 1999a), but this knowledge and these achievements must be reclaimed and reasserted in 'youth offending' practice. Such a call is not an anti-government statement, but a recognition that there are times when professional knowledge supersedes government policy and that to act professionally is not always the same as compliance with administrative requirements. How and when can we make the decision about when it is appropriate to act in such a manner? In part this decision is based upon the accumulated knowledge of what works in working with young people. Intervention must be based on solid, grounded, professional practice knowledge. But there is also a higher calling, and to this we must turn.

Fundamental principles for positive critical practice

Any attempt at an international comparison of youth justice practices will demonstrate the differences between systems across countries (Mehlbye and Walgrave, 1998). In the modern world, however, countries no longer operate solely within the boundaries of the nation state, but increasingly there is an international context which structures the behaviour of all countries. International texts concerning the special treatment that should be afforded to children, including juvenile offenders, have been developing over the last 100 years or so.

The Geneva Declaration of the Rights of the Child (1924) stated that particular care must be extended to children. This sentiment has been echoed in a range of international conventions (see, for example, Haines, 2000). The United Nations Standard Minimum Rules for the Administration of Juvenile Justice (the Beijing Rules, 1985) state that as a fundamental principle, the aim of the juvenile justice system should be the promotion of the well-being of the juvenile and that criminal proceedings (of any kind) should be conducted in the best interests of the juvenile. The Beijing Rules are not binding in domestic law, but the United Nations Convention on the Rights of the Child (1989) is legally binding on countries which have signed the declaration, and it includes the important statement, in article 3, that:

> In all actions concerning children, whether undertaken by public or private social welfare institutions, courts of law, administrative authorities or legislative bodies, the best interests of the child shall be a primary consideration.

In this instance, the definition of child is any young person under the age of 18 years (and the Convention makes no allowance for different considerations to be made in respect of some children who may be labelled as, for example, offenders – all children are to be treated according to the same principle). The definition of 'a primary' (as it appears in article 3 of the English version of the Convention) is intended to be 'the paramount' or most important consideration (as appears in article 21). These international conventions, therefore, firmly establish the principle that any action taken as a result of an offence committed by a juvenile must be in the best interests of the child.

Providing a universal definition of 'best interests' is, of course, no simple matter and deciding whether a particular action is in the best interests of the child is complex. However, the Convention itself provides some further guidance in these matters. For example, children have the right to education of a positive nature, to give their views and have their views listened to, not to be separated from their parents (unless it is in the child's best interests) or to have access to their parents where forced separation occurs, to leisure time and recreational activities, and to be protected from maltreatment, hazardous forms of employment (including that which interferes with school or play) and other forms of exploitation. These provisions have been established to give special recognition to the status of childhood and in particular the notion that childhood is a period of transition before adulthood and the nature of these transitions must be understood and acted upon (see Coles, 1995).

In thinking about work with young offenders, therefore, we must start from thinking about youth and about linking interventions with young people in difficulty into the range of provisions or activities that exists for all young people. In other words, international conventions establish the principle that interventions with young people, including those who have committed an offence, should be based on the premise of 'normalisation'. Thus, normalisation is a fundamental principle upon which all interventions with young offenders should be based and, in fact, this means reversing the trend of criminal justice interventions that have been recently developed in youth justice and probation.

In England and Wales, in recent years, the thrust of developments in offender interventions has been towards the development of ever more specialist, targeted and focused programmes. This trend is exemplified most strongly in the probation service, which, under particular pressure from the Home Office, has concentrated on 'evidence-based practice' (Hope and Chapman, 1998), cognitive programmes (McGuire, 2000) and accreditation for staff to conduct such activities, but similar developments are characteristic of youth justice also. In this manner staff are trained and programmes of intervention are developed which draw offenders away from the community and into closed, intensive, 'offender-oriented' and offence-focused activities. Even where the 'community' may be involved in such activities, as may be the case, for example, in young offender panels, it is not the offender or the young person that is inserted in the community, but representatives of the community are drawn into the closed programme.

Evidence from Massachusetts (Coates, 1981) has shown the value, in terms of reduced levels of reoffending, of programmes which are 'community linked', but the principle of normalisation urges us to go further. A fully operational normalised programme of interventions would eschew the provision of specialist activities for offenders. Instead, intervention would be based on (re)inserting young people into the full range of social and educational provision that exists for youth in general. This approach is no less specialist or challenging, but it requires a changed focus of intervention, away from intervening in the lives of young people and towards intervening in the mechanisms which link young people into social and educational services.

Such an approach is predicated on the exclusion experienced by many young people in trouble with the law. For example, local monitoring in Swansea (Haines et al., 1999) has shown that between 70 and 80 per cent of all young people made subject to criminal supervision orders were not engaged in meaningful daytime activities. For those receiving custodial sentences, the figure was in excess of 90 per cent. A survey of first time offenders indicated that over 20 per cent of the young people were either absent or excluded from school. Over half the young people, or their family, were in receipt of services from the social services department. It was also clear that the costs of exclusion continued into life after school, with higher numbers of young people who were disaffected and disengaged from education, training and employment involved in chaotic use of drugs and alcohol and lengthier patterns of involvement in offending behaviour.

A normalised strategy of interventions, therefore, is based on the promotion of social inclusion. The promotion of social inclusion is, in fact, an explicit policy of the current government, but, as this chapter has shown, it is difficult to visualise the principles or practices of social inclusion in the methods of intervention promoted by the government and the YJB. Youth justice policy has become increasingly politicised, which has not only led to vacillations in policy directions and the exploitation of youth for political advantage, but to the development of an approach to working with young people in difficulty which reduces social inclusion and promotes social exclusion. This is a strategy which the research evidence suggests is not only likely to promote further deviance and reduce the chances for young people to develop a positive life course, it is also contrary to the principles of international conventions. Before concluding this chapter, therefore, it is necessary to revise the key concepts, enshrined in international conventions, that shape critical practice in youth justice.

■ Interventions should be in the best interests of the child

■ Offence- or offender-focused programmes should be avoided

■ Work with young people (including those who have offended) should be based on the accumulated knowledge and experience gained through practice

■ Practice should be guided by the principle of normalisation and the promotion of social inclusion

■ Normalised and inclusive practice is characterised by: justice (not only in a formal legal sense, but according to the principles of natural justice); participation (of young people in the full range of social and educational provision for youth); and engagement (giving expression to the right of young people to make their own choices and decisions and to be fully involved in all matters concerning them).

CONCLUSION

This chapter has not focused on the details of interventions with young offenders or the range of new measures and changes to the youth justice system introduced by the current Labour government. The proliferation of new measures and so on renders such an approach beyond description and would also obviate the articulation of an alternative practice based on a critical approach, which has been the central objective here. Instead, this chapter has focused on an understanding of the dynamics of youth justice and the principles of intervention from which and upon which critical practice can be built and measured.

The central theme of this chapter has been that critical practice is based upon the accumulated professional knowledge about the effectiveness of approaches and methods of working with young people. It has been argued, further, that this knowledge must be placed in the context of international conventions concerning the treatment of young people and the principles set forth in these documents. Therefore the challenge for youth justice, as the full implementation of YOTs progresses, is not to find ways of meeting targets for the development of new measures, but to develop these new measures in a manner which protects and promotes the best interests of the child.

FURTHER READING

Goldson, B. (2000) *The New Youth Justice*, Lyme Regis: Russell House Publishing. A comprehensive and critical review of New Labour's youth justice and youth crime strategy.

Haines, K. and Drakeford, M. (1998) *Young People and Youth Justice*, Basingstoke: Macmillan — now Palgrave Macmillan. A critical appraisal of pre-youth offending team youth justice practice that repackages effective practices in a 'children first' approach.

Muncie, J. (1999) *Youth and Crime: A Critical Introduction*, London: Sage. Places the behaviour of youth in its social context and criticises approaches to youth criminality that do not take account of such factors.

Pickford, J. (ed.) (2000) *Youth Justice: Theory and Practice*, London: Cavendish. An edited collection of essays by academics, practitioners and magistrates exploring the theoretical and practice implications of the Crime and Disorder Act 1998 and the Youth Justice and Criminal Evidence Act 1999.

CHAPTER 15

Community Work

Keith Popple

CASE EXAMPLE

Parkwood is a housing estate some three miles from the centre of a declining industrial city in the English midlands. Built in the 1970s and comprising mainly council and social housing, the estate suffers from the neglect often seen in such areas, including above average levels of unemployment, crime, poor health, underachievement and minimal social provision. The local population is predominantly white, however there is a small but significant Asian community.

The local authority has established a community work project in Parkwood, under the auspices of the housing department. Two community workers, Ali and Henry, have been employed to work with residents, with the aim of involving them in tackling some of the neighbourhood problems. The workers operate from the refurbished church hall, part of which is designated as a neighbourhood advice and information centre. The community work project is advised by a management group comprising local professionals, including a social worker, a youth worker, a health visitor, the community police officer, a local councillor and a member of the Parkwood women's group.

Ali is annoyed at the concerns raised in a letter from a senior housing department official, Mr Daniel, who has criticised the project, stating that future funding is in jeopardy unless they adhere to their original brief of liaising with local community

---

CASE EXAMPLE cont'd

members and offering welfare rights advice. He warns them to refrain from encouraging local residents to take action on housing issues, as he sees this as outside their remit. Furthermore, Mr Daniel states that Ali and Henry are in danger of breaching the terms of their contract because people living in other parts of the city, having obtained a copy of their last newsletter, have started complaining to the local authority about similar issues in their neighbourhoods. He also complains that they did not adjourn a recent meeting when residents from a neighbouring estate attended seeking advice and support for their own petition to the housing department. The community workers are now considering their response. Their discussions encapsulate the classic problems for critical community work practice.

Introduction

The above scenario is not untypical of a dilemma that can confront community workers daily. A central issue that community workers constantly have to address is that of power relationships, as much of their activity is directly concerned with the political structure. For example, as in our scenario, community workers can be employed by the organisations whose policies they are enabling the residents to challenge. In the Parkwood scenario the community workers are faced with a dilemma which we will explore further throughout the chapter.

The central focus of the chapter is to consider what community work is and some of the dilemmas inherent in its practice. A helpful method for undertaking this is to consider the antecedents of community work. However, we begin with discussing the difficulties of defining community work and the term 'community'.

We will see that community work has evolved from the competing demands and contradictions inherent in a stratified society where considerable economic power and social prestige are located in discrete and defined areas. This has produced social divisions of inequality, the dynamic of which is frequently played out in community and neighbourhood life. This has produced dilemmas for community workers, which will be explored in the Parkwood scenario.

Defining community work and community

One of the problems facing community work is that it has no single definition and is frequently considered simply as a form of welfare work. For example, a wide range of activities, such as visiting housebound and older people, working in economically and socially deprived housing neighbourhoods (as in Parkwood), and intervening with young offenders, have all been described as community work. Because it encompasses such a wide area of work, 'community work' can be considered an umbrella term.

It has been argued, therefore, that the term 'community work practice' is imprecise and unclear. It can be almost everything (or anything) to everyone. For example, practitioners have been accused of lacking direction and certainty about their role (Thomas, 1983; Twelvetrees, 1991). Some of the questions frequently posed are; do community workers work *for* or *against* the local authority? Can/should community workers tread a middle path while maintaining both their professional standing and street credibility? As a significant amount of community work operates on short-term funding, can it therefore be considered as little more than experimental? These dilemmas are not clarified by much of the community work literature, particularly that derived from projects, which is often considered to be both descriptive and anecdotal. However, paradoxically, it can be argued that the experimental and creative approach of community work is its strength.

The view that the term 'community work practice' is imprecise and unclear is compounded by the numerous definitions used to analyse the concept of community. For example, Hillery (1955) found that there were 98 definitions of the term and the only thing that sociologists agreed on was that community had something to do with people! Sociologists appear therefore, to have problems agreeing a frame of reference, although Williams (1976: 66) claims that the term is nearly always used positively. Perhaps one of the most helpful contributions is that offered by Newby (1980), who defined community in three ways. First, as a social system (a set of social relationships), second, as a fixed locality (a geographical area) and third, as the quality of relationships (a spirit of community). These aspects of community are interrelated, although Newby claims that they are distinct, and evidence of one does not guarantee the presence of the others. For example, we cannot take for granted that people living in Parkwood automatically enjoy a warm spirit of community.

Similarly, although it can be claimed that 'community work' is an umbrella term, there have been many attempts to explain why and how it operates as it does, and to identify the models used. So, although 'community work' is an umbrella term or concept, it does have clear, albeit contested, boundaries and target groups, and it is informed by a range of disciplines that clearly place the activity in the education and welfare fields. Furthermore, definitions of community work have been devised by practitioners as well as academics and adopted by a range of organisations including the Association of Community Workers (ACW), the Association of Metropolitan Authorities (AMA), the Standing Conference for Community Development (SCCD), and the Federation of Community Work Training Groups (FCWTG).

The AMA (1993) has defined community work as being concerned

> with enabling people to improve the quality of their lives and gain greater influences over the processes that affect them.
>
> (AMA, 1993: 10)

Therefore we can see that, although the scope and nature of community work practice is large, diverse and dynamic, there have been attempts to describe and understand the activity. Furthermore, it has a delineated history, enjoyed considerable state funding and there is an accepted body of theories, methods and models used by practitioners (Popple, 1995).

Let us return to our community workers, Ali and Henry, who are struggling with the dilemma in which they find themselves. Ali proposes going along with the housing officer and abandoning ongoing work to raise the consciousness of the local residents. If the community workers take this stance, however, they are in danger of being identified with the policies of the local authority with which the residents have a number of arguments, rather than aligning themselves with the residents and their demands. Henry argues that Ali's view is too simplistic and claims there is no single solution to the problem. He points to the fact that they need to take into consideration their relationships with other professionals, particularly those on the management group, and the project's volunteers and the residents themselves. All these groups have a stake in the project and a right to influence its direction. If Ali and Henry do nothing, the situation may deteriorate rapidly and the housing department may close the project.

Ali and Henry face issues which commonly arise in community work practice and which cannot be isolated from various contexts, one of the most important being the rich history of community work. By examining the traditions of community work, we are able to understand its place in contemporary society and how it reflects the structural inequalities which determine the challenges for practitioners. Ali and Henry can inform their practice by a critical understanding of the lessons from history. For example, the community work project that employs Ali and Henry has been established within a framework that is designed to 'rescue' marginalised and disaffected sections of society. This approach has a long tradition in the UK and it could be argued that, in this situation, community work is acting as a 'buffer against disaffection, enhancing the weaker facets of social democracy and justifying the individualisation of poverty' (Popple and Redmond, 2000: 396).

Traditions of community work

Social inequality appears to be an ever-present feature of our society and in current times we have seen the rich gain while the poor continue to suffer. Historically and contemporarily, this dynamic has produced tensions in Britain that have led to those in powerful positions making (often calculated) concessions to less powerful groups, while introducing policies and structures to protect and extend their own interests and status. At the same time, less powerful groups and communities, frustrated by their own particular position or a specific issue that adversely affects them or wanting to safeguard their own situation, have collectively organised to protect themselves and attempt to secure an improved position. As community or neighbourhood is a central feature in people's lives, it is not surprising to note that it is here that the consequent dynamic of social inequality is frequently observed. As we have seen, community work can be a constituent of neighbourhood/community life and is therefore an element of this dynamic.

Top-down community work

One theme played out in community work practice reflects a major concern of Britain's ruling elite to incorporate and integrate groups into the dominant ideology in order to ensure its own security and sustainability. Within this concern, there has been an interest to rescue the 'deserving' poor and punish and reform those considered 'undeserving'.

The early settlement movement, which was overlaid with Christian and moral values, reflected these concerns and was a forerunner of community work. Unlike the work of the Charity Organisation Society (COS), which centred on an individual casework approach, pioneers of the settlement movement (established in 1894) argued that it was necessary for those who gave charity to become more familiar with the reasons for people's poverty. As well as observing and attempting to analyse people's experiences, the concerned bodies, usually linked to the Anglican Church and universities, established centres (that is, settlements) in poor neighbourhoods and offered educational and recreational opportunities for local communities (Parry and Parry, 1979). Although predating modern community work, the settlements had elements that resonate with contemporary practice, in particular attempting to enhance the social health of the locality in which they were situated and encouraging the development of responsible leadership. While intervention in working-class areas could be considered a response to growing social unrest (Jones, 1976), settlements were in essence an example of benevolent paternalism by socially concerned philanthropists.

In more recent times, local and central government has replaced the Church, universities and individual bourgeois philanthropists as the key actors in regenerating urban areas. In the UK, 'the inner city' has become synonymous with crime, unemployment, poor health, poverty, social dislocation and inadequate services and shopping facilities. In response, central government and local authorities have sought to implement methods aimed at tackling the resultant problems and claiming to reverse the experiences of inner-city areas. The urban programme, established by the Labour government in 1968 and administered locally, attempted to involve local people in taking greater responsibility for their neighbourhoods. The purpose has been to address social ills without spending the vast sums of public money needed to rebalance a society where poverty and social exclusion are a direct result of the pursuit and maintenance of profit and wealth. The types of project that have been established include tenants and residents associations, locally based and run cooperatives, parent and young children groups, youth projects and summer playschemes. At the same time, successive governments have sought to economically regenerate urban areas and encourage the industrial, service and retail sectors to locate and invest in the inner city.

So, a major theme of government-funded community work has been to integrate individuals and groups into mainstream society and make services and resources more sensitive to their needs, usually by involving people in the running and organisation of the projects. Parkwood, for example, is typical of areas targeted by local authorities that are concerned with what is now termed 'social exclusion'. However, as we have seen, the interventions and actions by the community workers with, and on behalf of, the residents may lead to consequences that the local authority would prefer to avoid. Top-down community work approaches are hampered by the overall need to maintain the status quo. At its core, however, critical community work practice has values of social justice and innovation, which often produce challenging approaches to local problems. This frequently sits uncomfortably with the philosophy and responsibility of local authorities, whose duties are broader than the perceived needs of one neighbourhood.

Voluntary organisations have played a major role in delivering services, employing community workers and establishing projects in deprived neighbourhoods. While there has been an element of 'doing something to' a neighbourhood, critical community workers have been keen to emphasise the democratic nature of their work. Evidence indicates that these workers recognise the state's desire to fund projects that incorporate and dissolve social dislocation, while supporting attempts to encourage people to manage their own communities. At the same time, community workers recognise that their practice occupies a unique position in civil society, where they can connect with people's individual experiences of poverty and marginalisation and offer a critique which provides an explanation of, and connection with, the structural (Jacobs and Popple, 1994; Ledwith, 1997; Lees and Mayo, 1984).

Bottom-up community work

The other major theme in community work has often been described as pressure from below, or collective community action. Historically, this can be traced back to resistance by groups to the dominant ideology and there have been a number of documented struggles within working-class communities, which attempt to secure improvements in their life chances.

One of the earliest recorded forms of community action was in the city of Glasgow. During the early part of the twentieth century, there were a number of struggles in the city against the Munitions of War Act 1915 and for the campaign demanding a 40-hour working week. In 1915 both working-class and lower-middle-class communities demonstrated against increases in rents and the lack of attention to slum housing. Thousands of Glasgow tenants were involved in a rent strike and protests spread to other British cities, leading to rent strikes and calls for lower rents and improved housing (Damer, 1980). Clydeside employers supported the workers' struggle because the higher rents were creating an unsettled workforce and deterring labour from moving to the area. The outcome was the Rent and Mortgage Interest (Rent Restriction) Act 1915 which restricted rent and mortgage interest rates (Melling, 1980). Working-class collective action was also prevalent in the 1920s and 30s with the growth of the national unemployed workers' movement (Hannington, 1967, 1977). Craig (1989) argues that this was the first attempt to link struggles in the home with those in the workplace. There is some evidence to support this, although Bagguley (1991: 108) reveals that women were marginalised by the dominance of men in the organisation of the movement.

In more recent times, examples of community action have been varied and include the squatting movement, the welfare rights movement and different forms of resistance against planning and redevelopment. In the past two decades, protests against the nuclear bomb, in particular the action by the women's peace movement at Greenham Common (Cook and Kirk, 1983; Finch, 1986; Harford and Hopkins, 1984) and widespread objection to the poll tax, introduced by the

Conservative government in the 1980s, have seen the mobilisation and action by many thousands of people (Hoggett and Burns, 1992).

However, most collective community action is relatively small-scale local attempts to negotiate with power holders over what is often a single issue. A significant text in this area is that by Jacobs (1976), in which he describes how residents in a housing clearance area in Glasgow organised themselves, with the help of outside community activists, into an organisation to protect their interests. This well-documented account argues that it is possible for community action successfully to take on local authority housing departments. One suggestion that could be made to Ali and Henry in our Parkwood scenario, therefore, is for them to reflect on the lessons that Jacobs draws from residents' experiences with their local authority housing department in Glasgow. It is possible that our two community workers may not lose their funding and will be able to continue facilitating the concerns of local residents in order to improve their estate. However, if the local authority do close the project, it could lead to a bitter struggle where local people are more forceful in their approach.

The role of women has been central in the majority of community actions and reflects the different experience of community for men and women (Dominelli, 1990). Cornell (1984) has argued that women appear more active in community life and occupy a greater range of communal spaces than men do. For example, whereas many men usually derive a sense of community from the local pub, women have a wider network including schools, shops and neighbours. The fact that women are key actors in informal community networks has led to the observation by Bornat et al. (1993) that it is women

> who are at the front line of negotiations over nurseries, schools, housing, health and other welfare agencies. Not surprisingly, then, women have also been central in community based actions to organise, defend or protest about such services.
>
> (Bornat et al., 1993: 383)

Returning to our Parkwood scenario, we note that a member of the community work management group was drawn from the local women's group. Her contribution to the debate over the threatened removal of funding is likely to be crucial. With children and young people needing facilities for constructive leisure time activity, the women's group representative is likely to articulate forcefully their concerns. Removal of funding from the project would threaten the drive to improve and increase facilities for all Parkwood's residents. At the same time, the community police officer, who will have first-hand experience of young people's 'antisocial' behaviour, is likely to advocate for the continuance of the project and the efforts of Ali and Henry.

Similarly, minority ethnic communities have used community work both to confront racism and discrimination and to forge alliances to protect and support cultural, religious and national groups. In Parkwood, the small Asian community could be considered to be socially excluded and therefore in need of intervention to enable them to integrate more fully into local life. The removal of financial support for the Parkwood community work project could result in their continued isolation.

In summary, we have seen that community work has evolved through, and continues to reflect, two major contradictory and distinct traditions inherent in British society. One is the top-down approach, which was a central aspect of the early settlement movement, and later the initiatives in urban areas, including the work of the present Labour government's Social Exclusion Unit. The other theme has been the bottom-up community action approach which has tended to be single-issue, locally focused attempts by groups to achieve change in policy and practice. With this understanding and the application to the present issues facing community work, and the dilemmas facing our two community workers, we move to consider the role of the community worker.

The role of the community worker

The tensions inherent in community work, which are reflected in the activity's traditions, have posed problems for practitioners employed by agencies based on the top-down approach. Most community workers are employed in the public sector, either by local authorities or the voluntary sector, which receives public finance. Increasingly, these agencies are required by funders to meet specific objectives, and those who do not meet these place themselves in a vulnerable position where their funding can be terminated or reduced. This can create difficulties for practitioners who experience a dilemma in terms of their personal goals, including ideas to be involved in change, and those of the agency that is required to meet performance targets. However, the role of the community worker reflects both the unique position that community work occupies and the resultant challenges for its practitioners.

As we noted in our consideration of the definitions of community work, the role of the practitioner is a complex one. Gilchrist (1994), for example, has identified five main roles: organiser, advocate, challenger, developer and supporter. However, if the community worker is based in a small organisation, he or she may have further tasks including fund raising and employing and managing workers.

We must remember that community work is about working with people in ways to encourage and empower them to do things for themselves. Therefore, the role of the worker centres on helping people to learn new skills, build self-confidence and develop talents and abilities. A good deal of community work focuses on gaining and disseminating information that can be applied by the neighbourhood or community. Usually this material is concerned with welfare and housing benefits. However, this may include strategic information, for example about local authority plans for the area. Hence, community work has often been associated with the slogan 'information is power'. With adequate and appropriate information, communities can make informed decisions and take action.

Returning to our scenario, one community work strategy that Ali and Henry can employ is to inform the Parkwood residents of the threat to remove the project's funding. With this information, the residents can then decide on their position. It may be that the threat is real and the housing department does want to silence the Parkwood community and neighbouring residents. If so, the Parkwood and nearby residents will have a view on this. However, there may be voluntary organisations with funding from other sources, including organisations with a national profile, who are prepared to situate a project in Parkwood and take a more challenging role.

So we can see that Ali and Henry have options. Like all community workers they have to juggle a series of demands and expectations. Their employers have one view, their management group another, the residents and volunteers yet another, and of course Ali and Henry have a position too. The key for community workers is to be certain of where they stand on issues, and to be clear from the outset how their role is to be defined and by whom. Finally, everyone, including their employers, needs to be cognisant of the sort of activities that community workers can engage in and what is off limits. Working as a community worker for a local authority has many advantages, such as appropriate 'core' funding and a certain security of position. However, community workers, like all employees, are accountable to their employers for their work. While Mr Daniel has a responsibility to ensure that Ali and Henry do not overstep the mark, he would be advised to consider engaging with the management group which can provide the workers with support and advice. This way it may have been possible to deal more effectively with the problems facing our two community workers.

CONCLUSION

Critical community work practice demands an awareness of the traditions of community work, including an understanding of the links with economic and political themes and structures that constitute contemporary society. Critical community work practice is concerned crucially with issues of powerlessness and disadvantage, and attempts to involve people in the process of social change. We have seen that critical community work practice is a process based on the sharing of knowledge, skills and experience. Therefore, it has an important role to play in enhancing and fostering a more democratic and just society. However, as we have noted from our scenario, this is not without problems. Organisations such as local authorities can feel threatened by the activity of community workers and communities that challenge its work. Critical community work practice is not easy, but it can have significant rewards for its participants and their neighbourhoods.

FURTHER READING

Dominelli, L. (1990) *Women and Community Action*, Birmingham: Venture Press. Explores issues of gender, race and class in community work and community action.

Freire, P. (1990) *Pedagogy of the Oppressed*, 3rd edn, Harmondsworth: Penguin. A powerful, classic account of the origins and use of informal 'liberating' education to challenge inequality and oppression.

Jacobs, S. and Popple, K. (eds) (1994) *Community Work in the 1990s*, Nottingham: Spokesman. An edited text that provides readers with critical accounts of the challenges facing community work after the Thatcher years.

Ledwith, M. (1997) *Participating in Transformation: Towards a Working Model of Community Empowerment*, Birmingham: Venture Press. Addresses issues of injustices and inequality central to the practice of community work.

Popple, K. (1995) *Analysing Community Work: Its Theory and Practice*, Milton Keynes: Open University Press. A key textbook that clearly sets out models and perspectives and draws attention to the interaction of community work theory and practice.

Twelvetrees, A. (2001) *Community Work*, 3rd edn, Basingstoke: Palgrave – now Palgrave Macmillan. Now in its third edition, this is a good introductory text for both students and practitioners of community work.

Care Management

16

Margaret Lloyd

Care management was formally introduced as the model for the delivery of health and social care services in the UK in 1993. It had been officially enshrined in policy in the 1989 White Paper, *Caring for People* (Department of Health, 1989a), which, together with its sister paper *Caring for Patients* (Department of Health, 1989b), provided the blueprint for the sweeping changes in the care of adults which have taken place throughout the 1990s. The National Health Service and Community Care Act 1990, codifying as it does changes in philosophy and political context as well as procedure and practice, is truly a watershed piece of legislation which has had a marked impact on the professions engaged in delivering health and social care services. None has been more affected than social work, the traditional deliverer of social care in the community; whose practitioners are employed in large numbers in those social services departments to which Griffiths (1988) gave the lead. This chapter examines the impact of care management on social work practice, connecting the tensions and dilemmas experienced by frontline practitioners and managers with analysis of the fundamental challenges to welfare services posed in the late twentieth century. Through close attention to the process of service delivery to the user, we shall explore a way forward for creative, 'best value' care management practice.

Social workers or care managers?

The complaint, 'We're not social workers anymore, we're just care managers', is commonly to be heard among practitioners.

CASE EXAMPLE

The case of Mrs Grant provides a typical example. She is an 85-year-old widow whose nearest relative lives 200 miles away. She lives alone in the house she has owned for 40 years and has been extremely socially isolated since her neighbour died a year ago. Following a fall at home she was admitted to hospital and has recently been discharged to an acute rehabilitation unit. Prior to the fall, she had a low-level care package and reasonable mobility. However, she has sustained shoulder and leg injuries which currently make her unable to stand and in need of a wheelchair and hoist. The pressure on the social worker in the multidisciplinary team is to free up her place in the rehabilitation unit as quickly as possible. Mrs Grant is determined to return home. Combining information from the medical assessment with review of the available services, the social worker considers that Mrs Grant could be discharged home if she were provided with a pendant alarm linked to 24-hour warden cover, an electric wheelchair (for which there is a 6-month waiting list) and increased home and daycare.

Underlying this case is the question of whether a social worker needs to be there at all. What are the knowledge base and skills required in organising a package of practical support services? There has been much comment on the deprofessionalising influences in the community care 'reforms' and the overriding of professional judgement by bureaucratic procedure (for example, Cochrane, 1993; Sheppard, 1995a; Clark, 1996; Lewis, 1996; Cowen, 1999). The claim that the reforms were driven by managerial rather than professional processes is a view shared by many commentators (for example, James, 1994; Sheppard, 1995a; Cowen, 1999). Lewis and Glennerster's study of implementation found some senior managers enthusiastically embracing the reforms, interpreting this enthusiasm as stemming from the new status afforded to them as developers and managers of locality information systems and plans. They found some frontline staff believing these new-style managers to be antipathetic to social work, with widespread agreement that the social work task was being redefined (Lewis and Glennerster, 1996).

Quite apart from the fact that there were other, including global, deprofessionalising influences (Foster and Wilding, 2000), to plunge into the debate at this point passes over the straightforward fact that what the new world of service delivery did was to *formally* blur professional roles and 'professionalise' new jobs. The 'old world' had been split between the established professions and care workers who undertook more practically oriented tasks deemed to require neither expert knowledge nor the exercise of professional judgement. Wilding's analysis (1982) demonstrates how the defence of separate professional territories had led to the organisation of separate services around the separate professions and their delineated skills. The new scenario resembled more of a job fair, with a world of 'workers', some of them with new labels, milling around newly configured tasks. At the heart of this mêlée was the question mark which was placed at the outset over who should be a care manager (Department of Health, 1989a). McDonald (1998) points out that while official guidance addresses the roles and responsibilities of the social services department, it never addresses what the job of the social worker was intended to be.

In an SSI overview, Welch confirms that most authorities have built care management onto a social work culture rather than a home care culture (Welch, 1998). He implies that this may have something to do with the problem of volume that has beset most care managers, and suggests that it is crucial that this 'professional variant' of care management be used only where it adds value that can be evaluated in a definable outcome. This angle has been crying out for further development and analysis ever since Challis (1994a) argued that intensive care management should be reserved for a relatively few complex cases, with the majority being held within a care management *system*, but not individually intensively care managed. There is more to this than the important questions of screening and targeting. There is also the neglected issue of defining *what the added value of the social work professional is*, and demonstrating when, where and how it should be incorporated into the overall care management process.

The early literature on care management was preoccupied with the search for a model, in the course of which some opposing approaches were identified (for example, Beardshaw and Towell, 1990; Biggs and Weistein, 1991; Huxley, 1993). If we consider these in the context of the history of British welfare services, the structure of social services departments and the tradition of social work – all of which have a bearing on the genesis of care management in the UK – the tensions which emerged seem almost predetermined. It is not hard to see how severe resource constraints might push social services departments towards a bureaucratic, administrative approach which separates the core elements for the purposes of budgetary planning and the monitoring of outcomes. This is clearly at odds with the social work tradition which cherishes the professional relationship and feels comfortable with a casework approach. Canadian advocacy and brokerage approaches were imported uneasily into a work context dominated by the two giants of health and social services. Fundamental changes in thinking and a rapid expansion of the options in health and social care services were going to be necessary if the exciting possibilities contained in the radical empowerment and entrepreneurial approaches were to be realised. Yet each of the approaches contains elements which critical practice applauds: accountability to outcomes, maintaining human continuity, creating choice for service users and facilitating individuals to identify and pursue their own 'best deals'.

Issues and dilemmas for the practitioner

What does the frontline practitioner or manager engaged in implementing care management make of this confusion, and is the search for a model of any real significance or value for those just 'doing the job'? In summary, a number of tensions and dilemmas have been experienced by social workers and their managers in adult services in the implementation of care management:

- How to negotiate user choice and creative responses to need in a resource constrained environment

- How to maintain the therapeutic elements of the professional relationship in a service delivery culture of measurable outcomes, weighed down by bureaucratic procedure

- How to provide continuity and attend to longer term processes in a system which appears to disrupt the dynamic interplay between assessment and intervention which social work has carefully nurtured.

There are no easy or complete answers to these questions.

CASE EXAMPLE revisited

Mrs Grant's case illustrates all three dilemmas. The medical opinion is that she will not regain her previous mobility and will need to use a wheelchair permanently. If she waits for a wheelchair to be provided she will either have to go into supported accommodation temporarily or return home to a situation where she is highly dependent on the home care support and severely restricted in her activities outside carer visits. There is not much flexibility in the formal service provision systems, for example there is no negotiation of the wheelchair waiting list around priority criteria or avoidance of more costly alternative care. Even once provided with a wheelchair, Mrs Grant will have to wait 12 months for a ramp to be built to gain access to the house. The care provided in the rehabilitation unit is designated 'acute', with the requirement to transfer to another setting and different professionals at the end of a six-week period.

The only easily measurable outcomes at this point, on the information currently collected by the health authority and social services department, are the length of time Mrs Grant remains in the acute unit and whether she returns home or enters residential or nursing home care. For the social worker to negotiate with Mrs Grant around accepting her reduced capacity and managing the risks in her situation, she needs time to build a relationship and for Mrs Grant to adjust to her changed situation. The assessment, to be accurate and user-centred, needs to take account of Mrs Grant's personality, how she was functioning before the fall, the impact of the crisis hospital admission, her willingness to engage with the rehabilitation unit and her feelings about the future. Yet there is no one worker who will have developed this dynamic assessment throughout the intervention.

Before considering some guidelines for a constructive way forward, it is worth 'taking stock' of the adult services scenario. Three factors should significantly temper our gloomy judgement of care management. First, community services for adults have never had a glorious era. The history of community care is one of underfunding, disadvantaged resource distribution within the personal social services and work with older people afforded low status in social work and usually assigned to unqualified staff (see for example, Means and Smith, 1998a). The fact that there were concerted efforts to develop the social work practice content of work with older people in the 1980s (for example, Rowlings, 1981; Bowl, 1986; Froggatt, 1990; Marshall, 1990) may have magnified the tensions experienced with care management, but in reality the theoretical developments had made few inroads into the negative picture in the field (Lymbery, 1998). The philosophy of tailored care packages, and the status afforded to care management in government policy, offered some potential to break out of this straitjacket, and this potential is cautiously applauded by disability groups (Priestly, 1999). Second, the forces of managerialism, bureaucratisation and technicism, which have emerged so strongly in the implementation of care management in the UK, are global trends with which social work must contend regardless of the system of service delivery in operation. Moreover, care management does not *of itself* embody the ideology of the market. It is partial and counterproductive to see the issues only in those terms, especially since there is no indication of government intention to reverse the marketisation of social care. Third, the situation may not be as bad as it initially seemed. Recent studies focusing on the carrying out of care management, rather than the overall implementation of the community care reforms, claim evidence of social work practice surviving and proving its value. For example, Hardiker and Barker (1999: 421) claim that social workers demonstrated 'skilled methods and proactive decision-making', adopting advocacy roles and identifying 'empower-ment' as a method to enable service users to negotiate around limited choices. The case studies showed utilisation of 'a wider range of individualised, imaginative solutions' (p. 425). Accepting that this study was concerned with people who were getting a service, and does not address the wider question of unmet need or those falling through the net, it nevertheless provides some counter to the picture of a deskilled, mechanistic response.

A comprehensive and recent picture of micro-level care management inter-actions is provided within the Personal Social Services Research Unit's reporting of its wide-ranging ECCEP (evaluating community care for elderly people) research programme. It provides important evidence of a 'fight back' by social work. Qualified social workers were responsible for the highest incidence of complex assessments and the guardians of the holistic assessment. They were spending a higher proportion of their time in face-to-face contact with the service user or in contact with other agencies directly associated with the care package. Only one-fifth of the worker's time was being spent on administration and form-filling, even in the setting up period. Care managers were undertaking direct work with service users and qualified social workers were more likely to provide counselling than other care managers. Moreover, the responses of the service users showed these 'social worker care managers' taking seriously the notion of user involvement and empowerment. For example, 87 per cent of the most 'dependent' category thought that their care manager understood their strengths as well as their problems. Sixty-nine per cent of all users felt that they could discuss alternatives, as equals, with their care manager (Bauld et al., 2000). This is not to gloss over the continuing problems, most notably in delivering a quality service with rising caseloads and the poor progress made in working together with health professionals. Nevertheless, the study identifies important areas of good practice.

A framework for good practice

Conceptual integration of analysis of the tensions experienced and those outcomes which are emerging as positive, provides us with the framework for good practice in care management.

Keeping the service user central

First and foremost must be a concern to maintain the centrality of the service user. A degree of cynicism about government esposal of 'empowerment' and 'user choice' may be justified, but it should not detract from a full-blooded determination to pursue user-centred objectives. In this respect it is important to acknowledge that the essential direction of the community care reforms is fundamentally 'what people want'. My own research found people, who were not service users and had no acquaintance with the care management system, expressing the desire for a needs-led, multidisciplinary assessment, an individually tailored package of care and a flexible balance between formal services and informal support (Lloyd, 2000). Staying focused on the user when resources are tight can foster creativity because it requires us to think through with the potential service user what exactly the need is, and what the essential element(s) is to meet that need. Overconsciousness of limited resources leads to a tendency to make a service-led assessment, not necessarily with any cost saving. Research into informal caring has long demonstrated that what carers actually want is often more low-key, cheaper alternatives than the sometimes underused schemes developed by service providers (for example, Haffenden, 1991). It is salutary that the ECCEP study found care managers realising that what had seemed an inadequate care package to them initially had actually made a significant difference to people's lives. The value of undertaking a user-centred assessment of need, with the user respected and involved in the process, should not be underestimated (Lloyd and Taylor, 1995). My own research demonstrated significant psychological benefits for carers of a community care assessment having been completed, independent of any ensuing service provision (Lloyd and Smith, 1998). Priestly points out that services which empower people to improve their own quality of life may have intrinsic value, even if this cannot be demonstrated through a measurable service outcome (Priestly, 2000).

This is not meant to cover up the inadequacies of service provision through dubious claims of therapeutic value. A user-centred process of assessment demands that it be part of an empowerment model of care management. This requires practitioners and managers to take risks in stimulating new responses and developing and reconfiguring existing services in response to locally defined user needs. It was my observation that those service managers and frontline practitioners who had got hold of this idea and were enthused by it were those who could see real possibilities to improve the quality of life of service users, despite struggling with the same implementation problems as those who were negative about the 'reforms' (Lloyd and Smith, 1998). Lyons et al. (1995) found that social workers who perceived positive potential in the changes and were willing to see themselves as change agents reported much greater job satisfaction. By contrast, Bland found that the inherent conservatism of most social workers in the Scottish case management experiment to be a major factor in limiting its success (Bland, 1994).

An empowerment model also requires care managers to take seriously the resources of the service user/carer in understanding and managing their own situations (see Chapter 6). The fact that these resources, even in the most resilient of people, can be undermined through lack of support or remain untapped through failure to access the system, should lead the empowering care manager to see her/his task as identifying what is needed in this particular situation, in order to facilitate a working partnership which goes beyond the 'in principle' commitment to involve the service user. Sometimes it should lead us as professionals to take the even bolder step of resourcing service users as managers of their own care pathways. Tanner is coldly realistic about the battle to work as an empowering care manager, but concludes with similar thoughts. The new professionalism implies a two-way sharing of knowledge, expertise and strength (Lloyd et al., 1996; Tanner, 1998a).

CASE EXAMPLE revisited

Mrs Grant is articulate about her needs and able to express her clear priorities. Recognising that formal services are not going to be able to deliver what Mrs Grant needs in the time available, the social worker immediately helps her to complete an application for a direct payment. Mrs Grant makes arrangements to have a ramp built and orders an electric wheelchair. Mrs Grant is fully involved in both individual assessment processes with the physiotherapist, occupational therapist and social worker and multidisciplinary planning meetings. Through these, Mrs Grant is able to see that her personal priorities of maintaining independence and mobility at home will only be achieved through attention to her excessive weight and compromising on accepting the pendant alarm for a trial period in order to reduce the risk arising from further falls. Importantly, the social worker advocates for Mrs Grant to stay in the acute unit while these arrangements are put in place rather than her having to move to another temporary unit.

Maintaining a holistic approach

This is not the first time that social work has faced a crisis of professional angst. Arguably, social work survived previous precarious moments because it managed to hold onto the 'whole person in total context' idea, despite the lure and challenge of psychotherapy, radical social work and community development. Yet it is that holistic approach which is most threatened by the culture of cost-effective task division and outcomes-focused accountability which has come to dominate the community care scenario. Cowen argues that the global forces of marketisation, bureaucratisation and managerialism, combined with the loss of the public sector ethic, have 'served to downgrade the status of holistic models and ethical caring in social work practice' (Cowen, 1999: 101).

The issue cannot be sidestepped, because it is at the centre of both the skills and values dilemmas in care management and is crucial to the effective integration of health and social care. A user-centred focus is, by definition, holistic. Holism is not concerned solely with the whole person, it is concerned with whole systems and *wholeness*, in both persons and systems and the interactions between them. The simultaneous engagement with individuals, families, organisations and social structures is what should mark out social work as a profession. A holistic approach to the assessment and meeting of the needs of individuals requires a focus on the social structures which shape their lives and the mechanisms which impact upon their experiences of services. Maintaining this holistic perspective and approach may seem to be the most impossible challenge of all, but, equally, holism – as concept and practice – may hold the key to the way forward on some of the seemingly intractable issues in health and social care. Hudson comments that the interagency collaboration envisaged in the newly created health action zones is premised on a notion of holism which embraces 'whole systems' change in order to effect 'whole person' health improvements (Hudson, 2000).

CASE EXAMPLE revisited

Using a biographical approach to assessment, the social worker discovers that Mrs Grant used to be a clerical officer in the civil service and is keen to deal with services direct. She needs to regain some control over her life and is unlikely to respond well to the rehabilitation programme without this. The relationships which she establishes with the different professionals, and their capacity to respond to her as a whole person interacting with the whole system, are crucial to the successful balancing of needs, resources, rights and risks.

An inclusive notion of quality

It is no accident that the emergence of 'quality talk' has been simultaneous with the community care changes. Each of the intrinsic agendas of care management connects with the notion of quality and its definition and measurement. The original emphasis within 'service quality' developed as a preoccupation with easily quantifiable outputs and performance indicators based on such measures. Nocon and Qureshi comment that a repeated finding in community care studies is that senior managers tend to prefer quantitative information which can be aggregated and used in budgetary planning, whereas the frontline professionals prefer qualitative outcomes which leave room for professional judgement and interpersonal processes (Nocon and Qureshi, 1996). The emerging evaluation of care management surely leads us to the conclusion that we must integrate both. Differences in what is valued, by whom and by what indicators it is measured lie behind the division between 'service quality' and 'quality of life' approaches. Yet service outcomes may be one indicator of quality of life just as enhanced quality of life may be one service outcome. Both quality of life and service quality may contain aspects which are amenable to quantitative measurement, but their significance may be a subjective judgement. Thus, practitioners and managers seeking to deliver quality through care management can only do so by a determined attempt to integrate subjective and objective indicators in relation to quality of life, and by finding ways to identify and demonstrate outcomes which are not easily measurable in respect of service quality.

CASE EXAMPLE revisited

Mrs Grant returns to her own home three months after her hospital admission and arrangements work well. The social worker feeds back to the service manager that without flexibility around the length of stay in the acute unit the outcomes could have been very different. Recognising other cases where this has been so, the manager begins to collect data to inform the development of more flexible use of the different rehabilitation and support units.

CONCLUSION

In order to move forward on care management, social work must do three things which it has repeatedly failed to do throughout its history. First, it must perceive research as an ally, not a threat or an irrelevance, and make detailed and active use of available evidence from the extensive research literature. Second, it must have confidence in the contribution which social work has made to the understanding of individual and social problems in health and social care, and actively promote its holistic model of assessment and integrated response to need on the multiprofessional stage of the 'new world'. Third, it must seek constructive avenues out of the impasses. It may even, as in the case of the refining of the definition and demonstration of quality outcomes, find improvement in so doing. These three strategies are connected, each underpinning and facilitating the other.

It is a bold claim, but an arguable one, that social work will survive or fall according to its response to care management. The critical issues for social work practice and social care management which have been examined here are at the heart of the challenge of delivering health and social care in technologically advanced societies in the twenty-first century. Moreover, care management contains within it all of the management themes discussed in Part III of this book, and connects with the critical values issues contained within professionalism, accountability, service evaluation, rights and empowerment, which have been covered in Part I. Focus in this chapter has been on those dilemmas which the reflective practitioner and service manager cannot avoid, because they are the working out of fundamental tensions and broader issues at the crucial point of service delivery to the user. Undoubtedly, underfunding, overproscribed directives and bureaucratic administration have contributed in no small measure to the implementation of care management failing to fulfil its positive potential and having a negative impact on many aspects of social work. Ultimately, however, if the 'community care experiment' fails, it will be for none of these reasons per se, but because those professionals concerned with its delivery have failed to engage with the fundamental challenges for welfare services in the postmodern world.

FURTHER READING

Challis, D. (1994) *Implementing Caring for People: Care Management: Factors Influencing its Development in the Implementation of Community Care*, London: Department of Health. A succinct review of the variants emerging in the early implementation of care management in the UK, with analysis of their significance, key issues and future challenges.

Gostick, C., Davies, B., Lawson, R. and Salter, C. (1997) *From Vision to Reality in Community Care*, Aldershot: Arena. Considers the development of care management in the overall context of the community care changes and overarching trends.

Payne, M. (1995) *Social Work and Community Care*, London: Macmillan – now Palgrave Macmillan. Written before the 1993 implementation could be properly evaluated, but makes a strong case for social workers as care managers and the defence of core social work skills.

Titterton, M. (ed.) (1994) *Caring for People in the Community: The New Welfare*, London: Jessica Kingsley. Useful discussion of a range of service contexts and the impact of the new arrangements, with examples of specific initiatives.

Cowen, H. (1999) *Community Care, Ideology and Social Policy*, London: Prentice Hall. Places discussion of the impact of the 1990s' policy developments on the health and social care professions in a political and global context.

Mental Health

Di Bailey

This chapter offers some suggestions to mental health social workers about how to develop critical practice as a way of responding proactively to the challenge of delivering contemporary mental health care within a context of paradox and conflicting discourse. Social work is only one contributing profession in the multidisciplinary mental health field that increasingly hinges on effective interprofessional working. For this reason, critical practice in mental health social work cannot be presented without reference to the multidisciplinary context which informs its delivery and to which it contributes.

Critical practice in mental health social work must incorporate an emancipatory social change orientation (Healy, 2000) which ultimately involves workers in the difficult task of adopting an activist approach. This is particularly problematic in mental health in the current political climate that perceives community care as a failure and prioritises public safety (Department of Health, 1999c), yet seeks to involve users and carers in partnership working (Department of Health, 2000c).

The challenge of writing this chapter is to present such an approach 'that engages critically and productively with what social work in mental health settings is rather than the received wisdom critical social science theory tells us it should be' (Healy, 2000: 77). As Hinselwood (1998: 25) claims, what is needed is not a 'simple "how to" manual' but an approach that encompasses the process of reflection in order to provide quality work in mental health that involves a 'human "being with", rather than an operational "doing to"' individuals with mental health problems.

The modernisation agenda in mental health policy and practice has fundamentally altered the provision of mental health care (Department of Health, 1999c; Department of Health, 2000c), replacing the bricks and mortar of the asylum with a different yet similarly constraining institution of care planning documentation and systems (Bailey, 2000) with community mental health teams (CMHTs) as the bedrock. As these teams have reconfigured to provide services such as assertive community treatment and crisis intervention (Department of Health, 1999e), a number of studies have revealed that the challenges of multidisciplinary working inherent in the institutions are still evident.

Community services are still delivered from an institutional philosophy, with mental health practitioners confused about the core skills and aptitudes that they bring to their role and those that are common and shared with other multidisciplinary colleagues. According to Hinselwood (1998: 21), 'what has emerged in providing community care is that the distortions found in the old large institutions recur within the organisations of agencies in the community'. He cites some of these processes which include staff demoralisation, stereotyped patients, scapegoating, a blame culture and schisms in the service.

Within this context, one possible approach to developing critical practice in mental health social work involves five stages and is helpful at several levels. In respect of individual practice, it potentially helps workers to feel more confident about exploring risky situations from the different perceptions of worker and user and enables workers to be more confident about delineating the respective responsibilities for risk management. At the team level, it helps mental health social workers to be clear about their role within integrated or single line-managed teams and allows for the identification of the professional social work contribution within a multidisciplinary domain.

The approach requires practitioners to:

■ Examine the situations that they encounter with service users from the individual's perspective as distinct from their own

■ Weigh up the options for intervening including the value base underpinning practice, and the practice context (theory, policy, power relations and legislation) together with their own previous experience

■ Make an informed judgement that is acted upon

■ Reflect on the outcome of their action/decision-making

■ Critically appraise what they have learned.

The remainder of this chapter will explore this approach and apply it to a case example where inherent tensions lie between either adopting an empowering and enabling approach or resorting to controlling interventions. Through the case example it is hoped to illustrate how the use of critical practice can redefine the power dynamics within the professional social work relationship, such that an intervention that has the potential to be coercive may actually involve the service user in working collaboratively with the practitioner to reach a shared responsibility for meeting care needs.

Exploring encounters with service users

The growth of the user/survivor movement in mental health has begun to change the balance of power within mental health services, although mixed views exist about the extent to which this has been achieved (Perkins and Repper, 1998a; Beresford, 2000).

Studies concerned with what users want from services reveal the importance of the ordinary aspects of everyday life, such as employment, housing and finances, over and above specialist mental health treatments and interventions (Estroff, 1998; Sainsbury Centre for Mental Health, 1997, 1998), although the latter are ascribed more significance by professionals, reflecting what they perceive to be an integral part of their role (Shepherd et al., 1995).

Users have also gone beyond articulating their expectations of services to describing 'lived' experiences of mental distress in their own terms, using a language that reinforces the concept of recovery (Polack, 1993; Carling, 1996) promoted through recovery groups and workbooks (see Leader, 1995; Coleman and Smith, 1997). Rather than focus on concepts such as 'cure' or being symptom free, the recovery approach encourages

> people to take stock and set new life paths [and it] provides a vision of moving from the despair of very changed circumstances on becoming a 'user' to hope. The hope is not about 'cure' but about leading a fulfilling life with mental health problems which are valued as part of experience.
>
> (Sayce, 2000: 132)

By exposing these different perceptions, critical practitioners can counter their complicity in the reproduction of oppressive conditions within the mental health system (Rojek et al., 1988; Sarri and Sarri, 1992), particularly in multidisciplinary contexts where a predilection for the medical model can result in people being labelled as 'cases of disease', dismissing their subjective experience of mental distress and the meaning this has for them.

The process of engagement as a foundation for such relationship building is probably by far the most important phase in reaching a negotiated perception of need. According to Perkins and Repper (1998a: 24), 'success will be measured by the quality of the relationship between mental health worker and client'. While they acknowledge the difficulties in defining what constitutes an 'effective relationship', they suggest that for people with severe and enduring mental health problems 'it might best be judged in terms of the extent to which the person is facilitated in living the life they wish to lead and achieving their own goals' (p. 24).

However, acting as an individual agent of change can be an isolating experience for practitioners within a multidisciplinary team, where the power struggles associated with competing mental health discourses have the potential to thwart emancipatory relationships with users. Social workers need their professional affiliation with the Central Council for Education and Training in Social Work as a means of safeguarding standards and offering solidarity through group identity (Richards and Horder, 1999: 450). By focusing on values and anti-discriminatory practice as part of the basic diploma in social work (Central

Council for Education and Training in Social Work, 1995), reinforced by the revised *Mental Health Act 1983: Code of Practice* (Department of Health/Welsh Office, 1999) and the ASW training framework (Central Council for Education and Training in Social Work, 2000), mental health social workers should feel confident in using their power and authority to initiate consciousness-raising in other disciplines regarding the potential contribution that users can make to their own care package and mental health services more generally, thereby reducing the need for a blame culture and schisms in care delivery.

Weighing options for intervention within the practice context

According to Walton (1999: 378):

> social work in the mental health field has traditionally occupied an unstable, ambivalent and ambiguous position, caught between the dominant theoretical and professional discipline of biological psychiatry and the psycho-socially oriented theory and practice of mainstream social work.

While the Mental Health Act 1983 provides the legislative context for considering options for intervention, Walton (1999) believes that it does little to assist social work's position, particularly by embedding the statutory role within a psychiatric model of illness and medical treatment.

The recent review of the mental health legislation (Department of Health, 2000b), together with the National Service Framework (Department of Health, 1999e) standards in respect of the Care Progamme Approach (CPA), indicate that the mental health care team will be required to play a much more systematic and coordinated role, providing mental health care from assessment and interventions (that may or may not include hospitalisation) to aftercare (Sainsbury Centre for Mental Health, 2001). Weighing the options will thus continue to be guided by the legislative framework but requires greater clarity regarding interprofessional working as the potential for professional role blurring increases.

An effective team approach will hinge on all workers being clear about the unique contribution that they offer as a result of their unidisciplinary training and professional affiliation, and also the skills, knowledge and philosophies they share with others. This respect for both uniqueness and diversity mirrors the approach outlined with service users in the previous section.

Within the team context, weighing the options for interventions will be hampered when team members cannot agree on a model of mental distress that draws from all contributing professions, together with the user's perspective, without losing something of the uniqueness of each profession's individualism. The biopsychosocial model (Kingdon, 2000; Watkins, 1997) is an increasingly favoured framework for understanding the causative factors that have contributed to the onset of mental distress in the first instance, together with those that sustain or compound difficulties. The model incorporates social factors as integral to a holistic approach which seeks to provide increased insight into relapse and individuals' coping strategies (Figure 17.1).

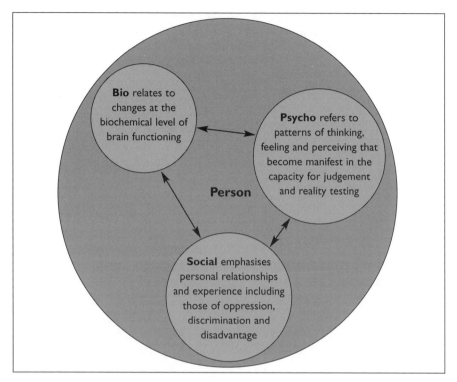

Figure 17.1 The biopsychosocial model

While some would argue that this combined theoretical framework may seem to contradict the emancipatory orientation of critical social work and allow the medical model to remain the dominant professional discourse (Walton, 1999; Tew, 1999), on reflection the author would assert that it adopts the activist stance of placing the users' experience as a determining factor in how the model is interpreted.

As Perkins and Repper (1998a: 25) highlight:

> different people adopt different models for understanding what has happened to them … organic constructions, psychological, social, religious or spiritual formulations. People have a right to define their own experiences for themselves and it is rarely helpful and more likely to be alienating for the clinician to insist that their understanding is correct.

For each individual, the respective elements of the model will feature to a greater or lesser extent in terms of their specific understanding and experience but also in relation to effective interventions. As Perkins and Repper (1998b: 92) elaborate, 'if a person wants to be able to cook then an understanding of their neurotransmitters or intrapsychic processes may not be particularly useful'. The author agrees with Perkins and Repper's view (1998a) that because an individual understands their distress with particular emphasis on one or more aspects of the model, this does not preclude interventions that are based on different parts of the model. Indeed, if a holistic approach to mental health care is to be developed, a combination approach should be the rule rather than the exception.

By continually questioning how the respective elements of the biopsychosocial framework can feature to a greater or lesser extent in understanding an individual's mental distress, and how a combination of interventions from one or more disciplines may meet the care needs, the power bases of the disciplines themselves become less intrinsically valuable. By working collaboratively with service users to define their mental distress from their perspective and using their language (even if, for some individuals, medical terminology is their preferred frame of reference), this optimises the chances of individuals taking responsibility for their mental health, using more effective coping and relapse prevention strategies than previously (Healy, 2000).

Making informed judgements: reflection and critical appraisal

Faced with the dilemmas of interprofessional working and the increasingly prescriptive policy framework in respect of risk management (Department of Health, 1994a, 1994b, 1995; Mental Health (Patients in the Community) Act 1995), critical practice in mental health can only aid a process of questioning and self-questioning in the quest for an emancipatory approach which recognises that statistics do not support the proposition that the majority of people with mental health problems pose a risk to others (Mullen et al., 1998; Steadman et al., 1998; Sayce, 2000).

As Davis (1996) explains, there is an element of risk assessment in most aspects of practice, spanning decisions that impact upon an individual's liberty to the amount of care they receive and policy decisions about the deployment of resources. Davis goes on to argue (p. 114) that:

> Risk taking ... is an essential element of working with mental health service users to ensure autonomy, choice and social participation. It is a means of challenging the paternalism and overprotectiveness of mental health services.

This is echoed by Sayce (2000: 227) who argues for 'a need to generate a more realistic debate about risk than at present' as 'it is impossible to predict every crime'. However, it must be acknowledged that 'mental disturbance in any of us makes us emotionally and behaviourally unpredictable' (Foster, 1998: 85).

In the context of this debate, how can critical social work be assisted in the self-questioning process to rise to the challenge of working with risk? First, being clear about what is meant by 'risk assessment' is important as, in the author's view, this misleading term relates to only one element of a cyclical process that in the interests of the individual needs to be ongoing.

In the absence of a coherent conceptual framework to guide the process described above, practitioners often resort to risk assessment checklists which, according to Davis (1996: 117), 'are only adjuncts to lengthier more detailed and time consuming work which is focused on getting to know an individual and building trust and confidence over time'. This links back to the importance of relationship-building highlighted earlier in the chapter as integral to the making of informed judgements.

Several recent 'risk' publications (Moore, B., 1996; Morgan, 1999) encourage the critical practitioner to go beyond collecting information to highlighting biases in decision-making and identifying specifically under what circumstances risks may be apparent. It thus becomes possible to design a risk management plan (Figure 17.2) that systematically delineates those risks that the service user has responsibility for managing and those that need to be managed by the multidisciplinary team. This approach requires the critical practitioner to work collaboratively with other team members to ensure that such biases are identified and addressed. Indeed Carson (1990) guards against risk work being left to isolated individual practitioners and advocates the need for flexible yet systematic assessments and responses that encourage collaborative decision-making with users. In the author's view this approach should be extended to colleagues within the multidisciplinary team in order that all relevant information can be shared and acted upon.

The importance of effective interprofessional communication has been highlighted as one of the most significant omissions in cases where mental health inquiries have been instigated (Ritchie et al., 1994). Thus such sharing of

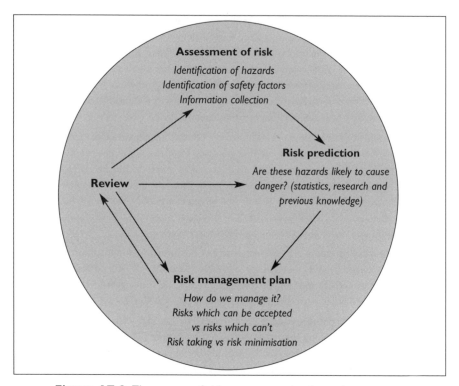

Figure 17.2 The process of risk assessment, planning and management showing the questions/issues to be considered at each stage

information is integral to collective decisions being taken, especially where it is unclear whether a risk taking or risk minimisation approach is adopted. Also, by adopting a collaborative approach to risk work, critical practitioners are encouraged to involve their multidisciplinary team colleagues in the process of reflecting upon a course of action taken irrespective of the outcome.

In an attempt to illustrate these issues together with those raised in the previous sections the following case example is presented as an illustration of critical social work practice in mental health.

CASE EXAMPLE

Sally is a 25-year-old woman who has been experiencing difficulties with anorexia nervosa since her late teens. Despite three previous admissions to hospital (two as an informal patient and the latter under section two of the 1983 Mental Health Act), therapeutic intervention has been effective only in terms of weight gain. Social difficulties remain, as on discharge Sally has moved back to the family home where she lives with her younger sister aged 22 and her mother. Sally has identified her mother as the perpetrator of emotional and physical abuse spanning the past 13 years since her father left when she was 12 years old.

Sally contends that relationships within the family are fraught with high levels of criticism, hostility and physical assaults from her mother, contrasted with an overprotectiveness that prevents Sally from holding down a job and restricts her finances and when she can see her friends. Sally's sister Ruth colludes with the mother's controlling behaviour as a way of sustaining her own role within the family, as the 'idealised daughter who can do no wrong' holding down a responsible job as a police officer, compared to Sally who is seen as a 'loser', intent on destroying herself with no hope of employment or independence.

An assessment of risk reveals at least two previous self-harm attempts motivated by Sally's despair connected to a need to get away from the home environment. One involved Sally taking an overdose of antidepressants prescribed by her GP, while the latter, which had prompted the most recent referral to the community mental health team, involved her superficially cutting her wrists in a public toilet in the local park where she jogs several times each day. On this latter attempt Sally was found by her sister who was routinely following her afternoon beat.

Both self-harm attempts are connected to periods of marked low self-esteem that stem from Sally's belief systems ('I am unlovable','I must try to be a perfect daughter like my sister' and 'It's my fault that my father left'), and are triggered by rows with her mother following episodes of emotional and physical abuse.

Sally's self-reports of the abuse are corroborated by a neighbour, Jan, who lives in the terraced house adjoining the family home and hears most of the arguments taking place. Sally's small social network includes Jan as an identified confidante and supporter together with Clare, an old school friend who lives ten miles away but visits in secret when Sally's mother is out at work.

Other risk factors include Sally's ritualised behaviour connected to her pursuit of weight loss, which is significant, but not life threatening. This involves eating little and taking excess exercise (jogging or swimming) together with abuse of laxatives for purging and a problematic addiction to cough medicine to aid sleep.

Until the overdose attempt with the antidepressants, Sally had maintained a good relationship with her GP. She is now frustrated that she has to visit the surgery weekly for a repeat prescription, feeling that this is an unnecessary infringement on her civil liberties.

She also sees previous involvement of mental health professionals as coercive, due to the admission under section and a confrontational relationship with her consultant psychiatrist.

The temptation to wade into this situation and instigate another assessment under the 1983 Mental Health Act as a means of minimising the risks by admission to hospital is great but smacks of Hinselwood's 'doing to' approach with little opportunity for reflection and consideration of alternatives.

Also, Sally's previous experience of professional involvement suggests that pursuing this course of action would do little to foster a process of engagement and relationship building that in the long term might achieve greater success in promoting recovery rather than just weight gain. As the ASW responsible, my preference was to pursue the latter option provided that, through the process of engagement, I could identify and contain some of the apparent risks until I had a more appropriate opportunity to address them in a more proactive way.

Emancipatory encounters with service users need to commence on their terms, in order to demonstrate the dignity and respect of one human 'being with' another. Meeting with Sally at her request at Jan's house immediately communicated my desire to collaborate rather than control. However, as a qualified ASW I was faced with a dilemma at this point: whether to be up-front about this added dimension to my role and the associated powers it entails, thus risking the process of engagement, or, alternatively, reserving the discussion until the engagement process was further underway, which could then be jeopardised because I would be seen to have withheld vital information.

It is worth pointing out that each individual user will respond differently to whichever stage of disclosure is adopted, thus this is the kind of example where I, as a critical practitioner, needed to make a judgement as to when to take action and then reflect upon its outcome with the help of supervision.

In Sally's case, because of her previous encounters with professionals, I considered it necessary to be honest about my ASW status and explore the power relationship collaboratively, being clear that just as easily as I could take a decision to pursue a formal mental health act assessment I could equally decide not to invoke my powers. Furthermore, to indicate that I actually preferred to work with Sally without recourse to legislative measures, but that this required some joint effort to establish a collaborative relationship on which we might start to build some trust. Interestingly, Sally's response to my disclosure was to offer her own negotiating position for our relationship. While she was willing to give such collaboration a try, her provisos were that we did not have to involve her mother in our discussions at this stage, or spend session after session focusing on the past emotional and physical abuse, as she had found this kind of therapy in the past of little use in terms of moving forward.

By engaging in an initial discussion that attempted to set some 'ground rules' for working together, we were able to move to an exploration of Sally's hopes and aspirations for the future, rather than focusing solely upon her eating disorder and self-harm attempts. Subsequent discussion revealed that Sally wished to leave home, live independently and have control over her own finances. She also expressed a wish to make contact again with her father whom she had written to in secret until she was 15 years old. Not surprisingly, a more in-depth discussion unearthed Sally's ambivalence about the costs required to achieve these goals, particularly her concerns that her mother would sabotage any attempt she made to leave the family home and the stress of managing financially and making the changes would exacerbate her eating disorder to a point where it would become out of control.

What became clear from discussing with Sally how the first steps towards this new 'life path' might be taken was that she had never been given the opportunity to reflect upon her own understanding and interpretation of what had happened in her life over the years and how this had contributed to her mental distress and despair. Working in accordance with the biopsychosocial framework, I recognised Sally's need to understand:

- How the biological effects of her anorexia, including the associated use of laxatives and addiction to cough medicine, could contribute towards her mental health

- The interrelatedness of her belief systems with her self-harming behaviour

- How the social factors of unemployment and financial dependence on the benefit system, coupled with domination and oppression within the family, featured in a complex presentation of interrelated need, such that previous strategies to extricate herself from this web were not surprisingly ineffective.

In order to address the above, the contributions from the GP and consultant psychiatrist were important not only in helping Sally and myself understand the biological contributions to Sally's presentation, but also in modelling for Sally that one professional group does not have a monopoly on explaining mental distress and thus she too has an element of choice in deciding how she interprets her own experience.

Thus, in order to facilitate the first steps towards the new life path that Sally had identified, I needed to work collaboratively with her, together with other multidisciplinary colleagues and members of Sally's social network, to begin to provide the support necessary for her to move into independent living. While the CPA framework would provide the vehicle for such collaboration, the timing of CPA meetings and their focus on Sally's needs rather than on interprofessional rivalry were paramount. For this to be achieved, I had to undertake some 'behind the scenes' work with Sally's permission prior to a full meeting being convened.

As the care coordinator responsible for implementing Sally's care plan, my subsequent interventions with her included:

- Accompanying Sally to the housing department to complete an application for supported accommodation *(being with as opposed to doing to)*

- Individual meetings with the GP and consultant to update them of the social work involvement on housing and finance issues, and also to highlight the need for effective medical treatment as part of a holistic approach *(role clarification in the interests of interprofessional working)*

- Joint discussions with GP and consultant to agree a collaborative approach to risk management, taking on board Sally's aspirations *(generating more realistic debate about risk and guarding against it being left to an isolated practitioner)*

- Meetings with Sally together with Jan and Clare to explore the social support available and to explain the CPA as a framework for care planning in preparation for a CPA meeting in which they would feel more able to participate *(encouraging collaborative decision-making)*

- Continuing individual sessions with Sally to foster the engagement process and monitor the risk issues as part of the care plan with the opportunity to reflect on the ongoing work and issues arising in regular supervision sessions *(providing a flexible yet systematic response)*

- Individual/joint sessions with Sally's mother and/or sister to explore family dynamics in more detail, facilitate Sally's move to independent living and promote ongoing support from close family members *(sharing of information and making informed judgements)*.

All of the above demonstrates how the use of professional power together with self-questioning and reflection can be used constructively to pursue an emancipatory approach, bearing testimony to the contribution that critical mental health social workers can make to 'the development of a perspective which empowers service users rather than labelling them as sick' (Braye and Varley, 1992: 46). Depending upon the nature of the relationship established with individual services users and multidisciplinary colleagues, the 'behind the scenes' work will be more or less necessary and there will be situations where collaborative joint meetings with users involve possible rights from the outset. Supervision is an obvious and important vehicle to allow the critical practitioner the opportunity to reflect on how they might 'stage manage' interprofessional working in order to promote optimum involvement for people like Sally.

CONCLUSION

Contemporary critical practice in mental health social work is shaped by a policy agenda that on the one hand promotes the involvement of users but on the other considers the importance of public safety. Thus critical practitioners in mental health are forced to explore the situations they encounter with users in the context of shifting power relations and the conflicting paradoxes apparent in the legislative and policy context. Only by working collaboratively with both service users and professional colleagues can critical mental health social workers rise to the challenge of making informed judgements that are proactive and underpinned by a bedrock of user-oriented values. Through the process of collaboration together with supervision, reflective social work practitioners can engage in a process of ongoing reflection and professional development that only serves to highlight the contribution of critical social work practice to contemporary mental health care.

FURTHER READING

Bailey, D. (ed.) (2000) *At the Core of Mental Health Practice*, Brighton: Pavilion. An in-depth look at current mental health issues and approaches.

Foster, A. and Roberts, V.Z. (eds) (1998) *Managing Mental Health in the Community: Chaos and Containment*, London: Routledge. A more theoretical book from a psychoanalytical perspective on current working in mental health, including a useful chapter on risk.

Healy, K. (2000) *Social Work Practices: Contemporary Perspectives on Change*, London: Sage. A useful analysis of more general critical social work practice.

18

Physical Disability

Bob Sapey

A key aspect of critical practice in any field is to ask questions such as: What am I doing? What am I taking for granted? My starting point in this chapter is to ask the question: Do disabled people *need* social work? This can be asked in two ways, first in terms of whether the administration of welfare requires qualified social workers to work with disabled people. The reorganisation of community care has led to the blurring of occupational boundaries with other welfare professions, a rise in the use of unqualified assessors and an emphasis on the management of care services. Second, in such an environment it is easy for social workers to question their own value and fail to ask the question, which in a sense is more important to the future of welfare: Do disabled people *benefit* from social work?

Disability and social work

Since the 1960s, disabled people have consistently criticised the organisation of welfare services and, more importantly, have questioned whether the provision of welfare, as opposed to access to the mainstream social and economic worlds, is an appropriate response to people who are physically impaired. In this sense, social welfare and social workers are seen as part of the process of the construction of a disabling society rather than as part of the solution. The social model of disability distinguishes between impairment and disability, the former referring to some form of physical loss, while the latter is taken as the disadvantages, restrictions and oppression that occur as a result of social responses to impairment. This model leads to an argument that, by its very nature, social work assumes that disabled people need to be 'cared for' and as such views them as unable to be in control of their own lives. If disabled people were full citizens of a society, there would be no need for a welfare system to offer care services as a substitute. Therefore, the receipt of care services through a welfare system is viewed as second best and any attempt to try and perpetuate it is seen as counter to the goals of citizenship.

However, the actions of many social workers are based on a belief in the collective provision of welfare, and their aim in practice is to deliver services in a non-stigmatising manner. While being aware of the academic and political debates about disability, many social workers would consider their own position to be supportive of the disability movement. They aim to help disabled people to empower themselves and gain access to services that would meet their care needs. They aim to counter the oppression and discrimination that disabled people experience by such actions as encouraging self-assessment of need, and they try to ensure that their practice does not contribute to the further disabling of people with physical impairments. Different social workers may take different approaches to these tasks, ranging from the politicisation of specific issues to personal counselling, but their aim is one of trying actively to help disabled people.

But, while social workers may use the term 'care' to signify positive attitudes and actions, it has been experienced by many on the receiving end as meaning some form of control or custody. We may see welfare as an indicator of a mature society but our clients often see it as no less than a form of apartheid, in that it singles out certain groups of people as needing to be dependent upon it. As part of the disability industry we may well understand these arguments, but we tend to temper them with the reality faced in local authority social service departments that welfare is basically a necessary and usually positive activity. The challenge is that while we may well try to make it positive, why should people with physical impairments be singled out to receive it?

Challenging practice

Thinking about two men, both with spinal injuries, may help to illustrate some of this. Stephen had recently become paraplegic following a road accident. After a period in a spinal injuries unit, he had returned home to resume his life. Stephen's father was an influential local businessman and the family were quite affluent. They had good access to medical advice and were well informed of the consequences of the accident. When the accident occurred, they were shocked, saddened and distraught and the social services manager wanted to ensure that all the help his department might be able to offer would be available. However, by the time that Stephen had returned from hospital, much of what could be done to make his previous life accessible to him had already happened. Because of the influence and efforts of his family, he was returning to a life in which he would be accepted rather than rejected, and in which his right to opportunity was ensured.

The social worker visited to establish what if anything would be required in the coming weeks. Stephen's father asked her what it was that she could do for him. This was an open question on one level, but it was also a challenge. The social services department expected this family and Stephen in particular to need their assistance. Over the years they had invested in a range of institutional provisions for younger disabled people in the belief that this was the way in which they should provide care. The social worker described the father's question as asking her if she represented a part of society that might treat his son as dependent. The consciousness-raising that had occurred over the past months was thorough and they were fully capable as a family of ensuring that he was not disadvantaged. Clearly, there was no role for social work with this family at that point in time, as they had no need of the services to which social workers act as gatekeepers and they had the wherewithal to deal with the changes that had occurred as a result of the accident. The social worker closed the case.

This contrasts with another man in his late teens who was resident in a local authority home. The home had some influence with the local housing department and at one case conference the staff were discussing how to help Philip to leave and live independently. Apart from being unemployed and homeless, he was not dependent on any other person and it seemed clear that what he needed was suitable accommodation. However, the senior manager who chaired these conferences made the observation that Philip had never appeared to have grieved his 'loss' and that until he had done so he would be at risk living independently. Therefore she was not willing to permit the social worker or staff in the home to liaise with the housing department. Philip remained in the home a further year until he left to live in a flat which he found for himself, but the point of telling this story is to illustrate the power that social services can have in restricting people when they expect them to conform to certain theoretical processes of adjustment. In Stephen's case, the social services may have thought this to be true but the social worker was able to act in an empowering way by closing the case, but for Philip his dependence in terms of his homelessness meant that he was unable to exercise the same choices.

However, while it may often be the case that disabled people do not need social workers to get involved with how they might live with their impairments, nevertheless they can experience considerable social inequalities. While those people with the financial freedom to provide for their own needs may be able to avoid state intervention in their lives, this is not the case for those who need the local authority to pay for services. For Philip, the price of being dependent was that the state assumed the right to involve itself forcefully in his life.

However, there are times when the authority of the state can be useful. David was involved in a motorcycle accident that resulted in severe brain damage. Following the accident, he was unconscious for several weeks and this necessitated several months of medical rehabilitation in hospital, after which he was considered ready to be discharged. This meant that he was functioning well enough to go to a specialist rehabilitation centre, but not that he had the ability to live at home without being quite dependent on others. As this was the time of the Falklands War, most head injury rehabilitation centres were too busy to take civilian patients. The only opportunity for David was to go to a local social services day centre. Within a few weeks, the staff at this centre decided that he was too disoriented to be productive and insisted that he leave. After a few weeks, he was found a place in a sports rehabilitation centre but within one week his disorientation resulted in his being rejected again. Reports were sent by all involved to a rehabilitation centre that specialised in head injuries in the hope that they would now consider helping him, but they responded by saying that all they could do was to recommend long-term nursing care.

In the meantime, David was living at home with his elderly parents and attending the physiotherapy department of the firm that had employed him. He was making steady progress in relearning a range of activities with the help of the physiotherapist, while the social worker supported his parents in learning to live with him. However, they were faced with a lack of any hope that he might get the specialist help he needed to make greater progress, which made the social worker look at the situation from a different perspective. He began to examine what help would actually be provided by these specialist centres and discovered that it would consist of sessions with various therapists. None of the services that would be offered within the rehabilitation centre would be different to those that could be offered locally, except that they would be coordinated. What the social worker then did was to talk to the therapists in the local community services and arrange for them to come together to form a rehabilitation team. While each person might have had a defined area of practice, what they achieved was a means of working together that was effective for David.

What this example demonstrates is the potential for social work to affect the institutionalised processes of treatment which was in turn useful to David. The services were inflexible and condemning of his potential for an autonomous life. The dominant social attitudes permitted people in positions of power to reject him and suggest that some form of incarceration in a nursing home was the best he could hope for. It was only by confronting the power of those organisations that the social worker was able to examine their actions and provide the services that would help this individual. This was made possible by the skills that social work brought to the problem because it was concerned with both his adaptation to the social world and the social world's adaptation to him. Most of the practical help he needed came from other sources but these professions work to particular functional responsibilities and would not find it easy to confront their own organisational control. The power relations of the rehabilitation industry were a major part of the problem and the social worker played an important role in understanding and changing these.

Despite policies based on the assumption that all disabled people need support and care, social services are generally provided for those people without the ability to survive or progress, particularly those who live in poverty. This raises some pertinent points regarding my initial question – do disabled people need social work? In an unjust society, poverty is more likely to hit particular groups of people and disabled people are one such group. Therefore, it is important to recognise why people need social work assistance and not simply claim this as being directly attributable to their impairment. In effect, part of the social process of being disabled is to be economically disadvantaged, so it is dishonest to say that people with impairments need social workers per se, rather that disabled people may need some form of help to fight the oppression that they are experiencing. The question remains, however, as to whether social work is or can be the right sort of help. There is clearly a legitimacy in the argument that social welfare and social work can contribute to the disablement of people with impairments, but it is also true that many people, both with and without impairments, need and benefit from the help that social work can provide. So how can this paradox be explained?

The argument that social work is part of the problem, in that it perpetuates the dependency of disabled people, is being made at a political level. This is the same argument that might be made against unemployment benefit as an insufficient substitute for employment, and, as a political analysis, it is sound. However, society cannot be examined from that perspective alone. As Thompson (1993) has argued, discrimination occurs within a complex interaction of the structural, cultural and personal levels of our social world. In this sense, we can begin to explain why it is that many people, both disabled and non-disabled, might subscribe to the view that people need to adjust to their disabilities. We are influenced by the cultural realities that we have grown up with, part of which is the construction of disability as a state of dependency and a personal problem. No matter how much we argue at a political or structural level that this is wrong, it will not change unless we also address the cultural influences on the personal.

While structural change will undoubtedly affect our cultural realities in the long term, in the immediate present we need some other means of dealing with the problems that individuals are experiencing. It is at this personal level that social work can help and be part of the solution. While the political arguments are made and before the changes they seek have occurred, there are individuals who will find that the only alternatives on offer are a life in institutions or inadequate and custodial care in the community. It is these individuals that social workers may be able to assist. What must be remembered, however, is that these levels are involved in a complex interaction and therefore social work practice at the personal level will have its influence on the cultural and structural level also. What is needed is an understanding of the whole which will lead to models of practice at a personal level that are consistent with and supportive of the change being sought elsewhere.

An example of this was a piece of work undertaken by a social work student while on placement with a social services department. The student was asked to deal with a referral from the mother of a 19-year-old with spina bifida. On leaving 'special' school at 17, Michael had spent some time at home and had attended the local day centre to ensure that he was not a 'burden' on his mother. He was then sent to a residential centre to learn the skills of independent living. This had largely concentrated on functional abilities and at the end of his stay he returned home. Like many teenagers, he continued to rely on his mother who, worried that this could be a lifelong dependency, had requested that he be readmitted to the day centre. The expectation of the social services was that this would be treated as a reasonable request and Michael would be offered a place, hence it was allocated to a student to learn how to carry out the administrative process of the task.

On first visiting the family, the student discovered that Michael did not wish to attend the day centre and he felt quite happy at remaining at home while his mother was out at work. On the other hand, his mother reported having to provide a range of help to Michael during the day and considered that he would be at risk if he was left alone. The assessment was made more complex by the fact that some of the activities that Michael was dependent on his mother for were not things that he was incapable of doing for himself, but things for which, as a teenager, he chose to rely on her for. The dilemma for the student was whether to help the mother or to accept Michael's right to refuse to be sent to the day centre.

The student initially attempted to get the authority to use the cost of daycare to purchase home support for Michael, but this was refused on budgetary grounds. The advice from the agency was to 'counsel' Michael towards accepting the day centre placement in order to give his mother a break. This would have been perfectly acceptable for passing a social work course and would be theorised as intervention in a situation of conflict in which both parties could not have exactly what they required. However, the student felt this would have made her part of the problem in relation to the structural aims of equal citizenship for disabled people.

What she did was to approach the problem from a different perspective. She felt that it was necessary to help Michael to understand the politics of his predicament so she did engage in counselling Michael, not in order to get him to accept the placement but to help him become aware of the ways in which he was being denied his dependency as a teenager. The aim of this was that it would help him to adopt a strategy that he would have a chance of succeeding with, because he would be better informed about the true nature of what was happening. The student also took him to meet with people from a nearby coalition of disabled people so that the politicisation could advance beyond that which could be offered by an able-bodied social worker.

This illustrates how it is possible to contribute at an individual level in a manner that is consistent with challenging the cultural and structural expectations of disabled people, and provides a sound basis for the way in which personal problems can be re-examined from a different perspective. However, Michael was receptive to the notion of developing a positive identity and this is not true for everyone.

John was 50 years old when he was diagnosed with multiple sclerosis. For him the diagnosis was devastating and he viewed it as the end of life. He gave up work and his relationships with friends and family began to deteriorate. He regarded other people's acceptance of his disability as pity. He left his wife and returned to live with his mother. His physical condition was deteriorating rapidly and he soon began to use a wheelchair and could no longer manage to live in his mother's small cottage. He requested that social services place him in a residential home. He had already spent two weeks in a nursing home and the staff complained that he seemed to find the sight of other disabled people repugnant.

Following a conventional approach to assessment, John's behaviour would be examined in relation to his failure to adjust psychologically towards accepting his debilitating illness. There would be little questioning of the view that the multiple sclerosis would cause him to have to abandon positive roles and, while being a disabled person would be seen as undoubtedly a negative experience, he would be expected to have the emotional capacity to cope with it. Any failure to do so would be treated as a lack on his part. He would be labelled as a problem because he was failing to conform to the goals of whatever rehabilitation had been planned. The focus of any intervention would be on getting John to behave in ways that would be acceptable to the services that he might need to receive.

I want to suggest another way of viewing John and his response to this illness. Throughout his life, John, like most other people, has been subjected to an education and socialisation which have caused him to believe that disability is a negative state. This is not just a passive piece of information that he held in his mind but a belief so strong that he had consistently thought of disabled people as lesser beings or part of another world. In short, he was a disablist person. Therefore, when he was diagnosed as having an illness that would result in his becoming increasingly impaired, he was only able to view this as the start of a negative phase of his life. While clearly he was subjected to a range of stigmatising stereotypes, the predominant ones were already in place within his own mind and he was in effect his own oppressor. We should try to understand this in terms of identity – John's identity as an able-bodied person was of such importance to him that, when it was threatened, it resulted in a range of self-damaging reactions.

Within this way of thinking, a number of questions arise as to how John might be helped. First, if he has been and continues to be influenced by a personal tragedy model of disability, then some form of consciousness-raising aimed at countering this, and providing him with an alternative way of understanding impairment and disability, may be of some value. However, is it possible that this can be achieved through contact with a social worker, when the probability is that she will be able-bodied and, regardless of this, likely to be representing an organisation that is embedded in an individual model approach to disability issues (Oliver and Sapey, 1999)?

It is possible that, as John retains his identity as an able-bodied person, he may find it easier to relate to an able-bodied social worker, albeit in order to strengthen his conviction that impairment is a problem. This is important, for if a social worker, whether they are disabled or non-disabled, is going to even begin helping in this situation, they are going to have to ensure that they do not reinforce these beliefs. There are various ways of doing this according to the style and approach to practice of the individual, but one thing that is important here is the recognition and understanding that disability can be a universal experience.

While many people are already disabled, those who are not could be at some point in the future and this makes disability somewhat different to other issues of oppression such as gender or race. Indeed, John represented precisely that, he was an able-bodied person who had become disabled and, while undoubtedly he faced many problems because of that, his first and perhaps most significant difficulty is his prior failure to acknowledge disabled people as part of the same society as himself. The problem therefore lies not just in the negative identity that John perceives disability has brought to him, but in his having a strong able-bodied identity prior to this.

Although individual social workers can be prepared for working in ways that do not reinforce the stigma which disabled people will experience, they also need to be able to provide people like John with some form of positive role models, and they need to consider how they do this while representing organisations that have traditionally been responsible for the large-scale segregation of disabled people. The problem here arises out of the ways in which social work agencies, in both the statutory and independent sectors, have developed their relationships with disabled people by treating them as 'other'. Finkelstein (1991) argues that such organisations have been practising an administrative model of disability in which social workers simply administer cures and care to disabled people who have already been deemed to be socially dead. But the process can be institutionalised in other ways. Social workers work in organisational structures which devalue direct work with clients. The rewards in terms of salary are in an inverse relationship to such contact, in that those jobs which have least direct contact pay most. In order to have a career in social work in the conventional sense of moving up the hierarchy and salary scale, social workers have to actively seek posts with reduced or no contact with their clients. If direct work is devalued, then so too are clients.

Individual social workers can resist such a culture, although it does make it personally difficult for them within their employment. However, even if social workers are individually able to resist pressures to conform to their agencies' view of disabled people, they may still have difficulty in presenting themselves to their clients in such a way. Social services departments will have some form of popular reputation and this will contribute to the way that the social worker is perceived from the outset of their working relationship, so it is important to try and establish a more personal basis for working together. This is not personal in the sense of being non-professional, but in terms of being symbolically separate from an oppressive organisation. The aim is to present oneself to John as someone whose identity is not determined by disablism, but by the idea that impairment can be part of a universal experience. Whether the social worker is disabled or not, this provides the potential of a positive role model.

CONCLUSION

All the examples I have discussed here are of men and therefore there may be other issues which should be considered in relation to disabled women, but nevertheless I am proposing that there is a possibility of positive social work practice with disabled people. Central to this is the recognition that the primary reason for that involvement is not the individual's impairment, but the ways in which society perceives people with impairments. This is made difficult by both the structure of social welfare agencies and the focus of social policy, in which disabled people are identified, defined and made separate from the rest of society. The task for the social worker will involve overcoming the structural, institutional, cultural, professional and personal barriers that contribute to the problem. However, none of this can be achieved effectively if social workers themselves hold onto an identity that devalues difference and impairment. Social work is an interpersonal activity and it cannot take place effectively if one person in the working relationship believes himself to be superior to the other.

FURTHER READING

Morris, J. (1993) *Independent Lives: Community Care and Disabled People*, Basingstoke: Macmillan – now Palgrave Macmillan. This is a study of disabled people's experience of receiving care which contains many important messages, both positive and negative, for anyone involved in organising support services for disabled people.

Oliver, M. and Sapey, B. (1999) *Social Work with Disabled People*, 2nd edn, Basingstoke: Macmillan – now Palgrave Macmillan. This is a key textbook, updated to include the major community care changes, which examines the relationship between the social model of disability and social work policies and practices.

Priestley, M. (1999) *Disability Politics and Community Care*, London: Jessica Kingsley. This book raises significant issues regarding the differences that exist between local authority services and disabled people's organisations in their understanding of what the outcomes of community care should be.

Thomas, C. (1999) *Female Forms: Experiencing and Understanding Disability*, Buckingham: Open University Press. This book develops social model theorising to include impairment effects and the psycho-emotional dimensions of disability alongside material issues, and in doing so raises some important questions about the role and practices of welfare.

Learning Disability

Tim Stainton

Introduction: constructing difference

CASE EXAMPLE

Jones, B, male, 18, profound mental handicap due to unspecified brain damage at birth, mental age of 3 years 10 months, poor motor control due to mild cerebral palsy on left side, no verbal or other forms of communication, frequent episodes of aggressive behaviour, incontinent and lacking all basic daily living skills.

Barry is a lively young man of 18 who has had a learning disability since birth. He walks with a slight limp on his left side. He does not speak nor has he had the opportunity to learn other formal means of communication, however, he communicates his likes and dislikes clearly through his facial expressions and behaviour. After being admitted to hospital due to the lack of community support systems, Barry has occasionally lashed out at staff. This invariably occurs after visits home and is usually directed at unfamiliar staff who are trying to rush him through one of his routines. Barry needs support to go to the toilet at regular intervals. Although he does very little in hospital, at his family home he enjoys helping wash the dishes or the car, going for long drives, listening to rock music, and has his own drum set which he uses regularly at home but has no access to at the hospital.

So which one is the real Barry Jones? Well, both of them, or at least they are as real as any of us get. They represent two different constructions of who Barry is. How he is constructed, though, has serious implications, not only for how we may perceive Barry but also how we as social workers might respond. While we are all socially constructed to some degree, people with a learning disability have been more vulnerable than most individuals or groups to negative, stigmatising and exclusionary constructions. A simple look at the labels used to describe learning disability illustrates this: *idiot; moron; imbecile; retard; defective; mentally handicapped,* and so on. These are all terms which jar our contemporary sensibilities, but which began their modern usage as 'scientific' terms or categories, but have been transformed into popular terms of derision in the English language. Such is the power of the construct that whatever term is used almost inevitably takes on an oppressive, derisory meaning. The power of any label to oppress is recognised by the movement of people who have a learning disability by their choosing *People First* as the name of their movement, inherently recognising how their humanity has been suppressed by this plethora of labels.

A key aspect of critical practice in this, or any other area of social work, is the ability to deconstruct imposed identities, to understand the power of various constructions and labels to oppress or emancipate. As social workers, we are both subject to, and part of, this process of identity construction. If we accept uncritically Barry number one, then we are likely simply to reinforce the oppressive and stigmatising identity that the description implies. We may choose to recommend more restrictive environments or more aggressive behavioural interventions which will themselves reinforce the spoiled identity described; a self-fulfilling prophesy. Or, we may ask ourselves how did this person get reduced to this litany of negative identity features? Who is the person behind this construction? How can we help Barry to overcome identity number one and embrace and build on identity two? This is not an easy challenge, as it requires both the skills and knowledge to deconstruct identities which are often mired in scientific complexity and the will to challenge systems, structures and professions which profit from the spoiling of Barry's identity.

In this chapter, we will look first at what we mean by learning disability and the difficulty in arriving at any specific definition. We will then look at the dominant models or approaches to learning disability: the medico-psychological model; normalisation; and a rights and citizenship perspective. The first two have been, and continue to be, widely used perspectives and we will briefly consider each and how one might respond in practice using these models. The third model, that of rights and citizenship, has only recently emerged and we will concentrate on this model and what it implies for critical practice in social work.

Defining learning disability

The simple task of naming the category of people we currently refer to as having a learning disability has often led to acrimonious debate and a large dose of political correctness. In the UK, *learning difficulty* or *disability* are the current 'correct' terms, while in the US the use of 'people first language' is de rigueur. Intellectual disability, developmental disability and older forms such as mentally handicapped, defective or retarded can all still be found in the literature and in practice. The reality is of course that there is no such thing as a neutral term, nor is any term perceived to be 'correct' today likely to remain so. Language is power and so will always reflect the shifting sands of power dialectics.

While the seemingly simple task of naming has proven complex, identifying exactly who we are talking about within whatever label we choose is equally complex and can have severe ramifications for those who are included or excluded. Over the years the category has expanded and contracted depending more on who was doing the categorising and why, than on any essential truth or scientific 'fact'. During the early part of the twentieth century, when the eugenics movement was at its height and intelligence tests were first being developed, the category expanded rapidly. H.H. Goddard's (1866–1957) rather poor interpretations of Binet's test created a situation where extreme numbers of persons were classified as 'mentally defective'. Goddard wrote:

> For many generations we have recognised and pitied the idiot. Of late we have recognised a higher type of defective, the moron, and have discovered he is a burden … a menace to society and civilization, that he is responsible in large measure, for many, if not all, our social problems.
>
> (Quoted in Abbott and Sapsford, 1987: 25)

Intelligence tests rely heavily on normative assumptions about what constitutes average or 'normal' functioning with little regard to social or cultural factors. The arbitrary nature of determining what constitutes 'normal' can be seen in the fact that when the American Association on Mental Deficiency reclassified its IQ levels, 'thousands of people were cured of mental handicaps overnight' (Blatt, quoted in Bogdan and Taylor, 1982).

So, the question of 'what is learning disability?' is neither simple nor without dangers. Being included in the definition has at different times meant a total loss of rights, being subject to sterilisation, incarcerated and, in some cases, killed. On the other side, being excluded may mean a lack of access to services or support. Therefore, the critical social worker must be aware of not only what the various definitions are, but also more critically, the implications for the person involved.

In general, we find at one end of the spectrum definitions which have an exclusive or predominant emphasis on the biological facts, the presence of a specific impairment such as Down's syndrome. The main problem with this type of definition is its exclusive focus on learning disability as a 'disease', an individual pathology, with little or no reference to the practical or social consequences which may be vastly different given the severity, the individual and the social context. A more specific problem is the magnitude of possibilities and range of degrees that may be present in a given case. Most learning disabilities cannot be attributed to a specific biological factor. Down's syndrome represents the largest single identified 'cause' and yet includes only 10 per cent of the entire putative 'class'. This does not even begin to tell us about the degree or severity of the impairment.

Other definitions have focused on various forms of intelligence or adaptive behaviour tests which purport to measure either intelligence or behavioural attributes or deficits. As noted above, these definitions rely heavily on normative assumptions about what constitutes average functioning or adaptive behaviour. They also tend to ignore the 'person' behind the behaviours or IQ levels and engender stereotypical responses and attitudes. Saying someone has a mental age of 13 gives the impression that they act like a 13 year old or can only do things that a 13 year old can. In fact, this tells us nothing about who the person is or what they want and are capable of.

These types of definitions generally are underpinned by what Oliver (1990) has termed the 'personal tragedy theory of disability' (see Chapter 18), where disability is seen exclusively as an individual, disease-based problem, thus encouraging a focus on the elimination of the impairment and a predominantly bio-psychological approach to policy and practice. For example, if you were working from this model, you might recommend for Barry more psychological or psychiatric intervention, the problem being exclusively 'in Barry'. Alternatively, a 'social model' of disability has begun to emerge, spurred on largely by the work of people with disabilities themselves and focusing not on the individual with a disability as the problem, but on social arrangements which 'construct disabilities'.

In this vein, some have attempted to deal with the problem by the conceptualisation of learning disability as purely a social construct. The central idea is that through processes such as labelling, segregation, stigmatisation, lack of access and a denial of citizenship we have constructed the disability. While these ideas seem relevant, they fail to give us the whole picture, and they do not seem to deal adequately with physical or intellectual difference. One may well be disabled because as a wheelchair user you cannot enter a building that does not have a ramp, but the fact still remains that physiological difference must be acknowledged if it is to be addressed. What we need is a conception that allows for some identification of difference if we are to justify differential treatment in terms of services and supports, allows us to engage in a process of empowerment and collective emancipation, but does not itself engender social devaluation and discrimination; a tall if not impossible order.

St Claire (1989) argues that we need to view three dimensions interactionally: impairments; subnormal performance; and role failures, in terms of failure to adequately fulfill socially defined roles or achieve statuses consistent with valued social roles. Social construction is seen as overlaying all three dimensions, encouraging an interaction between the elements. That is, identification of an impairment, and consequent labelling, may lead to inadequate education, stigmatisation and segregation, thus inhibiting development of social skills and resulting in devaluation and role failures. However, at the end of the day, the critical social worker must remember that definitions, of whatever type, are simply social constructs which help us to understand a general phenomenon, but tell us little about the person behind the label. But, the critical social worker must also remember that definitions are powerful tools which can be used for good or ill. A rose by any other name does not always smell as sweet.

Medical, psychological and normalisation approaches

As the above sections suggest, how we approach both the definition and process of supporting people with a learning disability has a major impact on our practice and, more importantly, on the outcomes for the people involved. The medical or psychological approaches discussed above engendered certain types of responses such as special classes, behavioural interventions, medical control, a focus on prevention and institutional or 'hospital' provision. The eugenics fears reflected in Goddard's comments engendered a response of control, regulation and exclusion which still haunts our current system of services and policy, although now the most explicit eugenic focus is on prenatal detection and elimination. The medical and psychological approaches are still common in practice today, particularly in cases where people are thought to have either 'challenging behaviour' – mental health difficulties in addition to a learning disability – or complex physical needs. Whether this justifies the continued use of these approaches is a question beyond the scope of this chapter, but one you may want to keep in the back of your mind as we look at other approaches which are more relevant to social work practice.

Normalisation or, as it has been renamed, *social role valorisation* was the dominant approach to learning disability from the 1970s through to the 1990s and is still common in practice today. The most influential version was developed by Wolf Wolfensberger. The normalisation principle as formulated by Wolfensberger is as follows:

> The utilisation of culturally valued means in order to establish and/or maintain personal behaviours, experiences and characteristics that are culturally normative and valued.
>
> (Quoted in O'Brien, 1981: 1)

Normalisation is based on social role theory and, as the name implies, is concerned with reversing negative roles and images and developing and enhancing more positive social roles for people with a learning disability. As such, normalisation is concerned with issues such as dress, the normal rhythms to people's day, the locations and company in which people spend their time and the things people spend their time doing. For example, normalisation advocates against large groupings of devalued people, segregated provision which reinforces their role as different, labelling and stigmatisation. In short, normalisation is concerned with ensuring that people with a learning disability fulfil roles which are both valued and non-stigmatising (see Brown and Smith, 1992, for further details on normalisation).

While the above brief review hardly does justice to what is a complex theory, you can see how this might influence practice, by, for example, ensuring that people have the opportunity to participate in meaningful activities, rather than spending their days in large day centres enduring endless, usually pointless training that only reinforces their differences. In short, it means ensuring that our interventions enhance people's positive roles in our community and minimise the occurrence of devalued or stigmatising activities and roles. Normalisation can also be a useful means of evaluating current or proposed services or interventions. In brief, we can ask ourselves 'does this activity encourage a positive identity or reinforce a negative image?'

In recent years, normalisation has come in for criticism from a number of directions (see for example Brown and Smith, 1992), but most of these can be summed up in two related questions: does normalisation simply reinforce existing ideas about normality and what is culturally accepted?; and, does normalisation simply encourage the appearance of normality without really giving the individual true choice and empowerment? In the former case, concerns centre around reinforcing societal prejudices about race, gender, sexuality, class and so on. In order for people not to be further stigmatised, are they encouraged to accept roles which may be oppressive either to themselves or others? In the second case, does normalisation encourage people simply to 'pass' rather than challenging their oppressors and embracing and celebrating their own identity? Space precludes a full treatment of these issues, but we can look at what has evolved as a 'next step', that is, the rights, citizenship and self-determination movement.

Rights, citizenship and self-determination

The concepts of rights, citizenship and self-determination (see Chapter 4) are increasingly seen as central to a new approach to learning disability. We are concerned here with ensuring that everyone can exercise their rights as citizens. Stirring words but ones which raise a host of questions, particularly for people with a learning disability as traditionally they have been considered to lack the basic prerequisites for both rights and citizenship. John Locke, a central figure in modern liberal political thought, was clear on this point in his *Two Treatises of Government*:

> But if through defects that may happen out of the ordinary course of Nature, any one comes not to such a degree of reason wherein he might be supposed capable of knowing the law, ... he is never capable of being a free man, ... So lunatics and idiots are never set free from the government of their parents.
>
> (1924: 145)

While this citation may seem of little relevance today, in fact it represents the very basis upon which people with learning disabilities have been, and continue to be, excluded from full citizenship rights. This is taken even further by many moral and political philosophers who question the very humanness of people with a learning disability. Ryle notes that 'specifically human behavior' is that 'which is unachieved by animals, idiots and infants' and Quinton, discussing the centrality of rationality in humanness, notes that 'defective human beings who look and are physically constructed like men ... are only marginally or by a sort of prudent and humane courtesy fully human beings' (both quoted in Goodey, 1992: 28ff.). Therefore, rights, citizenship and self-determination may seem a strange place on which to base an approach to learning disability. On the other hand, it may be that we are finally attacking the real root of their oppression and exclusion.

Rights in Western democratic states are grounded in the idea of autonomy or self-determination; that is, the ability to choose how to live one's own life either on our own or, as is the case with most of us, in collaboration with others whom we choose to live and work with. Self-determination is of course not a new term, having long been considered the core value of the social work profession. It is also a core value in Western liberal democratic societies. This connection is useful in helping us to understand what self-determination means, and does not mean, for practice and policy. We will return to this question shortly, but first, let us look at the concept of self-determination.

Put simply, it is choosing for oneself what one does or does not want to do, be or value. A slightly more complex definition of the related term 'autonomy' is *the capacity to formulate and pursue plans and purposes which are self-determined* (Stainton, 1994). This highlights a couple of key features which will help us to see what this means for practice. First, we are concerned here with *capacity* not outcome. In other words, our goal is not to ensure that people achieve some specific outcome we think is valid, but that they have the capacity to determine what they would like to do and an equal chance of achieving their goal as anyone else. Notice that we are concerned with equal opportunity, not outcome. In service terms, this means that we will focus more on supporting choice-making through our planning and assessment systems and other supports such as advocacy, rather than deciding what programme or service is best for a person.

Second, we are concerned not only that people are able to decide something for themselves, but also with their ability to act on their choices. Telling someone they are free to decide to go to college, but not providing the means for them to do so is no choice at all. We are not looking at special rights here, but simply ensuring that people with a learning disability are not inhibited by discriminatory practices and have an equal chance to benefit from college as anyone else. So our goals in practice are to ensure that people have the means to exercise their choices whether that means support staff, benefits, or simply knowledge and skills.

The idea of equality requires some clarification here. If equal means simply 'getting the same as everyone else', in essence that means we are ignoring difference that may require either a different way of doing things or additional support. This problem, sometimes called the 'difference dilemma', refers to the problem that what people require in order to achieve equal citizenship differs with each individual. In other words, 'equal treatment' does not equate with equal citizenship, since different people require different types of treatment to achieve the same basic capacity for participation. For example, a person who is paraplegic requires different means to achieve basic mobility than does a fully ambulant person. They are not getting 'more' mobility, they simply require more to achieve the same mobility as everyone else.

While the example above may be relatively easy, dealing with this dilemma becomes more acute as the nature and complexity of needs increases. This complexity makes it impossible to establish general universal provisions which will satisfy all needs. The challenge then for social work and policy is not to find better services, but to create a structure in which individuals can articulate their demands directly and which allows the state to adjudicate and meet legitimate claims. In essence, this is what the role of the local authority social worker is in a rights-based system, both helping the person to articulate their needs and determining if these are needs which a person has a right to have met. If so, then the social worker becomes the catalyst for both making sure that they are met and monitoring any changes in the person's needs.

The struggle to recognise and respect the autonomy, citizenship and rights of people with a learning disability is at heart a political struggle. It is not primarily a psychological concept concerned with changing the individual, but a political one concerned with changing the relationship between the individual and the state. On one level, this means focusing on obtaining basic legal equality and securing equality of rights. The new Human Rights Act 1998 is a good example. However, legal equality and rights are only one step towards equal citizenship for people with learning disabilities. On a more structural level, social policy must begin to allow for individually determined choices about the how, when and where support is provided. This is why policy developments such as direct funding and access to advocacy, which allow the individual to choose how their needs are to be met, are so critical to building self-determination and equal citizenship. They provide the means for the individual citizen to emerge, participate and grow as an individual citizen rather than a part of some excluded putative class. These types of change to the context of practice are critical if social workers are to be given the scope to truly recognise and support the rights and citizenship of people with a learning disability (see Stainton, 1998). The critical practitioner must be able to recognise where structural barriers exist and work to overcome them within their own communities and agencies.

On the level of practice, social workers' key roles as assessors and case managers are critical in determining if people are to be supported to be autonomous, rights-bearing citizens, or if they are to continue to be oppressed. From this perspective, critical practice requires a much sharper focus on the individual both in terms of our planning and assessment systems and in determining needs and how they are best met. Planning and assessment systems such as person centered planning (Sanderson, 1997) are useful tools in helping us to do this and help to break us out of existing ways of working with people.

In many ways, from a rights and citizenship perspective, critical practice is simply what has always been good practice in social work: making the user the centre of the assessment process; acting as a facilitator to help people to determine for themselves what they need and want, and not deciding for them; ensuring that they are supported to make decisions both with information and independent advocacy and advice, particularly important for people with more severe learning disabilities who may not be able to articulate formally their wants and needs. The critical social worker is not an 'expert' on intellectual disability, but a skilled professional able to support people both to determine and act on what they want and need in order to be the person they want to be. In the past, we predetermined outcomes for people by labelling them and then assigning them to 'services for the moderately mentally handicapped' and so on – a day centre, a group home, a special school. A rights-based approach means that we must reject any preconceived notions of what some illusory category of 'people with a learning disability' needs, and focus on the individual as an individual, who happens to require some support because he or she has a learning disability. What a person wants and needs are questions that must be addressed to the specific individual, not to a label or category.

CONCLUSION

So to return to Barry, our goal is to see past the labels, diagnoses and so on and see the person, to find ways of helping Barry to express what he needs and wants and support him in achieving this, even if it may not be what 'we' think is 'best for him'. The critical practitioner needs to be aware of both the often subtle ways in which Barry's identity has been distorted and the ways and means of helping him to reclaim his autonomy, rights and citizenship.

I have tried to outline what is required if we take the autonomy, rights and citizenship of people with a learning disability seriously. A foundation in rights and legal equality, a social policy structure which supports and enhances individual autonomy and participation, and practice which truly focuses on the person and who they are and what they want. As was noted, this perspective is at heart a political concept which is also concerned with eliminating the oppression experienced by people with a learning disability. Is not the social work response then too individualistic to bring about this change? First, as was noted, a social worker has an ethical obligation to work towards broader structural changes which counter oppressive structures and practices. But in terms of practice with specific individuals, it is founded on the belief that only empowered individuals can form the collective force necessary to bring about full citizenship for people with learning disabilities. As Lise Noel (1994) notes, 'Even though emancipation begins and ends with the individual, he or she has only collective means of ensuring its progress'. Critical practitioners must not only commit themselves to these goals, but arm themselves with the knowledge and tools to both identify means of oppression and support people to take their rightful place as full and equal citizens.

FURTHER READING

Atkinson, D. (1999) *Advocacy: A Review*, Brighton: Pavilion. An excellent review of the literature on advocacy.

Brown, H. and Smith, H. (eds) (1992) *Normalisation: A Reader for the Nineties*, London: Routledge. This volume provides a good overview of normalisation (Ch. 1), its applications (Ch. 3) and some of the key criticisms (Ch. 10).

Malin, N. (ed.) (1996) *Services for People With Learning Disabilities*, London: Routledge. This book remains the best overview of the history, definition and range of services for people with a learning disability.

Ramcharan, P., Roberts, G., Grant, G. and Borland, J. (eds) (1997) *Empowerment in Everyday Life: Learning Disability*, London: Jessica Kingsley. An excellent volume containing chapters on self-advocacy (Ch. 3), families (Ch. 5), legal aspects (Ch. 9) and citizenship and empowerment (Ch. 13).

Stainton, T. (1998) 'Rights and Rhetoric of Practice: Contradictions for Practitioners', in Symonds, A. and Kelly, A. (eds) *The Social Construction of Community Care*, London: Macmillan – now Palgrave Macmillan. This chapter, although not specifically on learning disability, outlines the basis of a rights approach and some of the contradictions and paradoxes this raises for practice in the current system of community care.

20

Older People

Mo Ray and Judith Phillips

This chapter will address some key critical debates and dilemmas in social work practice with older people. It discusses the role of critical practice in the development of positive social work practice with older people and proposes an agenda for change and development, which incorporates the key messages of critical practice. Finally, we identify what we believe to be an appropriate future agenda for gerontological social work practice. The issues we highlight draw on the following case study.

CASE EXAMPLE

Marjorie Wilson lives alone and has one daughter who lives locally. She is 76 years old and has worked all her life as a school cook. Marjorie's health and well-being are reported to have deteriorated very rapidly over the past year and she has become increasingly dependent on her daughter, Joan. She often feels intensely lonely and these feelings tend to be associated with drinking alcohol. She has significant memory difficulties and often appears disoriented. This is the case even when she is not drinking.

She has fallen several times and has been admitted to hospital. She has just been registered blind and diagnosed as having dementia. Marjorie is pressing to be discharged, saying that her daughter will provide the care she needs. Ian, the duty social worker, knows that this is not the case as both her daughter and her neighbours have telephoned the social work duty officer several times to complain about Marjorie being at risk and a risk to the community.

Critical debates in social work with older people

There are many dilemmas and challenges involved in developing the values and skills of social work within the current trends in practice. The social work practice arena with older people is not a straightforward one.

Policy dilemmas

Inequalities in service provision

There remain significant tensions in policy and practice in relation to the inequalities that exist in service provision for older people. For example, in the imperative to manage finite resources, the net amount of money available to be spent on each older service user often has a lower threshold than for younger people with physical or learning disabilities (Bradley and Manthorpe, 1997). The effect may be for social workers and care managers to continue to be influenced by the 'perverse incentive' towards admission for older people to care homes or for assessments of need to be service led. Older people may be particularly vulnerable to admission to residential care if the money available for their care needs is already being spent and their changing needs require more financial resources. How should social workers balance the aspirations of an older person, such as Marjorie, wishing to remain at home with the needs of the organisation to manage finite resources and avoid overspending? How can social workers cope with the reality that limits must be placed what can be spent on an individual person in order to make sure there is money for other people in need of social services?

Diverse needs of older people

Historically, policy has not addressed the needs of older people in relation to their potentially diverse range of needs. At its simplest level, community care services for older people were slow to develop (Means and Smith, 1998b). The provision of services for older people continues to focus on, for example, services such as home care and, once a person has reached a sufficiently complex level of need, residential or nursing home care appears to remain the primary service option. These are, of course, important services. But, the tendency to focus on the predictable denies the possibility of older people having needs as complex and diverse as the rest of the population. There is now a greater commitment towards the development of rehabilitative services (Sinclair and Dickinson, 1998), but preventive services remain underdeveloped or unavailable. There is a need for social work and care management to continue to move away from the 'one size fits all' approach to intervention and care planning. How this can be achieved in the context of increasing workloads and the failure to develop creative service options remains a crucial dilemma. In Marjorie's case there may eventually be a need for a more intense supportive environment, based on creative packages of care from public and informal sources.

Partnership

One of the key elements of developing critical practice in working with older people is the emphasis on partnership. Although this has become a buzzword (Thompson, 2000), in reality, different agencies providing different services often work within different theoretical and value frameworks and, consequently, tensions arise. Evidence so far of different approaches being adopted by health, as opposed to social work, professionals is not overly encouraging (Illife, 2000). Yet, the reorganisation – in some areas this means integration – of social work, health and housing departments is an important aspect of work in this area. The development of alternative partnership models of care and support remains on the edge of service provision and social workers have lacked a clear voice in their development.

Practice and professional dilemmas

The managerial process of assessment

It is argued that the NHS and Community Care Act 1990 has had the effect of promoting social work as a purely bureaucratic role, aimed at gatekeeping services for the most 'needy' (Phillips, 1992). Hughes (1995) highlights a potential tension between professional aspirations for assessment set against managerial imperatives towards eligibility, which can force a reductionist approach to assessment.

There is a tendency towards understanding assessment as a means of obtaining resources rather than of acquiring an understanding of the individual and his/her needs. The service-led or procedural assessment is alive and well and determining eligibility and the associated provision of services may remain, in the hearts and minds of budget-focused organisations, the most important aspect of assessment. This in turn poses an enhanced potential for the move towards standardised approaches to assessment, which reinforce a notion that assessment is not an activity which requires skill (Smale and Tuson, 1993). Such approaches are likely to result in an associated reduction in older persons' rights to start from their own ideas about their situation. Proving eligibility can carry with it a disincentive to highlight an older person's strengths, abilities and lifelong continuities which may be harnessed to cope with current challenges. Moreover, it may deny the possibility of developing assessment within appropriate theoretical frameworks (Milner and O'Byrne, 1998; see also Chapter 26) and with no reflection on the relationship between the social worker and the older person. How can or should social workers use their skills in assessment processes when they have an organisational imperative to prove eligibility? The potential for developing social work skill in assessment is in danger of being stunted and is a critical issue that strikes at the heart of social work provision with older people. Conducting a thorough assessment of Marjorie's and her daughter's needs may be complex and time consuming but an essential part of intervention. Services may not be the primary response to Marjorie's needs initially and an ongoing assessment to build up a picture of her life may require longer term work.

The concept of risk

Risk assessment and management is reinforced as a crucial issue in the current social care context with older people (see also Chapter 27). The skilful management of risk set in a context of working positively with the rights of an individual to continue to assert their own wishes, needs and aspirations is central to the skill and value of the social work role (Stevenson, 1989). This is inevitably complex work and is in danger of being routinised by procedural assessment practice. In this context, risk may be centralised in assessment in order to attempt to secure finite resources. The concept of risk is also in danger of being narrowly understood and defined and its central relationship to quality of life overlooked. How should social workers be enabled to work creatively in complex situations of risk and continue to develop practice skills appropriate to the needs and aspirations of older service users (Tanner, 1998b)? What are the relative risks to Marjorie in pursuing different options in her future care?

Ageist stereotypes

Routinised assessments may also serve to reinforce ageist stereotypes, which abound about older people and, perhaps in particular, older people who need to use social and health care services (see also Chapter 3). For example, a focus on individual dysfunction and problem states can reinforce notions about the inevitable dependency of older people. A failure to consider an older person in their biographical context can have the effect of separating older age from the rest of the life course and rendering the complexities and uniqueness of a person's life invisible. Finally, failing to consider strengths and abilities can imply that older people are helpless in the face of change. How can we avoid older people's biographies entering our field of vision only at the point that they become known to us in a social work or care management context?

Balancing carer and user needs

Over the past decade the central role of informal carers has been increasingly recognised (Twigg and Atkin, 1994). Social workers and care managers face the practice tensions of working with carers and older service users who may have very different views about their circumstances and aspirations for the future. For example, how should social workers manage the tension of a carer, such as Joan, telling them that their older relative should move into a care home, while the older person is indicating that their key aspiration is to remain at home? Carers roles are dynamic and diverse and there is a need for social work to develop practice insight into the ways in which the role may change, often dramatically, over a relatively short time period (Ray, 2000). There is a need to recognise and understand the ways in which carers and those people they care for bring meaning and understanding to their situations, informed by their existing relationship (Nolan et al., 1996; Parker, 1994). The strengths, skills and approaches that they use to manage their circumstances should also be a feature of assessment, intervention and care planning. The social work role should be focused on unpicking the complexity of these contexts and providing interventions which enhance and support service users and carers rather than providing services which, at best, can only substitute existing help or, at worst, be experienced as unhelpful. In the above case study, should Joan be supported in caring for her mother or should services be directly provided to Marjorie? Once again, these dilemmas point to a need for the ongoing development of practice skills and values aimed at being able to work positively with complex practice situations, including situations of conflict and disagreement. In what ways should the social work practice agenda inform practitioners in their ability to fully embrace the complexities of such work?

Crisis, change and transition

Social workers and care managers are inevitably engaged with older people at times of crisis, change and transition. They are faced with the goal of working positively with older people who are experiencing complex and frightening situations. In this context, social workers' skills and values must incorporate the ability to work with positive assessment but must also have the skill to provide positive and skilful interventions. This is a difficult issue as community care teams are increasingly driven towards short-term assessment and purchasing provision and there is not always a place where the short-term worker can refer an older person for longer term work. This is not a call for a return to long-term, open-ended 'casework'. But, we do challenge the notion that every service user has needs, which will inevitably be short term. A person with dementia, for example, may need time for a social worker to build a relationship with her/him. Difficulties with memory and communication, together with an appropriate concern about a 'stranger' intruding on a private life, may make it impossible for a social worker to engage in a short-term 'assessment relationship'. Older people bereft of lifelong partners may need time and skilful help to cope with, and manage in the aftermath of, their bereavement. Older people, like anyone else through the life course, may experience difficulties with alcohol and drugs, have sexual difficulties, find it hard to talk with their partner, be in an abusive relationship or face terminal illness. These life challenges can be as disabling as chronic physical or mental illness and do not necessarily lend themselves to a procedural assessment followed by the provision of off-the-peg interventions. How should social workers and care managers appropriately respond when they are faced with service users with complex needs requiring intervention beyond the provision of care services? What theoretical and practice bases should inform the gerontological social work agenda?

All these critical debates and dilemmas currently influence the social work role with older people. Social work must live with these tensions. Dealing with such complexities is the 'bread and butter' of social work. They highlight three important questions:

- What should constitute an appropriate social work practice agenda with older people?

■ How should a social work agenda take account of the central role of care management, while developing an appropriate social work practice with older people?

■ What critical practice do we need to develop to work with older people in the best possible way?

The contribution of critical practice

Brechin (2000: 27) defines key components of critical practice as:

> the capacity to handle uncertainty and change, rather than simply operating in prescribed ways in accordance with professional skills and knowledge. Practitioners must in a sense, face both ways, to be seen as appropriately knowledgeable and competent but at the same time be continually aware of the relative and contextual basis of their practice. A critical approach, of itself assumes no moral direction. If however, we assume that here is a fundamental assumption of social justice underpinning the provision of care for others, it follows that successful caring processes must be both empowering and anti-oppressive.

Brechin (2000) frames three domains of critical practice as:

■ Critical action

■ Critical reflexivity

■ Critical analysis.

How might these domains assist social workers in developing their practice skills within uncertain organisational contexts?

CASE EXAMPLE revisited

The case study in this chapter highlights some of the practice dilemmas that a social worker may typically face and the ways that the skills of critical practice may assist in complex practice situations. Ian faces uncertainty both in terms of Marjorie's future and also in relation to the impossibility of knowing with any certainty what he should do for the best to support her. For example, he has to live with the knowledge that Marjorie is in many ways at risk, but that while there are interventions that may alleviate the risk, he is unlikely to solve all the challenges that she faces. Ian has had to recognise and work with the realisation that other people may have different perspectives and has had to try to understand what, at first, may appear to be unsympathetic responses to Marjorie's deteriorating situation. Ian has also had to make use of his knowledge of social work theory and information about physical conditions (for example blindness) to assist and inform his interventions. An essential part of this process must involve evaluating the outcomes of his interventions and reflecting on the process of his involvement with Marjorie.

Critical action

Critical action should be at the heart of social work practice with older people. It highlights the importance of tackling inequalities and disadvantage and working towards the empowerment of service users (Brechin, 2000). As we have seen, a critical debate rests on the erroneous assumption that ageing is appropriately positioned along a dimension of dependence and independence. There are now signs of a shift away from pathologising older people. Theoretical contributions towards the empowerment of service users have come through a critical perspective in exploring the social construction of old age (Phillipson and Walker, 1987). The focus of a critical perspective is to challenge assumptions that many of the experiences commonly associated with ageing are driven by biological imperatives. Instead, it is argued, many key experiences generally associated with the experience of ageing are constructed, sustained and reinforced by policy, legislation and organisational procedures which create structural inequalities (for example, Townsend, 1996).

For example, it could be argued within a critical perspective that the assumption that the most appropriate form of care for an older person with physical or cognitive disabilities is in residential care, and fuelled by limited resources to invest in support of older people, both creates and reinforces the inequalities experienced by older service users. The assumption that people with dementia cannot participate in complex decisions about their lives can be reinforced by practices which display tunnel vision and do not make use of evidence which challenges these assertions.

Anti-discriminatory practice

The promotion of anti-discriminatory approaches to working with older people is at the heart of critical practice. A gerontological social work agenda should vigorously challenge the notion that such work is boring and amounts to little more than providing a limited range of off-the-peg services. As we have seen, such approaches do nothing to challenge the assumption that older people are an essentially homogeneous group with the same or similar needs (Bytheway, 2000). Age-based discrimination of this nature reinforces myths about ageing and perpetuates superficial explanations of complex situations together with standardised service responses. As individual social workers, we have a professional duty to challenge society's views and assumptions about older people. For example, social workers should seek to recognise and value the diversity among older people with whom they work. This includes obvious differences such as membership of diverse ethnic minority groups, cultural experiences and sexual orientation. It also includes recognition and value being placed on the uniqueness of individual lives. Booth (1993), in his discussion of empowerment and older people, highlights the importance of a principle of enablement, that is, the validation of people's coping abilities together with a principle of proactive intervention focusing on the positive qualities and competences of older people and not just their disabilities. He argues that commitment to such principles challenges and opposes age-based discrimination.

Empowerment

A commitment to critical action would also empower older service users. It is important to work with service users' own definition of the problems or challenges they face. If practitioners are genuinely able to engage with this process, it is a crucial step away from the tendency to begin assessment by sizing up what sort of services might be needed. Part of the assessment process must recognise the importance of understanding the skills, abilities and active reorganisation attempts that older people have engaged with in order to manage the threats or changes in their situations (Ray, 2000). It is important for Ian to work with both Marjorie and Joan to build on the strengths in their relationship, enable both to discuss the situation and empower Marjorie by making a difference.

Empowerment beyond the assessment process involves the participation of the service user in deciding upon interventions or plans to meet identified needs. Participation and empowerment are fraught with problems in a context of restrictions on public expenditure. Allen et al. (1992) have reflected on the disincentives that practitioners face in 'coming clean' about what is possible when it is at variance with the aspirations of older service users. Clearly, there is a continued need for organisations to shoulder the responsibility of communicating clearly with user groups about the demands on finite resources and what can and cannot be achieved. Ideally, too, service users should be enabled to participate in planning community care and social services. At an individual level, it is likely that service users will fare better within a social services setting if they are armed with appropriate information about what they can and cannot expect in the process. For example, in Marjorie's case, what rehabilitation can achieve in enhancing abilities, promoting well-being and dignity to life. Bringing older people's voices to the forefront of practice can provide empowering experiences for both social worker and older person, offering insights which will be of great value to practitioners in listening to, for example, marginalised groups of older women with dementia (Bornat, 1999; Mills, 1999).

Biography and life course

Inherent in this approach is a recognition of biography of an individual (Dant et al., 1989; Bornat, 1999). Older people may have lifelong continuities, which they wish to preserve. Understanding the importance of biographical continuity can challenge and prevent a social worker from, for example, constructing apparent intransigence as the 'stubbornness' bound to accompany old age.

Our current snapshot approach tells us little about the entrances and exits that older people experience in relation to a range of problems over the course of their lives, what would help them to balance or juggle different dilemmas, or assist them in care giving or transitions to care. A life course approach can illustrate the way in which continuities are used to construct current identities and explain the ways in which individual older people employ strategies for managing change.

In addition, there is a clear need for social workers engaged in critical action to have the knowledge base to mobilise appropriate resources. This may mean providing traditional community care services such as home care and daycare. In addition, however, there may be other creative ways in which needs may be met. In the case study, Ian eventually solved the need for Marjorie to have some regular contact at home by arranging for a volunteer from a local dementia care organisation to visit. The volunteer was able to work positively with Marjorie by connecting with her lifelong interest in cooking. Eventually, the relationship enabled Marjorie to accept additional formal help from the specialist home care team.

Clearly, not all older service users will be in a position to receive complex information, weigh up the costs and benefits of various courses of action or decide independently on the best decision for them (Brown, 2000). There is a social work role in advocating for the service user to ensure that they have access to appropriate support or getting an advocate.

Critical analysis

Brechin (2000: 30) defines critical analysis as 'the critical evaluation of knowledge, theories, policies and practice, with an in-built recognition of multiple perspectives and an orientation of ongoing enquiry'.

Social work practice with older people is notable for its lack of a demonstrable relationship with theoretical frameworks to inform, develop and evaluate practice. This is in part caused by the slowness of disciplines contributing to social gerontology to systematically develop theoretical frameworks. Sheldon and McDonald (1999) argue that professional beliefs not based on evidence and debate consequently stand in the way of developing reflective evidence-based practice.

CASE EXAMPLE revisited

What sorts of theory might usefully be applied to social work with older people? The answer to this is it depends on the nature of the need or situation the social worker is facing. Consider, for example, Marjorie's situation – what kinds of theory and knowledge base might inform Ian's assessment, intervention and practice? The following are possible responses:

- loss (for example visual impairment and dementia)
- continuity and management of change
- theories associated with addiction
- impact of dementia (for example person-centred approaches to care and support, cognitive behavioural interventions)
- legal frameworks (for example community care legislation and associated adult legislation, current national and local policy)
- risk and risk management
- biographical and life course perspectives.

Given the complexity of the individual lives of older people and the diverse situations likely to be encountered, it follows that social work assessment and intervention must be informed by a diverse and appropriate theoretical knowledge base, which can be transformed into practice that can be evaluated.

Critical reflexivity

Brechin et al. (2000) define critical reflexivity as:

> an aware, reflective and engaged self; the term 'reflexivity' implies that practitioners recognise their engagement with service-users and others in a process of negotiating understandings and interventions and are aware of the assumptions and values they bring to this process.

Developing reflective skills through reflecting on our own understanding of ageing is an important and often overlooked aspect of social work practice with older people. Working with older people sharpens our focus on our own ageing and our possible future selves. Although the ability to examine one's self is a central preoccupation in social work, reflecting on self-ageing can be challenging and can call into question our own stereotypes and negativities associated with old age. Examining one's biases is not a once and for all experience but needs attention throughout the social work process in order to understand the social worker's impact on the service user. Reflexivity is one way of analysing the power differential and the diversity within the relationship. It is a way of understanding our role in the process. In Ian's case, working with Marjorie may, for example, highlight his own emotional problems in caring for his own mother.

CONCLUSION

We have argued that one way of working positively in complex environments is to develop critical practice in the context of gerontological social work. Such a development should engage in a debate about what should properly and appropriately constitute social work with older people. Most importantly, it should acknowledge the importance of developing sound knowledge bases and theoretical frameworks to both underpin and evaluate practice. Such practice should engage in broad agendas on a number of levels. The agendas would reflect the diversity associated with the experience of ageing and should include an active commitment to developing theoretical and practical interventions based on evidence. We believe that there should be a clear distinction between social work and care management, in order to develop as a respected and legitimate activity in the twenty-first century.

FURTHER READING

George, M. (2000) Breaking the Cycle: The Risk Factor, *Community Care*, 24–30 August. Looks at how an assertive outreach mental health team attempts to improve the well-being of an older woman who has been going back and forth from her home to hospital for many years. Case notes as well as arguments for and against risk are presented.

Hughes, B. (1995) *Older People and Community Care: Critical Theory and Practice*, Buckingham: Open University Press. Covers both policy and practice in relation to older people. It questions the lack of attention given by professionals to issues of structural inequality in old age and looks at how community care practice can be based on anti-ageist values and principles. It also looks at social work skills and dilemmas that inevitably arise in this area of work.

Marshall, M. and Dixon, M. (1996) *Social Work with Older People*, 3rd edn, London: Macmillan – now Palgrave Macmillan. Outlines and discusses the complexity of the social work role, focusing particularly on assessment and care management.

Neysmith, S. (ed.) (1999) *Critical Issues for Future Social Work with Aging Persons*, New York: Columbia University Press. *Critical Issues* moves beyond traditional frameworks in which we practise to a new conceptualisation of ageing. It maps a new agenda for social work in the twenty-first century, particularly focusing on women and takes a critical feminist approach in discussing a number of issues.

Opie, A. (1995) *Beyond Good Intentions: Support Work with Older People*, Wellington: Institute of Policy Studies. This book from New Zealand offers an analysis of the effectiveness of social work practice to carers and people with dementia. It is a gold mine of issues that span the globe in relation to how social work is practised with older people.

Dying and Bereavement

21

Caroline Currer

This chapter rests on the premise that dying and bereavement are very clearly on the agenda for all workers in social care,[1] whatever their area of practice. It argues that two factors are essential for critical practice in this and other areas of social work. These are confidence about the social work role, and the habit of reflectivity. For both, up-to-date and broadly based theoretical understandings are necessary, therefore, the chapter outlines a number of relevant concepts and models, showing through the use of practice examples how these can be used as a basis for critical practice with people who are dying or bereaved.

Critical practice with people who are dying or bereaved

Social work with people who are dying or bereaved is not, outside specialist settings, a unitary or defining area of work. For the mainstream worker, these aspects of experience may not be the main focus of involvement. Moreover, dying and bereavement are very different events as, in any particular situation, they describe the situation of different actors, for whom the outcome of the crisis of death is totally different. In some instances, involvement may span the event of death, offering important benefits for service users who are bereaved. Nevertheless, it is still helpful to look separately at dying and bereavement if we are to understand both the experience of those concerned and the social work response to their situation.

Confidence about the social work contribution and reflective practice warrant some discussion at the outset. Parton and Marshall sum up the paradox inherent within them as follows: 'The contemporary challenge for social work is to take action, which demands that we have made up our mind, while being open minded' (1998: 245). In relation to work with people who are dying or bereaved, the issues that arise in relation to these two factors are different in specialist and mainstream settings.

Specialist social workers – usually working in palliative care settings – are in the forefront of thinking and writing about the social work contribution, particularly with people who are dying, but also in relation to bereavement (Monroe, 1998; Oliviere et al., 1998; Sheldon, 1997). Here the issue is often the ways in which social work is defined in relation to the roles of other workers. 'Psychosocial palliative care' is a term used to refer to those areas of work that might previously have defined social work with dying or bereaved people, but are not exclusive to it. There are issues too in relation to the boundaries between the work done by specialist, hospice-based social workers and their social work colleagues in the community. Questions about the social work contribution may therefore centre less on *what* is the appropriate response (although this always has to be worked out afresh in any instance) and more on *who* is best placed to offer this care (often with attendant questions of funding).

Mainstream social workers are often much less clear about the social work response to dying or bereavement that is desirable or possible in their situation. Some argue that 'real social work' (Lloyd, 1997) with people who are dying or bereaved needs more time than can be offered in the present climate of changes in social care. Concepts and understandings that apply in specialist palliative care settings have little relevance, some say, outside these protected environments. Along with Quinn (1998), I will refute this, arguing that current theoretical understandings do in fact form the basis for a strong remit for social workers in mainstream settings.

Reflective practice (Payne, 1998) is the other factor highlighted as essential for critical practice. Those who work with people facing death must be able to acknowledge and manage the strong feelings that this rouses in them. 'Our use of self is part of the service we offer to users and clients' (Lishman, 1998: 92). This cannot be sustained and developed without adequate training and supervision and – less often recognised – appropriate policies and structures. Managers have a key role in facilitating reflective practice on the part of workers meeting death and loss on a regular basis. Just as practitioners need to be able to hold their own emotions in balance, so their managers need to balance the pressures for measurable outcomes and 'results' against an awareness that process is as crucial as outcome and, in the last analysis, is part of it. Managers also need an understanding of the social work response to people who are dying or bereaved if they are to create policies and structures to facilitate it. It is in this respect that workers in specialist posts may be at an advantage, since the organisational culture is likely to be one where these aspects are recognised as important.

Two tasks then face the confident and reflective critical practitioner. First, theoretical understandings and general ideas about the social work role have to be interpreted and probably adapted within a particular practice setting. Second, practices, policies and structures that undermine or threaten this response have to be challenged. This is an ongoing process and it occurs at many levels. It can involve 'stopping the action' for just five minutes to acknowledge someone's need to cry or say goodbye to a deceased relative. It can be about asking why there is no place for relatives to stay in a residential care setting if this enables them to be with a dying person, or asking who will accompany children from a residential unit to attend the funeral of a staff member. It can involve explaining to those pressing for an empty bed in hospital that informed choices about where an older person will live (and probably die) have an emotional component and cannot be made on the spot. It can involve putting in place (and monitoring) strict expectations in relation to the training and levels of supervision that private companies must offer if contracts for home care or other services are to be awarded. It may involve challenging national policies. While challenge is a factor that is particularly linked with social work (Ramon, 1997), this is actually no different to the response of any worker confident about their contribution to care; it is part of professional practice to seek to ensure the conditions that make it possible.

Dying

Much of the theoretical work relating to dying is focused on those people who become aware, usually through medical diagnosis of a terminal illness, that they are dying. Attention has been paid particularly to the emotional responses of individuals to this knowledge; the most influential of the frameworks being that outlined by Elisabeth Kübler-Ross (1970), who described an emotional progression from denial and anger through bargaining to depression and possible eventual acceptance. Subsequent authors (Buckman, 1998; Corr, 1992) have proposed alternative, more flexible, frameworks (Sheldon, 1997).

Based in practice, this work has been enormously influential and has been strongly associated with the developing field of specialist palliative care, admission to which is also contingent upon a terminal diagnosis. There can be a tendency, however, for frameworks to be rigidly applied in practice, rather than critically interpreted (Sheldon, 1997: 56). Other problems relate to the limits of these models. First, there is a focus on only a part of the experience of the dying person – a part that I have referred to elsewhere as 'abandoning the future' (Currer, 2001). From the accounts of those who have written of their own dying (Picardie, 1998; Moore, O., 1996) and from research reports (Young and Cullen, 1996; Davies, 1995), we can see that 'managing the present' is also an important preoccupation. A part of this involves renegotiation of social boundaries and managing issues of dependence and independence. This is apparent in the three scenarios below, where much of the focus of social care needs to be on practicalities that help the dying person and their carers to manage the present.

Jane Truman is ten years old. She lives with her mother Sonia who has terminal cancer. A district nurse visits Sonia regularly. Sonia's current partner has refused to accept her illness and is rarely in the home. Jane is in effect the main carer. The district nurse has asked a social worker from the hospice to visit Sonia and Jane. Sonia is very worried about what will happen to Jane after her death, but this is a subject that Jane does not want to discuss.

Lisa Jones has been severely disabled from birth and needs constant physical care. Her parents are aware that she is unlikely to live very long. Lisa's two sisters help with her care. The social worker from the local children's disability team has arranged for respite care to enable the family to have a holiday.

Simon Shaw has AIDS. He is living at home with his partner. The social worker is arranging for a home carer to help the couple.

Further points will be made in relation to these scenarios later in this chapter.

A second limitation of these models or frameworks relates to the issue of awareness of coming death. As Field (1996) and Seale et al. (1997) note, many people with long-term chronic conditions that result in death are never actually defined as 'dying'. In England and Wales, most deaths occur when people are over 75 years old (Office for National Statistics, 1998). George and Sykes (1997) argue that the deaths of older people are often hard to predict. Sidell et al.'s study (1998) of residential care for older people makes it clear that deaths are both frequent and often not accurately predicted in such settings. In such instances, then, we need a broader basis for the definition of dying if theoretical understandings are to help the practitioner working with older people.

From a sociological perspective, Seale defines dying as severance of the social bond: 'Disruption of the social bond occurs as the body fails, self-identity becomes harder to hold together, and the normal expectations of human relations cannot be fulfilled' (Seale, 1998: 149). This is a useful starting point for the social worker. Residents may decline the invitation to attend a funeral due to worries about their physical ability to sit through the service: the body is no longer reliable. In the following example, from a community setting, Violet Oliver's attempts to maintain 'respectability' in the eyes of neighbours, and the shame that can accompany failure to do so, will be familiar to many working with older people.

Violet Oliver is a woman of 80, with a reputation for being immaculately dressed. Admitted to hospital following a fall, she is found to be badly undernourished. She is very reluctant to agree to her neighbour's request for the keys to her home so that the neighbour can prepare for her return. The social worker sees her to make arrangements for her discharge.

For Violet, hospitalisation threatens to expose her attempts to preserve self-identity and to fulfil the 'normal expectations of human relations'. Seale's definition can also be applied to younger people with a terminal illness (Young and Cullen, 1996).

For those working with older people, understandings relating to dying have an application that is much broader than may be realised (Quinn, 1998). In relation to community care assessments, many social workers are acutely aware that service users (such as Violet Oliver) see the point of leaving their own home as a form of 'social death'. This concept has been defined as 'the cessation of the individual person as an active agent in others' lives' (Mulkay and Ernst, 1991: 178). Sweeting and Gilhooly (1997) have used the idea of 'social death' in their research into the experience of those caring at home for relatives with dementia. We could argue that the assessment of Violet's needs may result in a diagnosis of social death, should she be unable to return home, yet the pressure in many areas is to conduct such assessments in a routine way for the sake of speed.

Many people do of course spend their last years in some form of residential care. Let us consider just one of many situations that commonly arises.

CASE EXAMPLE

Maria Reed has been a resident in Green Meadows home for two years. She is 88 years old and has recently become confused, aggressive and disoriented. Her friend Grace (also a resident) has become increasingly withdrawn since Maria's deterioration. At present, the district nurse visits Maria at Green Meadows, but she is advising a move to a nursing home.

In this instance, the issue for staff caring for Maria concerns whether she will be able to die in the place that has become her home, a dilemma that relates to the separation of social and nursing care for older people. Sidell et al. (1998) report on national practice in this area, with recommendations for the wider application of good practice derived from experience in palliative care. The challenge for social care is to use insights from palliative care without reinforcing a stereotypical and potentially ageist association between old age and death.

Bereavement

While the dying person must abandon the future, the bereaved person must redefine it. The present is a struggle, maybe feeling unreal (Ironside, 1996; Currer, 2001). Social relationships are problematic and must be renegotiated. Anthropological studies see this as a time of transition (Littlewood, 1993). All social workers in ongoing contact with service users will be in touch with some experiencing bereavement, since this is a normal life event. Fear of 'opening up more than I can deal with' may lead to avoidance of the subject, in effect denying their grief. This is a reflection of general cultural uncertainties about how to respond to bereavement (Walter, 1994), and also of a context of change in social care, with attendant devaluing of emotional work (Marsh and Triseliotis, 1996; Quinn, 1998; Lishman, 1998).

Like dying, until recently there has been a dominant body of research with a focus on issues of emotional adjustment to the death of a significant person. Rooted in attachment theory (Bowlby, 1969, 1973, 1980), 'stages' of grieving have been described by Parkes (1996) and 'tasks of mourning' by Worden (1991). This body of research and knowledge has, with minor refinements, passed into the 'received wisdom' concerning bereavement, and been incorporated into advice leaflets in a range of spheres (for example, Tebbutt, 1994; Help the Aged, 1996; BODY, 1995). Recent research has also focused on the experience of children who are bereaved (Silverman, 1996; Worden, 1996), and there are practice developments also in work with bereaved children (Hemmings, 1995; Smith and Pennells, 1995).

In the last decade, there has been what is described as a 'revolution' (Walter, 1997) in thinking about bereavement. Work by Stroebe and Schut (1999) and Walter (1996, 1999) extends the theoretical base in ways that have direct relevance for social care. First, the culture and gender blindness of earlier research and theory has been recognised (Stroebe, 1998; Stroebe and Schut, 1998). Second, there has been sustained criticism (not least from bereaved people) of the notion that you 'get over' bereavement (Wortman and Silver, 1989), with exploration of what it means to 'move on'. Early ideas (rooted in Freud) of 'detachment' from the relationship with the person who died have given way to ideas of 'relocation' (Walter, 1996).

Perhaps most significantly, Stroebe and Schut have proposed (1995, 1999) a dual process model of coping with bereavement, in which they suggest that the person who is bereaved is confronting two categories of stressor, the loss itself and the changes that result from it. There is, then, a dual orientation, to loss and restoration, with oscillation between these two. A particular point of relevance for social care is that we are often associated with 'restoration': helping people with practical changes and adjustments that arise from bereavement. In some instances, these changes are forced, as for Jane in the example already given above, and for Tom and Imran Malik in the situations described below. In each case, involving different services, death has already or may in future precipitate a need for alternative (possibly residential) care.

CASE EXAMPLES

Tom is a child of mixed race who is in residential care following the breakdown of a placement in foster care. Eight years old, he was admitted to care after the suicide of his stepfather, when his mother became severely depressed and was admitted to hospital. His sister died at the age of two in an accident in the home.

Imran Malik is 30 years old. He lives at home with his parents and his younger sister, helping in the family shop when he is not attending Wellton Resource Centre for adults with a learning disability, where he has a number of close friends. The sudden accidental death of both parents has led to a call to the department. Arrangements are being made for his sister's marriage after which she will no longer live in the family home.

In such instances, opportunities to focus on the loss itself may be blocked. Conversely, where there is discrimination, attempts to focus on restoration may be particularly difficult (Currer, 2001: 104), and the person is thrust back into loss when they seek to take new steps. Therefore, understanding the social work task in terms of this model both validates our work and also highlights areas of particular vulnerability for some clients. Oscillation is the key, in Stroebe and Schut's model, to 'adaptive coping'. However, this rather prescriptive phrase is perhaps indicative of an overall question about even the more recent models. Some authors (for example, Ironside, 1996) argue that such models may benefit professionals rather than those who are bereaved. Walter (1994, 1999) takes a broader sociological perspective, in which counselling and psychology (and presumably also social care) are reflections of 'neo-modern' society, providing templates which are a basis for the social regulation of grief.

Responding to grief: the social work role in relation to dying and bereavement

Writing from the perspective of a specialist practitioner, Monroe (1998) identifies a number of features of social work in palliative care. Intervention will include giving information, helping communication and freeing up people's confidence to act, sometimes through helping with resources. Newburn (1993, 1996) gives feedback from those who have been in touch with social workers following the Hillsborough and other disasters. On the basis of such reports and interviews with practitioners from a wide range of social care settings, a number of features can be identified (Currer, 2001) as central in social care work with people who are either dying or bereaved. Such features can offer a foundation for the confidence mentioned earlier. In all situations, the social work response is likely to combine *both emotional and practical support*, recognising that these are inextricably linked.

In relation to work with people who are dying, *dependability* is crucial, facilitating efforts to 'manage the present'. This is clearly important for Lisa's family, as it is for all informal carers who have help with looking after someone in the community. *Listening* is also key. Such listening may be part of an assessment, and a means to the end of understanding what other services may be required, but it may also be enough in itself. This aspect of the work of home carers needs to be acknowledged, alongside their practical tasks. *Encouraging and helping communication with others* is an aspect of work that has clear links with the focus of social work on social relationships. It relates directly to the threat that can be posed to social relationships by increased dependency. For Sonia and Jane, this is a major issue. It also relates to the definition of dying as 'severance of the social bond' (Seale, 1998), and a time when human relationships become both more important and more difficult to sustain. Smith's existential analysis of bereavement (1976) proposes that even the apparently individual 'journey' of 'abandoning the future' can only be worked out in the context of social relationships with significant others. Finally, *advocacy* is seen, ideally, as a defining aspect of social work with those facing death.

Turning to consider bereavement, three features can be identified. First, there is the need to *recognise and endorse the need to grieve*. Another example illustrates this powerfully.

CASE EXAMPLE

A member of the emergency duty team is called to a house where a middle-aged woman has died in bed. Her mother, who is without sight, is in the kitchen with a young police constable. The woman's body is about to be removed, and the social worker is asked to make arrangements for her mother's care. Although she has been informed of her daughter's death, the mother seems very confused.

For the emergency duty worker, it was essential to 'stop the action' and allow the mother time to be with her daughter before her body was removed. This involved challenge to those who wanted to 'get on' and avoid upsetting the mother. She did indeed burst into tears when she felt her daughter's face, but said later that she was enormously grateful that this opportunity for farewell had been created for her. Recognition of grief may be less dramatic. In the residential home referred to earlier Grace's withdrawal in the face of Maria's decline suggests that her own distress needs to be recognised.

Practitioners also see a role as 'witness'; offering *accompaniment* to the grieving person, as well as *support in relation to re-engagement*. These two factors may be particularly important in relation to Jane's situation and influence the help that is offered. Sonia's primary carer is the district nurse; the social work role focuses on Jane. As a young carer, Jane is in need of immediate practical support. In the long term, there will be a need for alternative accommodation and care. Her emotional needs in the present and in the future include the need for someone to listen and be able to 'witness' to her current care of her mother as well as help her to remake her own life in the future. There is also a need to respect Jane's current reluctance to discuss her mother's death. It may be possible to identify a key worker who can offer long-term support to Jane, perhaps a young carers worker or a member of staff from a residential care setting. The task for this worker would not be 'grief counselling' either before or after her mother's death, but recognition of her current need for support and future need to grieve. If this person could meet Jane and Sonia together at home, he or she would be in a position to share memories of Sonia with Jane later, and in this way, they could fulfil the role of witness and give ongoing support at a pace that Jane can manage. This may involve support around the time of the funeral, and challenge to any well-meaning adults seeking to 'protect' Jane by limiting her involvement. Jane is likely to need both a well-informed advocate and accompaniment at this time.

Imran Malik and Tom also need accompaniment in their grief. Daycare and residential services are well placed to provide this, once workers recognise its importance. This is an active process involving appropriate acknowledgement of distress. In Pakistan, visits of condolence are customary following bereavement. Are staff at the Resource Centre aware of this? If Imran's friends wish to visit, how can this be facilitated? Is there an opportunity to explore with Imran his understanding of death and for him to talk about his parents? Rituals can easily be introduced in many settings, giving opportunities to remember, say goodbye and endorse the view that grief can be talked about. Tom has encountered multiple deaths in his short life. Is awareness of this a part of the brief for those working with him? A variety of resources have been developed to facilitate memory work with children (see Smith and Pennells, 1995). The critical practitioner is one who is aware of the range of resources available and seeks to adapt and use these within his or her own situation.

CONCLUSION

It is tempting to think that responding to the grief of people who are dying or bereaved is no longer possible for social workers except in specialist palliative care settings. Such a view is mistaken. In so far as dying and bereavement are everyday events, they will arise in the course of social work practice in all areas. In many settings, we are ideally placed to respond appropriately – probably as members of a multidisciplinary team – given the necessary theoretical basis for intervention, and confidence concerning our part in care. It is part of the remit of those who work in specialist settings to encourage wider awareness of good practice with people who are dying or bereaved (Sheldon, 1997; Oliviere et al., 1998; Quinn, 1998). To learn from this experience, interpret it realistically (adapting as necessary) and defend good practice vigorously in the context of mainstream practice are the challenges facing the critical practitioner in mainstream social care.

Note

1. Social care is used here to underline the point that many of the arguments in this chapter are applicable to all social care workers, whatever their level of training or professional status. In what follows, I will, however, refer to social workers since this is the focus of this text. In some cases, the roles outlined here will be undertaken by people who are not social workers.

FURTHER READING

Currer, C. (2001) *Responding to Grief: Dying, Bereavement and Social Care*, Basingstoke: Palgrave – now Palgrave Macmillan. This book has been written specifically for social care workers in mainstream settings, although it does also include reference to specialist work.

Oliviere, D., Hargreaves, R. and Monroe, B. (1998) *Good Practices in Palliative Care*, Aldershot: Ashgate. A lively introduction for anyone interested in the current state and range of social work in specialist palliative care settings.

Sheldon, F. (1997) *Psychosocial Palliative Care*, Cheltenham: Stanley Thornes. Written by an experienced, specialist social work practitioner and lecturer, this text identifies both theory and practice issues in work with those who are dying and bereaved.

Smith, S. and Pennells, M. (1995) *Interventions with Bereaved Children*, London: Jessica Kingsley. This is a rich source of examples of practice with children who are bereaved.

Walter, T. (1999) *On Bereavement*, Buckingham: Open University Press. A compelling read for anyone willing to take a step back from practice and look at the ways in which grief has been managed over time and in different places.

PART
III
Managing and Organising Practice

22

Management

Malcolm Payne

Introduction – management and Mrs McLeod

Management faces us starkly with the conflicts of attempting critical practice in social work. First, management involves a clash between control and freedom. Classically, social work takes place in agencies and social workers are accountable to the policies of those agencies. They do not have the freedom of independent discretion in decision-making that we associate with some professions, such as medicine, the law and the Church, so they are not free to be critical. Management is often about controlling an agency and its employees in order to provide services within the resources and policies laid down by political decisions or pressed upon us by economic forces. 'Good management' seems to be about control on behalf of the 'powers that be' rather than 'powers for change'. If all this is so, should the critical social worker simply dismiss management as irrelevant to, or should they attack it as inherently opposed to, critical practice? One resolution of this issue is to create areas of freedom for critical thinking within the boundaries of controlling management forces, for example by a team leader supporting feminist practice within a local government agency. However, this only creates some areas of critical practice within an oppressive structure, rather than questioning the structure itself, supports critical practice for some clients, while maintaining unequal resources for others who do not have access to this area of freedom. Critical practice, therefore, needs to incorporate the duality that good service requires both control and freedom. The presence of both enables control to criticise excessive freedom, and the availability of freedom to criticise excessive control.

Second, management is clearly not social work, yet there are demands that social work must embrace management. We see this in ideas such as 'case management', 'care management' or 'managerialism' (Clarke et al., 2000; Payne, 2000a, Ch. 2) in social work organisations. Managerialism promotes techniques such as 'quality assurance' or 'performance indicators' in which predetermined requirements are set by the powerful, rather than encouraging flexible responses to the needs and wishes of the powerless. Yet the powerful would say that just such a flexible response is what they want.

CASE EXAMPLE

Mrs McLeod, an elderly, somewhat disabled and lonely woman in her early eighties illustrates how different understandings of management can seem irrelevant to good critical practice. As greater age restricted her horizons, she had had a limited community care assessment and received meals on wheels from a local voluntary organisation and home help service from a private operator contracted by the social services department. A few months later, she broke her collarbone in a fall and went into hospital for treatment, receiving physiotherapy, nursing care and a further assessment for adaptations to her old-fashioned cottage. Volunteers redecorated before she moved back home.

When Maria, a social worker acting as a care manager, visited on referral from her GP several months later, she found a community care 'case' typical of many thousands. By this time, a district nurse was visiting weekly to help with her physical care. Talking over the situation, Maria found that Mrs McLeod's son and daughter lived with their teenage families in different towns, visiting on family occasions and taking her out sometimes. Only a nephew who lived a few streets away dropped in regularly of an evening. His mother, Mrs McLeod's sister, had died a few months ago, just before Mrs McLeod's fall and hospital stay, and this had brought to the front of her mind the ache of the loss of her husband through cancer almost 20 years ago, which had been dulled by time.

Neither the twice-weekly visits to the Age Concern day centre that Maria arranged, nor the cheerful rota of drivers who took her there really abated Mrs McLeod's loneliness and depression. The GP said that medication for depression was 'over the top', when Maria enquired. On the social services department's priorities, Mrs McLeod was a long way from a residential care home place, which she quite liked the idea of, because there would be people around to talk to. She quite liked talking things over with Maria, but was coping well enough not to justify casework help for her depression and unresolved bereavement.

So, Mrs McLeod carried on 'managing' in a rather forlorn and unsatisfying final phase of her life. Maria was a care 'manager', implementing her department's priorities and fulfilling the objectives of community care. Her 'managers' were pleased by a sensitive and thoughtful assessment, which met government objectives and performance indicators by maintaining Mrs McLeod in the community. They noted the effective liaison with health service provision, the delivery of a fairly complex range of services from different sources. It was all very well 'managed', yet, these human needs might be better met, and this is so in many of the situations we deal with. Many children drift into residential care, many mentally ill people cannot make full use of their skills, many people with learning difficulties are excluded from social integration, many disabled people cannot take the fullest control of their lives.

If we are critical, therefore, our current service does not entirely satisfy us. By 'manage' we imply that we do just well enough, or that we juggle successfully with constrained resources and inadequate services. On the other hand, without managing it might be worse. We sometimes meet social workers whose practice does not impress, and we hope that some manager is keeping them up to standard.

Therefore, what we mean by management, what it means to be a manager in social work and what it means to incorporate a concern for management within social work raise complex issues. As always with critical practice, the first step in this chapter is to sort out the different aspects of meaning. This is the purpose of the next section, where I develop a practical model of management, which social workers may find useful. In the following section, I examine some basic theoretical positions within management, because I find that these help to establish the ideas we can use in critical practice.

The meaning of management

The word 'management' comes from the Latin word *manus*, meaning 'hand'.[1] Perhaps it implies that to manage is to 'handle', to cope, to get things done; perhaps to 'give a hand', to help things happen; perhaps to 'lay your hands on', to grasp and take action. All these aspects of meaning are present in Mrs McLeod's case.

Levels and skills of management

These meanings of management imply different levels of management action. In Figure 22.1, I call the 'coping' level 'management as taking up'. By this, I mean that the fundamental requirement of doing anything is to confront it, try to understand its implications and work on it. Avoiding, forgetting or missing things that we need to work on is the opposite of good management. We often criticise managers, for example, when they will not confront a colleague who is not pulling their weight, because we suspect this will lead to greater problems later on. By not confronting her grief about her husband, Mrs McLeod is putting herself at risk of adverse bereavement reactions later on; by not taking this up, Maria is not managing the full situation that Mrs McLeod faces.

The next 'giving a hand' level in Figure 22.1, I have called 'management as taking hold'. In order to work on a problem, we have first to gain a grasp of its implications and then participate actively in doing something about it. Good management means not leaping in without clear aims, thinking whether someone else is the right person to refer a problem to and helping them to take the right action. We criticise managers if they delegate the tough jobs and then make themselves scarce. We feel that Mrs McLeod's care is merely adequate, rather

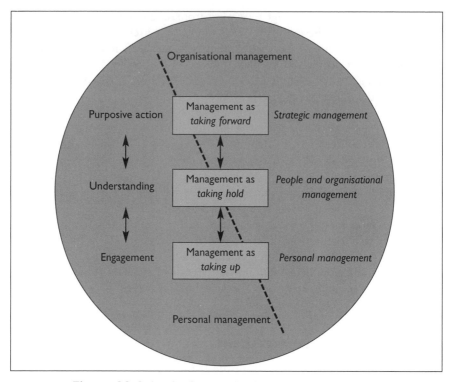

Figure 22.1 Levels of personal and organisation management

than good, because Maria is not able to pick up on the more complex interpersonal work that might be done.

I have called the third 'taking in hand' level in Figure 22.1: 'management as taking forward'. 'Doing things' is not enough, because good management means making good use of resources and developing our work strategically. Good management means thinking out our aims and planning the coordination of services. We criticise managers if they decide to create a new day centre and get service users' responses to the way they want it to run, and then find out that there are not enough resources to offer anything at all. This is because they should have suspected that they would raise expectations that they cannot fulfil. We are unhappy about the services in Mrs McLeod's care because they do not meet the full range of needs that we can envisage and society, through political decisions, is not prepared to go far enough to meet needs that we can identify.

Each of these levels of management is involved in many tasks that we undertake: we have to take them up, take hold and take them forward. On the left-hand side of Figure 22.1, I have described skills that are important at each of these levels of management. 'Taking up' requires engagement, 'taking hold' requires understanding and 'taking forward' requires us to take action in a purposive way. Each of these levels of work runs into each other. Being prepared to become engaged sets us off to make sure that we have understood all the implications of what we are about to do (taking up) and this means getting involved with the issues and exploring the problem more deeply (taking hold). As we do this, we begin to build up a conception of possible aims and strategies, and, very often, investigating the issues will start to resolve the questions that we are trying to deal with (taking forward).

Personal and organisational management

All these levels of management include two elements: personal management and organisational management. Personal management is about keeping ourselves organised and efficient through good decision-making, record-keeping, time or workload management. This is relevant to everyone in ordinary life, how Mrs McLeod organises her life, for example. Remembering what it takes to run a household, or buy a car, reminds us that everything involves personal management. We can transfer everyday experience in personal management to work and use management techniques we learn at work in everyday life.

Organisational management is about getting the organisation to work as you want it to. It involves things such as supervision (Chapter 24), teamwork and coordination (Chapter 25), organising (Chapter 23) and quality management (Chapter 29). The diagonal dotted line dividing Figure 22.1 represents the likelihood that the higher levels of management will involve more organisational management, while the lower levels will involve more personal management.

The comments on the right-hand side of Figure 22.1 suggest that this is also true when we look at the structure of organisations. People working at the lower levels will be mainly organising themselves, so their jobs will involve a greater proportion of personal management, whereas people in middle management will probably be organising other people and resources for most of their time, while people in senior management at the top will be mainly working on strategy. People at the lower levels will have to be strategic and purposeful about their work, while people at the top will need to organise their time and make decisions effectively, so that the skills and management levels will still apply to everyone. However, senior management will usually involve a higher proportion of strategic than personal management, and practitioners' work usually the opposite. So, discussing reorganising agencies in Chapter 30, a strategic activity, Peryer takes into account personal responses among staff and clients, while Milner and O'Byrne, in Chapter 26, discuss assessment not only as a personal activity for clients but also as raising implications for managers.

Ideas about management

Social work management involves three basic distinctions between different sorts of management activity, all of which are represented in the chapters in this section of the book:

- Between policy, public administration and management
- Between rational or scientific management and human relations management
- Between task, individual and group.

Policy, public administration and management

The first distinction is partly about lines of study and development of ideas and knowledge. The development and study of policy is concerned with how governments determine the direction and form of the actions to take in public affairs. Public administration is the process of organising and administering such services. Management derives more from the business and commercial world and is concerned with how to plan and organise the production and delivery of services and goods. This is relevant to public service and social services because social care is a service, and can use ideas about service delivery from the private sector.

The academic traditions of study in each of these areas have different origins and lines of development, but they overlap and influence each other to some extent. They also have different focuses. For example, a policy focus looks at the processes of, and factors involved in, making policy decisions, while public administration and management are more concerned with how decisions are carried out. Policy issues would suggest what services we should offer Mrs McLeod and whether they should all be in the public sector, or be part of a 'mixed economy of care' covering public, voluntary and private sectors. Public administration and management would be more concerned with, say, how services should be coordinated. Each of these traditions also has different underlying assumptions. For Mrs McLeod, public administration would want to know about the accountability of the different services, to local government or the NHS, for example. Management would be more concerned with whether the workers are well coordinated and motivated to provide a good service.

The first two parts of this book demonstrate that all these aspects need to be considered together. Part I shows that how we think about the issues that we face and the values that we want to implement in a service crucially affect what we do. Similarly, Part II shows us that social work requires a detailed critical analysis of social work purposes and actions in order to implement social work, so that simply setting up a service is inadequate. Returning to Mrs McLeod, we are dissatisfied with the social services policy that does not seek to deal with the bleakness of her existence and we are dissatisfied with the limited character of a social work that simply organises services rather than engaging with stimulating her dreary lifestyle. To practise management within both policy and social work contexts requires management to interact with policy choices and social work opportunities. It is no use organising things well, if the organisation does not achieve the policy objectives and does not allow social workers to take up the opportunities to practise their craft with service users.

Scientific and human relations management

The second distinction identified above was between rational or scientific management and human relations management. Scientific management focuses on management as a way of structuring organisations and the tasks they undertake, controlling the people within them so that the objectives of the organisation are met. Looking critically at this, however, I discussed 'organisations' and 'tasks', without acknowledging that organisations do not actually exist, they are collections of people. Consequently, tasks can only exist as thought out and done by people. Human relations management proposes that relationships between people carrying out tasks within the organisation are crucial to the success with which objectives are met. It emphasises aspects of the organisation such as 'culture', the collective identity of members of the organisation and formal and informal groups within it.

These two approaches represent, in some ways, the controlling and liberating aspects of management. For example, supervision in rational management involves designing appropriate tasks, checking that they are performed as required and paying more for better performance, while human relations management focuses on improving the skills and education of employees in order to improve services. Quality management in the rational view is about effective definition, planning and sequencing of tasks, while in the human relations view it is more concerned with involving people in organising their work effectively. In some respects, these approaches to management are appropriate for different kinds of tasks. For example, rational management might be suitable for more routine, repeated and mechanised tasks involved in factory assembly lines. Human relations management, on the other hand, might be more suitable for more creative, less repetitive and more service-oriented tasks.

The nature of work is changing, moving towards less routine activities requiring people to think creatively and flexibly, which might suggest that rational management approaches are less relevant in management nowadays. The nature of social work suggests a human relations style of management is appropriate, because of its varied nature and human interaction, which seems to need effective motivation of staff, who need a high degree of discretion. However, rational management control is not only oppressive and human relations management is not only liberating. In the case of community care work, for example, social workers must assess and process a range of information that is similar in most cases and come up with consistent decisions that service users and carers can accept as fair. The fairness and consistency are important to members of the public, and a more scientific/rational approach is therefore a valid contribution. Child protection work implies a consistent attention to detail and checking of information. Managing risk for someone who is mentally ill and may harm themselves also requires careful planning. Running a residential care home or day centre contains many programmed details. Supervising a student or staff member well means keeping careful records and checking information. Many aspects of social work, then, are susceptible to the processes of rational management and they provide for equality and justice. However, taking this too far would damage the flexibility and responsiveness that many social work tasks seem to require. The question for the critical social worker is where the boundary between programmed and flexible approaches lies, and how the two approaches interact.

The distinction between rational and human relations management helps us to judge the appropriate style of management for our daily activities and work organisation. When are you becoming too programmed, too controlled by the system? When are you using so much discretion and flexibility that you may act unfairly to different service users who have rights to similar treatment?

Task, individual and group

The third distinction outlined above was between task, individual and group (Adair, 1986). Clearly, there are *tasks* to be performed. Organisations and managers need to be clear about what these are. Part of management is defining the work and getting it done. Then there are *people* who will be doing the jobs and organisations and managers need to think about what they need to do the jobs well. Part of this is personal: finding the right people, supporting, training and supervising them (Chapter 24). What they need to do the job may be fairly concrete: a chair, a desk and a computer, for example. Or they may be fairly esoteric, as for example where managers consider strategically whether to switch assessments from paperwork to computers and what training and support are needed to achieve the move.

The third aspect is the *group*. People in organisations are by definition in groups because an organisation implies more than one person. Therefore, managers have to consider how the groups help or hinder individuals in carrying out their tasks. This may be quite concrete, such as organising systems for work flow from, say, the intake to the long-term teams. I have seen staff groups where this contributed to serious conflicts and, in one case, a strike. It is a classic problem in social services (Buckle, 1981), because the culture of such teams tends to differ. Intake teams focus on finishing off pieces of work quickly. Long-term teams sometimes think that work that needed more extensive activity was closed by intake teams, depriving them of work. On the other hand, intake teams sometimes think that long-term teams are rather precious about their therapeutic work and maintain high workloads, preventing them from taking on new cases and adding to the pressure on the intake team, which has to carry the case until it can be taken on long term or close it inappropriately.

Because much social work is multiprofessional, there are also networks of other professions or organisations to deal with. Moreover, social work clients are part of family, community and social networks, whose interests and concerns social workers have to deal with. I call reaching out and drawing in such networks of professional, family and community care 'open teamwork' (Payne, 2000b). The need to do this is a powerful support in critical management. For example, in Chapter 30, Peryer centres the issue of reorganising agencies as a problem of strategic organisation, looking at the needs of an agency. It would be equally possible to examine the problem of reorganisation by centring on the point of view of service users and workers. In this way, we may look at the freedoms and controls needed from a variety of points of view. Decentralisation may benefit users by making workers more accessible, but disadvantage them by separating specialist help from general community provision. As Peryer makes clear, there is no single complete answer, but a range of opportunities and disadvantages. Problems must be compensated for, in this example by organising effective links between community offices and specialist workers.

Managers are helped in making these people-related decisions by understanding the programmed systems and the organisational structures that they participate in and the policies, practices and values that come from the agency's decision-making processes and the professional values incorporated into the organisation. All these things together interact to help us to work with the person, task and group or network; that is the focus of our action as a manager. However, choices made among the distinctions discussed here construct our managerial practice and form what we do, how we do it and its effect on the people that we manage, our services and the people we serve.

Service management and the people served

Social work is a service, not the manufacture of a product. Many Western societies are increasingly becoming 'service societies' in which providing services and the social structures and behaviours involved in this are more important than the class and organisational structures of traditional manufacturing industry. Services are reflexive; that is, how the person served thinks and behaves affects how the worker can do their work and how the manager can organise the service, and how the worker and manager think and behave affects how the person served can make use of the service. For example, if Mrs McLeod is so depressed that she will not do anything for herself, Maria, her worker, will have difficulty in making her assessment and will have to organise services to respond to this. If Maria is brusque and unsympathetic, she may have difficulty in getting Mrs McLeod's nephew to do more than make the occasional visit.

Therefore, a crucial element of management in social work is how we manage the relationship between the service and the people served, whether we see them as citizens, clients, consumers, service users or customers. It is an important focus of critical practice because it embodies how we manage issues of oppression and empowerment. To the social policy and public administration traditions, citizenship is an important issue, because citizenship confers rights to participation, for example through voting and political accountability, that balance the potential oppression that comes from dependence.

To be a citizen is, in one way, more than to be a customer. A customer is entitled to what they are willing to pay for and to standards of service that may be legally defined but are often only set by the service provider. Mrs McLeod is a customer when buying groceries in her local shop, but in receiving social and health services, she is a citizen. A citizen has rights to service, whether or not they can pay and arising from the humanity that they have in common with service providers. To manage services as though Mrs McLeod is a customer who cannot pay and so receives services by the goodwill of society fails to perceive her rights as a sister human being and in particular fails to respond to her participation in society and as a voter. However, in another way, she may be excluded from services by a commonplace perception that older people, having had a good life, are less important than children or, being slow and frail, are irritating. So, she may benefit from an organisation that has inculcated among its staff a 'customer care' approach, which would overcome some of the ill-effects of these exclusionary attitudes. A worker's official and legal authority in some aspects of social work does not prevent their being open to influence and a client's direction and self-determination in many other aspects of the worker–client relationship and in their lives. The fact that Maria must assess Mrs McLeod for services, in a way that is partly legally defined, does not prevent her from respecting and responding to Mrs McLeod's preferences and attitudes.

Obviously, clients are 'users' of services, as Mrs McLeod is, and the role of the social worker is sometimes in relation to services. However, social work also develops positive helping relationships with clients; they do not just 'use services'. We saw that Mrs McLeod would benefit from a conception of social work like this. Carers have also become more important in social work thinking. An important social movement emphasises the role that carers play in providing for social need in all societies. Legislation and official guidance have sought to give them rights to contribute to assessments of services appropriate to the person they care for and to have their own position assessed (Mandelstam, 1999). However, looking at their position critically, their whole being should not be defined by the caring role; they are themselves citizens and members of wider communities. Therefore, they have a political role in social provision that transcends the limited role of 'carer'.

The language that we use about the people that we serve implies the approach that we take to the management of our service, our political conception of its nature and our attitude to the people involved. Whether it is oppressive and regulatory, or whether it is enhancing and empowering, is disclosed by the language of our management approach. We can use this language to understand the nuances of people's perception of their position and our role.

Organisational structure and culture

Much management thinking concerns how the organisation is structured (the traditional focus) and its culture and style (a more modern focus). This aspect of management is about accountability. When we think about structure, we are asking ourselves: 'How do I understand how I fit into this collection of people?' When we think about culture we are asking: 'In what historical and social traditions do I relate to these people and how do they relate to me?' So, our work is not bounded by the organisation. First, it relates to clients. Second, it derives from social interactions and policies. Third, it interacts with others' activities in our multiprofessional and community networks.

Traditionally, we ask these questions about the organisation internally. However, in recent years, management has also been concerned to see how these issues affect the organisation's relationship with people outside the organisation. This concern is both with 'partnerships' with other organisations involved in the network of activities, and with 'customer care', that is, how the organisation responds to the people it serves. Clear and positive relationships with customers and 'suppliers', such as people who refer clients to us, ease the work of an organisation, provided they are pursued genuinely, rather than as a veneer of responsiveness.

'New public management' is a recent conception of management within the public sector, treating the public organisation as the organiser, enabler and promoter of services, rather than always being the direct provider (Clarke et al., 2000). It seeks to disperse power over decisions, replacing it with public control over resources, exercised through setting targets and performance indicators to achieve compliance with policy objectives. Sometimes central government sets the targets and indicators mainly for local government, but the same conception informs contracts where local public authorities commission voluntary and private organisations to provide services.

This is important for social work management because social workers have become the assessors for new public management service provision. Their major relationship with the public is on behalf of managerialist approaches to their role and practice. However, it is possible to see organisations in a different way, so that while managerialism exerts surveillance and control, it also supports variety and alternatives. Rather than seeing the organisation as a machine, in which account-abilities are structured in linear ways, we can see organisations as systems of interacting groups, with many different cultures, relationships and influences (Bilson and Ross, 1999).

Newman (1996) suggests that organisational culture is not always (or perhaps ever) an integrated whole, closed to outsiders and outside influences and consensual in its decision-making. Culture may be a site of contested values, practices and symbols. It may be analysed and changed. A concern of modern management practice is to focus change where there are contested values and practices. In Mrs McLeod's case, the central conflict between the managerialist care management objectives of her managers and the practice possibilities open to Maria is a site of contested values and practices between the open possibilities of social work and the closed assumptions of centralised managerialism. However, within managerialism, there are also elements in tension. Identifying and presenting Mrs McLeod's needs effectively within the organisation offers opportunities for Maria to build on the importance of users' views in the managerial model of organisational practice.

Seeing organisations more flexibly, so that models of influence are possible which provide alternative sources of power for workers, users and carers, can help workers find ways to gain leverage on behalf of users. Similarly, seeing organis-ations not as monolithic (having a single, powerful centre) but as containing contending cultures offers a focus for critical thinking about organisations. Thinking critically leads on to finding alternative modes and sites of action within and outside the organisation. Thus, again, we may see the same management approaches as both containing control and opportunities for creativity on behalf of clients.

Work, management and social divisions

It may seem obvious that management is about work, but it is sometimes unconsidered. Everything about management connects with being in work. As soon as activities are carried out in an organisation, more than one person must be involved, because organisations are by definition a collectivity of people. Organisations require division of labour, responsibility and accountability among the people who work in the organisation. It also means that the people in the organisation must devise ways of ensuring that the organisation works together in some way.

The first point is that management takes place in relation to employment. Personal management involves organising our lives to report for work on time, wearing appropriate clothing, being efficient in keeping appointments with clients and using our skills to answer the telephone or emails appropriately.

Organisational management lays certain responsibilities upon the organisation and us. Among implied conditions of employment contracts in the UK are that we must cooperate with our colleagues, obey reasonable instructions and work as required. The organisation has a responsibility for organising and planning the work appropriately and protecting our health and safety while we are doing it. Buildings must be planned and laid out, heated and lit, furnished and equipped. Salaries and wages must be paid.

The second point is that work carries obligations, because we are paid and therefore are accountable to those who pay us for the work that we do. This may involve doing things that we do not want to do. It may also require us to account for our time to others, through the hierarchical system of an organisation.

The third point is that employment has social and psychological consequences. It provides personal support and validation and structures our time. Being part of important social structures, employment can also reflect and incorporate power relations and social divisions within wider society. Thus, many organisations face problems in offering equal opportunities for employment and advancement to employees. Employing organisations may be just as oppressive as other social structures within the societies in which we live, because they take their form and practices from other social structures and must interact with them. Women workers, workers from minority ethnic groups and disabled workers are disadvantaged in employment and so less able to use their shared experience with clients as part of their practice (White, 1995).

CONCLUSION

The aim of this chapter is to set the scene for the contributions that follow and to make connections with the preceding chapters. I have tried to make clear, first of all, that management is a practice, just as social work is a practice. Flowing from this point, critical thinking in management is just as relevant to management practice as to social work practice. Critical practice requires understanding context: the social structures and relationships within which the practice takes place. It also requires understanding meaning: what we mean by management and its different elements and how other people's meanings interact with our own. Does 'managing' mean 'coping' to Mrs McLeod, 'taking hold' to Maria's manager, 'taking forward' to Maria? How do these different meanings matter to the others? What do we do about them?

The succeeding chapters take this forward. They examine some important aspects of personal management and organisational management, the context in which they arise and how they may be carried out. Each in its own way raises questions about how aspects of management may be understood in different ways. In doing so, they put forward their own positions about the aspect considered. However, there are always opportunities for the reader to examine critically the material presented, using the principle of this chapter that management practice always incorporates both control and freedom. For example, many chapters focus on finding ways of increasing freedom from the constraint of conventional assumptions about their topic. For example, Milner and O'Byrne (Chapter 26) identify policy and management debate about the role of assessment in social work, and propose social constructionism as a mode of thinking that frees present practice from many of its oppressive constraints. We saw earlier, though, that assessment requires both creativity and fair decision-making so that care management decisions, for example, must be fair across a range of clients. How do the social constructionism techniques proposed permit adequate control of fair and equal decision-making in an organisational context? Another example is Peryer's discussion of reorganising agencies (Chapter 30). How does the requirement for consistency of service delivery through effective organisation balance against the opportunity for flexible response to clients?

Inevitably, in the complexity of the tasks undertaken in modern organisations, professions and communities, these different aspects of management will be contested. The accountability to her employer in her work role may constrain or liberate Maria's accountability to Mrs McLeod and her family and community as a citizen and human being, and her accountability to the values of a profession that requires critical and creative practice. Management means taking hold, taking on and taking forward those contests, those accountabilities.

Note

1. I am grateful to Lydia Meryll for this insight.

FURTHER READING

Balloch, S., McLean, J. and Fisher, M. (1999) *Social Services: Working Under Pressure*, Bristol: Policy Press. A stimulating research study of the organisational and other pressures on social workers.

Coulshed, V. and Mullender, A. (2001) *Management in Social Work*, 2nd edn, Basingstoke: Palgrave – now Palgrave Macmillan. A useful book thoughtfully covering the main practical issues in social work management.

Farnham, D. and Horton, S. (1996) *Managing People in the Public Services*, Basingstoke: Macmillan – now Palgrave. This book places social services management in the context of wider developments in the public sector and focuses on people management rather than structures.

Hill, M. (ed.) (2001) *Local Authority Social Services*, Oxford: Blackwell. A useful and up-to-date analysis of local public services, with a social policy focus.

Payne, M. (2000) *Anti-bureaucratic Social Work*, Birmingham: Venture. A short polemical book about the need to fight bureaucratic tendencies in social work, by understanding the social and organisational changes that underlie managerialism.

Managing the Workload

Joan Orme

Introduction

At its simplest, managing workloads requires ways of receiving, allocating and supervising the work undertaken within a social work agency. The aim is to ensure that tasks are performed effectively and that there are appropriate resources to undertake the work. This chapter briefly reviews the systems that have been utilised in social work agencies to help manage workloads but, in doing so, it highlights that there are a number of competing dilemmas in such schemes. Critical practitioners will not only become aware of the limitations of mechanistic attempts to quantify and organise work, but will also be alert to the different management theories and organisational values which can be reflected within them. They will understand that managing the workload is integrally tied to meanings of social work and the value bases on which it operates.

(Mis)managing the workload?

CASE EXAMPLE
A worker in an adult services team has had an unusually high number of referrals allocated to her in the week before she is due to go on leave. On her last day, she has a number of assessment schedules to complete in order to finalise care packages for

people she has already seen. This is a slow process, as she has to ensure that all the data is fed accurately into the computer. Also, local performance guidelines demand that the documentation is completed within a certain number of working days. Finally, she is aware of pressure on the provider agencies and she wants to ensure that the requirements of the individual packages are met as fully as possible.

However, she has to give priority to undertaking the assessment of an 89-year-old woman (Ms P) who has been referred by neighbours to the emergency duty team during the night. Action needs to be taken, not only because Ms P appears to be at risk, but also because this is not the first time that the neighbours have been disturbed by her behaviour and they are threatening to go to the local press. Previous workers have described her as a fiercely independent woman who wants nothing to do with social services. When the worker visits Ms P on this occasion she finds her in a distressed state. She is malnourished and it is difficult to assess whether her incoherence and disorientation are due to lack of food, or whether there are more substantial physical and mental health problems. Therefore the worker decides to set up a multidisciplinary assessment. While her presence is not absolutely necessary at this meeting, she becomes aware that she is the only person who, in the short time she has spent with her, has developed a rapport with Ms P and can give support and provide advocacy for her.

In the light of the various pressures on her, the worker makes the decision that she will have to cancel her leave to ensure that the needs of Ms P are properly identified, and that the other assessments are fully completed to secure the necessary services.

Some weeks later the worker has to take sick leave because of illness which her GP diagnosed as being stress related. Her personnel records show that for the past three years she has not taken her statutory leave entitlement.

This situation could have been handled differently. The worker could have routinised her tasks by spending less time with Ms P or deciding to be less conscientious about the paperwork (Moffat, 1999). She could have consulted with her team leader/manager at the time that the case of Ms P was allocated to her and shared her concerns about her workload. The agency could have had an effective workload management scheme which would ensure that the worker had a manageable workload, or that there were systems for dealing with cases at times of overload.

These possible alternatives illustrate that managing the workload has implications for all levels of the organisation. At the macro-level, ensuring systems for allocating work to individuals and balancing workloads between workers is an important part of the health and safety responsibilities of an organisation. This was evidenced by the decision of an industrial tribunal in 1994 to uphold a claim by a social worker that repeated stress-related mental health problems were caused by the failure of his employing social services department to monitor and allocate workloads appropriately. Research demonstrates that one cause of stress in workers in social services is role ambiguity: being exposed to conflicting demands, being expected to do things which are not part of the job and/or being unable to do things which are part of the job (Balloch et al., 1998). In the case of Ms P such conflicting demands are exacerbated by lack of time to undertake the tasks allocated.

At the micro-level, the individual worker has to make crucial decisions about competing needs, either between individual service users for whom they have responsibility, or between the needs of those on her caseload and her own needs (or those of any of her dependants). Such decisions reflect the freedom which the autonomous professional values. But if the consequences are overwork, sickness and resultant poor service, the value of such freedom may have to be questioned.

Workload, values and practice

Attention to issues of stress, worker safety and support are aspects of a more supportive culture, which sees individuals as part of the 'human resources' necessary for the organisation to perform its responsibilities, but also questions what those responsibilities are. Is a system of workload management designed to give a service, irrespective of the quality of the service? Is it in place to ensure high quality service to those whose needs are seen to be paramount, or are more deserving? Does it represent a welfare system which acknowledges the responsibility of the state to provide for the needs of all those who are not able to provide for themselves? Or is it designed to calculate the cost of each activity, and then analyse its value? These are some of the questions raised for the critical practitioner.

Decisions about workload impact on practice. Jordan (1989) has argued that practitioners have to make ethical choices on a daily basis. They have to make decisions about whether they are responsible for providing absolutely, or achieving the greatest good for the greatest number. But, as the case of Ms P illustrates, such decisions may be taken out of the hands of the worker if the political pressures are so great that an immediate response is required.

Equally, managing the workload and rationing resources are about balancing risk. Official enquiries into childcare cases illustrate that if a worker makes a professional assessment not to offer services, or not to intervene, it is often the individual worker who bears the consequences if the assessment is incorrect. Just as importantly, in situations where those in need of services are deluding or demonstrating aggression, the worker can be put at risk by having to refuse services. Effective management recognises organisational responsibility.

Organisational responsibilities

Within the literature on workload (Vickery, 1977; Glastonbury et al., 1987) there has been emphasis on organisational perspectives including:

■ how are decisions made about controlling the flow of work into an agency?

■ what measures can be taken to ensure the equitable distribution of workloads between workers?

- what constitutes a workload, and what are contributory pressures, for example performance indicators, record-keeping and so on?

- who decides what to prioritise, and when?

- how can the different needs of individuals (users or workers) be addressed in the systems which are introduced?

This reflects the fact that systems adopted by social work organisations to manage workloads have favoured principles of workload measurement, which involve attempts to quantify the work that has to be undertaken and ensure some kind of equitable distribution of this work between workers. Among the most sophisticated have been those developed by the probation service. Regular audits of work undertaken were used by the National Association of Probation Officers (NAPO) to calculate, on the basis of monthly statistics, the allocation of particular pieces of work to individual workers and negotiate staffing levels (Orme, 1995).

Workload measurement

The probation system used time per task as an analysis of the work to be done and workloads were measured against an agreed total of hours per working month. Such calculations are not uncommon, but the units of measurement can differ in order to reflect different aspects of the work (Bradley, 1987), although basically these units ultimately equate to time.

Practitioners consider measurement systems flawed. Calculations are criticised for not including all the aspects of the work to be done. For example, in our scenario, the increasing paperwork associated with community care assessments needs to be reflected in any calculation of the overall workload. Also, if the worker chose to meet the neighbours to try and both appease them and learn more about Ms P's behaviour, would that be a legitimate piece of work to be calculated in her workload?

Other criticisms of measurement systems are that they take no account of the quality of service which might be given (Orme, 1995). Questions are raised about whether measurements on a time per task basis can accurately reflect the complexity of social work tasks, when the focus is on micro-functions such as the number of reports to be written in a given period, or the number of people seen, rather than the purpose of the social worker being involved in the first place. Tasks such as assessment can lead to decisions which deprive people of their liberty. Alternatively, they may conclude that no intervention is necessary, which in community care assessments, such as that required in the case of Ms P, could lead to neglect and death. Such processes require time over and above task completion (that is, thinking time). The arguments are that they should be allowed appropriate weightings to allow professionals to make an informed judgement.

Having said that, some form of measurement is necessary in order to attempt to ensure equity of allocation between workers and, as the industrial tribunal decision highlighted, provide some protection for workers. Also, in the mixed economy of service delivery, workload measurement has contractual implications.

Workloads and markets

The introduction of the market into welfare has brought different emphases to workload management. Service providers have to calculate the resources necessary to undertake identified tasks in order to make realistic estimates of the cost of providing the services. Commissioners have to assess the tenders for service giving consideration to both cost and quality.

Additionally, in a culture of best value (see Chapter 30) and philosophies of total quality management (see Chapter 29), organisations are concerned about performance. In the case of Ms P, the worker was involved as a care manager in the statutory sector, and as such had to be concerned about response times and aware of the effect of her action or inaction on the public opinion of the organisation. For workers in provider agencies in the voluntary, independent and private sectors, their performance may also affect the success of future tenders and their own employment prospects. The workload calculations made in the original tender will dictate the time they have to provide a quality service.

The interplay of purchasers and providers is therefore focused on the assessment which becomes the blueprint (Orme and Glastonbury, 1994). At the organisational level, the problem is how to manage a system that can appropriately discern between how realistic the original assessment was and how accurate was the measurement of resources required to meet the need. It is the individual worker who has to operate at these margins, ensuring that the work is done, but not compromising their value systems. However, if they are successful, the outcome may be more contracts where the expectations are even higher, and more is expected of them. If they do not achieve what is required, the service user might suffer, or the worker may be held responsible.

Workload management

At the organisational level, therefore, workload issues are complex. Resources are allocated according to a variety of indicators. These may be certain populations in a particular area, or predictions based on past incidence of, for example, mental ill health. Budgets are allocated according to formulae which include raw data, predictions based on research evidence and political expediency. Statistical data is collected and used to make broadbrush decisions about the allocation of resources, but this is not always enough. In large organisations, different sets of data are often not cross-referenced. So, for example, a social services committee may at one meeting consider data about numbers of referrals, time lapses before cases are seen, number and cost of care packages and average number of cases per worker. At another meeting it may have data on staff sickness levels (or absenteeism as it is pejoratively called), or make decisions about holding posts vacant in order to balance the budgets. If these sets of data are not integrated, there is little sense of the conditions in which workers are operating. The potential of management information systems to cross-reference such data is great and has to be part of management responsibility.

Equally, decisions about what happens if demand exceeds supply have to be made at the organisational level. Ideally, the response to excess demand would be to deal with the causal factors which created the need (for example poverty, housing and so on) or allocate more resources in order to meet the demand. However, these depend on policies at governmental level. Alternatives include setting workload ceilings, rationing, prioritising or the creation of waiting lists as a means of ensuring that those in extreme need are dealt with, and that workers who provide services are not overloaded.

However, when such policies are introduced, the responsibility for operationalising them again falls to frontline workers. Those in assessment and emergency duty teams, in particular, faced with someone in distress, either at their own misfortune or at the condition of a relative, friend or neighbour, find it difficult to refuse services. The pressure to respond is great, even if this means that there will be fewer resources either in terms of hospital beds, daycare places or indeed the worker's own time to give to others who might come along in greater need.

Individual responsibilities

Whatever macro-systems are introduced, therefore, they have implications for the frontline worker. The basic tenet of social work, respect for persons, has to operate in all service provision. The individual worker's dilemma in a system of rationing is how to reflect such an ethic when having to refuse requests and not meet need.

Equally significant are the decisions about how time is spent. If a worker spends time with an individual, it may be possible to identify resources which maintain the person in their own home and avoid them becoming part of the welfare system. This might not always be the most streamlined intervention, but it may be more effective for the individual who otherwise might have to give up their right to privacy and autonomy by becoming a client or user. However, the consequences for the worker in the case of Ms P of setting up an appropriate and professional multidisciplinary assessment was that she had to forego her own leave because, in the light of competing pressures, there was not enough time available.

Allocation of time is therefore crucial, but frontline workers' criticisms of measurement systems were that they are retrospective, giving opportunity for relief once overload in workload has been identified (Glastonbury et al., 1987). This does not have to be the case, especially now that computers can input, analyse and give graphical representation of data within minutes. However, such systems are dependent upon workers being prepared to input the data and the systems being sensitive to the nuances of the task that they have to perform.

Management responsibilities

Computerisation brings further challenges. The introduction of measurement systems may be seen to give workers protection and ensure the quality of service to users. More effective management could ensure that when there was unexpected demand, as in the case of Ms P, the work could be dealt with in other ways, either diverted to other sources of help or emergency staff recruited. However, in order to achieve this workers would have to experience greater accountability, informing the supervisor exactly how time was being spent, justifying the work that was being done and why it was being done. However, all forms of overview of a worker's activities can represent a form of surveillance of the individual's work, and surveillance has been integrally related to issues of power (Foucault, 1972).

To achieve measurement there have to be exercises that log detailed activities to achieve a baseline (Orme, 1995). In imposing measurement there are expectations of normative practice which might not allow for individual differences. The positives of such systems therefore depend upon the management culture. It is also unhelpful if, as a result of analysis, the worker is made responsible either for the cause of the overwork because they 'took too much time' or 'got too involved', or for the solution, by multi-tasking, streamlining their systems or undergoing training in time management.

While there has to be an element of self-management, and advice available on how to cope with demands (Coulshed and Mullender, 2000) is important and helpful, what is crucial is the context. For example, where workload schemes have been used systematically and transparently, workers have welcomed the acknowledgement that they were doing 'too much', that they were working over their allocation. This was enough to relieve their stress and enabled them to keep going (Glastonbury et al., 1987). More importantly, it provided everyone with crucial information which enabled them as a team to look at where the pressures were coming from, and identify what could be done to relieve them.

At the individual level, systems such as case review involve allocation of work accompanied by close supervision by a manager. Ongoing supervision of allocated cases involves feedback and discussion which is part of ongoing professional development. It can offer support in decisions about the amount of time to be spent with cases and managerial accountability for rationing decisions and ongoing risk assessment. It can also provide information which can be fed into the organisational systems about the demands of particular work, or about the patterns of need which are emerging. Why, for example, did the worker in the case of Ms P have an unexpected demand before her leave? Was it because she had left some tasks to the last minute or because there were local circumstances which were unpredictable?

Simply advocating management involvement is not an easy solution. Healy (2000) warns that managerialist attempts to control, which might also relieve some of the pressures, often emphasise authoritarian and hierarchical power. The suggestion that everything can be measured, and in measuring can be quantified and controlled, is seen as part of rationalist, modernist assumptions associated with Weberian notions of formalised, hierarchical models of bureaucracy that are not always relevant to social work (Coulshed and Mullender, 2000). Such management styles have been seen to be oppressive. For example, they can be phallocentric because they are 'not the way of women' (Healy, 2000: 91), or impact negatively on workers who, because of culture, gender or disability, do things differently (Hough, 1999).

Critical practice

It is not necessary to reject all attempts at managing workload as part of a negative managerialist agenda. As has been said, worker protection and efficient operations are important aspects of positive management, leading to effective service delivery. Understanding and critically analysing the systems which are introduced helps workers to understand how different personal, professional and organisational identities are constructed by different managerial discourses (Hough, 1999). Positive practice involves localised activities which include networking, strategic alliances to allow for reflection on workday lives and the impact on workers' construction of their identity in the workplace (Hough, 1999: 51). Such reflection can involve individual users reflecting on how needs can be best met, workers reflecting on the way in which policies are implemented, and the impact of these on workers and service users. Active listening, feedback and achieving egalitarian relationships can support systems of workload management which are more discursive and interactional and will be more acceptable and fruitful than mechanical systems of measuring input and output.

Such interactional systems allow workers to exercise their rights and power by collective responses. They require that workers be consulted about the workload systems that are used, and the detail of the calculation. In the past, such activities might have been coordinated by trade unions or professional associations, now they are more likely to operate at the local level, where the specific conditions can influence the systems that are set up, but it is still necessary to network at national or UK level. Accurate information about workloads that reflect both the time and level of expertise necessary in social work interventions should inform policy decisions about funding, staffing levels and qualifications.

The disadvantage is that effective systems take time, a scarce commodity within social work resources. However, if time is not taken, the quality of services will be compromised and resources, including human resources, will be wasted. In social work this can have life-threatening consequences – for users and workers.

FURTHER READING

Bilson, A. and Ross, S. (1999) *Social Work Management and Practice*, 2nd edn, London: Jessica Kingsley. This text uses systems theory to analyse social work management.

Coulshed, V. and Mullender, A. (2001) *Management in Social Work*, Basingstoke: Palgrave – now Palgrave Macmillan. This text provides an excellent overview of the themes and issues relating to managing social work generally with specific sections on workload.

Orme, J. (1995) *Workloads: Measurement and Management*, Aldershot: Avebury in association with CEDR, University of Southampton. This text describes a research project undertaken with probation officers and explores in detail the complexities of trying to operate and refine workload measurement systems.

Payne, M. (2000) *Teamwork in Multiprofessional Care*, Basingstoke: Palgrave – now Palgrave Macmillan. This text explores how teams in care services can use networking and teambuilding to strengthen their practice with practical guidance on teambuilding and teambuilding activities – all necessary when managing workloads.

Supervision and Being Supervised

Julia Phillipson

Contemporary social work has been described as contested, compromised and challenged (Healy, 2000) and many believe that the social work profession, like others, is in crisis (Rossiter, 1996). The reasons for this buffeting are numerous and include the changing design and delivery of social work and an increasing dominance of managerialism, and the impact of imperatives of challenge and auditing embedded in best value and evidence-based practice as well as the destabilising that postmodernism has prompted (Leonard, 1997). Service users too continue to question social work practices and theories (Wilson and Beresford, 2000). Together, these challenges have unsettled social work's identity, purpose and processes.

Yet social work supervision, a fundamental plank in ensuring social work's focus and effectiveness (Brown and Bourne, 1996), appears to be largely untouched by these seismic upheavals. The steady flow of books and articles on supervision largely refine and develop it rather than question it fundamentally (for example, Hawkins and Shohet, 2000; Knapman and Morrison, 1998). Is this because all is well with supervision or might its very continuity be hindering the profession's ability to respond critically to the changes and develop critical social work practices that emphasise an emancipatory social change orientation (Healy, 2000: 3)? Might it be enhanced by being challenged itself? A preliminary excursion into reconsidering social work supervision is the focus of this chapter. It uses a questioning process that critical practice also requires and begins to consider supervision's potential to facilitate critical social work.

Uprooting the roots of supervision

Brockbank and McGill (1998) suggest three roots to contemporary supervision. First, industry, with its perceived need to oversee employees and their work. Second, therapy, where counsellors and therapists are regularly supervised to ensure the cognitive and emotional 'fitness' of the therapist and therefore the safety of the client. Third, academia, where learners are attached to a 'master' (p. 232). Each root emphasises different aspects of the functions of supervision: the control of the behaviour and output of the worker, support and 'fitness for purpose', and learning and development. The three roots find their way not only into conceptions of supervision's functions (for example, Kadushin, 1976; Richards and Payne, 1990) but also into many agency supervision policy documents and Diploma in Social Work handbooks. Together they are regarded as a key to ensuring social work's purpose and efficacy. Thus Brown and Bourne (1996: 9) argue that:

> supervision is the primary means by which an agency-designated supervisor enables staff, individually and collectively, and ensures standards of practice. The aim is to enable the supervisee(s) to carry out their work ... as effectively as possible.

'The provision of the best possible service to service users' is the ultimate aim.

(p. 10)

It is usually suggested that the effective implementation of the functions is ensured through mechanics such as recording proforma (which are often shaped by the functions), contracting and having a regular time, space and place for supervision. The role of authority and the supervisor's expertise in practice, management and in supervision itself are also requisites for effectiveness. This depiction of supervision is of a formalised, regulated and largely private process into which supervisors are trained, but where supervisees are infrequently offered parallel training in being a supervisee.

This portrait of supervision's purpose, functions and implementation, as already suggested, appears remarkably consistent in literature and policies while other realities are largely ignored. For example, workers and students also depend on 'on the hoof' supervision in the corridor or office, while supervision of large groups of workers at infrequent intervals, such as in domiciliary care, is rarely acknowledged or considered in detail. The latter is largely by and with women about an area of practice seen as relatively unskilled, although much appreciated by service users. What might these omissions suggest about the orthodoxies of supervision?

There is some acknowledgement in the supervision literature of difficulties with the formalised model. For example, Brown and Bourne point up the danger of assuming that supervision is a convenient hybrid of three different kinds of meetings, each with their allotted time on the supervision agenda. This 'runs the risk of reducing supervision to a rote practice capable of maintaining only minimum standards' (1996: 61). Hughes and Pengelly (1997) depict the functions as a triangle and thereby reveal a problem they describe as ' three into one won't go', where there is a danger of over- or underemphasising one of the corners/functions at the expense of the other two. The functions are not themselves queried. Power dynamics and aspects of identity are also increasingly acknowledged as an important issue in supervision. Concerns about the potential for the abuse of power embedded in the typically hierarchic structure of student and staff supervision are raised (for example, Evans, 1999; Hawkins and Shohet, 2000). In this author's experience, much practice teacher training rightly emphasises this potential and the need to be vigilant against it. However, this orthodoxy too may be problematic in practice, for Brown and Bourne (1996: 33) also suggest that social work supervisors are not comfortable with their authority and power and seek to sidestep it, thus confusing the supervisee. Maybe the models of power and empowerment espoused in the supervision literature and training also need questioning. Perhaps they do not adequately reflect the complexity and impact of identity aspects such as race, gender, disability and sexuality as explored by Carroll and Holloway (1999). For example, Lee Nelson and Holloway's review of gender relations in supervision shows complex and changing power dynamics over time which are affected by the gender alignments of supervisee and supervisor:

> Only dyads with male supervisees followed the path of becoming more collegial over time, while dyads with women supervisees over time, tended to reflect a greater imbalance of power.
>
> (1999: 30)

They quote Jordan's study which contended that power in supervision cannot be considered without also considering affiliation and women's need for a sense of mutuality and to 'participate with others in a mutual give and take of empathy and understanding' (1999: 31). While the study concerns counselling, it raises questions for student and staff supervision. Studies on the impact of sexual orientation, 'race' and disability in the same volume confirm the need to see power relations as complex, dynamic and affected not only by the structure of supervision but also by the wider societal structures and ideology such as medical and social models of disability (see also Thomas, 1999). Like Healy's contention that critical social work has developed its own orthodoxy in seeing worker power as essentially oppressive, maybe supervision also needs further work on exploring the positive dimensions of power imbalances, how power relationships change over time as well as different sorts of authority models such as proposed by Jones (1993).

So while there are some ripples of disturbance in the conventions of writing and thinking about supervision, what of the experience of supervision?

Experiencing supervision

Information from social work students, practitioners and managers suggests that while there are great expectations of supervision and some good quality supervision is experienced, many people are disappointed by either what they can offer or receive. Some examples suggest differing components to the dissatisfaction.

CASE EXAMPLES

It's quantity supervision, it's like a game of tag where you touch base and then shoot off again.

(Williams, 2000, personal communication)

❖

As the previous month's supervision had been cancelled, there were now 17 'cases' for update as well as other agenda items. Mrs J was one of them. She'd been in hospital for three months and was desperate to go home. The discussion was brief and focused on finding and contracting with care providers. The other 'cases' were also skimmed through; mutual support was offered about the workload pressures both worker and supervisor were experiencing; some agenda items were postponed. It was all that was possible in the hour and a half. Later, when the delay continued, the supervisor realised that no contingency plans had been discussed, neither had the worker's feelings, and as for research into the impact of delayed discharge on older women …

❖

The female senior manager described how when she went into supervision she seemed to spend a lot of time listening to her supervisor's problems with his senior management colleagues; till at last, fed up, she went outside the division for support and advice (Phillipson and Riley, 1991).

❖

It was a tense moment in what had seemed, initially, a positive supervision session. They'd exchanged news about their respective weekends and agreed the agenda and note-taking. Their shared discussion about theory teaching at college was lively. But then the practice teacher's verbal feedback on the student's written work was met with rebuttal. He'd commented gently on the way she sometimes seemed dismissive of her practice skills by writing statements such as 'I just let her talk'; his attempts to encourage her to enquire further about her thinking, feeling, and responses to the family were countered, laughingly, by 'you make it too complicated, you're too analytic …'

These examples highlight the difficulties of 'overseeing' the sheer volume of work; relationships that may be both enabling and oppressive, tensions between aspects such as speed and depth, support and challenge, thinking and feelings. For students there may be a tension between proving competence and acknowledging difficulties. The tensions experienced in supervision are not surprising for 'tensions and contradictions lie at the heart of much social work' (Lawson, 1998: 248). Social work practices include fleeting encounters as well as sustained relationships, they are about power and control as well as empowerment, they necessitate the often simultaneous performance of activities, some of which require considerable skills and others which do not. Both social change and conformity are demanded of social work. Social work supervision is likely to mirror these tensions and paradoxes (Mattinson, 1975). Supervision policies and rituals seem designed to contain and shrink these complexities and tensions, and maybe this too mirrors social work with its concern to 'manage risk' (Parton, 1998).

Using provocations to question how supervision might be different

Healy, as part of her critique of past attempts at critical social work, uses the postmodernist tools of querying, dismantling the orthodoxies and destabilising the ideas and practices of critical social work to move it forward. Being context-ually sensitive and self-reflective are two key tools. Applying this latter approach to my own work as supervisor and supervisee, I sought to disturb my own orthodoxies about supervision by questioning my own practice and reading accounts which provoked and helped me to do this. Three are offered below, not as essential reading but as exemplars of the process. A novel by A.S. Byatt (2000), research by Jan Fook (2000) and writing by Celia Davies on nursing (1995) all provided fertile provocation.

Davies' study of 'gender and the professional predicament in nursing' highlights the way in which the parallel developments of both organisational and professional development have been essentially a process of masculinisation. Her analysis leads her to point up the way gender is not only 'on the surface', in terms of aspects such as speech, dress, presentation and ways of interacting, but also a constitutive element in organisational structure and logic (pp. 45–6). The notion of a 'job', the concept of 'career', the supremacy of hierarchical organisational structures, the assignation of tasks and thereby status to different ranks are all gendered. This gendered organisational logic affects other aspects such as the expression and suppression of emotions, sexuality and even what counts as legit-imate knowledge. This analysis provokes consideration of the way in which the conception and practice of supervision might itself be gendered, for example in its own predominately hierarchical model, the content, focus and processes. Might this explain the lack of attention paid to 'on the hoof' supervision and group supervision for predominantly women workers? How might gendered organ-isational logic and expression impact on my experience as a woman supervisor and supervisee? And how might this link to the development and promotion of critical social work which espouses the importance of the wider structural context, change and standing alongside oppressed and marginalised peoples?

Fook's research into the development of social work expertise also uses postmodernist critiques and tools. Like Davies, she sets this within a feminist framework that attempts to characterise social work expertise in ways which are more representative of the experience of social workers and service users, many of whom are women. Her study showed that 'rather than entering situations with superior and fixed notions of desirable outcomes derived from the legitimacy of professional knowledge practitioners often engage in a mutual process of discovery with service users' (p. 114), they were context sensitive and used uncertainty and playing it 'by ear'. This echoes Parton and O'Byrne's description of practices they call 'constructive social work', where 'an ability to work with ambiguity and uncertainty in terms of process and outcome is key'. Such social work suggests a richness of practice that emphasises a 'plurality of knowledge and voice, the use of paradox, myth, enigma and narrative' (2000: 3).

Neither Fook nor Parton and O'Byrne discuss the implications of their research and practice accounts for supervision models and processes. But their work prompts the possibility of valuing and surfacing uncertainty, ambiguity, plurality and narrative in supervision as well as in practice. This may be 'counter culture' in organisations where 'getting the work done' is essential and where, like the White Queen in *Alice Through the Looking Glass*, people often feel that they have to undertake 'six impossible things before breakfast' and supervision (of any sort) is just one of these.

The third provocation is *The Biographer's Tale* by A.S. Byatt. The novel begins with her hero Phineas G. abandoning the 'stultifying' criticism and tortuous deconstructions of postmodernism that he has been studying.

> It was a sunny day and the windows were very dirty. I was looking at the windows and I thought I am not going on with this any longer ... I need a life full of things, full of facts.
>
> (2000: 3, 4)

Instead, he decides to become a biographer in search of uncontestable facts. The novel is redolent of the tension between facts and assumptions, the search for certainty and the discomfort of questioning. I recognise the temptations of looking for and assuming the solidity of facts, of leaving critical self-reflection and the uncertain 'swampy lowlands' described by Schön (1991) behind. Supervision is not exempt from such yearning or a pressure to deal in 'facts'.

Regrowing supervision for critical social work

These provocations encourage a reconsideration of how supervision might be used to develop and sustain critical social work in an era of challenge and contestation, and how supervision itself might model this approach.

If practice is to be flexible, pragmatic and undogmatic, supervision could model this in terms of its 'when', 'where' and 'how' without abandoning the more formal expectations and opportunities. Practitioners and managers reveal that much significant 'supervision' takes place spontaneously, often among peers, yet this is rarely formally acknowledged, recorded or used to expand the notions of supervision. Domiciliary care workers in particular are often dependent on a quick phone call to a supervisor for advice, support, workload management and even quality assurance. Supervision in its formalised, one-at-a-time version is likely to be unavailable or infrequent for such workers – new supervision models are needed that respect and problematise their work. Surely critical social work cannot be the prerogative only of social workers? New technology also offers the possibility of new models of supervision.

Fook's research suggests that there is a challenge to develop a new discourse of expertise derived from practitioner experience. The discourse of critical practice might include the contradictions and uncertainties of what it constitutes as well as developing some 'facts' about it. Emancipatory practice might well take place in the everyday activities of social work practices as well as the more usually assumed wider political spheres or indeed in both. How, for example, are practitioners engaged in identifying and recording the 'unmet need' of both service users and carers? How might they tackle people's unmet needs and at the same time promote social change? This is a practice, management and political issue, yet personal experience of supervision notes rarely show this being debated or recorded. What might it be like to have 'emancipatory practice' as an agenda item? The example of the supervision session in which Mrs J was briefly discussed might have thought about her not only in terms of 'setting up a package of care', but also in terms of how information about the shortfall of care might be collected, made known and acted upon individually and collectively. The possible impact of aspects such as ageism, sexism and racism and medical models of care might also be crucial. In this way the focus of the supervision 'lens' might itself be open to debate, such as, 'why are we discussing this aspect? What are we not looking at and why?' 'How are we talking about it?'

Critical social work requires an ability to be both self and politically reflective. If supervision's aim is to ensure the delivery of the 'best possible' service, then 'best possible' could also be contested in supervision in terms of beliefs, policy and practices. Johns' (2000) suggestion that a key aspect of reflection is to expose and understand the contradictions between what is desirable and actual practice could form part not only of the destabilising and contesting but also the construction of knowledge through telling the practice stories in supervision.

CONCLUSION

It has been suggested that the theory and policies of supervision have remained largely untouched by the debates about social work. This is perhaps not surprising, given its origins in the largely hierarchical organisational settings in which it is still mainly implemented, where questioning, contesting and political challenging are constrained. By using questioning and self-reflection, other possibilities for supervision have been suggested. And yet maybe this discourse of questioning is itself a new orthodoxy. Maybe supervision remains undisturbed because the definitions of its purpose, the analysis and implementation of its functions are apt and appropriate? The need for regular space and time for review, reflection, action planning and quality control continue to be what people say they want and hope for. Perhaps the roots should be cherished and nurtured, not questioned. But I am not convinced that this is enough for the development and enhancement of critical social work.

FURTHER READING

Bond, M. and Holland, S. (1998) *Skills of Clinical Supervision for Nurses*, Buckingham: Open University Press. A very detailed look at supervision as a 'working alliance' that offers a multitude of practical ideas as well as being thought provoking.

Brown, A. and Bourne, I. (1996) *The Social Work Supervisor*, Buckingham: Open University Press. A social work focused text on supervision which has very useful chapters on the necessary value base and the impact of difference for supervision.

Hawkins, P. and Shohet, R. (2000) *Supervision in the Helping Professions*, 2nd edn, Buckingham: Open University Press. A key book for understanding processes in individual and group supervision which has now been revised to include more debate on working with difference.

Healy, K. (2000) *Social Work Practices*, London: Sage. A book that challenges some of the orthodoxies of critical social work, highlights the importance of everyday practice and questions itself.

Lahad, M. (2000) *Creative Supervision: The Use of Expressive Arts Methods in Supervision and Self-supervision*, London: Jessica Kingsley. A small book rich with ideas and stories of imaginative ways of working in supervision which are fun and illuminating.

25

Coordination and Teamwork

Malcolm Payne

Coordination and teamwork are security against the risks of complexity in postmodern social work and welfare. With the mixed economy of care character-istic of the early twenty-first century, a variety of organisations in health and social care from different sectors of the economy, state, private and voluntary or third sector, provide different elements of service. They work with a range of social units, such as a family, a couple, a group or a community. This form of organisation has been politically chosen: it is a reaction against the trend of the 1960s and 70s for large state organisations. It has also been a response to social developments: people in a postmodern society seek individual directions among many alternatives. A one-size-fits-all philosophy is as unacceptable in the social services as it is in the high street. A dull-but-worthy style is as unacceptable in social care as it is at Marks & Spencer, the high street colossus that has been troubled by having a too-monolithic, traditional image for its products. However, the very individualism of a postmodern society everywhere demands integration. The care manager of the twenty-first century department store is the personal shopper, who, told of the customer's needs, collects the various items from the different floors.

The pattern of services built up in the 1970s was of one major agency, led by one major profession, providing a range of services linked by a common philos-ophy. The health service meant a medical model; social services, a social model; education, learning models. Some of the less central services overlapped with others, childcare with education welfare, social services area team with health services primary care team, so that connections needed to be managed. This requires workers to manage the relationship between their own organisation and others (interagency coordination) as well as between their profession and others (interprofessional coordination) and between their own professional knowledge and values and others (interdisciplinary coordination). In Northern Ireland, health and social services were combined and alternative arrangements were possible.

Agency, profession and discipline

Some of the issues that arise between agency, profession and discipline, as social workers in a health care setting carry out these different forms of coordination, appear in the following account of a period in the life of a team.

CASE EXAMPLE

In Ward 7, the long-standing social worker, June, arranged residential care home placements for service users requiring discharge through the purchasing unit at the social services department (SSD), organising the assessment visits by care home staff, making the arrangements, fixing the ambulance transport and filling in the purchasing contract information form for the SSD. Nursing staff sometimes became frustrated with her, because they referred patients and then experienced quite a delay before assessment visits were made; even then, the transfer did not seem to take place on any consistent basis. Patients and their relatives often pressurised nurses to know what was happening.

In Ward 3, the social worker, Karen, was new. She asked the purchasing officer's advice about process and organised herself a progress sheet. She left this on the patient's notes, asked the ward staff to contact the care home staff about the assessment visits, took the contract information form to fill it in together with nursing staff, and asked them to arrange the ambulance and organise arrangements with carers. June criticised this in the social work team meeting, because Karen was passing social work functions on to the nursing staff. June saw Karen as damaging the position of social work in the hospital.

The Ward 3 nursing and medical staff fed back to the team leader that Karen was magic – everything was so quick. The team leader looked at this and found that there was no difference in speed of discharge. The nursing staff thought Karen's process was quicker because they knew what was going on, so they did not experience mysterious delays. Because they had made the contacts themselves, they knew about the information required, which was mainly nursing information. They began to trust Karen more, and referred more work about patients' family problems, whereas the Ward 7 staff saw June as a not very efficient organiser of arrangements. Discussing it in the team meeting, Karen saw her approach as moving social work on from the more routine role of arranging external links. She hoped to develop towards the more satisfying and unique role of helping clients and their families understand and respond to what was happening in their lives because of the illness and disability that patients were facing.

These events represent very complex individual interprofessional relationships, relationships between agencies and between professions. Coordination and teamwork are modes of action in this situation, which help to provide a feeling of security. Coordination assumes that the alignment of structures or policies will reduce uncertainty. Teamwork assumes that effectiveness is improved by promoting good relationships among participants in service provision. As 'modes of action', coordination and teamwork are things people do. When a group of people are organised to work together, we call them a team with the hope and expectation that they will find ways of cooperating together. Services will clearly work better if they fit together with other services. In June and Karen's team, neither the social work team's way of working, nor the fit with the ward nursing teams is finally set. Tensions exist in the way June works with her ward team; changes are made in the way Karen works with hers. The social work team has a debate about different ways of working. Thus, coordination and teamwork require constant attention and management.

Because coordination and teamwork are about making things and people fit together well, there is sometimes a taken-for-granted assumption that they are good things and that they feel nice when they happen successfully. Looking at June and Karen's team, however, we can see that this is not so. There are conflicts and differences of view, played out in people's actions. June's way of working has led to difficulties, but these are coped with and any tensions repressed. Karen's way of working reduces these tensions but raises the possibility that there may be long-term consequences for relationships between the professions. When these issues turn into a conflict, the team examines what has happened; but we do not know about the final outcome. Does June or Karen change her practice? How is this achieved: is one persuaded by team agreement or do both compromise a bit, or does no change happen? Does the long-term issue about the role of social work take precedence over the apparently better relationships developed by Karen's approach? Whose view of the role of social work should be preferred? There are no simple answers to questions such as these, so therefore there are always conflicts to be resolved. Teams, whether they comprise people from a single profession or are multiprofessional, are a site where these issues may be worked out and an effective team often brings conflict to the surface and finds ways of dealing with it. As the team works them out, they have regard for their view about the direction of the agencies, disciplines and professions involved.

Social work in a multiprofessional team

Pushing for social work may seem to cut across the cooperative ideal of teamwork. However, one aim of teamwork is to bring issues and conflicts to the surface and have them resolved openly, rather than repressed and unconsidered. Therefore, if there are issues of difference between different professional, disciplinary or agency views, these need to be dealt with, not swept under the carpet. The team, being a cooperative endeavour, is the place to do this, rather than having conflicts resolved through bureaucratic processes.

Pushing for social work may also be difficult because we, and others, are not clear what it is and how we should value it. What positions might be legitimately taken? It partly depends on the context: it might be different in criminal justice as compared with health care. However, a number of general perspectives are often contributed by social work, set out in Table 25.1. These broad perspectives underlie many of the conventional tasks of social work and provide a basis for supporting the position of social work within teams. Many other professions have particular responsibilities and duties, to a patient in medical services, for example, or to the court and legal system. This often means that they do not focus on the considerations that are central to social work. It is not that they are unable to or unaware, necessarily, but their focus is different. For example, the social work approach to family and community involvement and the social model provide the value base for the role of social work in assessment. When someone asks: 'why do we need a social work assessment?', these principles provide an answer. They also provide the basis for social workers' roles in working with families and clients together in relation to their communities' expectations. Similarly, the welfare rights and social justice models provide the value base for social workers being effective in care planning and providing welfare rights help and advocacy. The welfare rights and family and community perspectives also provide the value basis for the social work role in liaison and developing community resources.

In the multiprofessional world of the twenty-first century, these roles have to be carried out within a broader model of coordination and teamwork, in which all participants have to help the others make their contributions to some degree. To do this, awareness of and responsiveness to a number of general issues in coordination and teamwork can help to retain a critical approach while remaining positive about

Table 25.1 Social work contributions in multiprofessional settings

Social work perspective	The social work approach	Service consequences
Welfare rights	Benefits and services are a right for clients, which should be actively pursued on their behalf	Welfare rights provision Effective planning for services
User participation	Clients to participate and if possible direct the services they receive and the way they receive them	Choices offered, where possible Wishes and values respected
Family and community involvement	People live in families and communities, whose interests in and concerns for particular individuals need to be taken into account	Concern for impact on family and community Concern for family and community influences
Social model	Medical, behavioural or criminal 'problems' may produce problems in people's lives, or may be influenced by social experiences	Concern for social influences Respond to social impact of 'problems'
Social justice	Many people have 'problems' or are 'difficult' because of the social divisions and social structures that have constructed their life experience	Avoid labelling Equality in service provision Anti-oppressive practice Empowerment – compensation for lack of life opportunities

the contribution that a social worker may make and about the work of coordination. In the next two sections, I examine these general issues in two groups: first, boundaries, identity and resources and then network, setting and community.

Boundaries, identity and resources

Social care and social work often have the role in multiprofessional activity of being concerned with managing boundaries between agencies, disciplines and professions for the benefit of clients and gaining resources from the state and communities for clients. Other professions, focusing on their patient, pupil or client, look to social workers to deliver support from family and community and services from other agencies. Pietroni (1994), looking at the history of interdisciplinary teams, characterises it as a 'quartermaster' role. Because most social work clients are in poverty, delivery of resources is crucial to the success of social work and clients' valuation of it.

Critical social work 'problematises' boundary, rather than just accepting or trying to overcome it. The benefits and values it may have are gladly embraced; its difficulties are sought and overcome. So June and Karen need to ask: where is the 'beneficial boundary' between nursing and social work in this task? Do we need to move our current boundaries to get there? Can we do that, or are there things getting in the way? If we can do it, are there further moves we can make that would create an even more beneficial boundary?

Identity can answer some of these questions. Boundaries help us to identify the limits of something. In this case, it is social work as compared with another profession such as teaching; the social care services as opposed to other agencies, such as the police; one worker's knowledge and value disciplines as against another's, such as nursing or occupational therapy. Limits are one aspect of the identity of a profession, agency or discipline, and being aware of boundaries alerts us to think about the point at which and the way in which we come into contact with others' agencies, professional concerns and disciplines. Thinking about limits is particularly useful in a postmodern society, because we are always cautious in postmodernism about considering the 'essence' of something. A psychological view of 'identity' assumes that there is something inherent in us, which gives us a personality and our lives meaning.

It helps us to change and stay flexible to think about boundaries as the white line on a sports pitch. It marks out the agreed territory and tells us what the social rules are, but it is easy to step across if we need to. If we think about boundaries in cricket, hitting a ball beyond the boundary scores the most runs; it is an achievement to be welcomed. So it is in social work, because going beyond the boundaries allows us meet up with our colleagues' work on the other side. June's approach is to maintain the boundary for clarity, in effect passing the patient across the boundary to another team member. Karen steps across it with the patient and works together with her colleagues. However, being aware of and recognising the boundary alerts her to risks: of offending others, of trespassing in areas where we do not have the expertise, for example. Maintaining the sports field metaphor, we cross the boundary knowingly in order to gain additional resources: more participants and more space to work in.

Staying within our boundaries may limit us and the resources of expertise and services available to our clients.

The model of multiprofessional coordination presented here, then, proposes making an issue of and thinking explicitly about:

- The boundaries between agencies, professions and disciplines

- The identity that agencies, professions and disciplines have for different participants

- The resources used and which agencies, professions and disciplines they are drawn from.

Multiprofessional network, setting and community

So far, I have assumed that multiprofessional work takes place around a case or a series of cases and that delivering resources from agencies, professions and disciplines is the crucial element of coordination and teamwork. However, critical thinking alerts us to the importance of historical and social context and the ways these construct different forms of practice. We have noted that different agencies represent particular professional and disciplinary models of action. Team members 'reach out' to 'draw in' resources from a network of agencies, professions and disciplines (Payne, 2000b). This task is made both easier and more complex by the extent of overlap or divisions between these elements of the multiprofessional network. For example, if the main tasks involve doctors using medical skill and knowledge in a health organisation, profession, discipline and agency are consistent and it is easy to organise the work. However, the very consistency of this situation may make occasional reaching out to find other resources, when it is required, difficult through lack of knowledge, understanding or authority. Where the main tasks are complex, a multiprofessional team may be set up. For example, many areas are establishing community mental health teams. These are tied in various ways to both social care and health organisations, involve a variety of social care and health professions and try to combine in various ways different knowledges and skills. While this may make coordination easier than in divided organisations, the people involved are faced with resolving conflicts about models of practice, knowledge and understandings, and professional and organisational authority.

This suggests that changing organisational structures does not automatically provide the answer to professional, agency and disciplinary conflicts. Equally, sharing professional skills and acting in positive professional ways do not necessarily overcome boundaries and identity problems. To achieve change in such situations requires thinking about the context in which our multiprofessional, multiagency and multidisciplinary work exists. There are three elements to be considered:

- The networks among agencies, disciplines and professions

- The social setting or environment in which they operate

- The community surrounding professional networks and social environments.

Networks are links between identifiable elements in patterns of work. We saw above that the networks of agencies, disciplines and professions do not always coincide, but may sometimes overlap. The crucial elements of organisation to be clear about are the elements and the links between them. Effective coordination and teamwork require understanding the role and boundaries of agencies, disciplines and professions and how they overlap and might substitute for one another (the elements) and how the links are formed and operate. June had a clear vision of the role and boundary of social workers and nurses in the hospital team. Karen saw that, in some aspects of planning discharges, nurses and social workers might substitute for each other. June operated a referral model of links, passing information in a structured way from one team member to another, Karen operated a sharing form of link in which roles were less distinct but defined by working together.

The social setting in this case is a hospital, where all the parties to the issue worked in the same building. Facing a similar conflict between primary care and social services teams in the community might be much more complex, because they are often geographically separate and loyalties to different agency disciplinary models might be strengthened by geographical division. Alternatively, they may be weakened by connections between the teams where they work together.

The network and social setting are further influenced by the community in which they are situated. This may be because of demographic pressures. For example, a court or youth justice team where the area experiences a serious problem of repeated youth theft and criminal damage may have opportunities and constraints from an area where theft is the main issue. A hospital covering a major city will focus on different issues from one in an isolated rural area and require different things of the contributions of their social workers.

Understanding, power and action

Making an issue of boundary, identity and resources may enable us to examine the relationship issues that we face in coordinating different agency, disciplinary and professional work. However, such an examination does not help us to know how to act. To do this, we must move beyond being critical and reflective to convert this first into shared understanding, so that different agency, disciplinary and professional analyses of the situation may be explored jointly and agreed upon. This will also draw on different but negotiable and debateable understandings of network, setting and community.

Shared understanding creates power, which may be used to support action in agreed directions. To arrive at an agreed understanding of the situation puts the power of knowledge behind taking action to resolve it. In June and Karen's social work team, understanding about the implications of their different approaches to work has emerged from the dispute about how team members should act. But we have seen from the questions raised above, however, that this does not overcome all the influences that may get in the way of change: the power of professional and disciplinary boundaries may counteract the power of better understanding and lead to inaction. Moreover, courses of action are supported by different powers. June's practice is supported by long-standing interprofessional practices, which, even though there are tensions, would need to be negotiated away. Karen's actions are supported by strong positive interprofessional reactions, but these may not influence a social work team fighting for a clear perception of its role in the hospital. Understanding and seeing where power lies, therefore, do not necessarily produce action to resolve differences of view.

The idea of *political agency* helps to draw these different aspects of coordination and teamwork together. It proposes that having an impact on a situation (that is, to have agency, in the sense that your actions can affect it) requires acting alongside transformation of political relationships, that is, structures that incorporate and mediate power. Thus, to change matters such as the boundary, identity or resources in a case we need to be aware of and change multiprofessional networks, and their social, environmental and community origins.

CONCLUSION

The social work team's response to the wider multiprofessional team's experiences of social work in June's and Karen's work illustrates the need for critical consideration of political agency in coordination and teamwork. To provide the best service for their clients, the team will need to consider not just how the boundaries, identity and resources of social work need to be managed, but how the multiprofessional networks, the setting of their team and the wider needs of the community need to change, and how these different factors have an impact on each other. Social work perspectives may only be contributed to the wider team, rather than developed independently as it is through shared understanding of the interaction of these different sets of factors that the team may gain the power to act on their situation. Failing to arrive at a shared understanding will mean that June and Karen will just continue to act in their own ways. Failing to include multiprofessional views, the centralised and dominating role of the hospital setting and the needs of their community may mean that their thinking about the proper boundaries and role of social work will not be able to have impact.

Coordination and teamwork are difficult because of the complexity of the interaction of these factors. Failing in coordination and teamwork, however complex, is not an option if we want to help service users and clients in a complex, postmodern world. Coordination and teamwork may seem to be security for anxieties for agencies and professional: it is better to see them as security for clients against the inadequacies of agencies and professionals.

FURTHER READING

Kaner, S., Lind, L., Toldi, C., Fisk, S. and Berger, D. (1996) *Facilitator's Guide to Participatory Decision-making*, Gabriola Island, BC, Canada: New Society. A very practical, skills development guide to helping groups and teams make decisions in a participative way, based on a well thought-out model of democratic decision-making.

Leathard, A. (ed.) (1994) *Going Inter-professional: Working Together for Health and Welfare*, London: Routledge. A good range of articles, with an emphasis on training and health care.

Øvretveit, J. (1993) *Coordinating Community Care: Multidisciplinary Teams and Care Management*, Buckingham: Open University Press. An important piece of research, developed through consultancy work, which brings together a vivid sense of practical management problems, with a good understanding of management issues.

Payne, M. (2000) *Teamwork in Multiprofessional Care*, Basingstoke: Palgrave – now Palgrave Macmillan. A text that includes discussion about teamwork models and practice, policy material on the development of teamwork and multiprofessional ideas and practical activities to help with team-building.

Soothill, K., Mackay, L, and Webb, C. (eds) (1995) *Interprofessional Relations in Health Care*, London: Arnold. Another good range of articles with a strong base in researched case studies, with an emphasis on training and issues of management and professionalisation, including a concern for user perspectives.

Assessment and Planning

Judith Milner and Patrick O'Byrne

Introduction

There is probably no area of social work where debate rages so fiercely as in assessment. Agencies have long been attempting to structure assessments, providing checklists and guidelines. Meanwhile government has redefined assessment with each new piece of legislation, sometimes stressing need, sometimes eligibility. The professional task itself is riddled with dilemmas and tensions. If a worker is too idealistic, recommendations, although laudable, will be too costly. Workers are trained to be needs led, but agencies seem to be risk and resource led. Workers are expected to apply theory to produce objective analyses but the theory is not always useful or does not fit. Assessment is supposed to be a process, not a one-off event, but time is rationed. Sadly, as Sinclair et al. (1995) discovered, assessments are frequently not even implemented and, of those that are, many do not contribute to positive outcomes.

There is much to question and reflect on; it cries out for the development of some critical thinking. We propose to show briefly what is involved in assessment and planning. We will touch on the main perspectives on assessment and the literature on which social workers draw. We will pick out the most problematic concepts associated with traditional and much of current assessment and we will introduce constructionism as one possible alternative and discuss the implications of its use.

> **CASE EXAMPLE**
>
> Meet Mark, a 12 year old with learning difficulties (from Milner, 2001). His social worker Kate has been in contact with him and his family for some time. Recently his mother has complained of his stealing, lying, kicking, biting, spitting and temper tantrums. She said, 'Either he goes into care or I'll put him six feet under. His dad won't even be in the same room as him and his sisters are not speaking to him. He can't concentrate for more than a few minutes.' The report traces the history and also sets out the views of teachers. It is a depressing story, getting worse. Explanations are sought: is he a family scapegoat? Is he just looking for attention/love? Does he feel empty inside? Has he just learned that he can get away with it? Is it down to poor parenting or poor resources? Do they need family therapy? Perhaps the marriage is on the rocks? The father is not very cooperative. Nothing seems to help. Perhaps Mark needs to be referred for special counselling?

What the work involves

We assume the social worker has collated much data on Mark, and tried to make sense of it, to search for the cause (to diagnose), to find the true explanation. She will have spent time talking not only with Mark but with several other people. She may have thought of behaviour modification (Skinner, 1953), client-centred interventions (Rogers, 1951), applied systems analysis perhaps (Pincus and Minahan, 1973), using transactional analysis ideas to understand the problem (Harris, 1981), or the task-centred ideas of Reid (1978). She may have been introduced to concepts of need located in white, adult, Eurocentric norms; she may have felt powerless in the face of Mark's learning difficulties, although they are not severe. She has found his father to be too angry to engage easily and his mother increasingly despairing. Do his parents take it all as a constant sign of failure? She is under pressure to show expertise, manage risk and save resources. The case looks as if it will be one of those endless costly sagas. How can she end her report and avoid selective attention and attributional bias? (For a full discussion of how these ideas and perspectives apply to social work assessment and the problems of report writing see Milner and O'Byrne, 1998). We will show later what actually happened.

But assessment in some areas of practice is much less theory based, relying on checklists for collating data and requiring very little judgement – what Smale and Tuson (1993) called 'the procedural model'. Their other two models are 'the questioning model' which is reflected in the description above (with the worker as expert), and 'the exchange model' with the service user as expert on the problem and seen as a primary resource for dealing with it.

Concepts to be questioned

For us, the first issue is the 'psy complex' (Rose, 1985). The practice of clinical psychology claimed it could define 'normal' children, families and parents and thereby single out the dysfunctional and the pathological, seeing the cause of problems within people and working mainly to treat these inner pathologies, playing down the social and cultural influences in lives which often overwhelm the social worker as much as the service user, failing to consider fully the impact of oppression and injustice and drifting dangerously near to being judgemental and generally disadvantaging women and children who present a softer target than men. This allows powerful professionals to define service users as 'oppositional', whereas service users have no power to define professionals as oppositional.

Next, the identification of deficit of one sort or another became a central thrust of assessments, which set out to study problems in great depth, seeking explanations and remedies. Much of the discussion with service users was/is problem focused and service users came to learn to talk knowledgeably about problems and identify with them, such as 'I am an alcoholic'. The main engagement was with the problem rather than the person and often the pictures that emerged were unbalanced, failing to bring to life the strengths and coping abilities of people.

Guidelines and formats for assessments were also biased towards the negatives and may have strengthened the pathologising tendency further. In reports, social workers can draw on theoretical language to set out a version of events in an impressive and apparently confident professional manner that implies it is the scientific truth. At least, it tends to strengthen the 'problem saturated story' and the whole problem. In line with the medical model, these assessments are usually made before any intervention takes place, are based on past performance and past reports, and perhaps presented as once-and-for-all judgements, lacking an appropriate uncertainty.

A further worrying aspect of such assessments is the suggestion that people are fixed in their problem identities, with a resultant lack of self-determination, and people are often categorised and denied the individualisation with which earlier social workers credited them. There is a tendency to blame and not address structural inequalities.

These are seriously questionable ideas which are still sometimes evident and which positivist/normalist notions, aspiring to mimic natural sciences, strengthen and perpetuate. If we were to rely on them, hope for Mark would probably be low.

Social constructionism and assessment

Constructionism maintains that language is central to human living, to any understanding of human nature or human difficulties, and to the creation of meaning and, to some extent at least, to the creation of realities, not just their description. If we diagnose, the naming makes it 'real'. Our language, as we participate in our social world, assigns meanings and thereby constructs what is being talked about and constructs even our identities; to talk in new ways is to construct new forms of social relations, new ways of being (for a full discussion see Parton and O'Byrne, 2000).

In Mark's case, the chances are that it has been said for many years that he IS a problem. As each of his faults have been discussed, his problem-identity has been strengthened. Reports setting out the difficulties have added to this. He has been 'authored' or 'storied' AS a problem and AS having many problems. But the 'A' changes to 'I', to make IS, what White (1995) refers to as 'totalising'. However, the other side of the coin is that people can be reauthored when they and others talk of them in new ways – new identities and solutions can thus be constructed.

Let us now look at how this happened with Mark.

CASE EXAMPLE revisited

Mark was referred to Judith for counselling. She started by asking him scaled questions, such as 'if 0 is an angel and 10 a devil, where are you?' He said '10'. 'If 10 is the best you could be and 0 the worst, where are you now?' '2 or 3'. 'If 0 is no stealing and 10 a lot, where are you on that scale?' '5 or 6'. 'If 10 is fully truthful and 0 fully dishonest, where are you?' '10'. His mother commented that this honesty amazed her and this led to discussion of other strengths: he is creative, imaginative, good with his hands and many more. Externalising the problem, Judith commented that it looks as if 'frustration' turns the talented person into a badly behaved one. Mark seized on this separation of the person from the problem and began to add detail, but he saw the problem as 'temper'. 'How long has temper been stopping you from being a good person?' '7 years'. 'Have you ever beaten it?' Yes, he was once good for five weeks at school and got a sticker book and some sweets. Mum could remember how 'over the moon' he was and she remembered other times when he beat the temper. The temper was discussed as having its own life and Mark said he got up with it each morning. They discussed what will be different when he gets up without it – how he would walk down the stairs with a smile and so on. Mum could help him to do this by reminding him to get his things ready the night before. He was asked to select three days next week when he would beat the temper and to have four ordinary days, not telling his parents which were which – they would have to guess. He liked this idea.

A week later, there was general agreement that he had greatly succeeded in excluding 'temper' from his life. Two more sessions were offered to strengthen the process and the progress. Twelve weeks later he was still behaving well and he was given a '12-year-old "silver" good-behaviour certificate'. (Sometimes service users are invited to select a gold, silver or bronze award to go for. It gives them a choice of goal and something to be cheered on and celebrated.)

The time taken to make this change was probably far less than the time taken in many assessments. It could have happened during assessment, long before matters deteriorated. It is only after intervention that we can write any 'true' assessment.

In the traditional/positivist frame the assessment goal was a diagnosis, to produce certain understandings of the nature of things and of normality, but in this century we inhabit a world that doubts if this is possible. If so much is socially constructed by words, how can our knowing be certain and independent of our language? The overarching 'grand narratives' (explanations) of modernism are seen by constructionists as unsound and unable to deliver truth. At least, we need to remain uncertain about them. It has come to be realised that there are invariably a plurality of truths and that 'local narratives' (the ideas and successes of Mark and his mother) are more important. Listening for what 'temper' means to service users reveals many personal meanings, such as upset, frustration, tension release, tears, stubbornness, shouting and so on – all of which are dependent on individual *social* and cultural situations. Further checking with the service user about what temper means in terms of being a man or a woman, a girl or a boy, reveals complex social constructions. In another example, Paul's temper was only evidenced in his interactions with other teenage boys and some teachers at his school as he rebelled against years of bullying and name calling. He exhibited an oppositional masculinity in these social situations in preference to his previous subordinated masculinity but, at home, he was a caring and responsible male; a side of his personhood which he wished to develop. Thus he occupied several masculine identities simultaneously, all of which were 'true' (for a more detailed discussion see Connell, 1995; Messerschmidt, 2000).

We cannot rely on positivist explanations and the good news is that we do not need to understand the cause of a problem before we start to construct a solution. We just need a minimum of motivation, some small exceptions with which to start, some imagination, and when workers ask constructive questions the possibilities are boundless. This can lead to an emphasis on personal agency – with the service user feeling in charge of his/her life.

Critics of social constructionism could argue that scientific classification is useful and should be retained. However, we consider that, while classifications of physical conditions and relationships are acceptable, classifications of persons are often not.

Implications for workers or managers

Resources

The constructionist approach, mainly using solution-focused and narrative ideas, seeing the service user as the main resource, has great potential for mobilising the resources within service users and it can do this in a short time.

Values

Empowerment of service users is facilitated, self-determination and choice is increased and cooperation is more easily gained, therefore service users no longer need be 'the enemy'.

Morale

There can be greater optimism over possibilities and staff morale can be much better as they use their skills and enjoy their successes.

Certainty

The burden of needing to show professional certainty is lifted – uncertainty is acceptable – we are not the only experts, we have the service users to help us. We need to listen to them more and collaborate with them. In this approach the worker's attitude is one of 'not knowing' rather than of being expert. Cade (1992) maintains that if he is expert in anything it is in knowing what does *not* work. It is not easy to take this stance without the confidence of experience. The grand narratives we are taught make us feel powerful and it takes courage to leave them behind and become virtually atheoretical. Freed from having to arrive at the *correct* explanation, we can settle for a *helpful* explanation and a story that has new possibilities. Yet, the paradox is that assessments can be *more reliable* because the worker has been closer to the service user and his/her language, views and resources. Critics may point out that while we support uncertainty we sound quite certain about our approach. We do not intend to be so. This approach is constantly developing and the implications of language are only beginning to be articulated. Therefore we strive to retain uncertainty, remaining open to any idea that is useful to service users.

Listening

The quality of our listening to service users will need to improve. What matters is how people perceive their relationship with the problem and those occasions when they stood up to it or managed to avoid it. There are always vital exceptions, when people resist the problem and it is less influential in their lives. In these 'unstoried' exceptions, lies the potential for change. People *do* know how to resist, because they were able to do it, but it is common to not know what one knows until one hears oneself answering the question 'how did you do that?'

Safety

Even in child protection work, it helps to ask people what they think is needed for safety and what the signs of safety are, rather than focusing exclusively on risk (Turnell and Edwards, 1999, is essential reading on this crucial topic). Our approach may sound naive to those who meet terrible abuse of children. It could sound as if we would believe whatever parents say. We believe, however, that the 'signs of safety' approach is as strict as any in child protection practice and can lead to outcomes that collaborate with most people's potential to care. It does not ignore signs of risk of harm.

Language

In all this work we need to watch our language very carefully. How we frame our questions will betray our assumptions, for example saying 'when you succeed', rather than 'if you succeed'.

The future

A shift from a past focus to a future focus is also needed. The past history (apart from the exceptions to the problem) is not as useful as we thought it was for building solutions and we can sometimes build future solutions without it, as Mark did.

Causes and explanations

In the constructionist approach, we question the notion of cause in the assessment of behavioural difficulties. In mechanical or physiological matters, cause may be clear and it may be necessary to find it, but in behavioural matters, because most people have a considerable degree of personal agency, we doubt if we can ever say with any certainty what causes actions. We find the term 'invitation' (White, 1993) more helpful than 'cause'. Various influences, the media, social practices, relationships, invite us to act in certain ways. The invitation may have varying strengths, but in the end it is we who decide to accept or reject it, or to do or not do something else. We cannot know to what extent the invitation influenced the decision, but we can explore what were the influences operating against the person, or the influence of the problem on relationships, for example. For assessment purposes, therefore, we need to gain some knowledge of the relationship between the person and the problem and whether any alienation is beginning to develop. This will usually enable us to assess motivation while empowering the person. In this view, people are essentially OK and caring, but social influences restrain their sense of responsibility, making it more difficult for them to make positive choices. The constructionist approach develops a sense of alienation from the problem.

Unlike White, who talks of invitations that restrain, de Shazer (1991) argues that *problems just happen* and that we need not worry about cause since we can understand and develop solutions without understanding cause, that we need to search for solutions in people's expectations and in their goals and their picture of the future without the problem, not in an analysis of the problem itself. The key assessment issues are: does the person have a goal? What will be happening day by day when the problem is solved? Is any of this beginning to happen already sometimes? These are more relevant questions than: 'what pathology is causing the problem?'

Greater responsibility

In both solution-focused and narrative approaches, the problem is seen as external to the person. The person is not the problem, the problem is the problem, and the problem is spoken of as having a detrimental effect on the person. This may sound as if there is a let-off for the person and that only the problem is taken to task. But in these approaches there is no let-off from accountability. However, blame is avoided. *Blaming* alienates and does not invite people to take responsibility. It attributes bad intentions. On the other hand, *accountability* promotes self-agency and responsibility for what is to be done next, and responsibility for the consequences of doing nothing. O'Hanlon (1995) says workers need to challenge stories of blame, invalidation and non-accountability; ideas of pathology make for excuses. However, he makes a useful distinction between feelings on the one hand and words and actions on the other. People are not accountable for the former, only the latter; feelings are always OK and to be validated, words/beliefs and actions may need to be challenged.

CONCLUSION

In maintaining that considerable critical thinking is needed concerning assessment and planning, we have attempted to contribute to critical practice, not only by questioning the questionable but by pointing towards an alternative. We have given little tasters of constructionist methods and we hope that readers will engage in further reading on this topic as they develop their critical practice.

For too long practice has been stuck with the 'psy complex', with false certainty and with failed solutions. There may have been an excessive focus on deficit and diagnosis and we have not always been clear as to how to empower service users to take charge of their lives. We have sometimes thrown resources at problems and we have tended to blame service users for not appreciating them. Talk has too often become oppositional. At times, our very language has built deficit rather than solutions and values may have slipped.

By less certainty, more listening to and respect for individuals' ideas, less trust in traditional explanations and more collaboration with service users, we can begin to draw on their massive reserves and potential, while lowering our own stress.

Divorce courts have stopped looking for the original cause of marital breakdowns; courts reading social work assessments of others' situations need to take the same leap. Assessment is moving on from checking hypotheses or finding correct explanations to rewriting more helpful narratives with people.

In the future, assessment and planning could be much more about co-constructing solutions with those we serve.

FURTHER READING.

Milner, J. (2001) *Women in Social Work: Narrative Approaches*, Basingstoke: Palgrave – now Palgrave Macmillan. Offers many case examples, discusses theory and techniques and examines the gender issues of these approaches to practice.

Milner, J. and O'Byrne, P. (1998) *Assessment in Social Work*, Basingstoke: Macmillan – now Palgrave Macmillan. Deals with all aspects of assessment and the theories on which it is founded. Chapter 10 provides the constructionist approach.

Parton, N. and O'Byrne, P. (2000) *Constructive Social Work*, Basingstoke: Palgrave – now Palgrave Macmillan. Provides a detailed account of constructionist ideas – leading to solution-focused and narrative practice. Chapter 8 specifically addresses assessment.

Managing Risk and Decision Making

Terence O'Sullivan

It has been argued that governments and agencies have directed much of social work towards differentiating high-risk from low-risk situations, so that limited resources can be more effectively used to protect people from harm (see for example Parton et al., 1997: 35; Parton, 1999: 121–2). This chapter examines some of the possibilities and pitfalls of refocusing risk assessment towards being an aid to professional decision making in uncertain social situations.

CASE EXAMPLE

Nazeen is an experienced social worker who has been involved in a review that discussed whether or not Zena, a young person on a care order, should return home. Zena is ten years old and has made remarkable progress since coming into care 18 months ago. A court made Zena the subject of a care order after years of emotional abuse by her mother, who had great difficulty coping with her daughter alone. Zena's mother wants her daughter home and the care order discharged. Zena is not sure what she wants, but Nazeen is concerned that Zena's placement home would soon breakdown and trigger Zena into a downward spiral. The review chairperson and Nazeen's line manager believe that Zena's needs would be better met at home, and if this is not feasible her care plan will need to be changed to working towards adoption. The review decided against the option of applying for a discharge of the care order and the chairperson requested a risk assessment of

➡

Zena being placed with her mother. Nazeen is sceptical of the vogue currently sweeping her agency for risk assessment as the answer to everything and is wary of placing too much confidence in the human ability to predict the future with certainty (Dingwell, 1989). Nevertheless, she is in favour of having a reasoned basis for making decisions, and sets about endeavouring to undertake a critical risk assessment.

Nazeen wants to promote the conditions of open discussion with Zena, her carers, her mother, the line manager and the review chairperson, so that communicative reason, rather than instrumental reason, can form the basis of decisions (Blaug, 1995). In deciding between courses of action, there are tensions between Zena's and her mother's right to live their lives free from interference and Nazeen's duty to protect Zena from self-harm and harm from others. Nazeen's starting point is that people need to be empowered to make their own decisions about their future but the nature of decision making in social work means there are different levels of client involvement (O'Sullivan, 1999). Zena's situation is typical of many in social work in which the right to take risks is not straightforward. Adult clients may be considered to have the right to take risks with their own bodies, if they have the capacity to take informed decisions, but not the right to harm others (Cupitt, 1997). So Zena's mother's wish to have her daughter home is important from a number of points of view but she is not considered to have the right to expose Zena to harm.

Nazeen poses herself four questions to be asked by critical practitioners involved in making decisions in uncertain situations:

- What is meant by risk?
- What are the social contexts of the decision making?
- How are the risks to be assessed?
- What approach to risk management is to be taken?

What is meant by risk?

One of the pitfalls for Nazeen is to take the concept of risk for granted. Risk is a contested concept, one aspect of which is the extent that *risk* has come to mean or is confused with *danger*. Douglas argues that 'the word *risk* now means danger' (Douglas, 1992 cited in Parton, 2001: 62). Alaszewski and Alaszewski (1998: 109) found that the professionals they interviewed defined risk in terms of danger. Nazeen recalls the review chairperson using the word risk as a synonym for danger, when she said, 'the risk is that Zena's placement will break down'. Within a professional decision making framework, there needs to be a clear conceptualisation and differentiation of risk from its related concepts of hazard, strength, danger and benefits. Nazeen is tempted to take the advice of Dowie (1999) and abandon the term 'risk' as redundant within decision analysis or substitute it for the concept of uncertainty as suggested by Parton (2001: 69). She settles on endeavouring to use the word in a more sparing, precise and careful way and thinks in terms of Carson's (1995: 75) definition of *a risk* as 'a course of action or inaction, taken under conditions of uncertainty, which exposes one [or more people] to possible loss in order to reach a desired outcome'. This definition involves key elements: course of action or inaction; uncertainty as to outcome; and exposure to possible loss in order to have the chance of benefit. This means that risk comes into play when deciding between different courses of action in conditions of uncertainty. Zena's situation is typical of those found in social work where all options involve possible dangers and benefits, there being possible dangers and benefits in both staying in care, returning home or being adopted. All three courses of action involve uncertainty with the possibility of sustaining a loss in order to achieve some benefit.

What are the social contexts of the decision making?

The sociocultural contexts of people's lives and social work practice are complex and multifaceted (O'Sullivan, 1999, Chapter 2). Nazeen lives in a modern global society that has been characterised by sociologists and anthropologists by its concern with risk (for example, Beck, 1998; Douglas, 1992; Giddens, 1998a). There are a number of important connections between the debate on a societal/global level and the work of Nazeen. At the core of the risk society are uncertainty and unpredictability (Ungar, 2001: 282), features that have always been present in social work in the sense that the outcomes of care plans cannot be predicted with certainty. Nevertheless, the hidden catastrophic dangers of global warming, nuclear accident and mass contamination of food generate different social anxieties than the negative impacts of being brought up in care. The observers of social anxieties would be forgiven for believing that the world has become more hazardous but, as Giddens (1998a: 27) has pointed out, they reflect a society increasingly preoccupied with the future and safety, rather than the world being a more dangerous place. Douglas (1992) argues that all societies, past and present, have systems of blame for misfortunes and that risk has taken on this function in modern society. In a blame culture there are pressures to proceduralise how uncertainty is dealt with, to ensure that there is always something or someone to blame when things go wrong. Workers can be blamed for not following the procedures correctly, or, if the procedures were followed, the procedures can be blamed for not being adequate. In such a safety climate, critical social work becomes a challenge, as Parton et al. (1997: 240) state:

> once concerns about risk become all pervasive, the requirement to develop and follow organisational procedures becomes dominant and the room for professional manoeuvre and creativity is severely limited.

Dangers are always in the background both in everyday social work and everyday life. For all these dangers to become the subject of decision making would disrupt one's own life and the lives of others. How some dangers come to the foreground of concern is related to, among other things, risk perception or, more accurately, danger perception. During periods of heightened sensitivity following the discovery or rediscovery of a social problem, there is a danger of excessive caution. The review chairperson's concerns about Zena remaining in care can be cast as being partly shaped by the latest agency panic engendered by the government's concern about the negative outcomes of care. Panic and deliberative decision-making do not go well together and an unintended consequence of legitimate government concern can be the generation of anxieties that translate into panicked agency responses. Many children are harmed by the experience of being in care, but this is different from saying that all children who are in care are inevitably harmed by the experience. The review chairperson and the line manager had accused Nazeen of not taking seriously enough the reality of being in care but this was to misunderstand her position. She, as an experienced social worker, knew better than most what the dangers were of remaining in care (Owen, 1997: 68). She did not question the reality of children being harmed, but was concerned about the engendering of fear and the potential for the perception of danger to be affected by panics that are generated from time to time through the activities of government or the mass media (Jenkins, 1992; Thompson, 1998).

How are risks to be assessed?

Assessment is a basis of decision making and different types of assessment can be distinguished by their purpose (Sinclair et al., 1995: 32). A risk assessment comes into play when there is concern that a person may be exposed to harm. Risk assessment identifies what the dangers are, how likely they are to occur and the likely extent of harm if they do occur. The result of any assessment is a particular representation of reality, which raises two issues in relation to risk assessment. First, is the focus on risk justified and, second, does the method of risk assessment give a distorted representation? An issue for Nazeen is whether the focus on risk becomes isolated from other concerns. No course of action is inherently a risk in itself but equally anything can be a risk (Ewald, 1991: 199). This means that any situation can be considered in terms of risk or alternatively seen through some other lens. Nazeen believes that risk assessment needs to be part of or built on a full assessment of Zena's situation, including her wishes and feelings, her progress in care, her needs and her mother's caring capacity and resources. Milner and O'Byrne have recognised that the development of an overarching framework for assessment in social work has been hindered by differing emphases on risk, needs and resources (Milner and O'Byrne, 1998: 25) and there is a need to see risk as only one side of a triangle, with needs and resources forming the other two sides.

The use of risk assessment instruments

Nazeen has witnessed a trend for all assessments to become more routine, sometimes being reduced to a number of tick boxes (Middleton, 1999). Her agency has just introduced a risk factor checklist for children under care orders returning home. Risk assessment instruments attempt to reduce difficult and complex decisions to a limited number of questions. In the past, risk assessment checklists have been taken seriously (for example, Greenland, 1987), only to have had their predictive validity subsequently questioned (Parton, 1991: 61). Even the most carefully researched predictive instruments are regarded as having too high an error rate to be relied on exclusively (Munro, 1999: 122; Sargent, 1999: 191). Nazeen and her colleagues have an ambivalent attitude towards checklists. On one hand they give a degree of protection to workers and can take much of the anxiety away from making difficult decisions. On the other hand they question the face validity of checklists, particularly when the prediction of harm occurring is reduced to the presence or absence of a limited number of factors. Using checklists can undermine the sensitivity to context and creative thinking needed to deal with the complexity and uncertainty of social situations. There is a danger that Nazeen uses the checklist in a mechanical routine way to give herself and her agency some protection from criticisms if things go wrong (Wald and Woolverton, 1990). Even when checklists are used to guide and focus professional judgement, the predictive validity of the featured factors needs to be questioned.

How is risk to be analysed?

Given the danger of reductionism in any process of analysing possible courses of action, Nazeen needs a way of analysing risk that does some justice to the complexity of social situations. One way of analysing options is through a *strengths/hazards analysis* (O'Sullivan, 1999: 140), which builds upon previous work on risk analysis (including Brearley, 1982: 82–91; Kemshall, 1996: 139–40). Strengths/hazards analysis is used to analyse options in terms of current strengths and hazards and possible future benefits and dangers. There is no agreement as to the precise use of terms in this area but *strengths* are factors thought to increase the chances of the benefits occurring, while *hazards* are factors thought to increase the chances of the dangers occurring. A distinction can be drawn between *specific situational factors* identified through careful assessment of the situation and the presence or absence of *risk* and *protective factors* reported by actuarial research.

The distinctive features of a strengths/hazards analysis are:

- a clear distinction between Zena's present situation (including her history) and her future

- being explicit about the feared dangers and the hoped-for benefits of each option

- clearly identifying both strengths and hazards within the present situation in relation to each option

- research-based protective and risk factors can be assessed for inclusion alongside specific situational factors

- all three options are subjected to analysis, whereas Nazeen was asked to focus on just one.

Nazeen endeavours to negotiate with Zena and her mother a strengths and hazards analysis of the three options: remaining in care, returning home and being adopted. One of the issues of carrying out such an analysis is the basis on which current strengths and hazards, and potential dangers and benefits are identified. Nazeen claims to be using her practice wisdom (Scott, 1990; Sheppard, 1995b: 279) accumulated through her own experience. For example, Zena's development being severely disrupted by the placement home breaking down is identified as a *danger* within the returning home option. A potential *benefit* of placement home was identified as the opportunity to build a family base for Zena's future development. The particular balance of hazards and strengths in Zena's present situation will influence the chances of these dangers and benefits occurring in the future. A *strength* in the current situation was thought to be the high degree of motivation her mother had to make the placement home succeed, while a *hazard* is the past history of a troubled mother–daughter relationship. Critical decisions such as Zena's future care plan need to involve deliberative processes, part of which is structuring or framing the decision situation (O'Sullivan, 1999: 103). The quality of Nazeen's practice wisdom and negotiating skills is crucially important in producing a well-reasoned frame of the decision situation that is based on carefully gathered and sifted information. Using checklists in a mechanical way shortcuts these processes and so reduces the sensitivity to context needed to make sound decisions under conditions of uncertainty and complexity.

What use to make of research findings?

Nazeen works in a context of mounting pressure to base decisions on research evidence but is aware of serious flaws in this approach (Webb, 2001). In considering the relevant factors, she reads some research that has been carried out in relation to returning home (Bullock et al., 1998), adoption (Quinton et al., 1998) and young people being bought up in care. Nazeen endeavours to take a critical approach to these research studies and the research methods used to produce their findings. She is quite willing to accept that they shed some light on factors that may be involved in certain outcomes occurring, but the danger is that such research is regarded as providing the whole answer or a definite conclusive answer. Research studies need to have a supportive rather than determining role in relation to decision making. For example, Nazeen discovers that the basis for the agency checklist is research carried out by Bullock et al. (1998) on children returning home from care and the five factors they found to be associated with a successful return home of children under 11.

The five protective factors were:

- The family are prepared for the anxiety generated by return and the disputes likely to occur.

- Family relationships are of a fairly high quality.

- The child is not an offender.

- There is evidence of highly competent social work.

- Professionals are entirely satisfied by voluntary arrangements with the family.

(Bullock et al., 1998: 207)

When making decisions in uncertain situations, there are serious flaws in relying solely on the number of research-based factors present (Howe, 1998c: 13). A mechanical, narrow and exclusive focus on the presence or absence of these five factors would not be warranted or likely to be advocated by the authors. The five factors are a product of a research process that involved gathering data on particular variables, operationalised in particular ways, and collected under particular conditions, and the searching for numerical associations between the presence or absence of the variables and particular outcomes. The construction of the five factors has been made possible by the application of computer technology to produce, from the deconstructed details of individual situations, 'statistical correlations of heterogeneous elements' resulting in 'a combination of factors liable to produce risk' (Castel, 1991: 288). The factors may give pointers to what *may* be influential in a majority of situations, but not what *will* be influential in a particular situation. In addition, there is a danger that users of checklists do not appreciate critically the need for interpretation, in addressing such questions as what indicates good social work practice and whether family relationships are of a fairly high quality. There is also the issue of the reductionism involved in focusing on the five factors to the exclusion of more specific situational factors. Nazeen, alongside Zena and her mother, can endeavour critically to assess the applicability of the factors to their particular situation, so that they can add the presence or absence of relevant factors to the strengths/hazards analysis, alongside the specific situational factors arrived at through their negotiated, holistic assessment. Nevertheless, there is always the danger that research-based factors will be given an unwarranted and exclusive status within risk assessment. This is not to deny that being familiar with this research has developed Nazeen's practice wisdom in some important ways (Klein and Bloom, 1995).

What approach to risk management is to be taken?

Nazeen completes her risk assessment which shows that all three options have associated dangers and benefits and considerable uncertainty as to their outcomes. Critical factors were considered to be Zena's negative attitude to adoption, promoting her continuing contact with her mother and maintaining the progress she has made since coming into care. Nazeen is aware how the future plans for Zena will be affected by the review chairperson's approach to risk management, particularly the prevailing attitude to risk-taking. Three approaches to risk management can be identified: defensive caution; informed risk-taking: and excessive risk-taking. Within *defensive caution*, the option perceived to be the safest is followed even when this causes unintended harm. Concerns with safety predominate, with fears about things going wrong and who will be blamed being more important than indirect negative consequences for clients (Harris, 1987). There is a danger that in the current cultural climate the review chairperson would take a safety first approach and uncritically regard Zena returning home as being the safest option.

Excessive risk-taking is when, either through overconfidence or the need to avoid a loss framed as certain (Whyte, 1998; Kelly, 2000), decision-makers take unjustified risks that can lead to disastrous outcomes. In the specific circumstances of Zena not wanting to be adopted, *the being adopted option* could be categorised as excessive risk-taking. The review chairperson can be cast as framing Zena remaining in care as a certain loss and if placement home was not viable, she would rather Zena had a chance to recoup these losses, even if it meant risking the even greater loss involved in an adoption disruption. Nazeen was advocating an *informed risk-taking* approach to decision making and risk management that had involved the careful analysis of the situation as a whole and a preparedness to take risks in order to have the chance of achieving benefits (Carson, 1996: 9). Nazeen was aware of the dangers of Zena remaining in care but considered these were outweighed by the chances of benefits. From the relative security of care, Zena has been able to develop her relationship with her mother in a way that is likely to extend well into adulthood. An issue for Nazeen is how to take practical steps to reduce the chances of the dangers of being in care occurring, while not significantly reducing the chances of achieving the benefits sought. Within the *remaining in care* option, she plans to take an active approach and do everything she can to reduce the hazards and build on the strengths, for example by providing supportive relationships and monitoring Zena's progress. A pitfall is that such actions can become overly intrusive and inadvertently bring about the feared dangers.

CONCLUSION

The review finally accepted Nazeen's analysis of the options in terms of the relative chances of dangers and benefits occurring in the three options. The chances of a bad outcome of the adoption and placement home options were accepted as too high in the present circumstances and that the present plan of Zena remaining in care, while the relationship with her mother is fostered, was considered the most likely course of action to produce a good outcome for Zena in the long term. Although pleased to have convinced the review, Nazeen was acutely aware that she had gone against current thinking and in doing so had exposed herself to future criticism if the situation develops in an unfavourable way for Zena. Despite the decision having been carefully thought through with a wide variety of factors and views taken into account, a bad outcome can still occur. A colleague responds to Nazeen's fear of being blamed if things go wrong, by reminding her that a desired future cannot be brought about in some definite way, but rather carefully nurtured and promoted in the face of complexity and uncertainty.

FURTHER READING

Alaszewski, A., Harrison, L. and Manthorpe, J. (eds) (1998) *Risk, Health and Welfare*, Buckingham: Open University Press. This edited collection considers the definition, assessment and management of risk in both health and social care settings.

Kemshall, H. and Pritchard, J. (eds) (1996) *Good Practice in Risk Assessment and Risk Management*, London: Jessica Kingsley. This edited collection considers risk in different social work settings.

Moore, B. (1996) *Risk Assessment: A Practitioners' Guide to Predicting Harmful Behaviour*, London: Whiting & Birch. This book provides a detailed and accessible guide to carrying out risk assessments in the context of endeavouring to predict harmful behaviour.

O'Sullivan, T. (1999) *Decision Making in Social Work*, Basingstoke: Macmillan – now Palgrave Macmillan. This book provides a framework for professional decision making in social work. Each chapter illustrates an aspect of the framework through a practice example.

Parsloe, P. (ed.) (1999) *Risk Assessment in Social Care*, London: Jessica Kingsley. This edited collection outlines theoretical issues of risk assessment in social care and social work.

Managing Finances

Jill Manthorpe and Greta Bradley

Introduction

How can social workers reconcile a desire to advocate for the poor and disadvantaged while, at the same time, being rationers of services and responsible for means testing care? This chapter explores these dual pressures. It does so in the context of a UK social work profession which has generally sought, unlike many others, to separate itself from income maintenance systems and maintain clear water between welfare and workfare.

In the UK, the twin services arising from the post-war welfare initiatives located welfare (and some health care) within local authorities and confirmed central government's control of most income-related systems such as national insurance, general taxation and national assistance (the Poor Law). Exceptions existed and continue to do so. Indeed Barnes and Prior (2000) have pointed to the growing numbers of central government initiatives to deal with unemployment in a more holistic sense, with initiatives to develop skills, enhance motivation and offer practical assistance and encouragement to those out of the current labour market. Such initiatives will compel a more personalised approach and blur, once again, the welfare role.

This chapter asks a number of questions about social work's role in finances, noting that few texts and guides tackle this subject, particularly at the level of social work practice, but also at the level of social services' overall financial resources (with the exception of Glennerster's seminal text *Paying for Welfare*, 1999). Its focus is on poverty, rather than social exclusion, since the authors would argue that this term has more meaning for service users.

Poor clients

Curiously, for a profession which evolved out of critical responses to the Poor Law, social work has an ambivalent relationship with poverty. Many of its origins stem from attempts to deal with problems of the urban poor and were a combination of acts of practical philanthropy and community development. Although closely associated with the Poor Law systems, early amateur social workers identified that the poor could be assisted by better housing, employment and cash provision. Many appreciated that social change would be necessary to challenge cycles of deprivation and systems of inequality.

While the slums of Victorian Britain were so central to the development of social work, the paradox of social work is its increasing distance from issues and experiences of poverty. This paradox arises despite considerable evidence that:

- poverty 'creates' social work clients

- the most common characteristic of social work clients is their poverty.

These two claims can be illustrated by specific examples. Becker (1997) chronicled the impact between the abolition of single (cash) payments to those on income support (supplementary benefit) and their replacement by the more stringent social fund. This led to a rise in demand on social services departments for help with financial emergencies, particularly section 1 (Children Act 1989) payments (section 12 Social Work (Scotland) Act 1962). He describes this as creating the 'new poor', a group of people who would not approach social services but for their poverty. At the time of these social security reforms, Becker and MacPherson commented: 'claimants are poor before they become clients but more and more are becoming clients because they are poor' (1986: 1).

Other research has focused attention on particular manifestations of poverty that drew people into the orbit of social services, notably fuel poverty (particularly disconnections), liaison with the DHSS/Benefits Agency (Balloch and Jones, 1988) and, more recently, help with funeral costs and water bills (Drakeford, 2000).

Despite social workers' daily encounters with poverty and its effects, responses remain similar to those of earlier decades. Becker (1997) is highly critical of social work's attempts to 'manage the poor'. He notes a collection of individualised responses to requests for help on discovery of poverty – aspects related to casework:

- advice on benefits

- referral to other sources

- tight criteria for assistance

- reliance on a working relationship between social services and the Benefits Agency.

These responses have their failings. A series of research reports has identified that many social workers are not trained and not interested in benefits. If they give advice or information it may be inadequate or erroneous. Their departments are ill-equipped to offer such advice and few social workers will advocate for users. Concern about this led in the 1980s to the development of welfare rights specialisms, often located within social services, where poverty problems could be separated off from matters of psychosocial functioning. As Hill (2000) outlines, such developments can combine advice to clients and their social workers, and a typical social services authority will mix information service and training for frontline staff with specialist referral points. For social workers three main dimensions arise for practice:

- the model officially embraced by their agency

- the culture of the office or team

- their personal inclination, knowledge and sympathy for the user.

These three elements draw on the discretion still open to social workers in determining the boundaries of their work. Thus, one practitioner may conceive his or her role as close to advocacy, while another may be quick to refer problems on in order to concentrate on the 'underlying pathology'.

The matter of referral can be seen as one way of 'managing the poor' in Becker's terms. Charities and self-help groups continue to receive supplicants for assistance, prompted and supported by their social workers. While social workers have generally been adverse to involvement in the priorities of the social fund, they have been less reluctant to push the merits of their clients for charitable relief. In practice this can involve dilemmas for social workers in heightening the claims of some individuals by portraying them as part of the 'deserving poor'. Key aspects of such a label may include:

- the person was 'not to blame' for their predicament (by implication, unlike others)

- the person is 'worthy' of one-off assistance (to get back on their feet)

- the person 'acknowledges' their position with due deference

- a sense of gratitude and/or apology.

In practice few social workers would so starkly represent this process but many feel forced to collude in respect of their client's/user's best or immediate interests. There is cold comfort, for example, in being without basic essentials but keeping one's dignity.

Social workers' management of the poor may also extend to other referrals, such as to welfare rights specialists, debt advice agencies or community legal services. In practice, the ever-changing and complex world of benefits, tax, bills and maintenance can defeat even those practitioners who wish to maintain expertise in the field. For some, the personal solution, or a strategy agreed with colleagues, may be to develop:

- particular expertise or specialism, for example on fostering allowances, the social fund, child support

- systematic screening for opportunities to provide initial advice on benefit claims

- regular audits of users' circumstances

- proactive information in conjunction with other agencies

- sound and appropriate referral routes to other agencies.

In such ways, individual practitioners counter Hill's allegation that they 'very often turn a deaf ear to material needs' (2000: 132).

Turning the screw

While social workers generally have a high awareness of service users' poverty, recent years have witnessed two countervailing approaches. First, social workers have increasingly become the agents of their local authorities in means testing service users and charging them for services. Second, they act within local authorities, many of which, simultaneously, have placed poverty on their corporate agenda. Such a position creates a series of multiple dilemmas.

Of course, there have been selective consumer charges for social care over many years. While central government has encouraged and enabled local authorities to charge, it permitted them to operate a discretionary system. Historically, fairly significant levels of income have been raised through charging. In 1975–76, for example, 11 per cent of personal social services expenditure was met through charging (Judge and Matthews, 1980: 5). Central government currently expects local authorities to raise 9 per cent of their income through charging (Bradley and Manthorpe, 1997: 9). As many research studies have shown (for example, Chetwynd and Ritchie, 1996; Baldwin and Lunt, 1996), charging systems can be confusing, contradictory and complex.

At practice level there are a number of dilemmas. These appear to account for many social workers' ambivalence at operating means-tested systems. We found, in recent research exploring financial assessment for residential care (Bradley et al., 2000), that practising care managers:

- felt caught up in conflicts of interest between older people, their relatives and the local authority

- were uncomfortable in giving information or advice and varied considerably in the extent they did so

- worried about distinctions between avoidance and evasion of charges

- felt unsupported by managers and politicians when they had suspicions of financial abuse or deception.

Half the care managers interviewed considered themselves inadequately trained but for many further training would appear more beneficial if it addressed ethical decision-making rather than knowledge-based skills. That care managers question the basis of financial assessment suggests they are alert to the sensitive nature of the processes. As the respondents observed, people undergoing financial assessments may be unwell, confused or extremely anxious. Social work skills may be very helpful in building relationships and presenting a holistic picture of people's needs and resources. For this reason we consider that financial assessment, in whatever form it is likely to take for social care in the short term, is best undertaken by care managers or social workers rather than by a separate workforce. New policies arising from the government's response to the Royal Commission on Long-term Care (Sutherland, 1999), as set out in the Health and Social Care Bill 2000, while offering some extension to free nursing care, will still entail financial assessment.

Means-testing systems demonstrate the dynamic link between social policy and social services. Theories from social policy provide the main basis for examining the social work task in respect of finance. They include, for example, the extent to which individual social workers can maintain some element of discretion (Baldwin, 2000) in the light of increased accountability and scrutiny. They offer a means of distinguishing the experiences of poverty, through, for example, insights into the feminisation of poverty (Lister, 2000; Williams, 1999) or the interrelationships between poverty and race (Craig, 1998).

Within social services, as noted above, a new interest in poverty, and a recasting of it as social exclusion, has emerged following the doldrums of the 1960s to the 1980s. This includes the moves to anti-poverty strategies and, at an individual level, the ability to respond to need with cash, not care.

More than a sticking plaster

While much of social work's origins lay in local responses to poverty, the development of anti-poverty work in the 1990s has broadened to include areas outside the inner cities and draw on a wider range of partners – both horizontally with partnerships of local agencies and vertically with links to government strategy – for social renewal, regeneration and inclusion. Social work's focus on individuals rather than groups and client status rather than locality has created some difficulty in aligning social work priorities with broader anti-poverty moves. The emphasis on risk and danger, which developed during the 1990s as a rationale for social work's focus on certain targeted groups, has also contributed to a reactive rather than preventive model of practice. In the new world of social inclusion initiatives, social services departments have been marginalised at times with Action Zones for Health and Education, Sure Start programmes emphasising multiagency approaches and regeneration schemes, generally the responsibility of the corporate local authority, within which many social services departments have lost autonomy and influence.

For social workers, however, anti-poverty strategies justify a renewed emphasis on combating poverty. Craig (2000) has identified practice implications including:

■ monitoring of service use to identify take-up or withdrawal by those living in poverty

- assessing the impact of policies in terms of reducing poverty through 'poverty proofing'

- pooling data with other agencies to monitor poverty levels locally

- listening to the voices of those 'on the sharp end of poverty' to hear their views of new approaches.

The initial priorities of the government's new Social Exclusion Unit were reducing truancy, provision for those sleeping rough and the renewal of deprived communities (1998). Such classifications again alert social workers to the artificiality and inappropriate labels of traditional client groups.

Developing skills

> Social workers ... have to engage with poverty in two ways. One involves a general response to its impact on their clients, with an obligation to describe and discuss for a wider audience whose concerns can be mobilised. The other ... requires the social workers to consider the most effective ways of helping the individual in poverty who is a unique person in unique difficulty.
>
> (Stevenson quoted in Hardiker and Barker, 1988)

Such views continue to represent 'practice wisdom' but have been refined into concrete skills such as advocacy. Bateman (2000) has usefully considered the extent to which social workers can develop their own practice in advocacy within the context of their employing agency and work. Briefly summarised, the skills include:

- understanding the 'best interests' principle

- purposeful and in-depth interviewing

- research skills

- organisational skills

- assertive, negotiation skills

- knowing when to act and when to refer.

These can be incorporated into placement opportunities or within social work curricula at pre- or post-qualifying levels.

Cash not care?

Increasingly central to the work of social services has been the provision of support to disabled people. The Community Care (Direct Payments) Act 1996 gave local authorities powers to make cash payments to service users to purchase their own assistance. Such schemes, in other forms, had proved popular and successful among disabled people. Users have valued the greater independence provided by cash and have argued that the staff they employ are more reliable, more flexible and personally suitable. As such, this form of cash assistance is said to be empowering.

It might be expected, therefore, that social workers too would welcome and encourage such schemes. Early research, however, points to the difficulties of translating the ideals of such schemes into practice. Leece's (2000) study of the early days of direct payments found that social workers did not always appear confident in the schemes or were reluctant to communicate information to potential participants. Dawson (2000) found that social services departments needed to change attitudes to risk management and learn to compromise in order to enhance the independence of service users.

Other research has pointed to practitioners' dilemmas in encouraging choice and user control while protecting disabled people from exploitation or neglect. Ryan (1999), for example, has developed frameworks to help practitioners to manage their own reservations about direct payments. These include:

■ accepting that service users can receive direct payments and assistance – the two are not exclusive

■ distinguishing between the 'willingness' to take on direct payments and the ability to manage such payments – other arrangements can be made to sort out administrative or practical matters

■ maximising the opportunities to learn about the scheme and respect that people may lack initial confidence

■ considering the use of independent living trusts and supported decision-making systems

■ establishing a range of safeguards to assess and manage risks.

Such critical points may provide social workers with greater confidence in the system of direct payments and new 'voucher' mechanisms for purchasing services such as short-break or respite care. Again, vouchers potentially offer service users and carers the opportunities to arrange support that is:

■ flexible in timing and extent

■ individually tailored

■ promoting a sense of control.

But, unlike direct payments, vouchers place more restrictions on users and carers, since they may only be used for specific purposes and much depends on which agencies will be willing to be and accepted as appropriate suppliers. Trusting poor people with cash has for many years been a difficult matter for state agencies, as the existence of subsidies or benefits in kind (for example free school meals and milk tokens) demonstrates.

Cash and capacity

This section moves to discuss social workers' roles in enabling individuals to maintain control over their own financial resources in the face of attempts to remove such abilities on grounds of ageism or disablism. For people whose mental capacity is becoming significantly impaired, social workers can play a key role in advising individuals about measures that can be taken and plans that can be made. Individuals who have been told that they have early dementia, for example, may be usefully supported by social workers in making legal arrangements for enduring powers of attorney and thinking about advance directives. For those without such arrangements, social workers may be involved in liaison with the Benefits Agency or the Court of Protection (Public Guardianship Office).

As Langan (1997) has shown, however, local authorities do not always support individual practitioners by setting up clear systems for the management of other people's money, and individual care managers can find themselves torn between acting in the user's best interests and those of the authority. Throughout the 1990s a series of critical reports from organisations such as the Law Commission (1995) outlined the confusions of the law in the area of decision-making about people's resources if mental capacity was seriously compromised. Little reform has followed, leaving individual practitioners advising service users and their families about systems which are widely agreed to be difficult to administer. Nonetheless, the Public Guardianship Office, in particular, has responded to criticism within the confines of existing legislation and it may be helpful for newly qualified practitioners not to be swayed by out-of-date impressions that it is too time consuming to 'do things properly'.

Evidence for the need to be alert to the possibility of financial abuse has come from a variety of accounts about the harm that may be caused by such betrayals of trust or deprivation of quality of life. Manthorpe (2000) provides numerous illustrations of such abuse from residential settings and domiciliary care as well as from family or acquaintances, while recent American research (Choi et al., 1999) notes that exploitation or deception can also be accompanied by physical threats or violence. Pritchard (2000) has suggested that financial abuse in later life for older women may be compounded by the lack of adequate response or support they receive should they disclose their predicament. Feelings of self-blame and helplessness were common among the women interviewed.

While deprivation of cash or possessions may be an important indicator that a person is being mistreated or abused, social work values and the law accept that people have a right to self-determination in all but the most extreme circumstances, generally if severe harm would be caused to themselves or others. At times social workers will find themselves respecting the rights of people to be 'foolish' and this may cause conflict with relatives. Similarly disabled people who are vulnerable to becoming involved in debt (Grant, 2000) may benefit from sustained support rather than crisis intervention. Such support, of course, is difficult when community care strategies focus on those in most need and may exclude those whose disabilities are classified as 'moderate'. The building up of relationships between service users and individual practitioners, which might provide a trusting, low level of help, appears to have declined over the 1990s with practitioners' focus on assessment rather than ongoing support.

CONCLUSION

In this chapter we have seen how social workers' ambivalence to working with finance reflects a desire to avoid crossing the boundary into matters of income and expenditure. New models of social care support combined with growing means testing mean that, like it or not, finance is central to the helping relationship. Similarly social workers' role in managing budgets and contracts with service providers means that ignorance of finance is untenable and unprofessional.

However, technical, financial skills are not sufficient for, as we have shown, money is central to the lives of social services' users. An understanding of the impact of poverty or financial abuse may contribute to a broader understanding of why individuals may react to their situation in certain ways and what might be the prompting to change. Listening to the experiences of people who are poor needs to be part of a continual process of reflection for practitioners, in respect of their work with individuals and families and with regard to the policies and resource allocations of the broader agency. And whatever new organisational structures arise for social work, managing to champion the interests of the most disadvantaged may be the one distinctive and enduring contribution of social work.

FURTHER READING

Bateman, N. (2000) *Advocacy Skills for Health and Social Care Professionals*, London: Jessica Kingsley. Presents discussion and practice advice on different advocacy strategies – including some useful problem-solving exercises and 'model' responses.

Becker, S. (1997) *Responding to Poverty: the Politics of Cash and Care*, Harlow: Longman. Surveys the major themes and research in respect of poverty and income maintenance, with particular focus on social services' roles.

Fairburn, Z. (1998) *Benefits*, London: Five Leaves Publications. Fiction can be one way of becoming more aware of the experiences of people living in poverty.

Gordon, D., Adelman, L., Ashworth, K., Bradshaw, J., Levitas, R. et al. (2000) *Poverty and Social Exclusion in Britain*, York: Joseph Rowntree Foundation. A report based on interviews and surveys about living standards and managing on low incomes. The particular focus is on 1980–2000.

Quality Assurance

29

Robert Adams

Quality and quality assurance are contested concepts whose application is as deeply enmeshed as any aspect of social work in the politics of its management. Quality assurance is an ambiguous concept, being both an empowering tool to improve the practice of social workers by giving clients a stronger role, and a means of regulating professionals. These functions may be compatible, but where they are not, assuring quality remains a problematic goal. The 'best value' culture of quality assurance in health and social services creates its own language of regulating bodies, standards, procedures and performance indicators against which practice is evaluated. The critical practitioner should not be swamped by the detail of these and just follow them slavishly, without an awareness of their inbuilt assumptions and limitations.

The context of practice, after all, ensures specific judgements cannot be clearcut. Robert Harris gives two examples of the ambiguity of societal attitudes towards children, reflected in the lack of stability about specific judgements in the context of the general principles of child protection policy as expressed in the Children Act 1989. First, the Act

> apparently permits those imbued with parental responsibility to impose forms of physical punishment on their children which would in almost any other circumstances be deemed criminal assaults, and hence themselves a legitimate ground for state intervention.
>
> (Harris, 1995: 35)

Second:

> although law and policy consistently demand that the child's interests come first, their practical application does not prevent families from providing for their children a physical and emotional environment of strikingly poor quality.
>
> (Harris, 1995: 35)

Quality assurance in social work

Quality assurance means many different things to different people. The lowest common denominator of quality assurance is as

> processes, procedures and techniques aiming to guarantee that social work services to clients and carers meet their needs through their appropriateness, consistency and excellence.
>
> (Adams, 2000: 279–81)

Quality assurance, laws, social services agencies and social work goals

The organisation and delivery of criminal justice and social services are extremely complex. The hundreds of functions which need performing have to conform with numerous acts of parliament and recognised procedures, reflecting not only the interests of professionals but also the public and special interest groups and organisations representing older people, people with disabilities, children in residential care and so on. Formal ways of organising such large-scale and complex services in order to ensure that they carry out laws in a consistent pattern across different geographical areas, require managers to ensure that they are delivered. Despite numerous checklists, audits, standards, reviews, inspections, evaluations and other equally rigorous and time-consuming techniques, the quality of social work remains problematic and subject to much criticism every time another scandal hits the mass media. A widespread perception of techniques of quality assurance is that by and large they are designed by civil servants, policy-makers and social service managers, in a direction dictated often by politicians. Managerialist trends increase the bureaucracy of quality assurance and make inroads into practitioners' territory, while not necessarily enhancing values and practices concerned with the empowerment of clients and carers. The situation is a potential battleground between managerial and professional interests and values, to the extent that these conflict in particular circumstances. The managed, some would say top-down, quality assurance techniques adopted by government, local authorities and social services managers may not achieve the objective of guaranteeing the quality of services when they conflict in some fundamental ways with the empowering goals of social work.

Four main approaches to quality assurance

The four main approaches to quality assurance (Adams, 1998a) are rectification of errors and shortcomings, maintenance through standard-setting, enhancement through audits and evaluation, and quality maximisation. Each has something positive to offer. None can be lifted off the shelf and applied with superglue, or as a bolt-on kit, to the workplace, with the guarantee that all will be well.

Rectification of errors and shortcomings in quality

The most widely publicised approaches to quality assurance in the personal social services are those arising from mistakes, problems and shortcomings of services. There has been a long succession of inquiries into disasters and scandals in Britain in childcare and mental health, in particular, since the early 1970s. The mass media tend to nurture the sparks of public interest in incidents and ensure that many of the small fires of concern become major conflagrations. The authorities in their turn often rely on inquiries and investigations as their main means of translating remedies into practice.

The history of emphasis in the social services on remedying shortcomings is unfortunate but some would say inevitable, given the poor quality of work in some areas. A so-called 'blame culture' may result from efforts by managers to identify blameworthy individuals. Failures are given a high profile in the mass media and the responsibility often focuses on faulty practice by individuals, including social workers. This has the effect of reinforcing a right-wing ideology which punishes individual weakness and rewards individual enterprise, responsibility and competition. Workplaces beset by scandals and subsequent investigations are understandably not happy places. Staff and clients, some of whom may have suffered from the effects of the original incidents, are likely to feel the depressing and stress-provoking impact of their aftermath.

Threaded through this chapter is an example, based on actual information supplied to the author. Details and names have been changed to protect the anonymity of those involved.

CASE EXAMPLE

Eleanor is a social worker, whose client, lone-parent Mary, takes her youngest child Stephanie to a nursery school within walking distance of her home. The nursery school has a new head, Gail, and is staffed by nursery nurses and teachers. Mary's widowed mother, who has had a stroke, has been admitted to a local privately run residential nursing home for older people.

We can see through this example the operation of this first approach to quality assurance. There has been a complaint about conditions in the residential home. An inspector from outside the local authority comes to interview Mary and visits Eleanor. Mary's mother has become seriously ill with food poisoning. The inspector wants to know whether Mary mentioned her worries about the physical deterioration in her mother since admission to the home. Eleanor admits that she didn't follow this up, or visit Mary's mother and check out the quality of care in the home. The inspector comments in passing that the most cursory visit to the toilets in the home would have revealed serious shortcomings in hygiene which would have been clues to other possible problems in the home.

Maintenance through standard-setting and inspection

Standard-setting is one of the main means by which quality is monitored. Quality assurance through the specification of standards of services is somewhat uneven in the personal social services, because of differences between authorities and between services. There are published standards of service in some authorities and in some aspects of the work, yet not in others. The Audit Commission and the Social Services Inspectorate, established in the early 1980s, have exercised an increasingly strong central government role in Britain in inspecting to ensure that financial and professional standards of services are being maintained and give 'best value'.

CASE EXAMPLE revisited

In the example referred to above, we can see how standard-setting and inspection operate. OFSTED has reported on the nursery. The new head of the nursery has come from a teaching background. She has decided to respond proactively to the report's observation that the first half hour of each day is not spent productively enough, and introduces a formal period of teaching for the first half hour of every day.

Mary's daughter Stephanie is causing problems. Parents used to stay with their children, but Mary now delivers Stephanie at nine am and leaves immediately because she feels in the way of the teaching. Stephanie has been extremely distressed every morning for two weeks. The work of seven other children in her group has been interrupted by her prolonged crying. Stephanie's keyworker nursery nurse asks the head if Stephanie can come half an hour later. The head refuses on the grounds that parents sign up for the entire curriculum or withdraw their children. There are not the resources to give Stephanie individual attention first thing in the morning. Stephanie must be unsuitable for nursery education, she comments.

Mary confides in Eleanor her distress at what is happening to Stephanie. Eleanor backs away from taking up the emphasis on schooling in the nursery, at the expense of care tailored to the individual needs of the children.

Our example raises a number of critical questions about the limitations of such quality assurance procedures. How far, for instance, can such measures recommend the resourcing of new and additional services where there is unmet need? How can they judge whether services are being delivered at prices that potential and existing clients can afford? How can the multiplicity of different standards for service provision in authorities throughout the United Kingdom be reconciled with the principle that all clients should have equal access to services of an equivalent quality which meet their needs? Where there is discretion, the variations in services offered will not always be ideal.

There is overlap between the roles of inspectors and investigators of specific allegations of shortcomings. Inspectors often stumble onto aspects requiring investigation. Key components of inspection should be independence of action, openness and accessibility. Additionally, inspection should have the power to comment on global issues affecting the parameters of the service, such as the overall adequacy of resources. For a number of reasons, largely due to human rather than technical factors inherent in the principle – it is a good one – of inspection itself, procedures for inspection as a means of imposing standards of service cannot of themselves assure quality. This is as true in criminal justice and social services as in schooling and the food industry, as the following illustration shows.

Quality Protects and care standards legislation

No-one can deny the positive benefits accruing from the present government's commitment to improving the quality of social services that people receive. The Quality Protects (Department of Health, 1998b) initiative is a banner for a range of different activities, many of which are bound to lead to beneficial outcomes. However, such an approach fails to address contextual issues such as the availability of resources, and the prevailing ideology of inspection commonly is constructed without any consideration of whether increased resources are necessary to deliver services at the required standard.

The task of adhering to published standards consumes huge amounts of collaboration, consultation, management and, of course, energy and commitment by staff and others who already are overburdened. There is much that is good about setting standards and attempting to measure performance by monitoring and inspecting, using them as benchmarks. But attained standards cannot be measured in social work and social care in an equivalent way to standards in clinical medicine, for example. The appearance of objectivity in published standards may offer false reassurance of quality being delivered.

To the extent that standard-setting and adherence to preformed agendas for action stifle initiative and flexibility in responding to the needs of individual people, they are hostile to the development of good, critical practice. There needs to be regulation of quality in probation and social services, but it needs to be good regulation. Attention should be paid to ensuring that regulation cracks the nut of poor quality. Finally, in today's rapidly changing world, the standards are always going to be out of date. The more listing we do, the more checklists we generate, the more they constantly have to be updated and revised.

Quality enhancement through audits and evaluation

A number of approaches to quality assurance move beyond maintaining existing levels of service, to enhancing them. There is overlap here with standard-setting and inspection, since some inspectorial systems have the brief of enhancement, whereas others are simply concerned to regulate the status quo.

Auditing

Auditing systems rely on an increasingly sophisticated array of quantitative and qualitative methods of collecting data, such as checklists, schedules, systematic monitoring using statistical and other management information, recurring and one-off audits and inspection activity designed to establish whether standards are being achieved. Audits may focus on seemingly more objective measures of performance, such as financial statistics concerning budgets and resources, relating these and other data to performance criteria developed by bodies such as the Audit Commission and Social Services Inspectorate. They may also focus on qualitative aspects such as relationships between staff and management, between staff and clients and teambuilding.

Clients' and carers' perspectives as users of services are important, but the ultimate responsibility for organising and delivering excellent, affordable services rests with staff. Even so, a balance is required, between sound internal procedures and external and independent audits and checks, to maintain public and professional accountability. Auditing also should include not just the financial affairs of the organisation, but all its activities.

Evaluation

Evaluation is an undervalued component of professional work. Basing quality assurance on evaluation greatly increases the likelihood of achieving the goal of enhancement of services. Often, evaluation can contribute to the development of critical practice. Evaluation helps to bring to bear on the task of making a judgement about the quality of service, the evidence from previous research. This introduces a necessary independence which can contribute to future sound judgements and effective decision-making. We can regard evaluative critical practice as a guardian of the professionalism of staff and the interests of clients, thereby increasing the chance of meeting clients' needs.

Quality maximisation

In most welfare organisations, rhetoric about standard-setting and quality indicators masks the cutting of resources, so that fewer staff work harder, experiencing greater stress, to sustain a growing range and depth of services, with ever-more risk that mistakes will occur and vulnerable people will suffer. The number of full-time staff in the core workforce declines and services are sustained by an increasing number of part-time, sessional staff. Meeting budgetary targets dominates the agenda. The pressure is on staff to accept working conditions. The implicit message, discouraging staff from looking critically at working practices in the organisation, is, 'if you don't like the job, leave and we'll find somebody else to do it'. In such circumstances, ironically, quality may actually decline.

Ideally, the workplace should be stress free. The goal of the stress-free working environment is to create flexible working arrangements – home and office – where managers encourage rather than punish staff. Valuing staff can lead to trusting them to organise their own work and providing facilities which meet their social as well as their work needs. An organisation with an autocratic management style will become autocratic in its culture. This cannot be remedied by introducing stress management and counselling for staff. What is needed is to change the culture of the organisation, inducing a nurturing rather than a blame culture. Professional staff need encouragement, support and space to develop creative and critical, rather than merely competent, practice.

The less professionally educated and experienced staff are, the less likely it is that they will assert professional values in a critical way, in order to benefit clients. The disempowering consequences for staff of being untrained in, say, residential settings impact on the clients with whom they work.

People receiving services need to be empowered so that they can have a stake in the quality of what they receive. Quality may be enshrined in the general principles of childcare as stated in legislation, but that does not ensure it is automatically present in the practice. Legislation which has the express purpose of protecting children does not always protect.

CASE EXAMPLE revisited

In our example, Eleanor is in a quandary. She knows she isn't helping Mary, Mary's mother or Mary's children. She is confused about what to do. She feels guilt at not picking up what was happening in the nursing home. Should she intervene proactively in the nursery school? A tutor on a quality assurance course she attended talked about quality maximisation, but she finds the implications of this – empowering practice with Mary and her family members – somewhat challenging and difficult to envisage in practice. Eleanor is not going to be popular with the head of the nursery if she insists on a meeting to examine the extent to which the needs of Stephanie are being met.

Eleanor reconsiders her situation. She looks critically at her practice in this case so far, and is aware that she has not been assertive enough on behalf of her clients. She decides to insist on the meeting, as her overriding priority is to achieve the highest possible quality of service for her client. She takes Mary into her confidence regarding her doubts, as part of her preparation for the next stage. She wants Mary to be as empowered as possible. She cannot predict what will happen.

Repeated evidence shows that clients' perceptions and views too often are ignored. Over decades, children, young people and adults have protested against the conditions in which they are incarcerated, schooled and 'cared for'. The examination of the strong tradition of protests by pupils (Adams, 1991) indicates that while those receiving services may protest, invariably their protests are not attended to. Their views should be taken seriously and not ignored or responded to punitively.

Empowerment can be too politically, financially and managerially dangerous. It is easier for the powerful to continue to manage the powerless in society. Empowerment could be about offering people informed choice, and thereby enabling exclusion to be challenged at the personal level. At the collective level, empowered people could tackle the political, social and economic causes of their and others' exclusion (Adams, 1998b). This is superior to top-down approaches where projects and programmes are designed without involving clients at all. In childcare, for instance, children could be offered greater control, choice and independence over when and what happens, at the expense, perhaps, of some protection. Immediate intervention may be traded off against providing the child with more support and scope to explore, with key adults including professionals, alternative strategies for addressing problems which may be ameliorated despite being complex and deep rooted.

Quality maximisation requires us to turn repeatedly to clients, carers, parents of children being looked after by the social services, and others receiving services, and ask them for their perceptions of those services. We should put them in the driving seat, as far as possible, of assessing and allocating resources. We should be prepared to be self-critical of our responses to them.

Implications for critical practice

Three general implications for critical practitioners can be drawn from this brief discussion of the four main approaches to quality assurance:

- We cannot maximise quality through quality assurance alone, or through approaches based on imposing regulation, standardisation, or one based largely on problem rectification. It is difficult to envisage how regulating a system which is not working will improve it significantly. Such a system needs reforms outside the quality assurance process and, probably, more resources.

- We cannot maximise quality without empowering clients and workers, including managers as well as professionals. A deskilled, demotivated, stressed, overworked workforce is not well placed to help other people.

- Professionals and managers will continue to have an uneasy, and potentially bumpy, relationship. The way to address potential conflicts between professional and managerial interests is for managers constantly to check out with social workers any implications for them of proposed new approaches to quality assurance. Likewise, practitioners have a responsibility to go beyond maintaining handed-down standards and to criticise approaches to quality.

═══════════════ **CONCLUSION** ═══════════════

Approaches to quality assurance based on rectifying shortcomings and maintaining present standards have little to offer in the rapidly changing circumstances facing our complex probation and social services organisations, in contrast with approaches based on enhancing professional practice and maximising quality through empowering all stakeholders in services.

To this end,

> organisational cultures which are equality-based, open and self-critical, rooted in client and carer participation, have a greater potential for maximising quality than techniques and procedures dominated by managers and professionals.

(Adams, 2000: 280)

Such open organisational cultures cannot automatically resolve conflicts of perspective and preference between adults and adults and adults and children. That complex task needs facilitating, among others, by social workers. But these open organisations have a greater potential for maximising quality than hierarchical settings where techniques and procedures are dominated by managers and professionals. The contribution of the empowered social worker is to make judgements, acting creatively, demonstrating expertise rather than skills alone.

We should empower clients and carers. There is a need to move beyond ideologically and procedurally driven analyses of problems and crisis-inspired responses to them. Empowerment is inherently problematic because it could be liberating or actually reinforce exclusion if imposed as a solution, or bestowed as a gift on people. We and our families are all potential clients of social services. In developing critical practice, we may be assuring the quality of services for ourselves.

FURTHER READING

Adams, R. (1998) *Quality Social Work*, Basingstoke: Macmillan – now Palgrave Macmillan. A critical examination of the four main approaches to quality assurance.

Evers, A., Haverinen, R., Leichsenring, K. and Wistow, G. (eds) (1997) *Developing Quality in Personal Social Services: Concepts, Cases and Comments*, Aldershot: Ashgate. A series of studies of quality assurance in a European context.

Kelly, D. and Warr, B. (eds) (1992) *Quality Counts*, London: Whiting & Birch/Social Care Association. A good spread of critical chapters on different aspects of quality in the social care field.

Kirkpatrick, I. and Miguel, A.L. (eds) (1995) *The Politics of Quality in the Public Sector*, London: Routledge. A diverse collection of studies providing a context for quality assurance in practice.

CHAPTER 30

Reorganising Agencies

David Peryer

Introduction: constant change

The NHS and Community Care Act 1980 required local authorities for the first time to consider commissioning home care services from independent agencies. Progress during the 1990s has been subject to joint review by the Audit Commission and the Social Services Inspectorate, now within national performance, quality and 'best value' frameworks. Local authorities have learned through this process to compete with independent agencies to provide home care services to the required standards at the lowest possible price. In the early twenty-first century, the Care Standards Act 2000 will give government new regulatory powers. The development of care trusts will add further to the pressure to review existing arrangements. The experience of the last decade is of constant change in legislation and organisation within the social and health care services.

A significant element of the service cost is the cost of the transactions involved in getting the appropriate worker to the right house at the right time, armed with the knowledge they need. Therefore the way in which rosters are organised, visits recorded, time sheets made up, clients charged and workers paid are key issues. Developments in information systems make it possible for care workers and first-line mangers to enter all this data directly, with subsequent transactions processed using integrated systems. That in turn provides managers with knowledge to review the organisation of services, identifying scope for greater efficiency and seeking opportunities to win new business.

These high-level changes will have personal consequences for managers and workers. Some existing providers will struggle with the technological, structural and cultural changes required. No doubt others will rise to the challenge. Some first-line managers will struggle with the role change required in working at a keyboard without the support of clerical staff whose jobs will disappear. Others will welcome the changes. But, sooner or later, national performance standards will lead most agencies to make changes that will:

■ mean middle managers taking a more entrepreneurial role in winning and keeping new business within a locality

■ demand a significant investment in new information systems, funded by savings on clerical support

■ place first-line managers in new roles working almost entirely hands-on down the line

■ thence provide opportunities for managers who do not fit the future to be redeployed or made redundant.

Such changes will allow departments commissioning services to specify their requirements in ways that give service users greater flexibility and choice and opportunities to redefine their personal priorities and needs on a daily basis, while allowing purchasers to retain control over spending and contract fulfilment. This in turn will require changes in the mindsets of administrators and solicitors who have to draft the contracts. Similar scenarios will emerge in the commissioning and provision of mental health, children's and other services.

The changes of the 1990s are not final, as the changes of previous decades were built on or displaced. Change is always a reaction or development to what went before, so we must focus on reorganisation in response to change as a continuous process in which organisational structure plays a relatively small but significant part.

There is no such thing as the perfect organisation. The way in which agencies are structured and managed always involves compromise, conflict and uncertainty for the people involved, and people, as we know, are never perfect. This chapter looks at some reasons why agencies reorganise, ways in which this can happen and the consequences and opportunities for the people involved.

Multiple objectives, structure and (re)organisation

The overriding concern of all social care agencies is to advance the interests of communities, families and individuals who are disadvantaged or have special needs, seeking to ensure the efficient and effective delivery of services to people seen to need them or known to want them. Such a concern instantly raises questions: among them, who are the agencies, the communities, families and individuals? What is disadvantage or special need? What is effective and efficient? Who defines need and want? What is the role of social care within a wider system? Every agency will have its own particular objectives and goals, which imply their answers and priorities in the face of such questions. All reorganisations have to be justified in terms of their contribution to the achievement of goals such as these, although the justifications for change may not always seem convincing to a hard-pressed social worker coping with the disruption that changes can cause or to members of an oppressed community or the taxpayer.

All reorganisations, being about structure, involve changes in the allocation of responsibilities, in lines of accountability, in the links between different functions and sectors of the agency, and in systems and processes from the relatively trivial to the more fundamental. And all involve people, and therefore changes in the distribution of power over resources and decisions.

Whatever the principal determinant, all reorganisations create opportunities to address issues around structure, systems, values, management capabilities and power. Thus, reorganisations are always political in the widest sense, although only some are political in the sense of being driven by changes in party political policies or control. When the need for reorganisation is justified by managers, the critical social worker may ask if the opportunities that change will bring are to be fully exploited for the benefit of service users, carers and the community. On the other hand, the reorganisation may bring disadvantages and losses to practitioners or service users or advantages to one but not the other.

All social care agencies, even the smallest, have multiple objectives and goals and will continuously be juggling priorities for the use of scarce resources, managing the tensions between different sectors of the agency, and balancing freedom of action for staff against the need to maintain control over standards within a political framework. Social workers within the social care system, whatever the organisational structure, will be required daily to manage paradox, multiple realities and conflict, balancing issues of freedom and control with a focus on the rights and needs of individuals with the needs of their families, carers and the wider community. Thus, for example, services for elderly people may aim at early intervention to help to maintain their capacity for independent living, whereas another goal is to give priority in using scarce resources for people with the highest dependency needs (see Chapter 20). In social work with children and families, a primary goal is to help children to remain in their own homes wherever possible. Another goal is child protection, which sometimes involves removing children from their home. Social workers supporting families with histories of significant problems are therefore expected to take substantial risks in selecting one objective rather than another, but without ever making serious mistakes (see Chapter 27). These conflicts can feel unfair and threatening to the survival of social work. Equally, it is the political reality that personal survival is also the ultimate consideration for most ministers, MPs and councillors, since managers may delegate to social workers the responsibility for action, but can never devolve responsibility for outcomes. Political and managerial leaders of all agencies, public or private, carry the ultimate responsibility for standards and therefore for the management of performance and risks. Therefore strong leadership is required if frontline workers are to be empowered to take major decisions, some of which have life or death implications. The critical social worker has the right to expect such leadership.

Social care agencies have to be organised around those multiple realities and tensions. There are no easy answers, only balances to be struck, or choices to be made. Thus, the structure of an agency will reflect, among other things, the chosen answers to conundrums such as the need to have separate sectors dedicated to work with particular client groups. This might concentrate skills and develop expertise within social work teams towards the achievement of high standards. On the other hand, it might be valuable to focus whole-agency support on the development of local communities, promoting social inclusion and seeking to ensure the integrated provision of a wide range of social care services. Equally, the need to give social care teams the information, resources and freedom of action that they require to work in flexible, sensitive and imaginative ways has to be balanced against having comprehensive procedures and sufficient controls to ensure comparable standards and levels of achievement across the agency and minimise the risk of serious failures.

Managers and practitioners will want it all ways in looking for structures and for practice that simultaneously liberate and constrain, that empower frontline workers and their managers but do so in ways that ensure prescribed outcomes are achieved and risks minimised. We cannot have it all ways. Critical social work implies clarity about expectations alongside freedom in professional decision-making. Within a command-and-control culture, defining the delegation of accountabilities in detail aims to ensure consistency and minimise predictable risks of failure. The downside is that potential creativity may be stifled, new initiatives thwarted and frontline staff demotivated. The organisation will then learn less than it might from staff delivering the service, and have difficulties dealing with new and unexpected demands.

By contrast, where substantial responsibilities are delegated to frontline teams and units providing services, and where the focus is on outcomes rather than prescribed ways of working, staff may be motivated to find innovative solutions to local problems and respond creatively to individual needs. This generates a strong commitment and much learning from experience, but, even within a framework of clear standards and procedures, it may lead to services delivered to different standards and in different ways at different points in the agency. Whether the differences are seen to demonstrate locally responsive social work services or unacceptable differences in standards will depend on the point of view.

So a balance has to be struck to try to ensure that the structure and culture within which staff take daily decisions are neither too 'tight' nor too 'loose'. That is a management judgement to be taken at a given point in time, and times change. Tight controls will be essential if the agency is seriously overspending, standards are slipping and staff are leaving as crises multiply. By contrast, it may be safe and wise to hold a much looser rein in better times. For example, greater flexibility may be possible where there are clear and widely shared expectations and organisational goals, most posts are filled, enough competent managers are in post to generate a trust that allows sharing of difficulties and failures, and systems allow timely monitoring of performance and outcomes. In social work with children and families, for example, where pressures are great and risks high, the capacity and capabilities of systems and the competence of team managers and the senior managers supervising them are crucial to decisions about how flexible or controlling management may be.

Reorganisation as a way of life

Reorganisations, therefore, always involve the exchange of one set of compromises for another, although it is unlikely that is the way the proposed changes will be presented. Reorganisations may be externally driven by national changes in policies, or by changes in local needs or the social care marketplace. They are also commonly driven by a need or the opportunity to deal with internal problems to improve effectiveness and efficiency.

Most past social services reorganisations have been locally determined, politically driven by a perceived need to improve services and address tragedies or failures highlighted by the media, or by a need to reduce expenditure. However, some have been driven directly by governments to meet political objectives. Thus, the Local Authority Personal Social Services Act 1970 following the recommendations of the Seebohm Committee (1968) brought local authority social services departments into existence, through the merger of children and welfare departments with elements of the former local health departments. The belief was that the new departments would promote an integrated response to individual and social needs within local communities, avoiding fragmented services.

Parallel legalisation stripped county boroughs of many powers and gave the new social services responsibilities outside metropolitan areas to enlarged county councils, in the belief that the range of resources at the disposal of counties would give them the critical mass required for the delivery of services to a high standard. Legislation 25 years later restored social services powers to smaller local authorities in many areas, creating a substantial number of new 'unitary' authorities, in the belief that smaller, all-purpose authorities would be better able to integrate service provision and respond to community needs in a different way. Early twenty-first century changes in the relationship between health and social care also have similar objectives. Looking at reorganisation reminds us of the old French proverb: *plus ça change, plus c'est le même chose* (the more things change, the more they remain the same).

This chapter opened with an aspect of Britain's move towards a contract culture focused on performance and outcomes. The relationship between central and local government has also shifted. To a lesser extent so has that between government and independent agencies. Through regulations, guidance and the use of hypothecated grants to local authorities (that is, grants with defined purposes), central government is increasingly specifying organisation and methods, rather than relying on setting performance standards and outcomes. Committees, boards, managers and practitioners now have to be able to deal with a succession of required developments, leading to consequential changes. For example, the government review of adoption practice (Cabinet Office, 2000) proposed changes in the way decisions are taken throughout the care system, not only changes in the organisation of permanency teams. New mental health legislation reform (Department of Health, 2000b) retains approved social workers, but requires them to work within a different organisational framework specified by government (see Chapter 17).

Values and beliefs lie behind the agency structures, justifying existing arrangements as being the best way of making the agency fit for purpose. Whatever the external determinants of change, most reorganisations reflect changes in these beliefs about the characteristics of successful organisations. Within any social care agency, only a minority of staff are likely to change their job, role or place of work in most reorganisations. However, sooner or later, most staff and many service users are likely to experience changes in priorities, or new ways of working that have a direct impact on their lives. Although structural changes can happen quickly, changes in working methods or values take much longer to achieve. Therefore, some time may pass before the effects of reorganisation are noticeable at the sharp end. Critical social workers might prepare for these, or seek ways of maintaining or incorporating current values within new developments. Alternatively, change may provide the opportunity to incorporate new desired values and objectives. Such is the pace of change that by then a further reorganisation may be on the way.

Leadership in the change process

Reorganisations come in all shapes and sizes. They may happen quietly and gradually, but are quite often highly visible, played as drama with a printed programme and cast list. As a reorganisation proceeds, the actors take new roles, the scenery changes and the plot unfolds.

It is relatively easy to reorganise an agency, redefining management responsibilities and lines of accountability and appointing managers to new posts. Most difficulties with implementation are likely to be around:

- management of the transition in ways that avoid loss of motivation and much precious energy being wasted

- the impact on day-to-day practice of new managers and practitioners and coalitions of interests with different or changing values and expectations

- the probable need for changes in systems and processes alongside changes in structure.

Plans to reorganise an agency need to be set in the context of existing or new standards and goals, the capacity of human and financial resources, organisational culture and openness to change, and the adequacy of systems for managing performance and sharing information.

As Chapter 22 suggests, employment and work issues are central to management. Within a contract culture, the terms and conditions of employment of staff, established through collective bargaining, are likely to come under particular scrutiny. Employers may press to move from a traditional approach to an approach based on partnerships with trade unions and agreements on protocols for flexible working and the management of change. One critical view may see this as a loss of trade union power that has to be fought. However, governments, supported by public opinion, seem likely to demand increasing flexibility in public services, mirroring changes in service industries generally, so that full social work services are available in the evenings and at weekends, as is increasingly the case in retailing, leisure and other services.

Reorganisations can use up massive amounts of energy and be draining. Leadership and drive therefore become key issues. Leadership may be seen as a form of oppression, imposing outcomes against conflicting objectives. In this view, for senior managers, leadership seeks scope for establishing coalitions of interests united in support of change, lest trade unions control the pace and possibly stall the process. Alternatively, leadership may focus on achieving a shared vision, together with a sense of urgency. Sharing proposals with staff at an early stage becomes important, engaging in consultation and sharing news of progress. The more clearly reasons for change are communicated once the aims are agreed, and the more transparent the process, the more likely it is that the changes will be understood if not welcomed. There also need to be enough perceived short-term gains (enough wins) to keep energy levels up, so that subsequent, possibly lengthy changes in culture and systems may be handled.

Reorganisations may be justified in terms of greater efficiency and effectiveness, but are never free of cost, both financial costs and disruption. The director and managers concerned therefore have to believe in what they are doing. Making changes means taking risks. Building a new structure means breaking up parts of the old. New beginnings involve endings, which are painful. As in families breaking up, so in organisations many staff will be working through the stages of relief or disbelief, anger and guilt, depression and maybe panic before reaching a position where the reality can be fully accepted.

Because reorganisations carry costs and risks, agencies need to justify significant changes to stakeholders. The reasons for change may be more complex than those drawn to public attention. Skilled politicians demonstrate how public presentation is the art of simplifying complex issues while sending out messages at more than one level of consciousness. A reorganisation is something tangible that can be sold on the basis of cost savings or greater effectiveness, with the implication of an 'action orientation' and a willingness to 'grasp the nettle' and make a 'fresh start'. If the reorganisation has been triggered by public concern around one or more perceived failures in the management of risks – say in child protection or mental health – a perceived 'firm response' in the shape of management changes may well be a managerial and political imperative. That may be so even if the issues are entirely around capacity, competence and process, not around structure.

Using the opportunities of change

When an opportunity or need for reorganisation arises, the ideal from the start is to use that opportunity to make progress on more than one front. Prudent managers and practitioners use the opportunity of reorganisation to address issues of four kinds as part of a continuous process of organisational development:

- required structural changes in management or team responsibilities
- changes required in organisational culture, values and ways of working
- improvements in systems and the management of process
- the need to move individual managers into or out of posts.

For elected members and senior managers of local authorities, where terms and conditions of employment are negotiated within a national framework, a reorganisation provides opportunities for management changes. Redundancies may be the easiest way of dealing with managers past their sell-by date who are not bad enough to be disciplined or retired on the grounds that their capability is seriously in question. Independent agencies may find it easier to pay off managers quietly on an individual basis, without needing the opportunity that a reorganisation brings.

Structural changes in responsibilities and lines of accountability change the distribution of power as managers move up, across, down or away. Staff studying the proposed changes will speculate over implied shifts in the distribution of power, making reorganisations a hot topic even for those not directly involved.

CONCLUSION

It was suggested earlier in this chapter that prudent reorganisations will be designed to address four kinds of issues simultaneously: structural changes; improvements in systems and the management of process; issues around the capability of individual managers; and changes in values and culture. Whatever the political imperatives for change, the critical social worker may reasonably expect this degree of prudence to be visible, with any reorganisation – small or large – set in the context of long-term plans for the development of the organisation that will be adequately funded and supported.

FURTHER READING

Bridges, W.R. (1995) *Managing Transitions: Making the Most of Change*, London: Nicholas Brealey. Describes the processes and opportunities of change.

Flynn, N. (1997) *Public Sector Management*, 3rd edn, London: Harvester Wheatsheaf. Considers developments and changes in the public sector, including local authorities.

Hadley, R. and Young, K. (1990) *Creating a Responsive Public Service*, London: Harvester Wheatsheaf. A case study of major organisational changes in a social services department.

Hudson, M. (1999) *Managing Without Profit*, 2nd edn, London: Penguin. An excellent study of organisation, management and change in the voluntary sector.

McKevitt, D. and Lawton, A. (eds) (1994) *Public Sector Management: Theory, Critique and Practice*, London: Sage. A reader that covers various issues raised in this chapter.

Concluding Comments: Facilitating Critical Practice

Robert Adams, Lena Dominelli and Malcolm Payne

From understanding theoretical debates to practising critically

This book has been a journey for us as editors and authors. It has continued the process we began in the first book, where we scrutinised theories and approaches in social work. In *Social Work: Themes, Issues and Critical Debates* (Adams et al., 1998), we argue that it is important for social workers to try to reach an understanding of the issues that they face, the methods that they try to use and the contexts in which they practise. It is impossible to practise without that alertness to the issues involved in practice.

In this book, we have journeyed further into the process of practice. Understanding, we say, has to be connected to action and the link between understanding and action is criticality. This is because action assumes a purpose, a direction in which we act. In Chapter 1, we referred to this direction as 'agency'.

Agency

Agency is the capacity of people to act, now and in future. Both the practitioner and the user have this capacity and use it in their activities, usually to meet certain objectives and goals. Agency involves interaction between people and engages them in negotiating their positions with one another. In realising their agency, users are able to stamp their own imprimatur (a mark of ownership) on their relationship with practitioners. This enables them to empower themselves, which ensures that no relationship is predetermined. However, power differentials between user and practitioner often complicate the sets of negotiations that can occur and disadvantage the user, who has less formal power and resources to draw on in the negotiation than does the practitioner.

When we say we have a purpose, we imply that our current position is not ideal. We want to change it in some way. This could be a small change, a minor correction of balance or stance, or a large change involving moving to a fresh position. Whatever our purpose, in order to justify our actions we need to understand what is inadequate and requiring change. That is the reason for being critical in practice.

So, in Part I of this book, we propose that considering our values is essential to deciding on our critical analysis. In Part II, we show that, in order to act, we must have a clear understanding of the prerequisites of practice arising from the needs of people receiving services – 'clients', 'service users', 'consumers', however we refer to them. In Part III, we examine the managerial and organisational contexts for being critical, and how management must itself be a critical practice, if it is to work well. This parallels our examination of the legal and agency contexts for practice in Part III of *Social Work: Themes, Issues and Critical Debates*.

We regard it as axiomatic that, for adequate understanding, we must examine practice directly and not consider it at one remove. For this reason, authors of many of the chapters in this present book have rooted their arguments in practice illustrations. Also, if critical practice is to be effective, we regard it as essential for our thinking and analysis to be examined minutely and systematically. This means devoting sufficient space to key areas and is reflected in our choice of topics in the foregoing chapters.

Critical practice and good practice: the example of diversity

We have reached the point where our argument that critical practice should be mainstream practice leads to the logical, if ideal, conclusion that all good practice should exemplify the principles of critical practice that we have set out in Chapters 1 and 9.

An example is the area of diversity. Not only critical practice, but all good practice, should be exemplified by a celebration of diversity. This is reflected in the diversity of approaches to the different areas of practice illustrated in this book. It goes beyond that, to the promotion of inclusion and citizens' rights as a means of engaging with anti-oppressive practice. The good practitioner is sensitive to attempts to attribute characteristics to people, in terms of their age, gender, race, geographical location and so on. Critical practice celebrates diversity, and thus regards it positively, but it extends further. The critical practitioners described in the previous section and throughout this book do not just acknowledge that diversity exists and do what is necessary, or just accept that they must behave correctly. Because critical practice involves careful attention to detail, diversities in the present situation need to be explored and understood and their implications for the people involved spelled out and acted upon.

Consequently, a critical practitioner is unable to polarise opinion about social groups, or stereotype people according to attributes of gender, role or ethnicity because such judgements will not survive critical analysis. They involve a form of essentialism, ascribing social behaviour to a particular essence of the individual, such as blackness or femaleness or disability. This results in a denial of diversity and difference, by assuming that all people who are socially constructed as black or old or disabled share the same experiences and aspirations.

But critical practice, since it requires agency, means acting in ways that value diversity, as well as awareness and analysis of it. Action presents more problems than analysis. For example, we may seek to represent the diversity of the workforce by ensuring reasonably equal numbers of people of both sexes in promoted posts in the management team, having become aware through analysis that this represents a problem about lack of diversity. Then, one or two appointments made by fair appointment processes lead to an imbalance of men, the traditional holders of power and management posts. Do we acquiesce? Do we accept a quota, which means that for individuals the appointment procedure may not be 'fair'? Do we take positive action and encourage and train women more actively? Do we look for hidden disincentives in the promoted posts? Or do we look for the incentives in practitioner posts, which leads us to accept that women might not want promoted posts of the present kind and look for different ways to enable them to take up seniority and influence? That there are so many possibilities for action demonstrates how critical practice needs to apply to action as well as analysis.

We would expect the critical practitioner to be concerned to locate the practice in its broader historical, social and policy context. By doing so, we offer alternative possibilities for explanation and action. So, in the example we have just given, power relations will emerge as immovably embedded in social structures. If we celebrate rather than stereotype people, their identities become multi-dimensional and complex. As a result, a greater range of alternatives for action arise. How could our services involve a wider range of people from different minorities to give flexibility and responsiveness to our services? Race, of course, is only one aspect of this, other aspects being gender, age, class, school, neighbourhood, friends, the perceptions of family members and so on.

The critical practitioner is aware of the contradictions and dilemmas inherent in adopting a merely tolerant approach. It is necessary to move beyond the multicultural essentialism which stereotypes people as though their diversity, both culturally and ethnically, has only one meaning: 'lazy Afro-Caribbean youth, cohesive street gangs, supportive extended families, oppressed Muslim women'. The so-called lazy youth is not motivated by things that officials such as social workers talk to him about, but an approach based on diversity suggests that there will be things that motivate him and can carry him forward, and they must be found. The cohesive street gang can use its cohesiveness in mutual support, if it can be helped to do so. The supportive family may need to explore the violence hidden in many families and understand the paradox that supportiveness may also be exploitative for some family members. Also family members may benefit from understanding the value of giving and receiving affection, help and support. People without experience of Islam may gain from seeing the oppression in all family relationships.

The critical practitioner will recognise, like other good practitioners, that difference is socially constructed and that oppression can be inherent in the way this happens. Power is distributed in many social networks, and may be taken up and used even by people who are usually in less powerful positions. Social constructions may inhibit us from using such opportunities, but may also offer certainty and shared understanding that will help us to deal with social changes. After all, everyone – individually and collectively – is working across differences all the time. Also, it takes many different perspectives to construct, and experience, a difference. But we would expect the critical practitioner to go further, for example into reconstructing individual and collective ideas and identities. Thus, the critical practitioner may be unhappy about the way masculinity is constructed in the locality and may envisage reconstructing it so as to assert male partners' roles as carers for children, and older and disabled people in the household. Thus, the critical practitioner attempts to achieve the reframing of qualities and activities associated with gender, on the basis that they are not attributes of gender but socially constructed cultural codes, valuable or disadvantageous in their own right as well as in their stereotypical identities. So, the critical practitioner questions dominant social constructions, resists or challenges oppressive constructions and seeks hidden certainties in social constructions that inhibit people's self-empowerment.

In this way, critical practice can be emancipatory practice, encouraging clients and carers also to reconstruct difference and thereby achieving the celebration of diversity. Thus, critical practice achieves the reconstruction of identities, valuing differences, and these values, which have been marginal or oppressed, now become dominant. The critical practitioner working across difference may tackle the reconstruction, for example, of black women working with white men, or gay men and lesbian women working with heterosexuals.

Changing emphasis: from reflective to critical practice

We would not dispute the claim of reflective practitioners to be critical. Just because we assert the need for the development of critical practice does not mean we are denying that other approaches to practice have a critical component. However, we argue that, for the critical practitioner, being critical is integral to the work and not something carried out incidentally or occasionally. Also, we have demonstrated in this book that shifting the territory of debates into practice has moved the centre of gravity of our discussion from 'being reflective' to 'being critical', because being critical involves action with a purpose as well as reflection. We have illustrated how critical practice is experienced by, and feels to, the practitioner, as well as touching the knowledge and skill bases.

Constructing bridges

We can use the metaphor of bridges to emphasise how our critical practice can link diverse aspects, not destroying those which are vulnerable, ignoring those which are marginal, and enabling them to interact with us and with each other. Critical practice may be a bridging activity, a means of reframing the different possibilities of our practice. Criticality can link alternative options. Being critical is powerful because it can enable us to reframe and treat as equivalent a diversity of options, including those which are part of the status quo and those which we otherwise might disregard as too problematic or risky. Critical practice offers bridges between the margins of possible practice and the centre. Through the medium of a diversity perspective, critical practice can bring the margins of our perceptions and experiences into the centre, the mainstream of our practice.

Critical practice also offers bridges between continuities and changes in the circumstances of our work, which enables us to transform both our view of situations and act transformationally. In other words, through criticality we can make connections between the past, the present and the future, and achieve change. We conclude this chapter by considering what is involved in these key ideas of *managing change and continuity* and *critical practice as transformational*. Inevitably, we engage with criticality as *an unfinished agenda* as we encounter the *paradoxes and dilemmas of practice*.

Managing change and continuity

Managing change is a difficult process. People, both practitioners and users, sometimes seek certainty. When this is so, ambiguous and constantly changing situations have to be managed in order to control and contain them. Anger and aggression must be calmed. Depression must be circumvented or overcome to permit progress. Without some form of order, it would be impossible to act. Thus, control and containment may have valued features of social situations as well as the oppressive elements that we often focus upon. The failing is to value either control or lack of it without a critical assessment of what people want and need in the situation. To value only control or only self-determination is to avoid being critical.

So it is with change and continuity. A problem with managing change is that people's fear of it often can leave them paralysed or disempowered. In those situations, a person with clearer ideas about what ought to be done may impose their views on another and reduce their potential to exercise agency or act in ways that take account of their own feelings and views. A problem with managing continuity is that frustration with it may lead them to seek change inappropriately. Sometimes, the answer to marital problems is to stay with it and work through them. That is sometimes a tougher option than seeking change.

Reflecting upon these alternatives and acting ethically, that is, in ways that do not abuse their formal power, is a critical stance that practitioners can adopt. Basically, to manage this tension, they need to be both critical in action and critical of action.

An unfinished agenda

Critical practice goes on forever. There is no end to the processes of analysis and action, continually deconstructing and reconstructing, reflecting constantly changing circumstances. We have deliberately avoided implying that critical practice is an end-point, but have presented it within traditions of social criticism and critiques of practice. It is fashionable to attach terms such as 'lifelong learning' and 'ongoing practice' to discussion of practice development. However, we would attach the aim of developing critical practice in social work to any programme of continuing professional development. It is significant that there is a lack of closure in our statements about the level of expertise that critical practice requires. Becoming a critical practitioner is easier to recognise than it is to accept somebody's claim to have achieved being a critical practitioner, as though it is a once-in-a-lifetime accomplishment.

We prefer to assert the need for the critical practitioner constantly to strive towards the accomplishment of becoming critical. There is an acceptable level of expertise, but whether there are 'experts' in critical practice is another matter. It is probably more realistic to assert that criticality continues to be affected by major critiques of power and those hierarchical structures of division and oppression – racism, sexism and class – which generate continually changing frameworks for critical analysis and action. Of course it is also affected by personal matters such as the level of energy a practitioner can apply today. The people we work with also have an impact on the degree of criticality that we apply. Colleagues, subordinates and managers, service users, carers and members of a multiprofessional team may all have a place in determining the extent of our criticality at any time and in any situation. Being critical means responding thoughtfully to the relationships we are working within, while also holding on to the idea that those relationships should not prevent the criticality that is necessary for ... what? We must critically decide.

Critical practice is transformational

In various ways, critical practice is a transformational activity. We suggested above that moving from understanding to criticality is an essential stage in moving eventually towards action. This is because deciding to intervene necessarily requires us to think that the present situation requires transformation. Criticality must, therefore, be transformational. However, it does not in itself transform: the final stage is to act on the critical decision. When we can practise critically, we can use these skills to advance our practice, for the benefit of those we work with and for the benefit of better social work and better services.

The diversity of fields for practice means that transformations can take place in various domains and at different levels. Advancing social work practice means helping the achievements in those fields to interact, so it is more generic in its progress. Initially, when the worker transforms understanding by making it critical, it becomes relocated in its wider contexts. Subsequently, understandings are revisited continually. This is not a one-off event, segregated from practice. But it may gain in emancipatory and empowering potential as the practice develops. The worker makes links with other areas of practice, in the light of analysis and action, and puts clients in touch with others in comparable situations, in a liberating fashion.

Critical analysis enables the practitioner to transform discovered anomalies into contradictions, making it possible to perceive oppressive features beyond ideologies and reconceptualising, which is integral to continuing critical action.

Paradoxes and dilemmas of practice

We have illustrated how paradoxes and dilemmas are embedded in practice. There are always alternatives for action and they always become more extensive if we are critical. Being critical creates dilemmas for us, but offers a wider range of opportunities. Being a critical practitioner is difficult in these circumstances because it involves accepting both constraints and freedom, in the context of everyday realities. While critical practice is emancipatory because it should transform lives and social structures and empower workers and clients, it takes place in the context of oppressive structures of racism, sexism and class, which have their impact at every turn, on the efforts of the practitioner. The dilemmas of practice are compounded by legal, organisational and practice requirements that further constrain the worker. Social work is more difficult because creative practice is possible in these circumstances, than if prohibitions existed against any such initiatives. It is part of the uniqueness of social work that such difficulties exist and that, paradoxically, they also present opportunities to resist oppression.

The pace of change in social work is such that this book, too, becomes part of social work's history, even in the year between its writing and publication. However, the notion of critical practice is like a template which can be brought to bear on any situation, enabling us as practitioners to remain optimistic and in control of our practice, in the face of dilemmas and contradictions. While acting, we learn to retain our grip on the dilemmas. We do not shy away from the fact that we cannot resolve them, but we can hold them while acting.

Moral hope for practitioners

The challenge for practitioners is to avoid being ground down by the constraints and becoming so undisciplined that they lose focus. The persistence of oppression in all its forms reinforces the need for an optimistic critical practice, which is not defensive or nihilistic in the face of prevailing social structures, but engages with them. Moral hope (Leonard, 1979), is a way of thinking that enables practitioners to do that by providing alternative ways of considering problems and possible solutions or ways forward. It provides a guarded optimism that is rooted in the belief that resistance and survival strategies can be utilised to formulate alternatives to what is currently available. Without moral hope, there is only burnout and despair. This book provides ammunition for this, in the form of ideas, knowledge and experiences. Carole Smith has written of the need not to abandon the traditional values of social work – the qualities of sensitivity, concern, reassurance, compassion and warmth – in striving to achieve the morally good (Smith, 2001). This offers a prospect beyond a view of practice advancing on the basis of evidence alone, where social work may be merely the tool of instrumental rationality.

The critical practitioner is at the opposite pole from the alienated worker. In this sense, critical practice is akin to a belief which has penetrated the ideological masking of oppressive features of the social situation. Critical practice engenders a sense of hope in the values that the worker seeks to establish and confirm, and in their application. Just as we have engaged in both dialectical and reflexive processes in writing and editing this book, so we invite you, the reader, as critical practitioner, to try using the chapters in this way and endorse this fundamentally critical approach to practice.

As editors, we are committed to exposing and challenging oppression, rather than presenting this book as a stock of already fixed knowledge. Both we and you, as critical practitioners in our own ways, are active participants in the development of this critical awareness, actions and practice. In pursuing this, we maintain the hope that social work practice may be transformed through its own actions to improve its helpfulness. In our first book together, *Social Work: Themes, Issues and Critical Debates* we focused on understanding. In this book, *Critical Practice in Social Work* , we have focused on skills in taking up our analysis and applying it to practice. It is an unending task, to develop that practice, so as to transform social work and its actions in positive ways.

Bibliography

Abbott, P. and Sapsford, R. (1987) *Community Care for Mentally Handicapped Children*, Milton Keynes: Open University Press.

Abel, E.M. (2000) 'Psychosocial Treatments for Battered Women: A Review of Empirical Research', *Research on Social Work Practice*, 10(1): 55–77.

Adair, A. (1986) *Effective Teambuilding*, London: Pan.

Adams, R. (1985) 'Truth and Love in IT', *British Journal of Social Work*, 15(4): 391–401.

Adams, R. (1991) *Protests by Pupils: Empowerment, Schooling and the State*, Basingstoke: Falmer.

Adams, R. (1998a) *Quality Social Work*, Basingstoke: Macmillan – now Palgrave Macmillan.

Adams, R. (1998b) 'Empowerment and Protest', in Lesnik, B. (ed.) *Challenging Discrimination in Social Work*, Aldershot: Ashgate.

Adams, R. (1998c) 'Social Work Processes', in Adams, R., Dominelli, L. and Payne, M. (eds) *Social Work: Themes, Issues and Critical Debates*, Basingstoke: Macmillan – now Palgrave Macmillan.

Adams, R. (2000) 'Quality Assurance in Social Work', in Davies, M. (ed.) *The Blackwell Encyclopedia of Social Work*, Oxford: Blackwell.

Adorno, T. and Horkheimer, M. (1979) *The Dialectic of Enlightenment*, London: Verso.

ADSS/SSI (1991) *Care in the Community Project: Care Management and Assessment*, London: SSI.

Ahmad, B. (1990) *Black Perspectives in Social Work*, Birmingham: Venture.

Alaszewski, H. and Alaszewski, A. (1998) 'Professional and Practice: Decision Making and Risk' in Alaszewski, A., Harrison, L. and Manthorpe, J. (eds) *Risk, Health and Welfare*, Buckingham: Open University Press.

Aldgate, J. and Tunstill, J. (1995) *Section 17 – The First 18 Months*, London: HMSO.

Allen, G. and Crow, G. (2000) *Families, Households and Society*, Basingstoke: Palgrave – now Palgrave Macmillan.

Allen, I., Hogg, D. and Peace, S. (1992) *Elderly People: Choice, Participation and Satisfaction*, London: Policy Studies Institute.

AMA (1993) *Local Authorities and Community Development: A Strategic Opportunity for the 1990s*, London: Association of Metropolitan Authorities.

Anderson, B. (1999) 'Youth Crime and the Politics of Prevention', in Goldson, B. (ed.) *Youth Justice: Contemporary Policy and Practice*, Aldershot: Ashgate.

Arnup, K. (1997) *Lesbian Parenting: Living with Pride and Prejudice*, Charlottetown: Gynergy Books.

Atkinson, D. and Warmsley, J. (1999) 'Using Autobiographical Approaches with People with Learning Difficulties', *Disability and Society*, 14(2): 203–16.

Audit Commission (1986) *Making a Reality of Community Care*, London: HMSO.

Audit Commission (1996) *Misspent Youth*, London: Audit Commission.

Bagguley, P. (1991) *From Protest to Acquiescence? Political Movements of the Unemployed*, Basingstoke: Macmillan – now Palgrave Macmillan.

Bailey, D. (ed.) (2000) *At the Core of Mental Health Practice: Key Issues for Practitioners, Managers and Mental Health Trainers*, Brighton: Pavilion.

Bailey, R. and Brake, M. (eds) (1975) *Radical Social Work and Practice*, London: Edward Arnold.

Baldwin, M. (2000) *Care Management and Community Care*, Aldershot: Ashgate.

Baldwin, S. and Lunt, N. (1996) *Charging Ahead; Local Authority Charging Policies for Community Care*, Bristol: Policy.

Balloch, S. and Jones, B. (1988) 'Social Services Responses to Poverty', in Becker, S. and MacPherson, S. (eds) *Public Issues, Private Pain*, London: Social Services Insight Books.

Balloch, S., Pahl, J. and J. McLean (1998) 'Working in Social Services: Job Satisfaction, Stress and Violence', *British Journal of Social Work*, **28**: 329–50.

Banks, S. (1995) *Ethics and Values in Social Work*, Basingstoke: Macmillan – now Palgrave Macmillan.

Banks, S. (1998) 'Professional Ethics in Social Work – What Future?', *British Journal of Social Work*, **28**: 213–31.

Banks, S. (2001) *Ethics and Values in Social Work*, 2nd edn, Basingstoke: Palgrave – now Palgrave Macmillan.

Bannister, A., Gordon, R. and Hendry, E. (eds) (1997) *Turning Points – a Resource Pack for Communicating with Children*, London: NSPCC.

Barber, J.G. (1991) *Beyond Casework*, London: Macmillan – now Palgrave Macmillan.

Barclay, P.M. (ed.) (1982) *Social Workers: Their Role and Tasks*, London: Bedford Square Press.

Barnes, C. (ed.) (1993) *Making our own Choices: Independent Living, Personal Assistance and Disabled People*, Belper, British Council of Organizations of Disabled People.

Barnes, M. and Prior, D. (2000) *Pivate Lives as Public Policy*, Birmingham: Venture.

Bateman, N. (2000) *Advocacy Skills for Health and Social Care Professionals*, London: Jessica Kingsley.

Batsleer, J. and Humphries, B. (eds) (2000) *Welfare, Exclusion and Political Agency*, London: Routledge.

Bauld, L., Chesterman, J., Davies, B., Judge, K. and Mangalore, R. (eds) (2000) *Caring for Older People: An Assessment of Community Care in the 1990s*, Aldershot: Ashgate.

Beardshaw, V. and Towell, D. (1990) *Assessment and Case Management : Implementation of 'Caring for People'*: Briefing Paper No. 10, London: King's Fund.

Bebbington, A. and Miles, J. (1989) 'The Background of Children who Enter Local Authority Care', *British Journal of Social Work*, 19(5).

Beck, U. (1992) *Risk Society: Towards a New Modernity*, London: Sage.

Beck, U. (1998) 'Politics of Risk Society' in Franklin J. (ed.) *The Politics of Risk Society*, Cambridge: Polity.

Becker, S. (1997) *Responding to Poverty: The Politics of Cash and Care*, Harlow: Longman.

Becker, S. and MacPherson, S. (1986) *Poor Clients: The Extent and Nature of Financial Poverty Amongst Consumers of Social Work Services*, Nottingham: Nottingham University Benefits Research Unit.

Beresford, P. (2000) 'What have Madness and Psychiatric Systems Survivors got to do with Disability and Disability Studies?', *Disability and Society*, 15(1): 167–72.

Berridge, D. (1997) *Foster Care: A Research Review*, London: Stationery Office.

Berridge, D. and Brodie, I. (1998) *Children's Homes Revisited*, London: Jessica Kingsley.

Biestek, F. (1961) *The Casework Relationship*, London: Allen & Unwin.

Biggs, S. and Weinstein, J. (1991) *Assessment, Case Management and Inspection in Community Care*, London: CCETSW.

Bilson, A. and Ross, S. (1999) *Social Work Management and Practice: Systems Principles*, 2nd edn, London: Jessica Kingsley.

Binney, V., Harkell, G. and Nixon, J. (1981) *Leaving Violent Men: A Study of Refuges and Housing for Abused Women*, Bristol: WAFE.

Bland, R. (1994) 'EPIC – A Scottish Case Management Experiment', in Titterton, M. (ed.) *Caring for People in the Community: The New Welfare*, London: Jessica Kingsley.

Blaug, R. (1995) 'Distortion of the Face to Face: Communicative Reason and Social Work Practice', *British Journal of Social Work*, **25**: 423–39.

Blom-Cooper, L. (1986) *A Child in Trust: The Report of the Panel of Inquiry into the Circumstances Surrounding the Death of Jasmine Beckford*, London: Borough of Brent.

Blumson, M. (1999) 'Better Provision for Offenders', in Violence Against Women Conference Report. Shrigley Hall Hotel, 24–25 November 1999, Liverpool: Home Office, Special Conferences Unit.

Blyth, E. (1998) 'Donor Assisted Conception and Donor Offspring Rights to Genetic Origins Information', *The International Journal of Children's Rights*, 6: 237–53.

BODY (1995) *The Gift of Life* (2), Booklet available from the British Organ Donor Society, Balsham, Cambridgeshire CB1 6DL. 01223 893636.

Bogdan, R. and Taylor, S. (1982) *Inside Out: The Social Meaning of Mental Retardation*, Toronto: University of Toronto Press.

Bonnemaison, H. (1983) Face à la Délinquance: Prévention, Répression, Solidarité: Rapport au Prime Ministre de la Commission des Maines sur la Sécurité, Paris, La Documentation Française.

Booth, T. (1993) 'Obstacles to User-centred Services', in Johnson, J. and Slater, R. (eds) *Ageing and Later Life*, London: Sage.

Booth, T. (2000) 'Parents with Learning Difficulties, Child Protection and the Courts', *Representing Children*, **13**(3): 175–88.

Booth, T. and Booth, W. (1995) 'For Better for Worse: Professionals, Practice and Parents with Learning Difficulties', in Philpott, T. and Ward, L. (eds) *Values and Visions, Changing Ideas in Services for People with Learning Difficulties*, Oxford: Butterworth Heinemann.

Booth, T. and Booth, W. (1998) *Growing Up with Parents who have Learning Difficulties*, London: Routledge.

Bornat, J. (ed.) (1999) *Biographical Interviews: The Link Between Research and Practice*, London: Centre for Policy on Ageing.

Bornat, J., Pereira, C., Pilgrim, D. and Williams, F. (1993) *Community Care*, Basingstoke: Macmillan – now Palgrave Macmillan.

Boswell, G. (1995) *Violent Victims: The Prevalence of Abuse and Loss in the Lives of Section 53 Offenders*, London: The Prince's Trust and the Royal Jubilee Trust.

Bottoms, A. (1995) *Intensive Community Supervision for Young Offenders: Outcomes, Process and Cost*, Cambridge: Institute of Criminology Publications.

Bottoms, A., Brown, P., McWilliams, B., McWilliams, W., Nellis, M. and Pratt, J. (1980) *Intermediate Treatment and Juvenile Justice*, London: HMSO.

Bowl, R. (1986) 'Social Work with Old People', in Phillipson, C. and Walker, P. (eds) *Ageing and Social Policy: A Critical Assessment*, Aldershot: Gower.

Bowlby, J. (1969) *Attachment and Loss*, vol. I: *Attachment*, London: Hogarth.

Bowlby, J. (1973) *Attachment and Loss*, vol. II: *Separation: Anxiety and Anger*, London: Hogarth.

Bowlby, J. (1980) *Attachment and Loss*, vol. III: *Loss, Sadness and Depression*, London: Hogarth.

Boyden, J. (1997) 'Childhood and the Policy Makers: A Comparative Perspective on the Globalization of Childhood', in James, A. and Prout, A. (eds) *Constructing and Reconstructing Childhood*, London: Falmer.

Boylen, J. and Wyllie, J. (1999) 'Advocacy and Child Protection', in Parton, N. and Wattam, C. (eds) *Child Sexual Abuse: Responding to the Experiences of Children*, Chichester: Wiley.

Bracken, P. and Thomas, P. (2000) 'Ethics and Self Injury', *Open Mind*, May/June.

Bradley, G. and Manthorpe, J. (1997) *Dilemmas of Financial Assessment: A Practitioner's Guide*, Birmingham: Venture.

Bradley, G., Penhale, B., Manthorpe, J., Parkin, A., Parry, N. and Gore, J. (2000) *Ethical Dilemmas and Administrative Justice: Perceptions of Social and Legal Professionals Towards Charging for Residential and Nursing Home Care*, Hull: University of Hull.

Bradley, R. (1987) 'Workload Management in an Area Team', in Glastonbury, B., Bradley, R. and Orme, J. (eds) *Managing People in the Personal Social Services*, Chichester: Wiley.

Braye, S. and Varley, M. (1992) 'Developing a Mental Health Perspective in Social Work Practice', *Social Work Education*, 11(2): 41–59.

Brearley, C.P. (1982) *Risk and Social Work*, London: Routledge & Kegan Paul.

Brechin, A. (2000) 'Introducing Critical Practice', in Brechin, A., Brown, H. and Eby, M. (eds) *Critical Practice in Health and Social Care*, London: Open University/ Sage.

Brechin, A., Brown, H. and Eby, M.A. (eds) (2000) *Critical Practice in Health and Social Care*, London: Sage.

Bridges, W.R. (1995) *Managing Transitions: Making the Most of Change*, London: Nicholas Brealey.

British Agencies for Adoption and Fostering (1991) Form F: Information on Prospective Substitute Parent(s), London: British Agencies for Adoption and Fostering.

British Association of Social Workers (1996) *A Code of Ethics for Social Work*, Birmingham: BASW.

Brockbank, A. and McGill, I. (1998) *Facilitating Reflective Learning in Higher Education*, Buckingham: SRHE and Open University Press.

Brown, A. (1992) *Groupwork*, 3rd edn, Aldershot: Ashgate.

Brown, A. and Bourne, I. (1996) *The Social Work Supervisor*, Buckingham: Open University Press.

Brown, H. (2000) 'Challenges from Service Users', in Brechin, A., Brown, H. and Eby, M.A. (eds) *Critical Practice in Health and Social Care,* London: Open University/Sage.

Brown, H. and Smith, H. (eds) (1992) *Normalisation: A Reader for the Nineties,* London: Routledge.

Brown, P., Hadley, R. and White, K.J. (1982) 'A Case for Neighbourhood-based Social Work and Social Services', in Barclay, P.M. (ed.) *Social Workers: Their Role and Tasks,* London: Bedford Square Press.

Brownlee, I. (1998) 'New Labour – New Penology? Punitive Rhetoric and the Limits of Managerialism in Criminal Justice Policy', *Journal of Law and Society,* **25**(3): 313–35.

Buckle, J. (1981) *Intake Teams,* London: Tavistock.

Buckman, R. (1993) *How to Break Bad News – A Guide for Health Care Professionals,* London: Macmillan – now Palgrave Macmillan.

Buckman, R. (1998) 'Communication in Palliative Care: a Practical Guide', in Doyle, D., Hanks, G. and MacDonald, N. (eds) *Oxford Textbook of Palliative Medicine,* 2nd edn, Oxford: Oxford University Press.

Bullock, R., Gooch, D. and Little, L. (1998) *Children Going Home: The Re-unification of Families,* Aldershot: Ashgate.

Bullock, R., Little, M. and Millham, S. (1993) *Going Home: The Return of Children Separated from their Families,* Aldershot: Dartmouth.

Burfoot, A. (1990) 'The Normalisation of a New Reproductive Technology', in McNeil, M., Varcoe, I. and Yearley, S. (eds) *The New Reproductive Technologies,* London: Macmillan – now Palgrave Macmillan.

Burton, M. and Kellaway, M. (1998) *Developing and Managing High Quality Services for People with Learning Disabilities,* Aldershot: Ashgate.

Burton, S., Regan, L. and Kelly, L. (1998) *Supporting Women and Challenging Men: Lessons from the Domestic Violence Intervention Project,* Bristol: Policy.

Butler, S. (1994) '"All I've Got in My Purse is Mothballs!" The Social Action Women's Group', *Groupwork,* **7**(2): 163–79.

Butler, S. and Wintram, C. (1991) *Feminist Groupwork,* London: Sage.

Butler-Sloss, L. (1988) *Report of the Inquiry into Child Abuse in Cleveland,* London: HMSO.

Butt, J. and Box, C. (1998) *Family Centred. A Study of the Use of Family Centres by Black Families,* London: REU.

Buttny, R. (1993) *Social Accountability in Communication,* London: Sage.

Byatt, A.S. (2000) *The Biographer's Tale,* London: Chatto & Windus.

Bytheway, W. (2000) 'Old Age', in Davies, M. (ed.) *The Blackwell Encyclopaedia of Social Work,* Oxford: Blackwell.

Cabinet Office (2000) *Adoption – Prime Minister's Review,* a Performance and Innovation Unit Report, London: Stationery Office.

Cade, B. (1992) 'I Am An Unashamed Expert', *Context,* **11**: 30.

Calder, M. (1995) 'Child Protection: Balancing Paternalism and Partnership', *British Journal of Social Work,* **25**: 749–66.

Calhoun, C. (1996) 'Social Theory and the Public Sphere' in Turner, B. (ed.) *The Blackwell Companion to Social Theory,* Oxford: Blackwell.

Cambridge, P. (1999) 'Building Care Management Competence in Services for People with Learning Disabilities', *British Journal of Social Work,* **29**(3): 393–415.

Campbell, J.C. (ed.) (1995) *Assessing Dangerousness: Violence by Sex Offenders,* London: Sage.

Campbell, J. and Pinkerton, J. (1997) 'Embracing Change as Opportunity: Reflections on Social Work from a Northern Ireland Perspective', in Lesnik, B. (ed.) *Change in Social Work*, Aldershot: Ashgate.

Campbell, T. (1988) *Justice*, Basingstoke: Macmillan – now Palgrave Macmillan.

Carling, P. (1996) *Return to the Community: Building Support Systems for People with Psychiatric Disabilities*, New York: Guilford.

Carroll, M. and Holloway, E. (eds) (1999) *Counselling Supervision in Context*, London: Sage.

Carson, D. (ed.) (1990) *Risk-taking in Mental Disorder: Analyses, Policies and Practical Strategies*, Chichester: S.L.E. Publications.

Carson, D. (1995) 'From Risk to Risk Management', in Braggins, J. and Martin, C. (eds) *Managing Risk: Achieving the Possible*, London: Institute for the Study and Treatment of Delinquency.

Carson, D. (1996) 'Risking Legal Repercussions', in Kemshall, H. and Pritchard, J. (eds) *Good Practice in Risk Assessment and Risk Management*, London: Jessica Kingsley.

Carter, P., Jeffs, T. and Smith, M.K. (eds) (1995) *Social Working*, Basingstoke: Macmillan – now Palgrave Macmillan.

Castel, R. (1991) 'From Dangerousness to Risk', in Burell, G., Gordon, C. and Miller, P. (eds) *The Foucault Effect: Studies in Governmentality*, Hemel Hempstead: Harvester Wheatsheaf.

Cedersund, E. (1999) 'Using Narratives in Social Work Interaction', in Jokinen, A., Juhila, K. and Poso, T. (eds) *Constructing Social Work Practices*, Aldershot: Ashgate.

Central Council for Education and Training in Social Work (1995) *Assuring Quality in the Diploma in Social Work – 1: Rules and Requirements for the DipSW*, London: CCETSW.

Central Council for Education and Training in Social Work (2000) *Assuring Quality for Mental Health Social Work: Requirements for the Training of Approved Social Workers in England, Wales and Northern Ireland and of Mental Health Officers in Scotland*, London: CCETSW.

Chadwick, R. (ed.) (1994) *Ethics and the Professions*, Aldershot: Avebury.

Challis, D. (1989) 'Case Management: Problems and Possibilities', PSSRU Discussion Paper 669, University of Kent.

Challis, D. (1994a) *Implementing Caring for People: Care Management: Factors Influencing its Development in the Implementation of Community Care*, London: DOH.

Challis, D. (1994b) 'Case Management: A Review of UK Developments and Issues', in Titterton, M. (ed.) *Caring for People in the Community: The New Welfare*, London: Jessica Kingsley.

Challis, D. (1994c) 'Care Management', in Malin, N. (ed.) *Implementing Community Care*, Buckingham: Open University Press.

Challis, D., Darton, R. and Stewart, K. (1998) 'Linking Community Care and Health Care: A New Role for Secondary Health Care Services', in Challis, D., Darton, R. and Stewart, K. (eds) *Community Care, Secondary Health Care and Care Management*, Aldershot: Ashgate.

Challis, D., Darton, R., Hughes, J., Huxley, P. and Stewart, K. (1998) 'Emerging Models of Care Management for Older People and those with Mental Health Problems in the United Kingdom', *Journal of Case Management*, 7(4): 153–60.

Chaput-Waksler, F. (1991) *Studying the Social Worlds of Children*, London: Falmer.

Cheetham, J., Fuller, R., McIvor, G. and Petch, A. (1992) *Evaluating Social Work Effectiveness*, Buckingham: Open University Press.

Chetwynd, M. and Ritchie, J. (1996) *The Cost of Care: The Impact of Charging Policy on the Lives of Disabled People*, York: Joseph Rowntree Foundation.

Children Act 1989, London: HMSO.

Children's Rights Development Unit (CRDU) (1994) *UK Agenda for Children*, London: CRDU.

Choi, N., Kulick, D. and Mayer, J. (1999) 'Financial Exploitation of Elders: Analysis of Risk Factors Based on County Adult Protective Services Data', *Journal of Elder Abuse and Neglect,* 10(3/4): 39–62.

Clark, C. (1996) 'Innovation, Tradition and Compromise: Ethical Issues in Community Care Practice', in Adams, R. (ed.) *Crisis in the Human Services: National and International Issues.* Selected Conference Papers, Kingston upon Hull: University of Lincolnshire and Humberside.

Clark, C. with Asquith, S. (1985) *Social Work and Social Philosophy*, London: Routledge & Kegan Paul.

Clark, C.L. (2000) *Social Work Ethics: Politics, Principles and Practice*, Basingstoke: Macmillan – now Palgrave Macmillan.

Clarke, J., Gewirtz, S. and McLaughlin, E. (eds) (2000) *New Managerialism, New Welfare?*, London: Sage.

Cleaver, H. and Freeman, P. (1995) *Parental Perspectives in Cases of Suspected Child Abuse*, London: HMSO.

Clifford, D. (1998) *Social Assessment Theory and Practice*, Aldershot: Ashgate.

Coates, R. (1981) 'Community-based Services for Juvenile Delinquents: Concept and Implications for Practice', *Journal of Social Issues,* 37(3): 87–101.

Cochrane, A. (1993) 'Challenges from the Centre', in Clarke, J. (ed.) *A Crisis in Care? Challenges to Social Work*, London: Sage/Open University Press.

Cohen, S. (1975) 'It's All Right For You to Talk: Political and Sociological Manifestos for Social Work Action', in Bailey, R. and Brake, M. (eds) *Radical Social Work and Practice*, London: Edward Arnold.

Coleman, R. and Smith, M. (1997) *Working with Voices: From Victim to Victor*, Gloucester: Handsall.

Coles, B. (1995) *Youth and Social Policy*, London: UCL Press.

Commission on Social Justice (1994) *Social Justice: Strategies for National Renewal*, London: Vintage.

Compton, B. and Galaway, B. (1975) *Social Work Processes*, Homewood, IL: Dorsey Press.

Connell, R.W. (1995) *Gender and Power*, Cambridge: Polity.

Connolly, M. and McKenzie, M. (1999) *Effective Participatory Practice: Family Group Conferences in Child Protection*, New York: Aldine De Gruyter.

Cook, A. and Kirk, G. (1983) *Greenham Women Everywhere: Dreams, Ideas and Action from the Women's Peace Movement.* London: Pluto.

Cooper, A. and Hetherington, R. (1999) 'Negotiation', in Parton, N. and Wattam, C. (eds) *Child Sexual Abuse: Responding to the Experiences of Children*, Chichester: Wiley.

Coote, A. (ed.) (1992) *The Welfare of Citizens: Developing New Social Rights*, London: Rivers Oram.

Corby, B. (2000) *Child Abuse: Towards a Knowledge Base*, 2nd edn, Buckingham: Open University Press.

Cornell, J. (1984) *Hard Earned Lives.* London: Tavistock.

Corr, C. (1992) 'A Task-based Approach to Coping with Dying', *Omega,* 24(2): 81–94.

Coulshed, V. and Mullender, A. (2001) *Management in Social Work*, Basingstoke: Palgrave – now Palgrave Macmillan.

Cowen, H. (1999) *Community Care, Ideology and Social Policy*, London: Prentice Hall.

Craig, G. (1989) 'Community Work and the State', *Community Development Journal*, **24**(1): 3–18.

Craig, G. (1998) 'Race, Poverty and Social Security', in Ditch, J. (ed.) *Social Security in the United Kingdom: Policies and Current Issues*, Routledge: London.

Craig, G. (2000) 'Poverty in Research Matters', *Research Matters*, London: Community Care, Reed Business Information, April: 62–4.

Croft, S. and Beresford, P. (2000) 'Empowerment', in Davies, M. (ed.) *The Blackwell Encyclopaedia of Social Work*, Oxford: Blackwell.

Crow, C. (1987) 'Women Want It: In Vitro Fertilisations and Women's Motivations for Participation', in Spallone, P. and Steinberg, D.L. (eds) *Made to Order: The Myth of Reproductive and Genetic Progress*, Oxford: Pergamon.

Crow, C. (1990) 'Whose Mind over Whose Matter? Women, In Vitro Fertilisation and the Development of Scientific Knowledge' in McNeil, M., Varcoe, I. and Yearley, S. (eds) *The New Reproductive Technologies*, London: Macmillan – now Palgrave Macmillan.

Cupitt, S. (1997) 'Who Sets the Agenda for Empowerment?', *Breakthrough*, 1(2): 15–28.

Currer, C. (2001) *Responding to Grief: Dying, Bereavement and Social Care*, London: Palgrave – now Palgrave Macmillan.

Dalrymple, J. and Burke, B. (1995) *Anti-oppressive Practice, Social Care and the Law*, Buckingham: Open University Press.

Dalrymple, J. and Hough, P. (eds) (1995) *Having a Voice: An Exploration of Children's Rights and Advocacy*, Birmingham: Venture.

Damer, S. (1980) 'State, Class and Housing: Glasgow 1875–1919' in Melling, J. (ed.) *Housing, Social Policy and the State*, London: Croom Helm.

Daniel, B., Wassell, S. and Gilligan, R. (1999) *Child Development for Child Care and Protection Workers*, London: Jessica Kingsley.

Dant, T., Carley, M., Gearing, B. and Johnson, M. (1989) *Co-ordinating Care: The Final Report of the Care for Elderly People at Home (CEPH) Project, Gloucester*, for the Department of Health and Social Welfare, The Open University, London: Policy Studies Institute.

Davies, B. and Fernandez, J. with Nomer, B. (2000) *Equity and Efficiency in Community Care*, Aldershot: Ashgate.

Davies, B. and Knapp, M. (1988) 'The Production of Welfare Approach: Some New PSSRU Arguments and Results', *British Journal of Social Work*, 18, Supplement.

Davies, C. (1995) *Gender and the Professional Predicament in Nursing*, Buckingham: Open University Press.

Davies, R. (1995) I Wanted a Pink Coffin, unpublished Report of the HIV/AIDS User Consultation Exercise for Norfolk Social Services, produced by Norfolk County Council Social Services Department.

Davis, A. (1996) 'Risk Work and Mental Health', in Kemshall, H. and Pritchard, J. (eds) *Good Practice in Risk Assessment and Risk Management* 1, London: Jessica Kingsley.

Dawson, C. (2000) *Independent Successes: Implementing Direct Payments*, York: York Publishing Services.

Day, P. (1987) *Sociology in Social Work Practice*, London: Macmillan – now Palgrave Macmillan.

De Shazer, S. (1991) *Putting Difference to Work*, New York: Norton.

Department of Health (1989a) *Caring for People: Community Care in the Next Decade and Beyond*, Cm 849, London: HMSO.

Department of Health (1989b) *Caring for Patients*, London: HMSO.

Department of Health (1989c) *An Introduction to the Children Act 1989*, London: HMSO.

Department of Health (1989d) *The Care of Children: Principles and Practice in Regulations and Guidance*, London: HMSO.

Department of Health (1990) *Caring for People: Draft Guidance: CC18 Assessment and Case Management*, London: HMSO.

Department of Health (1991) *Patterns and Outcomes in Child Placement: Messages from Current Research and Their Implications*, London: HMSO.

Department of Health (1994a) *Introduction of Supervision Registers for Mentally Ill People with a Mental Illness Referred to Specialist Psychiatric Services*, HSG(94)5, London: HMSO.

Department of Health (1994b) *Guidance on the Discharge of Mentally Disordered People and their Continuing Care in the Community*, HSG(94)27, London: HMSO.

Department of Health (1995a) *Child Protection: Messages from Research*, London: HMSO.

Department of Health (1995b) *The Care Programme Approach for People with a Mental Illness Referred to the Specialist Psychiatric Services*, HC90(23)/LASSL(90)II, London: HSMO.

Department of Health (1995c) *Looking After Children: Assessment and Action Schedules*, London: HMSO.

Department of Health (1995d) *Looking After Children, Essential Information*, Parts 1 and 2, London: HMSO.

Department of Health (1995e) *The Mental Health (Patients in the Community) Act*, London: HMSO.

Department of Health (1995f) *Looking After Children: Good Parenting, Good Outcomes.* Training Guide, London: HMSO.

Department of Health (1998a) *Modernising Social Services*, Cm 4169, London: Stationery Office.

Department of Health (1998b) *Quality Protects: Framework for Action and Objectives for Social Services for Children*, London: Department of Health.

Department of Health (1999a) *The Children Act Report 1995–1999*, London: HMSO.

Department of Health (1999b) *Adoption Now: Messages from Research*, Chichester: Wiley.

Department of Health (1999c) *Modernising Mental Health Services: Safe, Sound and Supportive*, London: HSMO.

Department of Health (1999d) *The Quality Protects Programme: Transforming Children's Services 2000/2001*, HS(99)237, LAC(99)33 and DfEE Circular No. 18/99, London: Department of Health.

Department of Health (1999e) *Our Healthier Nation, National Service Frameworks: Mental Health: Modern Standards and Service Models.* London: Department of Health.

Department of Health (2000a) *A Quality Strategy for Social Care*, London: Department of Health.

Department of Health (2000b) *Reforming the Mental Health Act: Part 1 The New Legal Framework*, Cm 5016 – I, London: Stationery Office.

Department of Health (2000c) *The NHS Plan: A Plan for Investment and a Plan for Reform*, Cm 4818 – I, London: Stationery Office.

Department of Health/Department of Education and Employment/Home Office (2000) *Framework for the Assessment of Children in Need and Their Families*, London: Stationery Office.

Department of Health/Home Office/Department for Education and Employment/ National Assembly of Wales (1999) *Working Together to Safeguard Children*, London: DoH.

Department of Health/Social Services Inspectorate (1991a) *Caring for People, Practice Guidance: Purchase of Services*, London: HMSO.

Department of Health/Social Services Inspectorate (1991b) *Care Management and Assessment: Managers' Guide*, London: HMSO.

Department of Health/Social Services Inspectorate (1991c) *Care Management and Assessment: Practitioners' Guide*, London: HMSO.

Department of Health/Social Services Inspectorate (1995) *The Challenge of Partnership in Child Protection: Practice Guide*, London: HMSO.

Department of Health/Welsh Office (1999) *Mental Health Act 1983; Code of Practice*, London: Stationery Office.

Dholakia, N. (1998) 'Ethnic Minorities and the Criminal Justice System. Exclusion by Choice or Design?', in Barry, M. and Hallett, C. (eds) *Social Exclusion and Social Work: Issues of Theory, Policy and Practice*, Lyme Regis: Russell House Publishing.

Dingwell, R. (1989) 'Some Problems about Predicting Child Abuse and Neglect', in Stevenson, O. (ed.) *Child Abuse: Public Policy and Professional Practice*, Hemel Hempstead: Harvester Wheatsheaf.

Dobash, R.E. and Dobash, R.P. (1992) *Women, Violence and Social Change*, London: Routledge.

Dobash, R.E., Dobash, R.P. and Cavanagh, K. (1985) 'The Contact Between Battered Women and Social and Medical Agencies', in Pahl, J. (ed.) *Private Violence and Public Policy: The Needs of Battered Women and the Response of the Public Services*, London: Routledge & Kegan Paul.

Dobash, R.E., Dobash, R.P., Cavanagh, K. and Lewis, R. (2000) *Changing Violent Men*, London: Sage.

Dominelli, L. (1986) 'The Power of the Powerless: Prostitution and the Reinforcement of Submissive Femininity', *Sociological Review*, Spring, pp. 65–92.

Dominelli, L. (1988) 'Thatcher's Attack on Social Security: Restructuring Forms of Social Control in the British Social Security System by Challenging "Welfare Dependency" in Claimants', *Critical Social Policy*, (23): 46–61.

Dominelli, L. (1990) *Women and Community Action*, Birmingham: Venture.

Dominelli, L. (1996) 'Deprofessionalising Social Work: Competencies, Postmodernism and Equal Opportunities', *British Journal of Social Work*, **26**: 153–75.

Dominelli, L. (2000) 'Empowerment: Help or Hindrance in Professional Relation-ships?', in Ford, D. and Stepney, P. (eds) *Social Work Models, Methods and Theories: A Framework for Practice*, Lyme Regis: Russell House Publishing.

Dominelli, L. and Gollins, T. (1997) 'Men, Power and Caring Relationships', *Sociological Review*, **45**(3): 396–415.

Dominelli, L. and McLeod, E. (1989) *Feminist Social Work*, London: Macmillan – now Palgrave Macmillan.

Dominy, N. and Radford, L. (1996) *Domestic Violence in Surrey: Developing an Effective Inter-agency Response*, Guildford: Surrey County.

Donnelly, A. (1986) *Feminist Social Work with a Women's Group*, Norwich: University of East Anglia, Social Work Monograph 41.

Douglas, M. (1992) *Risk and Blame: Essays in Cultural Theory*, London: Routledge.

Dowie, J. (1999) 'Communication for Better Decisions: Not about "Risk"', *Health, Risk and Society*, **1**(1): 41–53.

Drakeford, M. (2000) *Privatisation and Social Policy*, Harlow: Longman.

Durkheim, E. (1972) (ed. Giddens, A.) *Selected Writings*, Cambridge: Cambridge University Press.

Eekelaar, J. (1986) 'The Emergence of Children's Rights', *Oxford Journal of Legal Studies*, **6**(2): 177–82.

Egan, G. (1998) *The Skilled Helper*, 6th edn, Pacific Grove, CA: Brooks/Cole.

Ehrenreich, B. and English, D. (1979) *Witches, Midwives and Nurses: A History of Women Healers*, London: Writers and Readers Publishing Co-operative.

England, H. (1986) *Social Work as Art: Making Sense for Good Practice*, London: Allen & Unwin.

Estroff, S. (1993) 'Community Mental Health Services: Extinct, Endangered or Evolving?', in Perkins, R. and Repper, J. (eds) *Dilemmas in Community Mental Health Practice: Choice or Control*, Oxford: Radcliffe Medical Press.

Evans, D. (1999) *Practice Learning in the Caring Professions*, Aldershot: Ashgate.

Everitt, A. and Hardiker, P. (1996) *Evaluating for Good Practice*, Basingstoke: Macmillan – now Palgrave Macmillan.

Evers, A., Haverinen, R., Leichsenring, K. and Wistow, G. (eds) (1997) *Developing Quality in Personal Social Services: Concepts, Cases and Comments*, Aldershot: Ashgate.

Ewald, F. (1991) 'Insurance and Risk', in Burell, G., Gordon, C. and Miller, P. (eds) *The Foucault Effect: Studies in Governmentality*, Hemel Hempstead: Harvester Wheatsheaf.

Fahlberg, V.I. (1991) *A Child's Journey Through Placement*, London: British Agencies for Adoption and Fostering.

Fairbairn, G. (1985) 'Responsibility in Social Work' in Watson, D. (ed.) *A Code of Ethics for Social Work: The Second Step*, London: Routledge & Kegan Paul.

Fairbairns, Z. (1998) *Benefits*, London: Five Leaves Publications.

Featherstone, B., Fook, J. and Rossiter, A. (eds) *Practice Research in Social Work*, London: Routledge.

Feeley, S. and Simon, J. (1992) 'The New Penology: Notes on the Emerging Strategy of Corrections and its Implications', *Criminology*, **30**(4): 452–74.

Field, D. (1996) 'Awareness of Modern Dying', *Mortality*, **1**(3): 255–65.

Finch. J. with Mary, Cynthia, Linda, Colleen, Barbara and Jan from Hackney Greenham Groups (1986) 'Socialist Feminists and Greenham', *Feminist Review*, **23**: 93–100.

Finer, C. and Nellis, M. (eds) (1998) *Crime and Social Exclusion*, Oxford: Blackwell.

Finkelstein, V. (1991) 'Disability: An Administrative Challenge? (The Health and Welfare Heritage)', in Oliver, M. (ed.) *Social Work, Disabled People and Disabling Environments*, London: Jessica Kingsley.

Fisher, M. (1991) 'Defining the Practice Content of Care Management', *Social Work and Social Sciences Review*, **2**(3): 204–30.

Fletcher, A. (1999) *Genes are Us? Genetics and Disability*. RADAR Survey, London: RADAR.

Fletcher, K. (1998) *Negotiation for Health and Social Services Professionals*, London: Jessica Kingsley.

Flynn, N. (1997) *Public Sector Management*, 3rd edn, London: Harvester Wheatsheaf.

Fook, J. (1999) 'Critical Reflectivity in Education and Practice', in Pease, B. and Fook, J. (eds) *Transforming Social Work Practice: Postmodern Critical Perspectives*, London: Routledge.

Fook, J. (2000) 'Deconstructing and Reconstructing Professional Expertise', in Fawcett, B., Featherstone, B., Fook, J. and Rossiter, A. (eds) *Postmodern Feminist Perspectives*, London: Routledge.

Foster, A. (1998) 'Thinking about Risk', in Foster, A. and Roberts, V.Z. (eds) *Managing Mental Health in the Community: Chaos and Containment*, London: Routledge.

Foster, P. and Wilding, P. (2000) 'Whither Welfare Professionalism?', *Social Policy and Administration*, **34**(2): 143–59.

Foucault, M. (1972) *Discipline and Punish*, Harmondsworth: Penguin.

Franklin, J. (1989) 'Terminal Care Teams', in Philpot, T. (ed.) *Last Things; Social Work with the Dying and Bereaved*, Wallington: Reed Business Publishing/Community Care.

Freeman, M.D.A. (1979) *Violence in the Home*, Farnborough: Saxon House.

Froggatt, A. (1990) *Family Work and Elderly People*, Basingstoke: Macmillan – now Palgrave Macmillan.

Frost, N. and Ryden, N. (2001) *An Evaluation of the South Lakeland Family Support Service*, Barkingside: Barnardo's.

Fuller, R. (1996) 'Evaluating Social Work Effectiveness: A Pragmatic Approach', in Alderson, P., Brill, S., Chalmers, I. et al. (eds) *What Works? Effective Social Interventions in Child Welfare*, Barkingside: Barnardo's.

Garrett, P.M. (1999) 'Mapping Child-care Social Work in the Final Years of the Twentieth Century: A Critical Response to the "Looking After Children" System', *British Journal of Social Work*, **29**: 27–47.

George, M. (2000) 'Breaking the Cycle: The Risk Factor', *Community Care*, August: 24–30.

George, R. and Sykes, J. (1997) 'Beyond Cancer?', in Clark, D., Hockey, J. and Ahmedzai, S. (eds) *New Themes in Palliative Care*, Buckingham: Open University Press.

George, V. and Wilding, P. (1994) *Welfare and Ideology*, Hemel Hempstead: Harvester Wheatsheaf.

Gergen, K. (1999) *An Invitation to Social Construction*, London: Sage.

Gerth, H.H. and Mills, C.W. (eds) (1948) *From Max Weber*, London: Routledge & Kegan Paul.

Giddens, A. (1987) *Social Theory and Modern Sociology*, Oxford: Blackwell.

Giddens, A. (1998a) 'Risk Society: the Context of British Politics', in Franklin, J. (ed.) *The Politics of Risk Society*, Cambridge: Polity.

Giddens, A. (1998b) *The Third Way: The Renewal of Social Democracy*, Cambridge: Polity.

Gilchrist, A. (1994) 'Community Worker – Roles, Skills and Responsibilities' in Harris, V. (ed.) *Community Work Skills Manual*, Newcastle upon Tyne: Association of Community Workers.

Glastonbury, B., Bradley, R. and Orme, J. (eds) (1987) *Managing People in the Personal Social Services*, Chichester: Wiley.

Glennerster, H. (1999) *Paying for Welfare: Towards 2000*, 3rd edn, Hemel Hempstead: Prentice Hall/Harvester Wheatsheaf.

Goldson, B. (1999) *Youth Justice: Contemporary Policy and Practice*, Aldershot: Ashgate.

Goldson, B. (2000) *The New Youth Justice*, Lyme Regis: Russell House Publishing.

Gondolf, E. (1998) 'Do Batterer Programs Work? A 15-month Follow-up of a Multisite Evaluation', *Domestic Violence Report*, 3, June/July, pp. 64–5 and 78–9.

Goodey, C.F. (1992) 'Mental Disabilities and Human Values in Plato's Late Dialogues', *Archiv Für Geschichte Der Philosophie*, **74**: 26–42.

Gostick, C., Davies, B., Lawson, R. and Salter, C. (1997) *From Vision to Reality in Community Care*, Aldershot: Arena.

Grant, L. (2000) 'Disabled People, Poverty and Debt: Identity, Strategy and Policy', in Bradshaw, J. and Sainsbury, R. (eds) *Experiencing Poverty*, Aldershot: Ashgate.

Greenland, C. (1987) *Preventing CAN Deaths: An International Study of Deaths due to Child Abuse and Neglect*, London: Tavistock.

Griffiths, R. (1988) *Community Care: Agenda for Action*, London: HMSO.

Habermas, J. (1984) *The Theory of Communicative Action:* vol. 1 *Reason and the Rationalisation of Society*, Cambridge: Polity.

Habermas, J. (1987) *The Theory of Communicative Action:* vol. 2 *The Critique of Functionalist Reason*, Cambridge: Polity.

Hadley, R. and Young, K. (1990) *Creating a Responsive Public Service*, London: Harvester Wheatsheaf.

Haffenden, S. (1991) *Getting it Right for Carers: Setting Up Services for Carers: A Guide for Practitioners*, London: HMSO.

Hague, G., Mullender, A., Aris, R. and Dear, W. (2001) *Abused Women's Perspectives: Responsiveness and Accountability of Domestic Violence and Inter-Agency Initiatives*. End of Award Report to the ESRC, Bristol: University of Bristol, School for Policy Studies.

Haines, K. (1996) *Understanding Modern Juvenile Justice*, Aldershot: Avebury.

Haines, K. (1997) 'Young Offenders and Family Support Services: A European Perspective', *International Journal of Child and Family Welfare*, 2(1): 61–73.

Haines, K. (2000) 'Referral Orders and the New Youth Justice', in Goldson, B. (ed.) *The New Youth Justice*, Lyme Regis: Russell House Publishing.

Haines, K. and Drakeford, M. (1998) *Young People and Youth Justice*, Basingstoke: Macmillan – now Palgrave Macmillan.

Haines, K., Jones, R. and Isles, E. (1999) Promoting Positive Behaviour in Schools, Report submitted to the Wales Office of Research and Development.

Hall, D. and Hall, I. (1996) *Practical Social Research: Project Work in the Community*, Basingstoke: Macmillan – now Palgrave Macmillan.

Hanmer, J. (1996) 'Women and Violence: Commonalities and Diversities', in Fawcett, B., Featherstone, B., Hearn, J. and Toft, C. (eds) *Violence and Gender Relations: Theories and Interventions*, London: Sage.

Hanmer, J. and Statham, D. (1988) *Women and Social Work: Towards a Woman-centred Practice*, London: Macmillan – now Palgrave Macmillan.

Hannington, W. (1967) *Never on Our Knees*, London: Lawrence & Wishart.

Hannington, W. (1977) *Unemployed Struggles: 1919–1936*, London: Lawrence & Wishart.

Harder, M. and Pringle, K. (eds) (1997) *Protecting Children in Europe Towards a New Millennium*, Denmark: Aalborg University Press.

Hardiker, P. and Barker, M. (1988) 'A Window on Child Care, Poverty and Social Work', in Becker, S. and MacPherson, S. (eds) *Public Issues, Private Pain*, London: Social Services Insight Books.

Hardiker, P. and Barker, M. (1999) 'Early Steps in Implementing the New Community Care: The Role of Social Work Practice', *Health and Social Care in the Community*, 7(6): 417–26.

Harford, B. and Hopkins, S. (eds) (1984) *Greenham Common: Women and the Wire*, London: Women's Press.

Harris, N. (1987) 'Defensive Social Work', *British Journal of Social Work*, 17: 61–9.

Harris, R. (1995) 'Child Protection, Care and Welfare', in Wilson, K. and James, A. (eds) *The Child Protection Handbook*, London: Baillière Tindall.

Harris, R. (1997) 'Power', in Davies, M. (ed.) *The Blackwell Companion to Social Work*, Oxford: Blackwell.

Harris, T.A. (1981) *I'm OK – You're OK*, London: Pan.

Hart, R. (1992) Children's Participation from Tokenism to Citizenship, Innocenti Essays. No. 4 UNICEF.

Harvey, L. (1990) *Critical Social Research*, London: Unwin Hyman.

Hawkins, P. and Shohet, R. (2000) *Supervision in the Helping Professions*, 2nd edn, Buckingham: Open University Press.

Healy, K. (2000) *Social Work Practices: Contemporary Perspectives on Change*, London: Sage.

Healy, L. (2001) *International Social Work*, New York: Haworth Press.

Help the Aged (1996) *Bereavement*, advice leaflet. 207–21 Pentonville Road, London N1 9UZ. Telephone 0207 278 1114.

Hemmings, P. (1995) 'Social Work Intervention with Bereaved Children', *Journal of Social Work Practice*, 9(2): 109–30.

Heritage, J. (1983) 'Accounts in Action' in Gilbert, G. and Abell, P. (eds) *Accounts and Action*, London: Gower.

Hester, M. and Radford, L. (1996) *Domestic Violence and Child Contact Arrangements in England and Denmark*, Bristol: Policy.

Hill, M. (2000) 'Social Services and Social Security', in Hill, M. (ed.) *Local Authority Social Services: an Introduction*, Oxford: Blackwell.

Hill, M. and Tisdall, K. (1997) *Children and Society*, London: Longman.

Hillery, G. (1955) 'Definitions of Community', *Rural Sociology*, 20(22).

Hinselwood, R.D. (1998) 'Creatures of Each Other: Some Historical Considerations of Responsibility and Care, and Some Present Undercurrents', in Foster, A. and Roberts, V.Z. (eds) *Managing Mental Health in the Community: Chaos and Containment*, London: Routledge.

Hoggett, P. and Burns, D. (1992) 'The Revenge of the Poor: The Anti-poll Tax Campaign', *Critical Social Policy*, 33: 95–101.

Holdsworth, D. (1994) 'Accountability: The Obligation to Lay Oneself Open to Criticism', in Chadwick, R. (ed.) *Ethics and Professions*, Aldershot: Avebury.

Holman, B. (1983) *Resourceful Friends: Skills in Community Social Work*, London: Children's Society.

Holman, B. (1993) *A New Deal for Social Welfare*, Oxford: Lion Publishing.

Home Office (annual) *Criminal Statistics for England and Wales*, London: Home Office.

Home Office (1997) *No More Excuses*, White Paper, London: Stationery Office.

Home Office (1999) *Supporting Families*, London: Stationery Office.

Hope, M. and Chapman, T. (1998) *Evidence Based Practice: A Guide to Effective Practice*, London: Home Office.

Horkheimer, M. (1978) 'The Authoritarian State', in Arato, A. and Gebhardt, E. (eds) *The Essential Frankfurt School Reader*, Oxford: Blackwell.

Hough, G. (1999) 'Social Work in the Customer Culture', in Pease, B. and Fook, J. (eds) *Transforming Social Work Practice*, London: Routledge.

Howe, D. (1996) 'Relating Theory to Practice', in Davies, M. (ed.) *The Blackwell Companion to Social Work*, Oxford: Blackwell.

Howe, D. (1998a) Relationship-based Thinking and Practice in Social Work, *Journal of Social Work Practice*, 12(1): 45–56.

Howe, D. (1998b) *Patterns of Adoption*, Oxford: Blackwell.

Howe, D. (1998c) 'Adoption Outcome Research and Practical Judgement', *Adoption and Fostering*, 22(2): 6–15.

Hudson, B. (2000) 'Inter-agency Collaboration – A Sceptical view', in Brechin, A., Brown, H. and Eby, M. (eds) *Critical Practice in Health and Social Care*, London: Open University/Sage.

Hudson, J., Morris, A., Maxwell, G. and Galaway, B. (1996) *Family Group Conferences: Perspectives on Policy and Practice*, Leichardt: Federation Press,

Hudson, M. (1999) *Managing Without Profit*, 2nd edn, London: Penguin.

Hughes, B. (1995) *Older People and Community Care: Critical Theory and Practice*, Buckingham: Open University Press.

Hughes, G. (ed.) (1998) *Imagining Welfare Futures*, London: Routledge.

Hughes, L. and Pengelly, P. (1997) *Staff Supervision in a Turbulent Environment*, London: Jessica Kingsley.

Hugman, R. (1991) *Power in the Caring Professions*, London: Macmillan – now Palgrave Macmillan.

Human Rights Act 1998, London: HMSO.

Humphreys, C. (2000) *Social Work, Domestic Violence and Child Protection: Challenging Practice*, Bristol: Policy.

Humphreys, C., Hester, M., Hague, G., Mullender, A., Abrahams, H. and Lowe, P. (2000) *From Good Intentions to Good Practice: Mapping Services Working with Families where there is Domestic Violence*, Bristol: Policy.

Humphries, B. (ed.) (1996) *Critical Perspectives on Empowerment*, Birmingham: Venture.

Huxley, P. (1993) 'Case Management and Care Management in Community Care', *British Journal of Social Work*, **23**: 365–81.

Ife, J. (1997) *Rethinking Social Work: Towards Critical Practice*, Melbourne: Longman.

Illife, S. (2000) 'Commissioning Services for Older People: Make Haste Slowly?', in Tovey, P. (ed.) *Contemporary Primary Care: The Challenge of Change*, Buckingham: Open University Press.

Inman, K. (1998) 'Generation Eggs', *Community Care*, 26 November–2 December, p. 29.

Ironside, V. (1996) *'You'll Get Over It'; The Rage of Bereavement*, Harmondsworth: Penguin.

Island, D. and Letellier, P. (1991) *Men Who Beat the Men Who Love Them: Battered Gay Men and Domestic Violence*, Binghamton, NY: Harrington Park Press.

Jack, R. (ed.) (1995) *Empowerment and Community Care*, London: Chapman & Hall.

Jackson, S. (1998) 'Looking After Children: a New Approach or just an Exercise in Formfilling? A Response to Knight and Caveney', *British Journal of Social Work*, **28**: 45–56.

Jackson, S. and Morris, K. (1999) 'Family Group Conferences: User Empowerment or Family Self Reliance? – a Development from Lupton', *British Journal of Social Work*, **29**: 621–30.

Jackson, S. and Thomas, N. (1999) *On the Move Again? What Works in Creating Stability for Looked After Children*. Ilford: Barnardo's.

Jackson, S., Fisher, M., and Ward, H. (2000) 'Key Concepts in Looking After Children: Parenting, Partnership, Outcomes', in DoH *A Child's World*, London: HMSO.

Jacobs, S. (1976) *The Right to a Decent Home*, London: Routledge & Kegan Paul.

Jacobs, S. and Popple, K. (1994) *Community Work in the 1990s*, Nottingham: Spokesman.

James, A. (1994) *Managing to Care: Public Service and the Market*, London: Longman.

James, J. and Prout, A. (eds) (1997) *Constructing and Reconstructing Childhood*, 2nd edn, London: Falmer.

James-Hanman, D. (1995) *The Needs and Experiences of Black and Minority Ethnic Women Experiencing Domestic Violence*, London: London Borough of Islington, Women's Equality Unit.

Jenkins, P. (1992) *Intimate Enemies: Moral Panics in Contemporary Great Britain*, New York: Aldine De Gruyter.

Jessup, H. and Rogerson, S. (1999) 'Postmodernism and Teaching and Practice of Interpersonal Skills', in Pease, B. and Fook, J. (eds) *Transforming Social Work Practice: Postmodern Critical Perspectives*, London: Routledge.

J.M. Consulting (1999) Review of the Diploma in Social Work: Report on the Content of the DipSW Conducted as Part of the Stage Two Review of CCETSW, London: J.M. Consulting Ltd.

John Baptiste, A. (2001) 'Appropriateness of Social Work Practice with Communities of African Origins', in Dominelli, L., Lorenz, W. and Soydan, H. (eds) *Beyond Racial Divides: Ethnicities in Social Work Practice*, Aldershot: Ashgate.

Johns, C. (2000) *Becoming a Reflective Practitioner*, Oxford: Blackwell.

Johnson, H. (1998) 'Rethinking Survey Research on Violence Against Women', in Dobash, R.E. and Dobash, R.P. (eds) *Rethinking Violence Against Women*, Thousand Oaks, CA: Sage.

Jones, G.S. (1976) *Outcast London*, Harmondsworth: Penguin.

Jones, K.B. (1993) *Compassionate Authority: Democracy and the Representation of Women*, London: Routledge.

Jordan, B. (1989) *Social Work in an Unjust Society*, London: Routledge.

Judge, K. and Matthews, J. (1980) *Charging for Social Care*, London: Allen & Unwin.

Jupp, V. (1989) *Methods of Criminological Research*, London: Unwin Hyman.

Kadushin, A. (1976) *Supervision in Social Work*, New York: Columbia University Press.

Kaner, S., Lind, L., Toldi, C., Fisk, S. and Berger, D. (1996) *Facilitators' Guide to Participatory Decision-Making*, Gabriola Island, BC, Canada: New Society.

Kanter, J. (1999) Remembering the Child in Child Care: The Life and Legacy of Clare Winnicott. Unpublished paper given at the Making a Difference Conference, Southport, BASW and University of Central Lancashire.

Kelly, D. and Warr, B. (eds) (1992) *Quality Counts*, London: Whiting & Birch and Social Care Association.

Kelly, L., Regan, I. and Burton, S. (1991) *An Exploratory Study of the Prevalence of Sexual Abuse in a Sample of 16–21 Year Olds*, London: Polytechnic of North London.

Kelly, N. (2000) Decision Making in Child Protection Practice, unpublished PhD thesis, Huddersfield: University of Huddersfield.

Kemshall, H. (1996) 'Offender Risk and Probation Practice', in Kemshall, H. and Pritchard, J. (eds) *Good Practice in Risk Assessment and Risk Management*, London: Jessica Kingsley.

Khan, P. and Dominelli, L. (2000) 'The Impact of Globalization on Social Work in the UK', *European Journal of Social Work*, 3(2): 95–108.

Kingdon, D. (2000) 'Schizophrenia and Mood (Affective) Disorder', in Bailey, D. (ed.) *At the Core of Mental Health Practice: Key Issues for Practitioners, Managers and Mental Health Trainers*, Brighton: Pavilion.

Kirkpatrick, I. and Miguel Artinez L. (eds) (1995) *The Politics of Quality in the Public Sector*, London: Routledge.

Kitzinger, J. (1997) 'Who Are You Kidding? Children, Power and the Struggle Against Sexual Abuse', in James, A. and Prout, A. (eds) *Constructing and Reconstructing Childhood*, 2nd edn, London: Falmer.

Klein, R. (1989a) *Infertility: Women Speak Out about their Experiences of Reproductive Medicine*, London: Pandora.

Klein, R. (1989b)' The Exploitation of Our Desire: Women's Experiences with *In Vitro Fertilisation*', Paper presented at the Women's Studies Summer Institute, Deakin University, Victoria, Australia.

Klein, W.C. and Bloom, M. (1995) 'Practice Wisdom', *Social Work*, **40**(6): 799–807.

Knapman, J. and Morrison, T. (1998) *Making the Most of Supervision in Health and Social Care*, Brighton: Pavilion.

Kübler-Ross, E. (1970) *On Death and Dying*, London: Tavistock.

Langan, J. (1997) 'In the Best Interests of Elderly People? The Role of Local Authorities in Handling and Safeguarding the Personal Finances of Elderly People with Dementia', *Journal of Social Welfare Law*, **19**(4): 444–63.

Langan, M. (1998) 'Radical Social Work', in Adams, R., Dominelli, L. and Payne, M. (eds) *Social Work, Themes, Issues and Critical Debates*, Basingstoke: Macmillan – now Palgrave Macmillan.

Lankshear, G., Giarchi, G. and Hodges, V. (1999) 'The Placement of a Social Service Care Manager in a GP Surgery as a Way to Improve Carer Access to Services and Improve Liaison between Statutory Agencies', *Health and Social Care in the Community*, 7(3): 206–15.

Law Commission (1995) *Mental Incapacity*, No. 231, London: The Law Commission.

Lawson, H. (ed.) (1998) *Practice Teaching – Changing Social Work*, London: Jessica Kinglsey.

Leader, A. (1995) *Director Power: A Resource Pack for People who want to Develop Their own Care Plans and Support Networks*. Joint Publication by the Community Support Network, Brixton Community Sanctuary, Pavilion Publishing and MIND.

Leathard, A. (ed.) (1994) *Going Inter-professional: Working Together for Health and Welfare*, London: Routledge.

Ledwith, M. (1997) *Participating in Transformations: Towards a Working Model of Community Empowerment*, Birmingham: Venture.

Lee Nelson, M. and Holloway, E. (1999) 'Supervision and Gender Issues', in Carroll, M. and Holloway, E. (eds) *Counselling Supervision in Context*, London: Sage.

Leece, J. (2000) It's a Matter of Choice. Making Direct Payments Work in Staffordshire, *Practice*, 12(4): 37–48.

Lees, R. and Mayo, M. (1984) *Community Action for Change*, London: Routledge & Kegan Paul.

Leonard, P. (1975) 'Towards a Paradigm for Radical Practice', in Bailey, R. and Brake, M. (eds) *Radical Social Work*, London: Edward Arnold.

Leonard, P. (1979) 'In Defence of Critical Hope', *Social Work Today*, 10(24).

Leonard, P. (1997) *Postmodern Welfare: Reconstructing an Emancipatory Project*, London: Sage.

Lewis, J. (1996) 'The Paradigm Shift in the Delivery of Public Services and the Crisis of Professionalism', in Adams, R. (ed.) *Crisis in the Human Services: National and International Issues*. Selected Conference Papers. Kingston upon Hull, University of Lincolnshire and Humberside.

Lewis, J. and Glennerster, H. (1996) *Implementing the New Community Care*, Buckingham: Open University Press.

Lindley, B. (1994) *On the Receiving End: Final Report*, London: Family Rights Group.

Lishman, J.(1998) 'Personal and Professional Development', in Adams, R., Dominelli, L. and Payne, M. (eds) *Social Work: Themes, Issues and Critical Debates*, London: Macmillan – now Palgrave Macmillan.

Lister, R. (2000) 'Gender and the Analysis of Social Policy', in Lewis, G., Gewirtz, S. and Clarke, J. (eds) *Rethinking Social Policy*, Buckingham: Open University Press.

Littlewood, J. (1993) 'The Denial of Death and Rites of Passage in Contemporary Societies', in Clark, D. (ed.) *The Sociology of Death*, Oxford: Blackwell.

Lloyd, M. (1997) 'Dying and Bereavement, Spirituality and Social Work in a Market Economy of Welfare', *British Journal of Social Work*, **27**: 175–90.

Lloyd, M. (2000) 'Where Has all the Care Management Gone? The Challenge of Parkinson's Disease to the Health and Social Care Interface', *British Journal of Social Work*, **30**: 737–54.

Lloyd, M. and Smith, M. (1998) *Assessment and Service Provision under the new Community Care Arrangements for People with Parkinson's Disease and their Carers*, Research Report No. 13, Manchester: University of Manchester.

Lloyd, M. and Taylor, C. (1995) 'From Hollis to the Orange Book: Developing a Holistic Model of Social Work Assessment in the 1990s', *British Journal of Social Work*, **25**(6): 691–710.

Lloyd, M., Preston-Shoot, M., Temple, B. with Wuu, R. (1996) 'Whose Project is it Anyway? Sharing and Shaping the Research and Development Agenda', *Disability and Society*, **11**(3): 301–15.

Locke, J. (1924) *Two Treatises of Government*, London: J.M. Dent.

London Borough of Hackney (1994) *Good Practice Guidelines: Responding to Domestic Violence*, London: London Borough of Hackney, Women's Unit.

London Borough of Hounslow (1994) *Domestic Violence: Help, Advice and Information for Disabled Women*, London: London Borough of Hounslow.

London Borough of Lewisham's Community Safety Team in conjunction with the Lewisham Domestic Violence Forum (1998) *Survey of Domestic Violence Services in Lewisham*, London: London Borough of Lewisham.

Loosley, S., Bentley, L., Lehmann, P., Marshall, L., Rabenstein, S. and Sudermann, M. (1997) *Group Treatment for Children Who Witness Woman Abuse: A Manual for Practitioners*, London, Ontario: The Community Group Treatment Program. (Available from: The Children's Aid Society of London and Middlesex, P.O. Box 6010, Depot 1, London, Ontario, Canada N5W 5R6.)

Lorenz, W. (1994) *Social Work in a Changing Europe*, London: Routledge.

Lupton, C. and Nixon, P. (1999) *Empowering Practice? A Critical Appraisal of the Family Group Conference Approach*, Bristol: Policy.

Lupton, C. and Stevens, M. (1997) *Family Outcomes: Following Through on Family Group Conferences*, Report No. 34, Portsmouth: University of Portsmouth.

Lupton, C., Barnard, S. and Swall-Yarrington, M. (1995) *Family Planning?: An Evaluation of the Family Group Conference Model*, Report No. 31, Portsmouth: University of Portsmouth.

Lymbery, M. (1998) 'Care Management and Professional Autonomy: The Impact of Community Care Legislation on Social Work with Older People', *British Journal of Social Work*, **28**(6): 863–78.

Lyons, K., La Valle, I. and Gramwood, C. (1995) 'Career Patterns of Qualified Social Workers: Discussion of a Recent Survey, *British Journal of Social Work*, **25**: 173–90.

Macdonald, G. (1996) 'Ice Therapy: Why we Need Randomised Controlled Trials', in Alderson, P., Brill S., Chalmers, I. et al. (eds) *What Works? Effective Social Interventions in Child Welfare*, Barkingside: Barnardo's.

McDonald, A. (1998) *Understanding Community Care: A Guide for Social Workers*, London: Macmillan – now Palgrave Macmillan.

McGibbon, A., Cooper, L. and Kelly, L. (1989) *What Support? An Exploratory Study of Council Policy and Practice, and Local Support Services in the Area of Domestic Violence within Hammersmith and Fulham*. Final Report, London: Polytechnic of North London: Child Abuse Studies Unit.

McGlone, F., Park, A. and Smith, K. (1998) *Families and Kinship*, York: Joseph Rowntree Foundation.

McGuire, J. (2000) *Cognitive Behavioural Approaches: An Introduction to Theory and Research*, London: Home Office.

McKevitt, D. and Lawton, A. (eds) (1994) *Public Sector Management: Theory, Critique and Practice*, London: Sage.

McNamee, S., Gergen, K. and Associates (1999) *Relational Responsibility: Resources for Sustainable Dialogue*, London: Sage.

McWilliams, W. (1992) 'The Rise and Development of Management Thought in the English Probation System', in Statham, R. and Whitehead, P. (eds) *Managing the Probation Service: Issues for the 1990s*, Harlow: Longman.

Malin, N. (ed.) (1994) *Implementing Community Care*, Buckingham: Open University Press.

Malin, N., Manthorpe, J., Race, D. and Wilmot, S. (2000) *Community Care for Nurses and the Caring Professions*, Buckingham: Open University Press.

Mama, A. (1996) *The Hidden Struggle: Statutory and Voluntary Sector Responses to Violence against Black Women in the Home*, London: Whiting & Birch.

Mandelstam, M. (1999) *Community Care Practice and the Law*, 2nd edn, London: Jessica Kingsley.

Manthorpe, J. (ed.) (2000) *Bags of Money: The Financial Abuse of Older People*, London: Action on Elder Abuse.

Marcuse, H. (1964) *One-Dimensional Man*, London: Paladin.

Marsh, P. and Crow, G. (1998) *Family Group Conferences in Child Welfare*, Oxford: Blackwell.

Marsh, P. and Fisher, M. (1992) *Good Intentions: Developing Partnership in Social Services*, York: Joseph Rowntree Foundation/Community Care.

Marsh, P. and Triseliotis, J. (1996) 'Social Workers: Their Training and First Year in Work', in Connelly, N. (ed.) *Training Social Services Staff: Evidence From New Research*. Report of a conference, Research in Social Work Education, No 4. London: National Institute for Social Work.

Marshall, L., Miller, N., Miller-Hewitt, S., Sudermann, M. and Watson, L. (1995) *Evaluation of Groups for Children who have Witnessed Violence*, London: Ontario: Centre for Research on Violence Against Women and Children.

Marshall, M. (1990) *Social Work with Old People*, London: Macmillan – now Palgrave Macmillan.

Marshall, M. and Dixon, M. (1996) *Social Work with Older People*, 3rd edn, London: Macmillan – now Palgrave Macmillan.

Marx, K. (1972) (ed. McClennan, D.) *Selected Writings*, Oxford: Oxford University Press.

Mattinson, J. (1975) *The Reflection Process in Casework Supervision*, London: Institute of Marital Studies.

Means, R. and Smith, R. (1998a) *Community Care: Policy and Practice*, 2nd edn, London: Macmillan – now Palgrave Macmillan.

Means, R. and Smith, R. (1998b) *From Poor Law to Community Care: The Development of Welfare Services for Elderly People 1939–1971*, 2nd edn, Bristol: Policy.

Mehlbye, J. and Walgrave, L. (1998) *Confronting Youth in Europe*, Copenhagen: AKF.

Melling, J. (1980) 'Clydeside Housing and the Evolution of State Rent Control', in Melling, J. (ed.) *Housing, Social Policy and the State*, London: Croom Helm.

Messerschmidt, J.W. (2000) *Nine Lives, Adolescent Masculinities, the Body and Violence*, Boulder, CO: Westview Press.

Middleton, L. (1999) 'Could Do Better...', *Professional Social Work*, November pp. 8–9.

Mills, M. (1999) 'Using the Narrative in Dementia Care', in Bornat, J. (ed.) *Biographical Interviews: The Link Between Research and Practice*, London: Centre for Policy on Ageing.

Milner, J. (2001) *Women in Social Work: Narrative Approaches*, Basingstoke: Palgrave – now Palgrave Macmillan.

Milner, J. and O'Byrne, P. (1998) *Assessment in Social Work*, Basingstoke: Macmillan – now Palgrave Macmillan.

Mirrlees-Black, C. (1999) *Domestic Violence: Findings from a New British Crime Survey Self-Completion Questionnaire*, Home Office Research Study 191, London: Home Office.

Moffat, K. (1999) 'Surveillance in Government of Welfare Recipients', in Chambon, A.S., Irving, A. and Epstein, L. (eds) *Reading Foucault for Social Work*, Chichester: Columbia University Press.

Monroe, B. (1998) 'Social Work in Palliative Care', in Doyle, D., Hanks, G. and MacDonald, N. (eds) *The Oxford Textbook of Palliative Medicine*, 2nd edn, Oxford: Oxford University Press.

Mooney, J. (1994) *The Hidden Figure: Domestic Violence in North London*: London: Islington Council, Police and Crime Prevention Unit.

Moore, B. (1996) *Risk Assessment: A Practitioners' Guide to Predicting Harmful Behaviour*, London: Whiting & Birch.

Moore, O. (1996) *PWA – Looking AIDS in the Face*, London: Picador.

Morgan, S. (1998) 'The Assessment and Management of Risk', in Brooker, C. and Repper, J. (eds) *Serious Mental Health Problems in the Community: Policy, Practice and Research*, London: Baillière Tindall.

Morgan, S. (1999) *Assessing and Managing Risk. A Training Pack for Practitioners and Managers of Comprehensive Mental Health Services*, Brighton: Pavilion.

Morley, R. and Mullender, A. (1994) *Preventing Domestic Violence to Women*, Police Research Group, Crime Prevention Unit Series, Paper 48, London: Home Office.

Morris, J. (1991) *Prides Against Prejudice: Transforming Attitudes to Disability*, London: Women's Press.

Morris, J. (2000) *'Having Someone Who Cares?' Barriers to Change in the Social Care of Children*, London: National Children's Bureau/Joseph Rowntree Foundation.

Morris, K. and Shepherd, C. (2000) 'Quality Social Work with Children and Families', *Social Work*, 5: 169–176.

Morris, K. and Tunnard, J. (1995) *Family Group Conferences: Messages from UK Practice and Research*, London: Family Rights Group.

Morris, K., Marsh, P. and Wiffen, J. (1998) *Family Group Conferences: A Training Pack*, London: Family Rights Group.

Morrow, V. (1998) *Understanding Families: Children's Perspectives*, London: National Children's Bureau.

Mulkay, M. and Ernst, J. (1991) 'The Changing Profile of Social Death', *Archives of European Sociology*, 32: 172–96.

Mullaly, B. (1997) *Structural Social Work, Ideology, Theory and Practice*, 2nd edn, Oxford: Oxford University Press.

Mullen, P., Wallace, C., Burgess, P., Palmer, S., Ruschena, D. and Browne, C. (1998) 'Serious Criminal Offending and Mental Disorder: Case Linkage Study', *British Journal of Psychiatry*, 172: 477–84.

Mullender, A. (1994) 'Groups for Child Witnesses: Learning from North America', in Mullender, A. and Morley, R. (eds) *Children Living with Domestic Violence: Putting Men's Abuse of Women on the Child Care Agenda*, London: Whiting & Birch.

Mullender, A. (1996) *Rethinking Domestic Violence: The Social Work and Probation Response*, London: Routledge.

Mullender, A. and Burton, S. (2000) 'Dealing with Perpetrators', in Taylor-Browne, J. (ed.) *Reducing Domestic Violence: What Works?*, London: Home Office.

Mullender, A. and Hague, G. (2000) 'Women Survivors' Views on Domestic Violence Services' in Taylor-Browne, J. (ed.) *Reducing Domestic Violence: What Works?*, London: Home Office.

Mullender, A. and Humphreys, C. (2000) *Children and Domestic Violence*, Totnes, Devon: Dartington Social Research Unit.

Mullender, A. and Morley, R. (eds) *Children Living with Domestic Violence: Putting Men's Abuse of Women on the Child Care Agenda*, London: Whiting & Birch.

Mullender, A. and Ward, D. (1991) *Self-Directed Groupwork: Users Take Action for Empowerment*, London: Whiting & Birch.

Muncie, J. (1999a) *Youth and Crime: A Critical Introduction*, London: Sage.

Muncie, J. (1999b) 'Auditing Youth Justice', *Prison Service Journal*, **126**: 55–60.

Munro, E. M. (1999) 'Protecting Children in an Anxious Society' *Health, Risk and Society,* **1**(1): 117–27.

National Association for Youth Justice (forthcoming) *Good Practice Guidelines*, NAYJ.

National Foster Care Association (1994) *Safe Caring*, London: National Foster Care Association.

National Foster Care Association (2000) *A Competence-based Approach to the Assessment of Foster Carers*, London: National Foster Care Association.

National Foster Care Association UK Joint Working Party on Foster Care (1999a) *Code of Practice on the Recruitment, Assessment, Approval, Training, Management and Support of Foster Carers*, London: National Foster Care Association.

National Foster Care Association UK Joint Working Party on Foster Care (1999b) *UK National Standards for Foster Care*, London: National Foster Care Association.

Newburn, T. (1993) *Disaster and After*, London: Jessica Kingsley.

Newburn, T. (1996) 'Some Lessons from Hillsborough', in Mead, C. (ed.) *Journeys of Discovery; Creative Learning from Disaster*, London: National Institute for Social Work.

Newby, H. (1980) *Community*, Milton Keynes: Open University Press.

Newman, J. (1996) *Shaping Organisational Cultures in Local Government*, London: Pitman/Institute of Local Government Studies.

Newman, T., Roberts, H., and Oakley, A. (1996) 'Weighing up the Evidence', *Guardian*, 10 January.

Neysmith, S. (ed.) (1999) *Critical Issues for Future Social Work with Aging Persons*, New York: Columbia University Press.

Nixon, S. (2000) 'Safe Care, Abuse and Allegations of Abuse in Foster Care', in Kelly, G. and Gilligan, R. (eds) *Issues in Foster Care: Policy, Practice and Research*, London: Jessica Kingsley.

Nocon, A. and Qureshi, H. (1996) *Outcomes of Community Care for Users and Carers: A Social Services Perspective*, Buckingham: Open University Press.

Noel, L. (1994) *Intolerance: A General Survey*, Montreal: McGill-Queen's.

Nolan, M., Grant, G. and Keady, J. (1996) *Understanding Family Care*, Buckingham: Open University Press.

Norwood, R. (1986) *Women Who Love Too Much*, London: Arrow Books.

Nosek, M.A. and Howland, C.A. (1998) 'Abuse and Women with Disabilities', accessed through VAWnet, a Project of the National Resource Center on Domestic Violence. Fax 717-545-9456 (USA), tel. 800-537-2238 or 800-553-2508.

Novak, T. (1997) 'Poverty and the Underclass', in Lavalette, M. and Pratt, A. (eds) *Social Policy: A Conceptual and Theoretical Introduction*, London: Sage.

O'Brien, J. (1981) *The Principle of Normalisation*, London: Campaign for Mental Health.

Office for National Statistics (1998) *Mortality Statistics (Registrations), England and Wales*, London: ONS.

O'Hagan, K. and Dillenburger, K. (1995) *The Abuse of Women Within Childcare Work*, Milton Keynes: Open University Press.

O'Hanlon, B. (1995) Breaking the Bad Trance. London Conference.

Oliver, J., Huxley, P., Bridges, K. and Mohamad, H. (1996) *Quality of Life and Mental Health Services*, London: Routledge.

Oliver, M. (1990) *The Politics of Disablement*, London: Macmillan – now Palgrave Macmillan.

Oliver, M. and Sapey, B. (1999) *Social Work with Disabled People*, 2nd edn, Basingstoke: Macmillan – now Palgrave Macmillan.

Oliviere, D., Hargreaves, R. and Monroe, B. (1998) *Good Practices in Palliative Care*, Aldershot: Ashgate.

Opie, A. (1995) *Beyond Good Intentions: Support Work with Older People*, Wellington: Institute of Policy Studies.

Orme, J. (1995) *Workloads: Measurement and Management*, Aldershot: Avebury in Association with CEDR, University of Southampton.

Orme, J. and Glastonbury, B. (1994) *Care Management: Tasks and Workloads*, Basingstoke: Macmillan – now Palgrave Macmillan.

O'Sullivan, T. (1999) *Decision Making in Social Work*, Basingstoke: Macmillan – now Palgrave Macmillan.

Øvretveit, J. (1993) *Coordinating Community Care: Multidisciplinary Teams and Care Management*, Buckingham: Open University Press.

Owen, H. (1997) 'One of the Hardest Jobs in the World: Attempting to Manage Risk in Children's Homes', in Kemshall, H. and Pritchard, J. (eds) *Good Practice in Risk Assessment and Risk Management 2: Protection, Rights and Responsibilities*, London: Jessica Kingsley.

Packman, J. (1986) *Who Needs Care? Social Work Decisions about Children*, Oxford: Blackwell.

Parker, G. (1994) *Where Next for Research on Carers?*, Leicester: Leicester University.

Parkes, C.M. (1996) *Bereavement*, 3rd edn, London: Routledge.

Parry, N. and Parry, J. (1979) 'Social Work, Professionalism and the State', in Parry, N., Rustin, M. and Satyamurti, C. (eds) *Social Work, Welfare and the State*, London: Edward Arnold.

Parsloe, P. (ed.) (1999) *Risk Assessment in Social Care*, London: Jessica Kingsley.

Parton, N. (1985)*The Politics of Child Abuse*, London: Macmillan – now Palgrave Macmillan.

Parton, N. (1991) *Governing the Family: Child Care, Child Protection and the State*, Basingstoke: Macmillan – now Palgrave Macmillan.

Parton, N. (1997) *Child Protection and Family Support: Tensions, Contradictions and Possibilities*, London: Routledge.

Parton, N. (1998) 'Risk, Advanced Liberalism and Child Welfare: The Need to Rediscover Uncertainty and Ambiguity', *British Journal of Social Work*, **28**: 5–27.

Parton, N. (1999) 'Reconfiguring Child Welfare Practices: Risk, Advanced Liberalism and the Government of Freedom', in Chambon, A.S., Irving, A. and Epstein, L. (eds) *Reading Foucault for Social Work*, Chichester: Colombia University Press.

Parton, N. (2001) 'Risk and Professional Judgement', in Cull, L.-A. and Roche, J. (eds) *The Law and Social Work*, Basingstoke: Palgrave – now Palgrave Macmillan.

Parton, N. and Marshall, W. (1998) 'Postmodernism and Discourse Approaches to Social Work', in Adams, R., Dominelli, L. and Payne, M. (eds) *Social Work: Themes, Issues and Critical Debates*, London: Macmillan – now Palgrave Macmillan.

Parton, N. and O'Byrne, P. (2000) *Constructive Social Work: Towards a New Practice*, Basingstoke: Palgrave – now Palgrave Macmillan.

Parton, N., Thorpe, D. and Wattam, C. (1997) *Child Protection: Risk and the Moral Order*, Basingstoke: Macmillan – now Palgrave Macmillan.

Pawson, R. and Tilley, N. (1997) *Realistic Evaluation*, London: Sage.

Payne, M. (1996) *What is Professional Social Work?*, Birmingham: Venture.

Payne, M. (1997) 'Change, Poverty and Power in Social Work', in Lesnik, B. (ed.) *Change in Social Work*, Aldershot: Ashgate.

Payne, M. (1998) 'Social Work Theories and Reflective Practice', in Adams R., Dominelli, L. and Payne, M. (eds) *Social Work: Themes, Issues and Critical Debates*, Basingstoke: Macmillan – now Palgrave Macmillan.

Payne, M. (2000a) *Anti-bureaucratic Social Work*, Birmingham: Venture.

Payne, M. (2000b) *Teamwork in Multiprofessional Care*, Basingstoke: Macmillan – now Palgrave Macmillan.

Peled, E. and Edleson, J. L. (1995) 'Process and Outcome in Groups for Children of Battered Women', in Peled, E., Jaffe, P.G. and Edleson, J.L. (eds) *Ending the Cycle of Violence: Community Responses to Children of Battered Women*, Thousand Oaks, CA: Sage.

Pence, E. (1987) *In Our Best Interest: A Process for Personal and Social Change*, Duluth, MN: Minnesota Program Development Inc.

Pence, E. and Paymar, M. (1990) *Power and Control: Tactics of Men Who Batter: An Educational Curriculum*, rev. edn, Duluth, Minnesota: Minnesota Program Development, Inc. (from 206 West Fourth Street, Duluth, MN 55806, USA).

Perkins, R. and Repper, J. (1998a) 'Principles of Working with People who Experience Mental Health Problems', in Brooker, C. and Repper, J. (eds) *Serious Mental Health Problems in the Community. Policy, Practice and Research*, London: Baillière Tindall.

Perkins, R. and Repper, J. (1998b) *Dilemmas in Community Mental Health Practice: Choice or Control*, Oxford: Radcliffe Medical Press.

Peters, A. (1986) 'Main Currents in Criminological Law Theory', in van Dijk, J., Haffmans, C., Ruter, F., Schutte. J. and Stolwijk, S. (eds) *Criminal Law in Action*, Arnheim: Gouda Quint BV.

Phillips, J. (1992) 'The Future of Social Work with Older People', *Generations Review*, 4: 12–15.

Phillipson, C. and Walker, A. (1987) 'The Case for a Critical Gerontology', in di Gregorio, S. (ed.) *Social Gerontology: New Directions*, London: Croom Helm.

Phillipson, J. and Riley, M. (1991) Women for a Change. Unpublished M.Phil, Cranfield Institute.

Picardie, R. (1998) *Before I Say Goodbye*, London: Penguin.

Pickford, J. (ed.) (2000) *Youth Justice: Theory and Practice*, London: Cavendish.

Pietroni, P.C. (1994) 'Interprofessional Teamwork: Its History and Development in Hospitals, General Practice and Community Care (UK)', in Leatherd, A. (ed.) *Going Inter-Professional: Working Together for Health and Welfare*, London: Routledge.

Pincus, A. and Minahan, A. (1973) *Social Work Practice: Model and Method*, Ithaca, IL: Peacock.

Pinkerton, J. (2001) 'Developing Partnership Practice', in Foley, P., Roche, J. and Tucker, S. (eds) *Children in Society: Contemporary Theory, Policy and Practice*, Basingstoke: Palgrave – now Palgrave Macmillan.

Pinkerton, J. and Houston, S. (1996) 'Competence and the Children Act', in O'Hagan, K. (ed.) *Competence in Social Work Practice*, London: Jessica Kingsley.

Pinkerton, J. and McLoughlin, J. (1996) 'Ethical Dilemmas in Practice – Some Thoughts on the Children (NI) Order', *Child Care in Practice*, 1(4): 40–51.

Pinkerton, J., Scott, B. and O'Kane, P. (1997) *Partnership Practice with Parents and Carers: An Approach to Practitioner Self Evaluation*, Belfast: Centre for Child Care Research, Queen's University.

Pinkney, S. (2000) 'Children as Welfare Subjects in Restructured Social Policy', in Lewis, G., Gewirtz, S. and Clarke, J. (eds) *Rethinking Social Policy*, London: Sage.

Pitts, J. (2000) 'The New Youth Justice and the Politics of Electoral Anxiety', in Goldson, B. (ed.) *The New Youth Justice*, Lyme Regis: Russell House Publishing.

Pitts, J. and Hope, T. (1998) 'The Local Politics of Inclusion: The State and Community Safety', in Finer, C. and Nellis, M. (eds) *Crime and Social Exclusion*, Oxford: Blackwell.

Polack, P. (1993) 'Recovery from Mental Illness: The Guiding Vision of the Mental Health Service System in the 1990s', *Psychosocial Rehabilitation Journal*, 16(4): 11–24.

Polanyi, M. (1983) *The Tacit Dimension*, Magnolia, MA: Peter Smith.

Popple, K. (1995) *Analysing Community Work: Its Theory and Practice*, Milton Keynes: Open University Press.

Popple, K. and Redmond, M. (2000) 'Community Development and the Voluntary Sector in the New Millennium: The Implications of the Third Way in the UK', *Community Development Journal*, 35(4): 391–400.

Pratchett, L. and Wingfield, M. (1994) *The Public Service Ethos in Local Government*, London: Commission for Local Democracy and Institute of Chartered Secretaries and Administrators.

Priestley, M. (1999) *Disability Politics and Community Care*, London: Jessica Kingsley.

Priestly, M. (2000) 'Dropping "E"s: The Missing Link in Quality Assurance for Disabled People', in Brechin, A., Brown, H. and Eby, M. (eds) *Critical Practice in Health and Social Care*, London: Sage/Open University.

Pritchard, J. (2000) *The Needs of Older Women*, Bristol: Policy.

Quinn, A. (1998) 'Learning from Palliative Care: Concepts to Underpin the Transfer of Knowledge from Specialist Palliative Care to Mainstream Social Work Settings', *Social Work Education*, 17(1): 9–19.

Quinsey, V.L. (1995) 'Predicting Sexual Offences', in Campbell, J.C. (ed.) *Assessing Dangerousness: Violence by Sexual Offenders, Batterers, and Child Abusers*, London: Sage.

Quinton, D., Rushton, A., Dance, C. and Mayes, D. (1998) *Joining New Families: A Study of Adoption and Fostering in Middle Childhood*, Chichester: Wiley.

Rai, D.K. and Thiara, R.K. (1997) *Re-defining Spaces: The Needs of Black Women and Children in Refuge Support Services and Black Workers in Women's Aid*, Bristol: WAFE.

Ramon, S. (1997) 'Building Resistance Through Training', *Breakthrough*, 1(1): 57–64.

Ray, M. (2000) Continuity and Change: Sustaining Long-term Marriage Relationships in the Context of Emerging Chronic Illness and Disability. Unpublished PhD thesis, University of Keele.

Reder, P., Duncan, S. and Gray, M. (1993) *Beyond Blame – Child Abuse Tragedies Revisited*, London: Routledge.

Reid, T. (1977 [1788]) *Essays on the Active Powers of Man*, New York: Garland.

Reid, W.J. (1978) *The Task Centred System*, New York: Columbia University Press.

Renzetti, C.M. (1992) *Violent Betrayal: Partner Abuse in Lesbian Relationships*, Newbury Park, CA: Sage.

RESPECT (The National Association for Domestic Violence Perpetrator Programmes and Associated Support Services) (2000) *Statement of Principles and Minimum Standards of Practice.* (Held at DVIP, PO Box 2838, London W6 9ZE).

Richards, G. and Horder, W. (1999) 'Mental Health Training: The Process of Collaboration', *Social Work Education,* 18(4): 449–57.

Richards, M. and Payne, C. (1990) *Staff Supervision in Child Protection Work* , London: National Institute for Social Work.

Ritchie, J.H., Dick, D. and Lingham, R. (1994) *The Report of the Enquiry into the Care and Treatment of Christopher Clunis,* London: HSMO.

Robson, C. (1993) *Real World Research: A Resource for Social Scientists and Practitioner-Researchers,* Oxford: Blackwell.

Rogers, C. (1951) *Client-centred Therapy,* London: Constable.

Rojek, C., Peacock, C. and Collins, S. (1988) *Social Work and Received Ideas,* London: Routledge.

Rose, N. (1985) *The Psychological Complex: Psychology, Politics and Society in England 1869–1939.* London: Routledge & Kegan Paul.

Rossiter, A. (1996) 'Finding Meanings for Social Work in Transitional Times: Reflections on Change', in Gould, N. and Taylor, I. (eds) *Reflective Learning for Social Work,* Aldershot: Avebury.

Rossiter, A., Prilleltensky, I. and Walsh-Bowers, R. (2000) 'A Postmodern Perspective on Professional Ethics' in Fawcett, B., Featherstone, B., Fook, J. and Rossiter, A. (eds) *Postmodern Feminist,* London: Routledge.

Rowe, J. and Lambert, L. (1973) *Children Who Wait,* London: British Agencies for Adoption and Fostering.

Rowlings, C. (1981) *Social Work with Elderly People,* London: Allen & Unwin.

Royal Society (1992) *Risk: Analysis, Perceptions and Management: Report of Royal Society Study Group,* London: Royal Society.

Ryan, M. (1994) *The Children Act 1989 – Putting it into Practice,* London: Macmillan – now Palgrave Macmillan.

Ryan, T. (1999) *Able and Willing,* London: Values Into Action.

Sainsbury Centre for Mental Health (1997) *Pulling Together: The Future Roles and Training of Mental Health Staff,* London: Sainsbury Centre for Mental Health.

Sainsbury Centre for Mental Health (1998) *Keys to Engagement: Review of Care for People with Serious Mental Illness Who are Hard to Engage with Services,* London: Sainsbury Centre for Mental Health.

Sainsbury Centre for Mental Health (2001) *The Capable Practitioner: A Framework and List of the Practitioner Capabilities Required to Implement the National Service Framework for Mental Health,* London: The Training and Practice Development Section of the Sainsbury Centre for Mental Health.

Sanderson, H. (1997) *People, Plans and Possibilities: Exploring Person Centred Planning,* Edinburgh: Scottish Health Services.

Sargent, K. (1999) 'Assessing Risks for Children', in Parsloe, P. (ed.) *Risk Assessment in Social Care and Social Work,* London: Jessica Kingsley.

Sarri, R. and Sarri, C. (1992) 'Organisation and Community Change through Participatory Action Research, *Administration in Social Work,* 16(3–4): 99–122.

Sayce, L. (2000) *From Psychiatric Patient to Citizen: Overcoming Discrimination and Social Exclusion,* Basingstoke: Palgrave – now Palgrave Macmillan.

Schön, D. (1991) *The Reflective Practitioner: How Practitioners Think in Practice,* Aldershot: Avebury.

Scott, D. (1990) 'Practice Wisdom: The Disregarded Source of Practice Research', *Social Work,* 35(6): 564–68.

Scott, M. and Lyman, S. (1970) 'Accounts' in Lyman, M. and Scott, M. (eds) *A Sociology of the Absurd*, New York: Meredith Corporation.

Seale, C. (1993) 'Demographic Change and the Case of the Dying 1969–1987', in Dickenson, D. and Johnson, M. (eds) *Death, Dying and Bereavement*, London: Sage.

Seale, C. (1998) *Constructing Death: The Sociology of Dying and Bereavement*, Cambridge: Cambridge University Press.

Seale, C., Addington-Hall, J., and McCarthy, M. (1997) 'Awareness of Dying: Prevalence, Causes and Consequences', *Social Science and Medicine*, 45(3): 477–84.

Seebohm Committee (1968) *Report of the Committee on Local Authority and Allied Personal Social Services*, Cmnd 3703, London: HMSO.

Seed, P. and Lloyd, G. (1997) *Quality of Life*, London: Jessica Kingsley.

Sellick, C. and Thoburn, J. (1996) *What Works in Family Placement?*, Ilford: Barnardo's.

Sevenhuijsen, S. (1998) *Citizenship and the Ethics of Care: Feminist Considerations on Justice, Morality and Politics*, London: Routledge.

Sewpaul, V. (1998) The New Reproductive Technologies in South Africa. Unpublished PhD for the University of Natal, Durban.

Shardlow, S. (1998) 'Values, Ethics and Social Work', in Adams, R., Dominelli, L. and Payne, M. (eds) *Social Work: Issues, Themes and Dilemmas*, London: Macmillan – now Palgrave Macmillan.

Sheldon, B. and Macdonald G. (1999) *Research and Practice in Social Care: Mind the Gap*, University of Exeter: Centre for Evidence-based Social Services.

Sheldon, F. (1997) *Psychosocial Palliative Care*, Cheltenham: Stanley Thornes.

Shemmings, Y. (1996) *Death, Dying and Residential Care*, Aldershot: Avebury.

Shepherd C. (1996) The Haringey Family Group Conferences Programme. Unpublished report to the Department of Health.

Shepherd, C. (1998) Haringey Family Group Conference. Unpublished report to the Department of Health.

Shepherd, G. Murray, A. and Muijen, M. (1995) 'Perspectives on Schizophrenia: A Survey of User, Family Care and Professional Views Regarding Effective Care', *Journal of Mental Health*, 4: 403–22.

Sheppard, M. (1995a) *Care Management and the New Social Work: A Critical Analysis*, London: Whiting & Birch.

Sheppard, M. (1995b) 'Social Work, Social Science and Practice Wisdom', *British Journal of Social Work*, 25(3): 265–93.

Shotter, J. (1996) *Representing Reality: Discourse, Rhetoric and Social Construction*, London: Sage.

Siddell, M., Katz, J. and Komaromy, C. (1998) Death and Dying in Residential and Nursing Homes for Older People: Examining the Case for Palliative Care, Unpublished Report of Research: The Open University.

Silverman, P. (1996) 'Children's Construction of their Dead Parents', in Klass, D., Silverman, P. and Nickman, S. (eds) *Continuing Bonds: New Understandings of Grief*, Philadelphia: Taylor & Francis.

Simon, B. (1990) 'Rethinking Empowerment', *Journal of Progressive Human Services*, 1(1): 27–39.

Sinclair, A. and Dickinson, E. (1998) *Effective Practice in Rehabilitation: The Evidence of Systematic Reviews*, London: King's Fund.

Sinclair, R., Garnett, L. and Berridge, D. (1995) *Social Work and Assessment with Adolescents*, London: National Children's Bureau.

Sissons, P. (1999) *Focus on Change: Report on Consultation Carried Out with Women Survivors of Domestic Violence for the Lewisham Domestic Violence Forum*, London: Lewisham Domestic Violence Forum.

Skinner, B.F. (1953) *Science and Human Behavior*, New York: Macmillan.

Smale, G., Tuson, G. and Statham, D. (2000) *Social Work and Social Problems*, Basingstoke: Macmillan – now Palgrave Macmillan.

Smale, G. and Tuson, G. with Biehal, N. and Marsh, P. (1993) *Empowerment, Assessment, Care Management and the Skilled Worker*, London: NISW.

Smith, C. (2001) 'Trust and Confidence: Possibilities for Social Work in "High Modernity"', *British Journal of Social Work*, 31(2): 287–305.

Smith, C.R. (1976) 'Bereavement: The Contribution of Phenomenological and Existential Analysis to a Greater Understanding of the Problem', *British Journal of Social Work*, 5(1): 75–92.

Smith, D. (1991) *Family Decision Making: Family Group Conferences: Practitioner Views*, Lower Hutt, New Zealand: Practitioners Publishing.

Smith, D. (1995) *Criminology for Social Work*, Basingstoke: Macmillan – now Palgrave Macmillan.

Smith, S.C. and Pennells, M. (1995) *Interventions with Bereaved Children*, London: Jessica Kingsley.

Snowdon, R. (1980) 'Working with Incest Offenders: Excuses, Excuses, Excuses', in *AEGIS: Issues on Child Sexual Assault*, No. 29, Autumn.

Social Exclusion Unit (1998) *Bringing Britain Together: A National Strategy for Neighbourhood Renewal*, London: Stationery Office.

Social Services Inspectorate (1998) *Partners in Planning: Approaches to Planning Services for Children and their Families*, London: HMSO.

Social Services Inspectorate (1999) *Inspection of Services to Support Disabled Adults in their Parenting Role; Cornwall County Council*, Bristol West Inspection Group: Department of Health.

Spallone, P. (1987) 'Reproductive Technology and the State: The Warnock Report and Its Clones', in Spallone, P. and Steinberg, D.L. (eds) *Made to Order: The Myth of Reproductive and Genetic Progress*, Oxford: Pergamon.

Spallone, P. (1992) *Generation Games: Genetic Engineering and the Future of Our Lives*, London: The Women's Press.

Spandler, H. (1996) *Who's Hurting Who? Young People, Self-harm and Suicide*, Manchester: 42nd Street.

Spratt, T. and Houston, S. (1999) Developing critical social work in theory and practice: Child protection and communicative reason, *Child and Family Social Work*, 4(4): 315–24.

St Claire, L. (1989) 'A Multidimensional Model of Mental Retardation: Impairment, Subnormal Behavior, Role Failures, and Socially Constructed Retardation', *American Journal on Mental Retardation*, 94(1): 88–96.

Stainton, T. (1994) *Autonomy and Social Policy: Rights, Mental Handicap and Community Care*, Aldershot: Avebury.

Stainton, T. (1998) 'Rights and Rhetoric of Practice: Contradictions for Practitioners', in Symonds, A. and Kelly, A. (eds) *The Social Construction of Community Care*, London: Macmillan – now Palgrave Macmillan.

Stanko, E., Crisp, D., Hale, C. and Lucraft, H. (1998) *Counting the Costs: Estimating the Impact of Domestic Violence in the London Borough of Hackney*, Swindon: Crime Concern.

Stanworth, M. (ed.) (1987) *Reproductive Technologies: Gender, Motherhood and Medicine*, Cambridge: Polity Press.

Steadman, H.J., Robbins, P.C. and Monahan, J. (1998) *The MacArthur Risk Assessment Study: 1 Executive Summary*, Charlottesville: University of Virginia.

Stein, M. (1997) *What Works in Leaving Care*, Barkingside: Barnardo's.

Steinberg, D.L. (1997) *Bodies in Glass: Genetics, Eugenics, Embryo Ethics*, Manchester: Manchester University Press.

Stevenson, O. (1989) *Age and Vulnerability: A Guide to Better Care*, London: Age Concern.

Stevenson, O. (1998) *The Neglected Child*, London: Blackwell.

Stroebe, M. (1998) 'New Directions in Bereavement Research: Exploration of Gender Differences', *Palliative Medicine*, **12**: 5–12.

Stroebe, M. and Schut, H. (1995) *The Dual Process/Model of Coping with Loss*, Paper Presented at the International Work Group on Death, Dying and Bereavement, St Catherine's College, Oxford, 26–29 June.

Stroebe, M. and Schut, H. (1998) 'Culture and Grief', *Bereavement Care*, **17**(1): 7–11.

Stroebe, M. and Schut, H. (1999) 'The Dual Process Model of Coping with Bereavement: Rationale and Description', *Death Studies*, **23**: 197–224.

Sutherland, S. (1999) *With Respect to Old Age* – Royal Commission on Long Term Care, London: Stationery Office.

Sweeting, H. and Gilhooly, M. (1997) 'Dementia and the Phenomenon of Social Death', *Sociology of Health and Illness*, **19**(1): 93–117.

Tadd, W. (1994) 'Accountability and Nursing', in Chadwick, R. (ed.) *Ethics and the Professions*, Aldershot: Avebury.

Tam, H. (1998) *Communitarianism: A New Agenda for Politics and Citizenship*, Basingstoke: Macmillan – now Palgrave Macmillan.

Tanner, D. (1998a) 'Empowerment and Care Management: Swimming Against the Tide', *Health and Social Care in the Community*, **6**(6): 447–57.

Tanner, D. (1998b) 'Jeopardy of Assessing Risk', *Practice*, **10**(1): 15–28.

Taylor, C. and White, S. (2000) *Practising Reflexivity in Health and Welfare: Making Knowledge*, Buckingham: Open University Press.

Tebbutt, C. (1994) 'After Suicide', *CRUSE Chronicle*, July/August, 3–4. CRUSE Bereavement Care, CRUSE House, 126 Sheen Road, Richmond, Surrey, TW9 1UR Telephone: 020 8940 4818, Helpline: 0870 167 1677.

Tew, J. (1999) 'Voices from the Margins: Inserting the Social in Mental Health Discourse', *Social Work Education*, **18**(4): 433–48.

Therborn, G. (1983) *The Power of Ideology and the Ideology of Power*, London: Verso.

Thoburn, J. (ed.) (1992) *Participation in Practice – Involving Families in Child Protection*, Norwich: University of East Anglia.

Thoburn, J. (1994) *Child Placement: Principles and Practice*, 2nd edn, Aldershot: Arena.

Thoburn, J., Lewis, A. and Shemmings, D. (1995) *Paternalism or Partnership? Family Involvement in the Child Protection Process*, London: HMSO.

Thomas, C. (1999) *Female Forms: Experiencing and Understanding Disability*, Buckingham: Open University Press.

Thomas, D.N. (1983) *The Making of Community Work*, London: Allen & Unwin.

Thompson, A. (2000) 'The Body Politic', *Community Care*, 2–8 November, pp. 20–1.

Thompson, K. (1998) *Moral Panics*, London: Routledge.

Thompson, N. (1993) *Anti-Discriminatory Practice*, Basingstoke: Macmillan – now Palgrave Macmillan.

Thompson, N. (2000) *Understanding Social Work: Preparing for Practice*, Basingstoke: Palgrave – now Palgrave Macmillan.

Thornton, D., Curran, L., Grayson, D. and Holloway, V. (1984) *Tougher Regimes in Detention Centres: Report of an Evaluation by the Young Offender Psychology Unit*, London: HMSO.

Thorpe, D. (1994) *Evaluating Child Protection*, Buckingham: Open University Press.

Thorpe, D., Smith, D., Green, C. and Paley, J. (1980) *Out of Care – The Community Support of Juvenile Offenders*, London: Allen & Unwin.

Tisdall, K., Lavery, R. and McCrystal, P. (1998) *Child Care Law: A Comparative Review of New Legislation in Northern Ireland and Scotland*, Belfast: Centre for Child Care Research, Queens University.

Titterton, M. (ed.) (1994) *Caring for People in the Community: The New Welfare*, London: Jessica Kingsley.

Townsend, P. (1996) 'Ageism and Social Policy', in Phillipson, C. and Walker, A. (eds) *Ageing and Social Policy: A Critical Assessment*, Aldershot: Gower.

Trinder, L. (1996) 'Social Work Research: The State of the Art (or Science)', *Child and Family Social Work*, 1(4): 233–42.

Triseliotis, J., Borland, M. and Hill, M. (2000) *Delivering Foster Care*, London: British Agencies for Adoption and Fostering.

Triseliotis, J., Shireman, J. and Hundleby, M. (1997) *Adoption: Theory, Policy and Practice*, London: Cassell.

Tunnard, J. (1991) *The Children Act 1989. Working in Partnership with Families*, London: FRG/HMSO.

Tunstill, J. (1997) 'Family Support Clauses of the 1989 Children Act', in Parton, N. (ed.) *Child Protection and Family Support: Tensions, Contradictions and Possibilities*, London: Routledge.

Turnell, A. and Edwards, S. (1999) *Signs of Safety*, New York: Norton.

Tutty, L. M., Bidgood, B. A. and Rothery, M. A. (1993) 'Support Groups for Battered Women: Research on their Efficacy', *Journal of Family Violence*, 8: 325–43.

Twelvetrees, A. (1991) *Community Work*, 2nd edn, London: Macmillan – now Palgrave Macmillan.

Twigg, J. and Atkin, K. (1994) *Carers Perceived: Policy and Practice in Informal Care*, Buckingham: Open University Press.

Ungar, S. (2001) 'Moral Panic versus the Risk Society: The Implication of the Changing Sites of Social Anxiety', *British Journal of Sociology*, 52(2): 271–91.

United Nations (1989) Convention on the Rights of the Child. Geneva: United Nations.

Vanstone, M. (1995) 'Managerialism and the Ethics of Management', in Hugman, R. and Smith, D. (eds) *Ethical Issues in Social Work*, London: Routledge.

Vickery, A. (1977) *Caseload Management: A Guide for Supervisors of Social Work Staff*, London: NISW.

Violence Against Lesbians in the Home (1998) *Lesbians' Own Accounts*, JJ Publications.

WAFE (1989) *Breaking Through: Women Surviving Male Violence*, Bristol: WAFE.

Wald, M.S. and Woolverton, M. (1990) 'Risk Assessment: The Emperor's New Clothes?', *Child Welfare*, 69(6): 483–511.

Walter, T. (1994) *The Revival of Death*, London: Routledge.

Walter, T. (1996) 'A New Model of Grief: Bereavement and Biography', *Mortality*, 1(1): 7–25.

Walter, T. (1997) 'Book Review', *Mortality*, 2(2): 73–4.

Walter, T. (1999) *On Bereavement*, Buckingham: Open University Press.

Walton, P. (1999) 'Social Work and Mental Health: Refocusing the Training Agenda for ASWs', *Social Work Education*, 18(4): 375–88.

Ward, D. (2000) 'Totem not Token: Groupwork as a Vehicle for User Participation' in Kemshall, H. and Littlechild, R. (eds) *User Involvement and Participation in Social Care, Research Informing Practice*, London: Jessica Kingsley.

Waters, M. (1994) *Modern Sociological Theory*, London: Sage.

Watkins, T.R. (1997) 'Mental Health Services to Substance Abusers', in Watkins, T.R. and Callicutt, J.W. (eds) *Mental Health Policy and Practice Today*, Thousand Oaks, CA: Sage.

Wattam, C. (1999) 'Confidentiality', in Parton, N. and Wattam, C. (eds) *Child Sexual Abuse: Responding to the Experiences of Children*, Chichester: Wiley.

Webb, S.A. (2001) 'Some Considerations on the Validity of Evidence-based Practice in Social Work', *British Journal of Social Work*, **39**: 57–79.

Welch, B. (1998) 'Care Management and Community Care: Current Issues', in Challis, D., Darton, R. and Stewart, K. (eds) *Community Care, Secondary Health Care and Care Management*, Aldershot: Ashgate.

Wendell, S. (1996) *The Rejected Body: Feminist Philosophical Reflections on Disability*, London: Routledge.

Weyts, A., Morpeth, A. and Bullock, R. (2000) 'Department of Health Research Overviews – Past, Present and Future: An Evaluation of the Dissemination of the Blue Book', *Children and Society*, **5**: 3.

Wheal, A. (1999) 'Family and Friends who are Carers', in Wheal, A. (ed.) *The RHP Companion to Foster Care*, Lyme Regis: Russell House.

Whitaker, D. and Archer, J.L. (1989) *Research by Social Workers: Capitalizing on Experience, Study No. 9*, London: CCETSW.

White, M. (1993) 'Deconstruction and Therapy', in Gilligan, S. and Price, R. (eds) *Therapeutic Conversations*, New York: Norton.

White, V. (1995) 'Commonality and Diversity in Feminist Social Work', *British Journal of Social Work*, **25**(2): 143–56.

Whyte, G. (1998) 'Recasting Janis's Groupthink Model: The Key Role of Collective Efficacy in Decision Fiascoes', *Organisational Behaviour and Human Decision Processes*, **73**(2/3): 185–209.

Wilcox, R., Smith, D. and Moore, J. (1991) *Family Decision Making: Family Group Conferences*, New Zealand: Practitioners Publishing.

Wilding, P. (1982) *Professional Power and Social Welfare*, London: Routledge & Kegan Paul.

Williams, F. (1991) 'The Welfare State as Part of a Racially Structured and Patriarchial Capitalism', in Loney, M., Bocock, R., Clarke, J., Cochrane, A., Graham, P. and Wilson, M. (eds) *The State of the Market – Politics and Welfare in Contemporary Britain*, 2nd edn, London: Sage.

Williams, F. (1999) 'Good-enough Principles for Welfare', *Journal of Social Policy*, **28**(4): 667–87.

Williams, R. (1976) *Keywords*, London: Fontana/Croom Helm.

Wilson, A. and Beresford, P. (2000) 'Anti-oppressive Practice: Emancipation or Appropriation', *British Journal of Social Work*, **30**(5): 553–73.

Wilson, M. (1993) *Crossing the Boundaries: Black Women Survive Incest*. London: Virago.

Winnicott, C. (1964) *Child Care and Social Work: A Collection of Papers*, Oxford: Codicote Press.

Winston, R. (1987) *Infertility: A Sympathetic Approach*, London: Optima.

Wistow, G., Knapp, M., Hardy, B. and Allen, C. (1994) *Social Care in a Mixed Economy*, Buckingham: Open University Press.

Worden, W. (1991) *Grief Counselling and Grief Therapy – A Handbook for the Mental Health Practitioner*, 2nd edn, London: Routlege.

Worden, W. (1996) *Children and Grief*, London and New York: Guilford Press.

Wortman, C.B. and Silver, R.C. (1989) 'The Myths of Coping with Loss', *Journal of Consulting and Clinical Psychology*, **57**: 349–57.

Young, M. and Cullen, L. (1996) *A Good Death*, London: Routledge.

Youth Justice Board (1999) Corporate Plan 1999–2000 to 2001–02, http://www.youth-justice-board.gov.uk/who/corporate99.htm

Author Index

Subject Index

A

abuse 22 34 64–5 102 133
abused children 101
abused women 25 65 66–7
access to child care services 121–2
accountability 28–37
Action Zones for Health and
    Education 282
adoption 106–15 300
advice workers 131
advocacy 119 161 163 278 283
advocate 55
African-American 33 75
African-Caribbean 306
Afrocentric 17
age 66 102 108
Age Concern 224
ageism 202
agency/ies 109 304–5 306
agency reorganisations 296–303
alcohol 203
alcohol abuse 104
allegations of abuse 113 114

ambiguity 308
America 101
American 33
American Association on Mental
    Deficiency 192
anthropological research 214
anti-discriminatory approach 92
anti-discriminatory practice 205
anti-nuclear protests 154
anti-oppressive 91
anti-oppressive practice 305
anti-poverty strategies 282
Approved Social Worker (ASW)
    172 177–9 300
artificial insemination by donor
    (AID) 73
Aryan 76
Asian 149
assessment 36 109 129 164
    187 261–8 272–3
Association of Community Workers
    (ACW) 151